DANGEROUS TALES

BIBLE AND ITS RECEPTION

Robert Paul Seesengood, General Editor

Editorial Board:
Lisa Bowens
Brian Kolia
Andrew M. Mbuvi
Hannah M. Strømmen

Number 9

DANGEROUS TALES

Genesis 34 and Its Literary Descendants

Carrie A. Cifers

SBL PRESS

Atlanta

Copyright © 2025 by Carrie A. Cifers

All rights reserved. No part of this work may be reproduced or transmitted in any form or by any means, electronic or mechanical, including photocopying and recording, or by means of any information storage or retrieval system, except as may be expressly permitted by the 1976 Copyright Act or in writing from the publisher. Requests for permission should be addressed in writing to the Rights and Permissions Office, SBL Press, 825 Houston Mill Road, Atlanta, GA 30329 USA.

Library of Congress Control Number: 2025933674

Cover image courtesy of the Phillip Medhurst collection of Bible prints. See https://tinyurl.com/SBLPress6710x1.

For Dinah

Contents

Acknowledgments ix
Abbreviations xi

1. Introduction 1

2. Dinah Decides: The Ethics of Multiperspectivity and
   Reticence in Genesis 34 19

3. The Ethics of Re-presentation in Jubilees 30 and *Judean
   Antiquities* 1.337–341 81

4. The Agent(s) of an Ethical Shift: The Re-presentation of
   Genesis 34 in Manuscripts A and F of *Aseneth* 183

5. Conclusion 235

Appendix: Translation of Chapters 1, 22–29 of *Aseneth*
   Manuscripts A and F 247

Bibliography 269
Ancient Sources Index 281
Modern Authors Index 297

Acknowledgments

The research and completion of this book would not have been possible without the institutions and individuals who have supported this endeavor in many ways.

Special thanks to Heather McMurray, who directed me toward SBL Press's The Bible and Its Reception series, and to Robert Seesengood, who welcomed the project with enthusiasm. Thank you also to Nicole L. Tilford for answering all of my many questions and making sure all the proverbial i's were dotted and t's were crossed along the road to publication.

I am thankful to the Association for Jewish Studies, which provided financial support through the final stages of writing. Also, the Religious Studies Department of the University of Virginia provided various research grants that granted me access to much-needed resources. Thank you especially to Jenny Geddes and her advocacy.

Thank you to Martien Halvorson-Taylor, who provided regular guidance and encouragement, especially when the vastness of the task that I had set for myself seemed too overwhelming. Thank you also to Janet Spittler, whose love of ancient Greek narratives is infectious and who helped me work through some difficult Grecian knots while translating the Joseph and Aseneth manuscripts. Thank you to Larry Bouchard, who encouraged me to delve deeper into Newton's Narrative Ethics and agreed to take time out of his retirement to review my finished product. Thank you also to Caroline Rody, who was willing to engage with this research during a busy year and offer a valuable perspective from outside the field of religious studies.

A special thank you also to Elizabeth Shanks Alexander, who has supported this project with guidance and enthusiasm from its earliest stages.

The community at Union Presbyterian Seminary has also undergirded the success of this dissertation. Unending thanks to Sam Adams for his continued mentorship and enthusiastic encouragement. Thank you also to Lisa Banes at the Union Presbyterian Seminary library for her moral support and for forgiving my overdue library fines, and to Mengistu Lemma, who sent me necessary resources through the mail while dealing with the confusions of my ever-changing patron status.

I am greatly indebted to Arthur Frank, who not only unwittingly sparked a wildfire of intellectual fervor in me through his scholarship but also graciously corresponded with me in the early stages of this work regarding one of its most thorny quandaries: What makes a story dangerous?

Many thanks to my students, who unwittingly spurred me on to this path of research. Special thanks to Maddie Pannell, Jenna Stanley, Jacob Bushey, and McKinley Verlik, who wittingly engaged in extracurricular conversations about the gritty details of Gen 34 in support of this project.

To the members (however loosely defined) of the Judaism and Christianity in Antiquity Graduate Colloquium, I am thankful for your keen editorial eyes, your humor, and your moral support: Helen Byler Buckwater, Rebecca Bultman, Abigail Emerson, Kerwin Holmes, Jon Holste, Peter Morris, Jeannie Sellick, and Avi Schwartz.

Much gratitude to Teddy Blanks, Molly Young, and Christian Hill, who acted as both fans and critics in the writing stages.

To Mom and Joe, whose support helped to make this possible. Especially to Mom, who cheered me on and saved the day again and again during my daughter's school closures and sick days.

Kisses and hugs to Chloe and Alice, who didn't make it easier but certainly made it sweeter.

Finally, I thank Robbie, whose myriad sacrifices over the past ten years have been a true example of a life laid down for another. Whatever time, energy, or resources I have devoted to this journey, he has given more to ensure that I had the time, energy, and resources to devote in the first place. You keep my feet on the ground and my heart full of faith, and I thank you.

Abbreviations

4Q216	4Q Jubilees^a
4Q252	4Q Commentary on Genesis^a
4Q320	4Q Calendar Document Mishmarot A
4Q321	4Q Calendar Document Mishmarot B
4Q322	4Q Mishmarot A
4Q323	4Q Mishmarot B
4Q324	4Q Mishmarot C
4Q325	4Q Calendar Document Mishmarot D
4Q326	4Q Calendar Document C
4Q328	4Q Mishmarot F
4Q329	4Q Mishmarot G
4Q330	4Q Mishmarot I
4Q337	4Q Calendar Document F
A.J.	Josephus, *Antiquitates judaicae*
AJEC	Ancient Judaism and Early Christianity
ANET	Pritchard, James B., ed. *Ancient Near Eastern Texts Relating to the Old Testament*. 3rd ed. Princeton: Princeton University Press, 1969.
Arm	Armenian
B. Bat.	Bava Batra
BHQ	Biblia Hebraica Quinta
BHQ Gen	Schenker, Adrian, et al., eds. *Genesis*. BHQ 1. Stuttgart: Deutsche Bibelgesellschaft, 2004–.
B.J.	Josephus, *Bellum judaicum*
BT	*The Bible Translator*
C. Ap.	Josephus, *Contra Apionem*
CBQMS	Catholic Biblical Quarterly Monograph Series
ch(s).	chapter(s)
Chron.	Syncellus, *Chronological Excerpts*
CSCO	Corpus Scriptorum Christianorum Orientalium

CurBR	*Currents in Biblical Research*
EHGIH	Europäische Hochschulschriften, Reihe III: Geschichte und ihre Hilfswissenschaften
EJL	Early Judaism and Its Literature
Ep.	*Epistula(e)*
Eth.	Ethiopic/Ge'ez
FJTC	Flavius Josephus: Translation and Commentary
fol(s).	folio(s)
frag.	fragment
FSBP	Fontes et Subsidia ad Bibliam Pertinentes
Gk.	Greek
GKC	Kautzsch, Emil, ed. *Gesenius' Hebrew Grammar*. Translated by Arthur E. Cowley. 2nd ed. Oxford: Clarendon, 1910.
GOTR	*Greek Orthodox Theological Review*
GRBS	*Greek, Roman, and Byzantine Studies*
Heb.	Hebrew
HCRSR	*The Hastings Center Report: Special Report*
Hist.	Lucian, *Quomodo historia conscribenda sit*; Polybius, *Historiae*
HTR	*Harvard Theological Review*
HUCA	*Hebrew Union College Annual*
IDB	Buttrick, George, A., ed. *The Interpreter's Dictionary of the Bible*. 4 vols. New York: Abingdon, 1962.
IJCT	*International Journal of the Classical Tradition*
Ios.	Philo, *De Iosepho*
JBL	*Journal of Biblical Literature*
JHS	*Journal of Hebrew Scriptures*
JNFT	*Journal of Narrative Family Therapy*
Jos. Asen.	Joseph and Aseneth
JPS	*Tanakh: The Holy Scriptures: The Jewish Publication Society Translation according to the Traditional Hebrew Text*
JQR	*Jewish Quarterly Review*
JSHRZ	Jüdische Schriften aus hellenistisch-römischer Zeit
JSJ	*Journal for the Study of Judaism in the Persian, Hellenistic, and Roman Periods*
JSOT	*Journal for the Study of the Old Testament*
JSP	*Journal for the Study of the Pseudepigrapha*
JTS	*Journal for Theological Studies*

Jub.	Jubilees
KJV	King James Version
KritHer	Reconstructed text in Burchard, Christoph, assisted by Carsten Burfeind and Uta Barbara Fink. *Joseph und Aseneth*. PVTG 5. Leiden: Brill, 2003.
LAB	Liber antiquitatum biblicarum (Pseudo-Philo)
Lat.	Latin
LD	*Lectio Difficilior: European Electronic Journal for Feminist Exegesis*
LSJ	Liddell, Henry George, Robert Scott, Henry Stuart Jones. *A Greek-English Lexicon*. 9th ed. with revised supplement. Oxford: Clarendon, 1996.
LXX	Septuagint
MFS	*Modern Fiction Studies*
Midr.	Midrash
Migr.	Philo, *De migratione Abrahami*
MS	*Memory Studies*
MS A	Manuscript Vaticanus Greek 803, fols. 133r–147v. Rome, Vatican Library.
MS B	Manuscript Palatinus Graecus 17. Vatican City, Vatican Library.
MS C	Manuscript Baroccianus Greek 148, fols. 298v–303v. Oxford, Bodleian Library.
MS E	Manuscript Vatopedi 600. Mount Athos, Konstamonitou.
MS F	Manuscript Greek 966, fols. 126r–140v. Bucharest, Biblioteca Academiei Române.
MS Lat. 436	Manuscript Latin 436 (C 37), fols. 119r–134v. Uppsala, Uppsala University Library.
MS O	Manuscript Greek 504. Sinai, Saint Catherine's Monastery.
MS P	Manuscript Greek 14, pp. 597–702. Mount Athos, Konstamonitou.
MS Q	Manuscript Palatinus Greek 364, fols. 293r–310v. Rome, Vatican Library.
MS R	Manuscript Greek 530, fols. 13v–17r. Sinai, St. Catherine's Monastery.
MS W	Manuscript Greek 1976, fols. 57r–102v. Sinai, St Catherine's Convent.
MT	Masoretic Text

Mut.	Philo, *De mutatione nominum*
Ngr	New Greek
NRSV	New Revised Standard Version
Off.	Ambrose, *De officiis ministrorum*
OG	Old Greek
OTE	*Old Testament Essays*
OTP	Charlesworth, James H., ed. *Old Testament Pseudepigrapha*. 2 vols. New York: Doubleday, 1983, 1985.
QJS	*Quarterly Journal of Speech*
QS	*Qualitative Sociology*
PAAJR	*Proceedings of the American Academy for Jewish Research*
Phil	Reconstructed text in Philonenko, Marc. *Joseph et Aséneth: Introduction, texte critique, traduction et notes.* SPB 13. Leiden: Brill, 1968.
Pirqe R. El.	Pirqe Rabbi Eliezer
Praep. ev.	Eusebius, *Praeparatio Evangelica*
PTL	*A Journal for Descriptive Poetics and Theory of Literature*
PVTG	Pseudepigrapha Veteris Testamenti Graece
Rab.	Rabbah
RevQ	*Revue de Qumran*
RP	*Research in Phenomenology*
Sacr.	*De sacrificiis Abel et Caini*
SCS	Septuagint and Cognate Studies
Slav	Slavic
SP	Samaritan Pentateuch
Spec.	Philo, *De specialibus legibus*
StPB	Studia Post-biblica
StBibLit	Studies in Biblical Literature
Syr	Syriac
T. Levi	Testament of Levi
T. Naph.	Testament of Naphtali
T. Job	Testament of Job
T. Reu.	Testament of Reuben
Tg. Onq.	Targum Onqelos
Tg. Neof.	Targum Neofiti
ThSoc	*Theory and Society*
Thuc.	Dionysius of Halicarnassus, *De Thucydide*
USQR	*Union Seminary Quarterly Review*
VT	*Vetus Testamentum*

VTSup	Supplements to Vetus Testamentum
Vulg.	Vulgate
WGRW	Writings from the Greco-Roman World
y.	Jerusalem Talmud
ZAC	*Zeitschrift für Antikes Christentum*
ZAW	*Zeitschrift für die alttestamentliche Wissenschaft*
ZNW	*Zeitschrift für die neutestamentliche Wissenschaft*

1
Introduction

> We live by stories, we also live in them. One way or another we are living the stories planted in us early or along the way, or we are also living the stories we planted—knowingly or unknowingly—in ourselves.... If we change the stories we live by, quite possibly we change our lives.
> —Ben Okri, *A Way of Being Free*

1. Genesis 34 as a Story Encountered

From ancient times, as generations have encountered the narrative of Gen 34, there has been a lack of agreement about its ethical message regarding the violent retribution of Simeon and Levi. Indeed, differing understandings of Simeon and Levi's actions at Shechem are evinced in works as early as the Second Temple period. As James Kugel concludes in response to such diversity, the ancients seemed to assume that "the story must contain some kind of moral lesson but if so, the message was unclear."[1]

---

1. James Kugel, *Traditions of the Bible: A Guide to the Bible as It Was at the Start of the Common Era* (Cambridge: Harvard University Press, 1998), 404. Throughout this book, I use the terms *story* and *narrative* somewhat interchangeably, although various theories of literature maintain a distinction between the two. For instance, certain theorizations maintain that *narrative* is the broader term, referring to templates of plotlines, motifs, and characters from which storytellers draw from, while *story* refers to specific tellings. See Marie-Laure Ryan, "Toward a Definition of Narrative," in *The Cambridge Companion to Narrative*, ed. David Herman (Cambridge: Cambridge University Press, 2007), 22–35; Anne Harrington, *The Cure within: A History of Mind-Body Medicine* (New York: Norton, 2008), 24–25; Arthur Frank, *Letting Stories Breathe: A Socio-narratology* (Chicago: University of Chicago Press, 2010), 199–200. I agree with Frank's assertion that "the words *narrative* and *story* overlap so frequently that sustaining this distinction in consistent usage proves impossible" (*Letting Stories Breathe*, 200).

The same can be said about modern scholarship. In the late twentieth century, a vigorous debate among biblical scholars was inspired by the ambiguity engendered by the formal features of Gen 34.[2] This debate included whether the text endorsed the retributive violence of Simeon and Levi on the Shechemites. One thing scholars could agree on was that the violence of the narrative is shocking and its lack of explicit evaluation puzzling. Many approached the text with an assumption that the narrator's evaluation is hidden within, discoverable through the tools of various interpretive methods.[3] Interpreters who argued for the narrator's approval of the retribution took an intertextual approach that prioritized certain texts or made claims to historical contextualization or the function of rhetorical cues.[4] On the other hand, interpreters who claimed that the

---

2. See Meir Sternberg, *The Poetics of Biblical Narrative* (Bloomington: Indiana University Press, 1985), 441–81; Danna Nolan Fewell and David M. Gunn, "Tipping the Balance: Sternberg's Reader and the Rape of Dinah," *JBL* 110 (1991): 193–211; Meir Sternberg, "Biblical Poetics and Sexual Politics: From Reading to Counterreading," *JBL* 111 (1992): 463–88; Lyn Bechtel, "What if Dinah Is Not Raped? (Genesis 34)," *JSOT* 62 (1994): 19–36; Mary Anna Bader, *Sexual Violation in the Hebrew Bible: A Multi-methodological Study of Genesis 34 and 2 Samuel 13*, StBibLit (New York: Lang, 2006), 9–122, 176–79.

Chapter 2 further expounds on the nature of these features. In one way, Gen 34 became a battleground where different methods of literary criticism were tested and pitted against one another. See Adele Berlin, "Literary Approaches to Biblical Literature: General Observations and a Case Study of Genesis 34," in *The Hebrew Bible: New Insights and Scholarship*, ed. Frederick E. Greenspahn (New York: New York University Press, 2008), 45–75.

3. E.g., Meir Sternberg, who posits a theory of the Hebrew Bible's "foolproof composition." While readers may bring to the text their own assumptions and "counterread" it, Sternberg strongly asserts that the rhetoric and art of the biblical narrative *always* points the reader to the emotional and moral sympathy of the "right" characters and the "moral point" made by the narrative. See Sternberg, *The Poetics of Biblical Narrative: Ideological Literature and the Drama of Reading* (Bloomington: Indiana University Press, 1985), 54–55, 194. Lyn Bechtel holds, along with Sternberg, an assumption that the narrative has an implicit evaluation that the careful scholar can uncover with the right methodology. Where Sternberg attends to the subtle clues of poetics to reveal it, Bechtel employs the X-ray of anthropological studies ("What if Dinah Is Not Raped?").

4. Like Sternberg, Bader assumes that the narrator has a side he is on and crafts the story in a way that betrays his partiality. By reading Gen 34 in conversation with 2 Sam 13, Bader's assessment accords much with Sternberg's (see n. 3 above). She asserts that the narrator, by depicting Jacob as inactive, discredits the father and champions his

narrator denounced the violence took intertextual approaches that prioritized *other* texts or supplied data from anthropological studies in support of their claims.⁵ Others abandoned the search for an implicit evaluation, choosing to provide their own evaluations based on the features of the narrative but informed by self-conscious ideological agendas.⁶ Some noted

---

sons instead—an assessment that she finds paralleled in the more explicitly evaluative story of 2 Sam 13 (Bader, *Sexual Violation*, 177–79). For an approach that makes claims to historical contextualization, see, e.g., Alison Joseph, "'Is Dinah Raped?' Isn't the Right Question: Genesis 34 and Feminist Historiography," *JHS* 19 (2019): 27–37. Like Joseph, Claus Westermann primarily follows a theory of the text that allows for multiple layers of redaction and believes the final layer that has shaped the text upholds Simeon and Levi as examples of godly zeal that accords with the Torah commands of Deut 7. See Westermann, *Genesis 12–36: A Commentary* (London: SPCK, 1986), 544–45. Concerning rhetorical cues: in conversation with Wayne Booth's theories on the role of rhetoric in fiction, Sternberg offers a reading of Gen 34 attentive to its every detail, in which he suggests "the rhetorical manipulation" of the narrator in burgeoning careful and calculated support for Simeon and Levi (Sternberg, *Poetics of Biblical Narrative*, 446).

5. Although acknowledging the ambiguity in Gen 34 resulting from its covert narration, Robin Parry claims that the biblical narrator condemns the violence of Simeon and Levi, which is supported by an intertextual reading of Gen 34 with Gen 49:5–7 and several New Testament texts. See Robin Parry, *Old Testament Story and Christian Ethics: The Rape of Dinah as a Case Study* (Milton Keynes, UK: Paternoster, 2004), 218. Bechtel argues that Gen 34 cannot be properly understood unless what happens to Dinah is considered from within an ancient Israelite mindset, which operated under a "thinking pattern" of group orientation ("What if Dinah Is Not Raped?," 20). By applying the lens of social-anthropological studies to every element of the story, Bechtel asserts that the group-orientation thinking pattern is native to the text: "Ancient Israel fits generally into the category of a group-oriented society" (21). The characters' individual actions and assumed motivations, read within the context of a group-oriented society, shift the stakes. Israelites Dinah and Jacob and Shechemites Hamor and Shechem are positively assessed as pursuing negotiation and cooperation between groups, while Simeon and Levi are negatively assessed as endangering the well-being of the Israelite group, even though their motivations can be understood through a group-oriented concern for pollution and boundary maintenance (34–36).

6. Danna Nolan Fewell and David M. Gunn provide an attentive reading of Gen 34 that opposes Sternberg's reading at various points, in which they "press for more self-consciously ideological readings of biblical narrative" and are explicit about their own value system, which they describe as "feminist." See Fewell and Gunn, "Tipping the Balance: Sternberg's Reader and the Rape of Dinah," *JBL* 110 (1991): 194. In their reading, Jacob's silence is a calculated response to be valued more highly than Simeon and Levi's rash action and excessive violence (198).

points at which the narrative design fosters ambiguity, but most offered readings that attempt to resolve that ambiguity with varying degrees of finalization.[7] Furthermore, within this framework that considers Gen 34 as a text to be interpreted, the prevailing trend of Second Temple period scholarship has been to look at later re-presentations of Gen 34 as evidence of biblical interpretation, such as those found in Jub. 30; Josephus, *A.J.* 1.337–341; and Jos. Asen. 22–29.

What this scholarship has failed to account for fully, however, is *why* this narrative in particular has had such a rich history of reader reception and fiery debate. Although previous scholarship has helped to highlight certain areas of semantic or syntactic ambiguity in the narrative,[8] it has not yet accounted for why Gen 34 as a whole has proved so resistant to finalization and why later generations have returned to it again and again as a story that audiences have felt the need to grapple with and retell.

The theoretical lens of narrative ethics and socionarratology offers a step back from interpretive assessment by considering Gen 34 as a story encountered rather than a text to be interpreted. Although the term *narrative ethics* has come to be used in a variety of ways in a wide range of fields of study, my use of the term derives from Adam Zachary Newton's *Narrative Ethics*, which posits a union of literary and ethical inquiry that considers "narrative *as* ethics." Basing his claims on the work of philosopher Emmanuel Levinas, Newton resists the linear theorization of narrative as a discourse "from author through text to reader" but proposes

---

7. For an example of the former, see Fewell and Gunn, "Tipping the Balance," 194, 198; Parry, *Old Testament Story*, 123–78; Bader, *Sexual Violation*, 35–37, 84. Notable exceptions to the latter include James Kugel (*Traditions of the Bible*, 404) and Rhiannon Graybill, *Texts after Terror: Rape, Sexual Violence, and the Hebrew Bible* (Oxford: Oxford University Press, 2021). Graybill deals with inherent ambiguities of Gen 34 in service of a larger project that aims to foster positive ethical engagement with issues of sexual violence through the reading of Hebrew Bible texts. She strongly resists the propensity of scholarship to clarify what is essentially "fuzzy" in the text (13–14). In particular, Dinah's story, for Graybill, becomes productive in problematizing modern discourse regarding consent. For Graybill, the ambiguity in the representation of Dinah "accurately represents the ambiguity and fuzziness that attends many reports of sexual violence, ancient and modern alike" (13–14). Part of Graybill's overall project is to destabilize conceptualizations of consent that are *not* fuzzy or complex and to push back against readings of texts that uphold a false "red light, green light" view of sexual consent.

8. See ch. 2 for further discussion.

the meeting of narrative and audience to be an encounter between others, in which both are vulnerable in the confronted presence of the other. This encounter is inherently ethical, as each exerts its own force on the encounter.[9] In this relational space of encounter, narrative ethics attends both to the claims that a text makes on its readers and to the ethical responsibility on the reader as witness to the text. As Amy Cottrill synthesizes:

> The encounter between text and reader makes a claim upon the reader that creates an ethical responsibility long before one rationally decides about the ethical value of such an exchange.... According to Newton, textual encounter forces response.... Every text exacts a price of its reader, a certain kind of involvement, obligation or demand. Reading a text leaves a pre-rational mark on the reader that makes one accountable, even in the act of reading, to what transpires before [them]. Readers are obligated.[10]

Through this framework, then, narrative becomes more than the means through which messages are communicated or the dirt from which morals are extracted by the wise and discerning like prized gems. Rather, narratives are alterous beings in their own right—performances or acts—with power that is exerted on the audience in the confrontation.[11] Thus, it stands to reason that as much as the audience may influence the nature of this confrontation through its contextualization or theorization of the narrative other (e.g., as text to be interpreted, as revelation, as cultural artifact), the narrative itself shapes the nature of the confrontation through its own faculties, which also exert a shaping force on the identity of its audience.

Newton's tripartite theorization also offers insight into the myriad ways in which Gen 34 acts on its audience. Narrative ethics holds that narratives are inherently ethical on several levels, including in the craft of both form and content (narrational ethics), in the representation of selves (representational ethics), and in encounter or reading (hermeneutical ethics). Rather than seeking to finalize what Gen 34 leaves unfinalized, approaching the story through narrational ethics in particu-

---

9. Adam Zachary Newton, *Narrative Ethics* (Cambridge: Harvard University Press, 1995), 7, 65, 105–6.

10. Amy Cottrill, *Uncovering Violence: Reading Biblical Narratives as an Ethical Project* (Louisville: Westminster John Knox, 2021), 36–37.

11. Newton, *Narrative Ethics*, 7, 65.

lar can help us attend to the interlocking web of Gen 34's formal features that structurally craft and connect elements of ambiguity on multiple levels—features that individually and collectively make ethical demands on the audience. Narrational ethics is concerned with how the "formal design of the storytelling act" not only shapes a narrative's ethical content but also creates relational ties between "teller, tale, and person(s) told."[12] In this sense, the ethics of narration is not only ethical content within the narrative but the ethical relationships formed by the telling of narrative. Narrational ethics can attune us to the unique demands that Gen 34 places on its audience.

The tripartite aspects of narrative ethics, however, are interlocking and interactive. For instance, assessment of the ethical force of a narrative's formal features on the reader can be considered in the realm of hermeneutical ethics, while the formal features in question may be details of narrative representation, thus also intersecting the inquiry with the arena of representational ethics. Together, these aspects of narrative ethics can provide an attentiveness to the unique ties with which the covert narration, ambiguity, multiperspectivity, and reticence of Gen 34 bind its audience. Furthermore, they can help us to understand why this story has proved so resistant to finalization and why audiences have felt the need to tell it afresh in ways that engage with the unanswered ethical questions of violence and retaliation with which Gen 34 confronts its audience.

Considering Gen 34 as a story encountered also allows us to reframe the way in which we consider the literary evidence from Jewish and Christian communities that have grappled with and retold this story. Responding to the unique ways in which the narrative positions its audience as active participants, generation after generation of authors and storytellers have made it their own in creative ways.[13] The ancient Judean histories of Jubilees and Josephus's *Judean Antiquities*, for instance, retell the story as a

---

12. Newton, *Narrative Ethics*, 25.

13. See ch. 2. For example, Theodotus (ca. second century BCE) puts the account to verse as an epic poem, while the Testament of Levi tells it through Levi's perspective (T. Levi 2.1, 5.1–7.4). In the Jewish novella Judith, the heroine makes passionate reference to the biblical tale in her prayers (Jdt 9:1–14), while in *Migr.* 39.223–225 and *Mut.* 36.193–200, Philo of Alexandria re-presents it as an allegory. Both the ancient rabbis and early church exegetes interpreted the biblical story for their disciples and made use of it for ethical exhortation (e.g., Gen. Rab. 80; Jerome, *Ep.* 22.25, to Eustochium; and Ambrose, *Off.* 1.25).

formative event in the nascent years of their *ethnos*.[14] By re-presenting the ancient clash between Israelites and Shechemites to their contemporary audiences as a formative historical event, they each explicitly weigh in on the retributive violence of Simeon and Levi in ways that promote an ethos to their contemporary readers.[15] This ethos is unique to each history, but for both it is bound up in the narrator's assertion of the audience's identity.

The roughly contemporary Hellenistic Jewish romance[16] Joseph and Aseneth (hereafter *Aseneth*)[17] also engaged with the ethical problem of

---

14. See ch. 3 for arguments about the generic categorization of these texts. By using the term *ethnos*, I aim to convey the many aspects of corporate identity that can be interchangeably and mutably bound up in the ancient term: ethnic, geographic, political, religious, and cultural. See Shaye J. D. Cohen, *The Beginnings of Jewishness: Boundaries, Varieties, Uncertainties* (Berkeley: University of California Press, 1999), 109.

15. I use *ethos* here and throughout the book to refer to the sum of a subject's character, habits of choice, and collection of virtues in the Aristotelian sense. I use the term in this manner whether the subject is a character or narrator in a work of literature, a writer, a reader, or a culture. My use of the term *ethos* is influenced by ancient Greek composition instructional books from George A. Kennedy, trans., *Progymnasmata: Greek Textbooks of Prose Composition and Rhetoric*, WGRW 10 (Atlanta: Society of Biblical Literature, 2003), and Wayne Booth's discussion of the terminology of ethical criticism in *The Company We Keep: An Ethics of Fiction* (Berkeley: University of California Press, 1988), 8–17.

16. Joseph and Aseneth was first presumed to be an ancient Christian text in the late nineteenth and early to mid-twentieth century by scholars following Pierre Batiffol, who published his edition of family *a* in 1889. By the late twentieth century, a majority of scholars held that the text originated in the Judean diaspora in Hellenistic times, following Christoph Burchard. Within this near-consensus, there are a variety of arguments for the work's geographic or temporal provenance, based on the shaky grounds of internal textual evidence from reconstructed texts. Ross Kraemer and Rivka Nir argue, based on Philonenko's reconstruction, for a late antique Christian provenance. See Kraemer, *When Aseneth Met Joseph: A Late Antique Tale of the Biblical Patriarch and His Egyptian Wife, Reconsidered* (Oxford: Oxford University Press, 1998); Nir, *Joseph and Aseneth: A Christian Book* (Sheffield: Sheffield Phoenix, 2012). I find Patricia Ahearne-Kroll and Gordon Zerbe's arguments for the dating of Joseph and Aseneth as a Hellenistic or early Roman Jewish/Judean work to be most compelling. See Ahearne-Kroll, *Aseneth of Egypt: The Composition of a Jewish Narrative*, EJL 53 (Atlanta: SBL Press, 2020); Zerbe, *Non-retaliation in Early Jewish and New Testament Texts: Ethical Themes and Social Contexts* (Sheffield: Sheffield Academic, 1993). An Egyptian provenance, however, is not *necessitated* by the story's setting in Egypt and its artful use of Egyptian symbols from the Ptolemaic period (see Ahearne-Kroll, *Aseneth of Egypt*, 187–241), though it is certainly possible.

17. The manuscript tradition attests to several names for this ancient work, two

Simeon and Levi's retributive violence. *Aseneth*, however, does so by casting the brothers as characters in a new story that parallels the plot of Gen 34 in several ways.¹⁸ Through various episodic circumstances, *Aseneth* explores the question of when and how one who worships God (ὁ θεοσεβής) should wield the sword or "repay evil for evil." These were not just interpretations of a text but living stories "in their own right,"¹⁹ like children

---

of which are discussed in ch. 4. Modern scholarship has adopted the name Joseph and Aseneth, but Kraemer argues that *Aseneth* is more fitting, as the narrative centers on the female protagonist throughout (*When Aseneth Met Joseph*, 3), and Ahearne-Kroll follows suit (*Aseneth of Egypt*, 1 n. 1). I agree that *Aseneth* is a more fitting title for the work, and it reflects the earliest attestation of its title found in the Syriac, which was simply labeled "Of Aseneth."

18. See ch. 4 for further discussion.

19. Eva Mroczek, *The Literary Imagination in Jewish Antiquity* (Oxford: Oxford University Press, 2016), 7. Mroczek pushes back on the "biblical centrality" often assumed by Second Temple period scholarship, which takes the literary remains of Second Temple Judaism primarily as "witnesses to early biblical interpretation" and either "mines" them for "biblical allusion" or combs them through for "clues about the views of scriptures and canonicity its authors held" (7). Both methods of inquiry, she argues, do a disservice to the literature, which is our window into the rich culture of Second Temple Judaism, in which literary production flourished, since "most of these texts are [not read] as literary products in their own right" (7). Andrew Teeter similarly challenges the narrow focus of scholarship that seeks to understand Second Temple period literature that "rewrites" its Scriptures for their "exegetical function" alone: "Examples of 'rewritten Bible' are not merely compilations of anthologies of exegetical tradition. They are, instead, full-fledged literary works in their own right, each with its own distinct profile and its own specific compositional aims." See Teeter, "On 'Exegetical Function' in Rewritten Scripture: Inner-biblical Exegesis and the Abram/Ravens Narrative in Jubilees," *HTR* 106.4 (2013): 375. Teeter uses Jub. 11's re-presentation of Gen 15 as a case study and argues that Jub. 11 is *not* primarily an "interpretation" of Gen 15 but is part of a larger compositional strategy that both responds to Mesopotamian traditions and parallels Abraham with the portrayal of other patriarchs—Adam, Noah, and Joseph more specifically ("On 'Exegetical Function,'" 401). Mroczek's and Teeter's arguments, which destabilize scholarly assumptions of Bible centrality and open up new channels of inquiry into these diverse expressions of Second Temple Jewish culture, form a welcome corrective to the field. Yet, even Mroczek concedes that certain texts, not officially canonized until the second century CE, *were* authoritative and central among a wide range of Jewish communities during the Second Temple period: "To be sure, most of the texts treated as authoritative and extensively copied in the Second Temple period were quite close to the biblical books we now have. Among the Qumran manuscripts are texts that look very much like the Masoretic Text—the authorized texts of biblical books in the rabbinic Bible—as well as the Hebrew texts

birthed from encounter with Gen 34 into a new generation. Furthermore, *Aseneth* went on to have many children of its own, as Christian scribes encountered and retold the story for their own generations in ways that uniquely engaged with its ethical messages. As stories encountered, these later narratives—Jubilees, *Judean Antiquities*, and the various iterations of *Aseneth*—had their own unique force that they exerted on their audiences.

Assessing and reflecting on the force exerted by these ancient stories can provide insight into the ethical potentials—for better or for worse—of our own generation's stories. Socionarratology helps us to attend to the ways in which stories not only encounter their audiences but act to shape who they are and their conceptions of who they can become. In the late twentieth century, sociologist Margaret Somers reported that a growing corpus of cross-disciplinary research was

> showing us that stories guide action; that people construct identities (however multiple and changing) by locating themselves or being located within a repertoire of emplotted stories; that "experience" is constituted through narratives; that people make sense of what has happened and is happening to them by attempting to assemble or in some way to integrate these happenings within one or more narratives; and that people are guided to act in certain ways, and not others, on the basis of the projections, expectations, and memories derived from a multiplicity but ultimately limited repertoire of available social, public, and cultural narratives.[20]

---

that underlie the Septuagint—the Greek translation of the Hebrew Scriptures that was later used by early Christian communities. Many of the texts now in the Bible had pervasive cultural influence, especially such texts as Genesis, Exodus, Deuteronomy, and Isaiah, which were widely copied and invoked in other writings. This is unmistakable" (*Literary Imagination*, 11). That the authors of Jubilees, *Antiquities*, and *Aseneth* inherited the same stories from Genesis and retold them in unique ways is undeniable and remains central to my investigation of them.

20. Margaret Somers, "The Narrative Constitution of Identity: A Relational and Network Approach," *ThSoc* 23 (1994): 614. See also Edward Bruner, "Introduction," in *The Anthropology of Experience*, ed. Victor W. Turner and Edward M. Bruner (Chicago: University of Illinois Press, 1986), 3–32; Bruner, "Ethnography as Narrative," in Turner and Bruner, *Anthropology of Experience*, 139–55; Marshall Ganz, "Public Narrative, Collective Action, and Power," in *Accountability through Public Opinion: From Inertia to Public Action*, ed. Sina Odugbemi and Taeku Lee (Washington, DC: World Bank, 2011), 273–87; Julie Hansen, "The Ethics of Storytelling: Narrative Hermeneutics, History, and the Possible," *MS* 13 (2020): 350–54; Arthur Frank, "Notes on

In other words, stories have the capacity to shape individual and social consciousness, to draw social boundaries, to inform people's conceptualization of what is and what is possible, to shape their identity, and to guide their behavior. These capacities of story contribute to what Hanna Meretoja terms the "ethical potential of narratives."[21] Arthur Frank has dubbed the growing interdisciplinary conversation about these capacities of story *socionarratology*. Socionarratology is a multifaceted, interdisciplinary inquiry into the symbiotic relationship between humans and stories.[22] Primarily, it investigates *how* stories work in the lives of humans; specifically, socionarratology asks how stories shape the perception and action of humans who are caught up in them. These concepts of social epistemology and social ontology, inspired by philosophical theories about narrative, hermeneutics, and selfhood, acknowledge that not only do people create and shape stories, but stories themselves are actors and shapers of human consciousness.[23] Thus, attending to the shaping power of stories is no mere

---

Socio-narratology and Narrative Therapy," *JNFT* 2 (2017): 3–19; Frank, "Philoctetes and the Good Companion Story," *Enthymema* 16 (2016): 119–27; James Phelan, "Narrative Ethics," in *Handbook of Narratology*, ed. Peter Hühn, Jan Christoph Meister, and Wolf Schmid (Berlin: de Gruyter, 2014), 531–46; Francesca Polletta, "Contending Stories: Narrative in Social Movements," *QS* 21 (1998): 419–41; Michael White and David Epston, *Narrative Means to Therapeutic Ends* (New York: Norton, 1990); Julie Cruikshank, *The Social Life of Stories: Narrative and Knowledge in the Yukon Territory* (Lincoln: University of Nebraska Press, 1998), 39, 43.

21. Hanna Meretoja, *The Ethics of Storytelling: Hermeneutics, History, and the Possible* (Oxford: Oxford University Press, 2017). Meretoja suggests six aspects of the ethical potential of narratives: to "cultivate and expand one's sense of the possible," to "contribute to personal and cultural self-understanding," to "provide an ethical mode of understanding other lives and experiences," to "create challenge, and transform narrative in-betweens," to "develop one's perspective-awareness and capacity for perspective-taking," and to "function as a mode of ethical inquiry" (89).

22. Frank, *Letting Stories Breathe*, 15. "Stories need humans in order to be told, and humans need stories in order to perceive the world, to gain a sense of agency in that world, and to bond with others in relationships and groups" (Frank, "Notes on Socio-narratology," 10).

23. Frank, *Letting Stories Breathe*, 14–15. In Somers's words, "It is through narrativity that we come to know, understand, and make sense of the social world, and it is through narratives and narrativity that we constitute our social identities ... [and that] all of us come to be who we are (however ephemeral, multiple, and changing) by being located or locating ourselves (usually unconsciously) in social narratives *rarely of our own making*" ("Narrative Constitution of Identity," 606). See also Arthur P. Bochner, *Coming to Narrative: A Personal History of Paradigm Change in the Human Sciences*

academic exercise. The stakes are no lower than our very lives and the lives of our families, communities, and nations.

Socionarratology acknowledges that stories can act as good companions to human life and that they can be dangerous.[24] If stories indeed have the power to shape human consciousness and to "refine the human capacity to simulate possible futures," then they can do so for better or for worse.[25] A narrative told one way can rally a disparate group of people to collective action for the betterment of a community, while told another way can drive a nation to war.[26] Dominant cultural narratives, sometimes called "public narratives" or "canonical narratives,"[27] have a particularly strong shaping effect on a large number of people within a society and are therefore charged with greater potential for good or for danger. As a strategy of mitigating the potential dangers of a story, Frank "recommends

---

(Walnut Creek, CA: Left Coast, 2014). Concerning philosophical theories about narrative, hermeneutics, and selfhood, see especially Paul Ricoeur, e.g., "The Human Experience of Time and Narrative," *RP* 9 (1979): 17–34; Ricoeur, *Time and Narrative*, trans. Kathleen McLaughlin and David Pellauer, vol. 3. (Chicago: University of Chicago Press, 1988).

24. Modern feminist interpreters of the biblical stories have also taken this axiom for granted. Renita Weems argues the dangers of the metaphorical portrayal of God as vengeful husband by the biblical prophets in *Battered Love: Marriage, Sex, and Violence in the Hebrew Prophets* (Minneapolis: Fortress, 1995). Ezekiel 16 and 23's "full-fledged drama" is a metaphorical narrative that casts Israel in the role of adulterous wife and YHWH in the role of avenging husband. The intended effect is to shape the audience Israel's response (a return to the sole worship of YHWH, as a faithful wife was expected to be the sole partner of her husband), but the dangerous effect that Weems argues is that it has the potential to be read (and *has* been read) as divine legitimation for wife battering in human relationships. Aware, often in personal ways, of the dangerous consequences that the interpretation of certain stories has had on women throughout history, many feminist interpreters have offered learned readings that aim to heal rather than harm.

25. Frank, *Letting Stories Breathe*, 22.

26. Polletta, "Contending Stories," 419–46. Philip Smith, in his research of twentieth-century war and media coverage, has identified three genres or "narrative templates" of conflict situations. See Smith, *Why War? The Cultural Logic of Iraq, the Gulf War, and Suez* (Chicago: University of Chicago Press, 2005). He examines the rhetoric and role casting of each of these genres, and the effects they have on the inflation or deflation of violent conflict.

27. Derek M. Bolen and Tony E. Adams, "Narrative Ethics," in *The Routledge International Handbook on Narrative and Life History*, ed. Ivor Goodson et al. (New York: Routledge, 2017), 619.

a mode of interpretation that is dialogical" in the Bakhtinian sense. No speaker and no voice is to be singular or allowed to be finalized as having "the last word."[28] Socionarratology investigates stories by means of dialogical narrative analysis, often studying the retelling of stories in different contexts and to different audiences and how stories are adapted to different environments and purposes.[29]

Perhaps the shaping power of stories is nowhere more potent than when one understands oneself or one's contemporary others to be represented within an ongoing story. Within the realm of narrative ethics, representational ethics is concerned with the narrativizing of individuals, which "shift[s] their ontological status from persons to characters in a story."[30] In other words, representational ethics attends to how persons or groups are characterized, that is, how they are crafted as characters.[31] Representational ethics acknowledges that, due to the shaping power of narrative, the characterization of individuals or groups may function to inform or shape an audience's conception of the self and other. By extension, representations can function, for example, to center or decenter, to liberate or oppress, to humanize or dehumanize. There is a danger inherent in dehumanizing or oppressive narrative representation when it is accepted as truth rather than as a limited construction by those who are caught up in a story. The dehumanizing capacity of representation in narrative is worth attending to, for the ramifications for narratives with authoritative force[32] affect the lived experience of those who are influenced by them. Indeed, at times it is a matter of life and death. For example, when European conquerors came to the "New World" of the Americas, there was a wide stream of narrative self-representation in writings and sermons that the God of the Europeans (also the God of the Bible) had adopted *them* as the new Israel, with the promised land of America stretching out before them, waiting to be conquered.[33] Biblical readers and preachers

---

28. Frank, *Letting Stories Breathe*, 16.
29. Frank, *Letting Stories Breathe*, 16.
30. David Richter, "Review of *Narrative Ethics*," MFS 42 (1996): 249.
31. Newton, *Narrative Ethics*, 25.
32. That is, narratives that are "taken up" and thus have power of influence over their audience's sense of self-identity and conceptualization of the world. "Texts tax readers with ethical duties which increase in proportion to the measure with which they are taken up" (Newton, *Narrative Ethics*, 292).
33. Sylvester Johnson, "New Israel, New Canaan: The Bible, the People of God, and the American Holocaust," *USQR* 59 (2005): 25–39.

took up the narrative from Deuteronomy and Joshua, casting themselves as nascent Israel, full of hope and promise, and the native First Nations as the diabolical Canaanites destined for annihilation.[34] As European settlers and their descendants took up the biblical past as a divinely approved narrative template for their present, the blood of countless millions of Native American men, women, and children paved the road of westward expansion. Representation in narratives, especially dominant cultural narratives, can be dangerous indeed.

Stories therefore can act to restrict and define, but they can also expand and inspire. By shaping the relational space in which audience and narrative encounter each other, stories invite their audiences to consider new possibilities of being and doing. As a dimension of narrative ethics, hermeneutical ethics in one sense grapples with the nature of this encounter and the agency that both text and reader bring to it. Meretoja, basing her claims on the work of philosophers Hannah Arendt and Adriene Caverero, calls the space of encounter between text and reader the "narrative in-between." This "shared relational space," or "common world" that storytelling creates for its audience, comes with a sense of connection and community that is built by the act of storytelling itself. In this narrative in-between, the possibility of "what is thinkable and sayable, ... experienceable and doable within different subject positions" becomes fluid and shaped by the shared encounter with a story.[35] The narrative in-between is, in essence, "a space of possibilities" where "new vocabularies and modes of expression can also open up new possibilities of experience, thought, and action."[36] According to Meretoja, "the ontological, epistemological, ethical, and social are integral and interconnected aspects of the sense of the possible" that narratives offer in this space.[37] Essential to the conceptualization of the narrative in-between is the idea that both reader and text have shaping power over the space of their encounter. It stands to reason that, just as contextual space affects the nature of human encounters, so too the space of encounter between text and audience influences *how* interaction takes place and what *sort* of force a text may have on its audience, or an audience

---

34. Abiel Abbot, *Traits of Resemblance in the People of the United States of America and Ancient Israel*, repr. in *The American Republic and Ancient Israel*, ed. Moshe David (New York: Arno, 1977).

35. Meretoja, *Ethics of Storytelling*, 117.

36. Meretoja, *Ethics of Storytelling*, 117, 93.

37. Meretoja, *Ethics of Storytelling*, 92.

on the text. Rhetorical features, generic choices, and other textual features help to shape the relational space in which a narrative meets its audience, setting the stage, as it were, for the encounter. Audiences, of course, may respond with their own degree of power and influence over this space, with presence, resistance, vulnerability, or interpretation.

Thus, considering Gen 34 through the lens of narrative ethics and socionarratology as a story encountered and retold can open up possibilities of understanding that previous methods missed. Narrative ethics invites us to consider the unique force that Gen 34 places on its audience and why the narrative has resisted finalization while continuing to inspire generational engagement. By taking up the ethical quandaries of Gen 34, the later stories of Jubilees, *Judean Antiquities*, and variations of *Aseneth* are as much in dialogue with that previous narrative as they are inviting their own audiences into dialogue with themselves.[38] Each of these later stories engages with one of Gen 34's central informational gaps: the lack of an explicit evaluation of the retributive violence of Simeon and Levi. These later re-presentations of Gen 34 are crafted with strong evaluations of the actions of the biblical characters. They use techniques of emplotment, representation, and alteration of the narrative in-between to shape the identity of their audience, including their ethos toward outsiders and retributive violence. Considering the literary children of Gen 34 through the lens of socionarratology enables us to consider not only evidence to exegesis but the ethical potentials and problems of re-presenting biblical stories in various contexts, and the power of readers to respond to and shape their inherited cultural narratives.

An underlying concern of primary importance in the analysis of these narratives is the ethics of re-presenting biblical characters and narratives today. Although these stories were first told in antiquity, they can offer insights for multimedia modernity, in which tellings and retellings of biblical narratives reach the masses through digital pulpits, internet-streamed dramatizations, movies, blogs, children's books, novels, podcasts, and other media. Through the lens of narrative ethics and socionarratology, I aim to offer a nuanced critical engagement with the biblical narrative and its ancient re-presentations that can provide productive reflection on the power of biblical storytelling in this generation.

---

38. Perhaps with the exception of Jubilees, which precludes dialogue by various methods, favoring the promotion of a monological re-presentation of Gen 34 to be adopted by its audience. See further discussion in ch. 3.

2. An Introductory Outline of this Book

The following chapters demonstrate the merits of applying the interpretive theory of socionarratology and Newton's tripartite theorization of narrative ethics to the study of Gen 34 and four of its literary descendants. Although the three aspects of narrative ethics are overlapping and inseparable, each part of this book forefronts a particular area of inquiry from Newton's tripartite structure.

In chapter 2, through the lens of narrational ethics, I argue that Gen 34 is composed in a way that fosters dialogical engagement. I attend to the form of the ancient Hebrew text of Gen 34, in particular its covert narration, semantic ambiguity, multiperspectivity, and reticence. By *reticence*, I refer to the "permanent suspension of information" as a narrative feature.[39] In chapter 2, I argue that this unique combination of formal features works together in a way that heightens the ambiguity of the narrative on multiple fronts and demands the reader's creative and evaluative engagement with the many perspectives represented within the narrative. Dinah, whose name means "judgment" or "she decides,"[40] is silent in her own story, as is, I argue in chapter 2, the final verdict of the narrator on the perspectives and ideas contested in the narrative. I posit that the narrator's mediation of the events and description of the characters does not offer an ethical evaluation of any character's actions.[41] Rather, the formal structure of the narrative in effect places the demand for engagement and evaluation on the reader. Genesis 34 leaves questions unanswered through the ambiguity constructed by its formal features, inviting the audience to consider the various perspectives and ethics in tension, including that of violent retribution.

Chapters 3 and 4 turn to later texts that took up the story of Dinah in the Second Temple period and centuries after, retelling the narrative and

---

39. Leona Toker, *Eloquent Reticence: Withholding Information in Fictional Narrative* (Lexington: University Press of Kentucky, 1993), 15–16. Toker argues that the informational gaps created through reticence invite the reader into the creation of the narrative (5). See further discussion in ch. 2, §2.6.

40. דינה is a feminine name derived from the verb with judicial connotations, דון, meaning "to execute judgment," or "decide a legal case," or from the related noun דין, meaning "legal judgment," "plea," "cause," or "condemnation." See further discussion in ch. 2, §2.6.

41. Contra Sternberg, Bechtel, Parry, and A. Joseph.

re-presenting its characters in ways that provide judgment on the events and actions of the characters that the original text left unresolved. Chapter 3 compares Jubilees and *Judean Antiquities*, and chapter 4 compares two manuscripts of *Aseneth*. The precise dating of the text of Gen 34 remains as elusive as ever, yet the cultural and historical contexts of Jubilees, Josephus's *Judean Antiquities*, and MSS A and F of *Aseneth* can be discerned to a degree. Each later text is therefore a witness to how Gen 34 was encountered, adapted, and told within four different contexts over time. Thus, these chapters analyze four ways in which later generations engaged with, retold, or renewed the story and its characters to grapple with contemporary ethical issues and to shape their respective audiences. In particular, I attend to the ways in which all four later texts provide and promote an evaluative judgment regarding the retributive violence of Simeon and Levi through the re-presentation of the events and characters of Gen 34.

Chapter 3 considers the role that representation plays, for better and for worse, in shaping identity and ethos in two prominent ancient Judean histories, Jubilees and *Judean Antiquities*. I make a case for the study of these ancient texts as authoritative national histories, defining what I mean with the use of that generic distinction and addressing why this generic distinction matters to the force of the representations they exhibit. This comparative analysis focuses on the re-presentation of Gen 34 in Jub. 30 and *A.J.* 1.337–341 while considering those sections within the literary context of the full historical narratives they are embedded within. While the interests of socionarratological inquiry are as vast and varied as human life and narrative expression itself, chapter 3 engages two concerns within the growing field connected to representational ethics. First, how does national history telling do the work of corporate identifying, or shaping the identity and actions of a people group by emplotting them temporally in an ongoing story? Second, how does the representation of the corporate self and other(s) in national narratives influence the relational ethos of a nation?

Chapter 4 looks at how two Christian manuscripts of *Aseneth* (MSS A and F) re-present the characters and plot structure of Gen 34, and how each uses rhetorical framing to inspire its audiences with new possibilities of responding to offense and offenders, upholding certain characters recast from Gen 34 as ethical models. I chose MSS A and F for this dialogical analysis because they each represent a popular iteration of the story that was transmitted across several communities and centuries. MS A is the earliest full text manuscript of *Aseneth* in family *a*, a group of

Byzantine Greek manuscripts that share MS A's framing of the tale as a hagiography, and MS F represents the form of *Aseneth* that passed into the Romanian vernacular by the eighteenth century.[42] The two manuscripts of *Aseneth* re-present the plot of Gen 34,[43] with Aseneth in Dinah's role as endangered daughter of Israel, and Simeon and Levi once again in their roles as avengers (ἔκδικοι). Although Dinah's voice is never heard in Gen 34, Aseneth's voice resounds in both MSS A and F, wielding power and influence, shaping the events and characters around her. In chapters 22–29 of *Aseneth* A and F, Aseneth's character, words, and actions are centralized in unique ways, put forth into the narrative in-between as paramount. I observe how each manuscript shapes the audience's encounter with the character of Aseneth and her voice, and how that shaping affects the unique force or claim that each text exerts on its audience. In conversation with Meretoja's theorization of hermeneutic ethics, I attend to how the formal features of each of these narratives craft a relational space between text and communal audience, a narrative in-between, in which the audience is invited to consider and adopt the unique ethos of nonretaliation presented by its exemplary characters. With varying degrees of force determined by generic markers or rhetorical shaping, these manuscripts work to expand a sense of not only what is possible but also what is preferable for the God-worshiper (θεοσεβής) when faced with various types of offense.

In chapter 5, which concludes this book, I offer comparative reflections on the power of each narrative to shape its audiences' ethical identities through its unique re-presentation of Gen 34. I first consider each later text as a reader of Gen 34 that responds to its gaps and ambiguities in different ways. I pay attention to how each text provides its own evaluation of Simeon and Levi's retributive violence—or "decides *dinah*"—in a way

---

42. Jonathon Stuart Wright, "After Antiquity: Joseph and Aseneth in the Manuscript Transmission: A Case Study for Engaging with What Came after the Original Version of Jewish Pseudepigrapha" (PhD diss., University of Oxford, 2018), 1:140; Christoph Burchard, "Joseph and Aseneth in Rumania," *JSJ* 39 (2008): 542–45. Furthermore, "Family *a* [was] the most popular Greek version of the story by the number of manuscripts preserved" (Wright, "After Antiquity," 140). Though MS F's title is not preserved due to damage, in the four extant Romanian manuscripts, the story is titled "The Very Useful Story of Joseph and Aseneth," signaling its reception in this stream of tradition as instructive for Orthodox monastics. See Christoph Burchard assisted by Carsten Burfeind and Uta Barbara Fink, *Joseph und Aseneth*, PVTG 5 (Leiden: Brill, 2003), 17.

43. See ch. 4 for further details.

that promotes a specific ethos to its contemporary audiences. The conclusion also comparatively considers the ways in which each text acts to shape the identity of its readers. Reading these later re-presentations of Gen 34 in conversation with one another serves to illuminate and mitigate potential dangers of biblical storytelling.

2
Dinah Decides: The Ethics of Multiperspectivity and Reticence in Genesis 34

> Stories always pose that question: what kind of truth is being told? Stories never resolve that question; their work is to remind us that we have to live with complicated truths.
> —Arthur Frank, *Letting Stories Breathe*

1. Introduction

Genesis 34 forces its readers to encounter a situation rife with complexity. Woven together by the threads of semantic ambiguity, covert narration, multiperspectivity, and reticence, the narrative of Gen 34 is crafted in a way that places a "constitutive force" on the reader,[1] bringing the reader into dialogical engagement with its characters and their ethical relationships. This story, which has resisted finalization for millennia, ends with an open debate between Jacob and his sons, inviting those who receive the tale to join in the conversation, assessing and evaluating the characters' perspectives and choices in the wake of the kernel event.[2]

The annotated translation of Gen 33:18–34:31 below highlights the points of multiperspectivity, reticence, and ambiguity that are discussed throughout the chapter.[3] The following analysis of the verbs in the crucial

---

1. Newton, *Narrative Ethics*, 29.
2. See introduction, §1. This is a term that describes events that "are so essential [to a narrative] that they could not possibly be removed without destroying the logic of the narrative." See Mark Allan Powell, *What Is Narrative Criticism?* (Minneapolis: Fortress, 1990), 36. Bader asserts, and I agree, that the kernel event of Gen 34 is the encounter between Shechem and Dinah (*Sexual Violation*, 5).
3. I begin in chapter 33 because the last sentences of that chapter serve as exposition for the rest of the story.

verse, Gen 34:2, which contains the kernel event of the story, demonstrates that there is a degree of semantic ambiguity regarding what happened between Shechem and Dinah. This is supported by the fact that interpreters have brought various biblical cotexts into dialogue with Gen 34 in their efforts to comprehend the kernel event and the chain of events it incites. Each cotext shades the interpretation of both what is at stake in the narrative and what ethical standards are assumed by it, often to drastically different effects.

That readers have felt the need to appeal to other texts for aid in assessing Gen 34 draws attention to a felt lack, that of the narrator's evaluation. I argue below that the narrator presents the characters and events of the story without explicit evaluative assessment of them. Furthermore, the rich multiperspectivity through which this story is crafted, combined with reticent characterization techniques and the absence of evaluation, produces ambiguity that compels reader engagement while giving rise to equivocal readings.

Yet in the midst of this openness and uncertainty, an artful connection is made that gestures to where the reader can look for the evaluation lacking in the narrative. The permanent withholding of Dinah's voice or perspective is centralized along with the essential but absent element of evaluation that readers for millennia have sought and debated. Thus, the structure of the narrative communicates that the key to unlocking the evaluation of the story's characters and events is hidden within the voice of Dinah. Yet in the text as it stands, her voice remains forever unheard, leaving readers to grapple in their own unique ways with the complex ethical maze that Gen 34 sets forth.

2. Annotated Translation: Genesis 33:18–34:31

The purpose of this translation is principally to demonstrate the multiperspectivity, reticence, and ambiguity inherent in the text. The annotations offer explanations for translational choices and also serve to draw attention to moments of ambiguity that later interpreters take in different directions. I also make note of any significant variations in the telling present in the LXX.[4] The authors of the second-century BCE Jubilees and Jose-

---

4. Many scholars agree that the LXX, a third-century BCE Greek translation of the Pentateuch, may offer us a glimpse at an earlier form of the biblical text than the MT. While this chapter will mainly make its argument based on the Hebrew, the LXX

phus's first-century CE *Judean Antiquities*, addressed in chapter 3, likely had Hebrew copies that predate the MT but are no longer extant. There is evidence, however, to suggest that Josephus also made use of the LXX when composing the *Antiquities*.[5] For the author(s) of the Greek romance *Aseneth*, discussed in chapter 4, the LXX was a source of inspiration, as supported by numerous allusions to and quotations from LXX texts and the heavy use of septuagintisms.[6]

This translation aims to represent the laconic nature of this text (something that is also carried over into the Greek of LXX Genesis). This narrative, as with many in the Hebrew Bible, is strung together most frequently through the use of *vav*-consecutive verbal forms. This heavy use of the simple *vav* conjunction produces "loose and indefinite connections" in the original language.[7] It is common in English translations to assign a more distinct value to the conjunctive marker *vav*, but I share Robert Alter's opinion that representing the pervasive conjunctions of biblical narrative in translation does not diminish the artistry of the original text; rather, it brings over into English a sense of both the cadence and simplicity of Hebrew narrative.[8] My translation below seeks to convey the parataxis of the Hebrew so as to give a sense of the pacing of the narrative and its artful use of this

---

is our earliest witness to this text, for the copies of Gen 34 among the Dead Sea Scrolls are so fragmentary that they give enough evidence that something about "Shechem son of Hamor" was included on a scroll at Qumran, but little else. The differences between the MT and LXX versions of Gen 33:18–34:31 are slight, and though I have marked those that are of interest when considering the later texts addressed in this book, they are not discussed in the body of the chapter.

5. Christopher Begg, "Genesis in Josephus," in *The Book of Genesis: Composition, Reception, and Interpretation*, ed. Craig Evans, Joel N. Lohr, and David L. Petersen (Leiden: Brill, 2012), 303–5.

6. Marc Philonenko, *Joseph et Aséneth: Introduction, text critique, traduction et notes*, StPB 13 (Leiden: Brill, 1968), 28–30, 101; Zerbe, *Non-retaliation*, 72–97; Gerhard Delling, "Einwirkungen der Sprache der Septuaginta in 'Joseph und Asenneth,'" *JSJ* 9 (1978): 29–56; Patricia Ahearne-Kroll, "*Joseph and Aseneth* and Jewish Identity in Greco-Roman Egypt" (PhD diss., University of Chicago Divinity School, 2005), 218–39; Samuel D. Giere, *A New Glimpse of Day One: Intertextuality, History of Interpretation, and Genesis 1.1–5* (Berlin: de Gruyter, 2009), 232–25; Ahearne-Kroll, *Aseneth of Egypt*, 8.

7. GKC, 270.

8. Robert Alter, *The Art of Bible Translation* (Princeton: Princeton University Press, 2019), 16–17, 28–30. Alter compares the narration of the Hebrew Bible to the English prose of such acclaimed authors as Margaret Atwood, Philip Roth, James

simple conjunction.⁹ Furthermore, this artful simplicity limits the communication of causation or temporal relations, a feature that in places adds to the text's openness to various interpretations.¹⁰ Biblical Hebrew has at its disposal a range of subordinate clause markers, few of which are employed in this story. Where they are present, I have noted them, and where they are absent, I have refrained from supplying them as much as possible.¹¹

2.1. Genesis 33:18–34:31

> ³³:¹⁸And Jacob came safely¹² to the city of Shechem (which was in the land of Canaan) when he came from Padan-Aram, and he camped in front of the city. ¹⁹And he purchased a piece of the field on which he had stretched

---

Joyce, William Faulkner, Ernest Hemmingway, and Virginia Woolf—all "masters of English prose"—who also "cultivated parataxis as a resource of expression" (17).

9. By translating the majority of the *vavs* as "and," I also reflect the LXX, which renders 79 of the 86 connecting *vavs* as either καί (60x) or δέ (18x). In a handful of sentences, either in the voice of the narrator (34:2, 25) or in direct speech (34:9, 17, 21), either these simple conjunctions are excluded (when imperatival, in 34:9, or preceded by a temporal clause, in 34:25) or a compound sequence of verbs is rendered into a participial phrase, which is more common in Greek narrative. The form of the LXX text thus also reflects an intentional restraint and inclination toward literalness in its attempt to render the Hebrew syntax, with a few exceptions.

10. See Eugene Nida, "Principles of Translation as Exemplified by Bible Translating," *BT* 10 (1959): 159; Nida, "Fewer Words and Simpler Grammars Mean More Headaches," *BT* 33 (1982): 135; Robert Alter, *Pen of Iron: American Prose and the King James Bible* (Princeton: Princeton University Press, 2010), 158–60.

11. Additionally, when variations in verb form between coordinated clauses or introductory temporal clauses indicate subordinate relationships (e.g., temporality, conditionality, purpose, or result), I have translated this accordingly (e.g., Gen 34:5, 12, 16, 23, 25, 30). The *vav* of Hebrew can also be disjunctive or epexegetical, depending on context, and I have sought to communicate moments of clear disjunction with "now" or "but" (e.g., 34:5, 17, 30, 31) and clarifying constructions with "that is" (e.g., 34:29).

12. Heb. שלם. Just before this in Gen 32–33, Jacob survives an encounter with his brother, Esau, who had previously wanted to kill him (Gen 27:41–45). In that context, the adverbial שלם highlights Jacob's safe return to the land of Canaan. The adverb could also indicate that Jacob came "peacefully," signaling that his approach toward Shechem was done in peace, not with any intention of hostility. This sense of peacefulness is echoed in Hamor's speech about the Israelites to his countrymen in 34:21, "These men, they are peaceful [שלמים] with us." The LXX renders this a place name, "And Jacob came to Salem, the city of the Shechemites [καὶ ἦλθεν Ιακωβ εἰς Σαλημ πόλιν Σικιμων]." The author of Jubilees indicates *both* the manner in which Jacob

2. Dinah Decides

out his tent from the sons of Hamor,[13] father of Shechem, with a hundred kesitas.[14] [20]And he erected an altar there and called it El Elohe-Israel.[15]

[34:1]And Dinah, the daughter of Leah, whom she had borne to Jacob, went out to see the daughters of the land. [2]And Shechem, the son of Hamor the Hivite,[16] the prince of the land, saw her. And he took her, and he lay with her, and he debased[17] her. [3]And his whole being[18] clung to

---

arrived and a place name: "During the first year of the sixth week, [Jacob] went up safely to Salem, which is on the east side of Shechem, in the fourth month" (Jub. 30.1).

13. Or "Hamorites." LXX παρὰ Εμμωρ πατρὸς Συχεμ ἑκατὸν ἀμνῶν, "from Hamor, father of Shechem, with a hundred lambs." There is no mention of the "sons of Hamor" or "Hamorites" in Greek; rather, Jacob deals directly with Hamor, just as his grandfather Abraham and father, Isaac, dealt with other landowning princes in their day (Gen 20; 21:22–34; 26). This little difference establishes a direct relationship in the Greek between Jacob and Hamor before the events of ch. 34. In the later texts of Jubilees, *Judean Antiquities*, and *Aseneth*, this sale is not included or referenced.

14. A unit of money.

15. Or "El, the God of Israel," or "God, the God of Israel." Other instances of altar naming may be found in Exod 17:15 and Judg 6:24. This finds parallel in other instances of naming places in association with God (e.g., Gen 22:14, 28:19, 32:30, 35:15). Alternatively, with the altar naming passages and here in Gen 33, one could read the masculine singular direct object as referring to God, which finds parallel with non-altar-related naming of God by Hagar in Gen 16:13. The LXX has "he called upon the God of Israel [ἐπεκαλέσατο τὸν θεὸν Ισραηλ]." As with the sale of the land, this moment is not referenced by the later texts discussed in this book.

16. Some LXX manuscripts have Συχεμ ὁ υἱὸς Εμμωρ ὁ Χορραῖος, "Shechem, the son of Hamor the Horite." Though likely due to a reading of ההוי as the similarly shaped ההרי, this would potentially make a significant difference to later interpreters reading this story through the lens of the later laws; the Horites are not explicitly listed in Exodus or Deuteronomy's lists of prohibited intermarriages in Exod 34 or Deut 7 (see §5.5.1 below). The Horites were not considered "the sons of Canaan" by the genealogy of Gen 10:15–19 but rather the dwellers of the hill country of Seir before Esau and the Edomites took that land (Gen 14:6, 36:20, 36:29; Deut 2:12, 22). This designation of the Shechemites as Horites, however, is unattested in the later works of Jubilees, *Judean Antiquities*, and *Aseneth*. It makes more sense that the original designation would be that the Shechemites were Hivvites, as they dwelled "in the land of Canaan" (Gen 33:18). This is the designation that is dominant throughout the literary record.

17. See the thorough discussion of this string of transitive verbs below.

18. Heb. נפשׁו. This word refers to a person's seat of desire, life force, or being (e.g., Gen 35:18) and is often associated with emotions, passions, and verbs of desire. LXX "and he attached himself to the soul [or life] of Dinah [προσέσχεν τῇ ψυχῇ Δινας]." In both texts, this conveys Shechem's deep and strong attachment to Dinah, stated after the narration of intercourse.

Dinah, daughter of Jacob. And he loved the young woman[19] and spoke to the heart of the young woman. ⁴And Shechem said to Hamor his father, "Get[20] this young woman[21] as a wife for me."

⁵Now Jacob heard that he had defiled Dinah his daughter,[22] but his sons were with the livestock in the field, so Jacob kept silent until they came.

⁶And Hamor the father of Shechem went out to Jacob to speak with him. ⁷Now the sons of Jacob came in from the field when they heard,[23] and they were deeply grieved and greatly angered because he did an outrageous thing[24] in Israel by sleeping with a daughter of Jacob—it is not done this way.[25]

---

19. Heb. נערה, used twice in this verse to depict Dinah. Elsewhere, this term is used in the Hebrew Bible to depict a young woman, no longer a child, either unmarried (1 Sam 9:11, Esth 2:4), newly married (Deut 22:19), or a young, childless widow (Ruth 2:6). Also used for female slaves or attendants (Gen 24:61, Exod 2:5). The LXX uses the coterminous παρθένος in this verse. Dinah's precise age is not communicated in Gen 34, but later retellings have sometimes supplied one. Jubilees 30, for example, offers Dinah's age as twelve. James Kugel notes that this vulnerable age not only "increas[es] the pathos of the incident" but also "may have had some particular legal significance" to the author, but what that significance may have been is unknown. See Kugel, "Jubilees," in *Outside the Bible: Ancient Jewish Writings Related to Scripture*, ed. Louis H. Feldman, James L. Kugel and Lawrence H. Schiffman (Lincoln: University of Nebraska Press, 2013), 394.

20. Lit. "take." See discussion of לקח below.

21. LXX τὴν παῖδα ταύτην, "this girl."

22. LXX Ιακωβ δὲ ἤκουσεν ὅτι ἐμίανεν ὁ υἱὸς Εμμωρ Διναν τὴν θυγατέρα αὐτοῦ, "And Jacob heard that the son of Hamor had defiled Dinah, his daughter."

23. While I have rendered this sentence with a decisive sequential order, grammatically, the sequence of events in this verse is ambiguous and has been noted as such for almost two millennia, as the rabbis considered this an "undecidable text" in Gen. Rab. 80:5 (see Sternberg, *Poetics of Biblical*, 451). The syntax may be grammatically segmented to render several constructions: (1) Jacob's sons were in the field, "heard" something (either that Dinah was "defiled" *or* that Hamor and Shechem were approaching), and then learned of what had transpired, sparking their strong emotional response, or (2) Jacob's sons returned from the field, and upon hearing that Dinah was "defiled," they were filled with strong emotion. In other words, the sequence of events could be "news followed by homecoming" or "homecoming followed by news" (452). This "chronological duplicity" allows for two mutually exclusive understandings of the timeline of events at this moment (452).

24. Heb. נבלה, LXX ἄσχημον, "a shameful thing." A thorough discussion of this term, its translation, and its use in this sentence is found below.

25. Heb. וכן לא יעשה, LXX καὶ οὐχ οὕτως ἔσται. This phrase is often translated, "this should not be done" or "such a thing is not done." I have tried to convey the

⁸And Hamor spoke with them, saying, "Shechem my son, his whole being²⁶ longs for your²⁷ daughter. Please²⁸ give her to him as wife and ⁹intermarry with us—give your daughters to us, and our daughters you may take for yourselves—¹⁰and you may dwell among us and the land will be before you:²⁹ dwell and move about and be settled in it."

¹¹And Shechem said to her father and to her brothers, "Let me find favor in your eyes—and whatever you say to me I will give. ¹²Make the bride-price and gift exceedingly high for me so that I may give just what you say to me, just give me the young woman as my wife!"

¹³And the sons of Jacob answered Shechem and his father Hamor with deceit, and they spoke, because he had defiled Dinah, their sister. ¹⁴And they³⁰ said to them, "We are not able to do this thing, to give our

---

emphasis on the manner of action that both כן and οὕτως lend to this phrase. I consider this statement below as representing the perspective of Jacob's sons and as providing somewhat of an explanation for their strong emotional reaction preceding the phrase. Kugel notes, however, that some ancient readers, including the authors of Jubilees and Judith (e.g., Jub. 30.5, Jdt 9:2), took this phrase to be an authoritative statement from heaven (Kugel, *Traditions of the Bible*, 411–12).

26. See note 18 above. LXX προείλατο τῇ ψυχῇ τὴν θυγατέρα ὑμῶν, "he has chosen your daughter with his soul."

27. The second-person pronouns are plural throughout Hamor and Shechem's speeches to Jacob and his sons.

28. Heb. תנו נא אתה לו לאשה. LXX δότε οὖν αὐτὴν αὐτῷ γυναῖκα, "Therefore give her to him as a wife." The LXX has rendered the precative particle נא as the conjunctive adverb οὖν, meaning "therefore." While this is a very slight distinction, Hamor could be read as more supplicating in the Hebrew, and more demanding in the Greek. Neither of the later works of Jubilees and *Judean Antiquities* convey the direct speech of Hamor. Jubilees narrates that Shechem alone begged Jacob and his sons (Jub. 30.3) and Josephus only mentions Hamor's "request" and that he was "hoping that Jacob would grant the marriage" (*A.J.* 1.339).

29. LXX καὶ ἡ γῆ ἰδοὺ πλατεῖα ἐναντίον ὑμῶν, "and look! The land is wide before you."

30. LXX καὶ εἶπαν αὐτοῖς Συμεων καὶ Λευι οἱ ἀδελφοὶ Δινας υἱοὶ δὲ Λειας, "And Simeon and Levi the brothers of Dinah, Leah's sons, said to them." In the Greek, Simeon and Levi are singled out as primary agents early on in the narrative, and their status as Dinah's uterine siblings is made explicit at this early point in the narrative (see discussion on maternal ties below). Though "the sons of Jacob" all "answered Shechem and Hamor with deceit" in LXX Gen 34:13, only Simeon and Levi are depicted as speaking in LXX Gen 34:14. Whether Josephus was influenced by this version of the story is uncertain, for his own telling of it is unique, as ch. 3 explores in detail; however, he depicts Simeon and Levi as the sole agents of the plan against the Shechemites (*A.J.* 1.339–140). This is not dependent on Josephus's knowledge of a Genesis text with Simeon and Levi as the sneaky spokesmen of the clan, however, for in *Antiquities*,

daughter to a man who has a foreskin, for it is a disgrace to us. [15]Only by this will we agree with you:[31] If you become like us by circumcising yourselves—every male—[16]then we will give our daughters to you and your daughters we will take for ourselves,[32] and we will dwell with you and become one people. [17]But if you do not obey us by being circumcised, then we will take our daughter and go."

[18]And their words were good in the eyes of Hamor and in the eyes of Shechem, son of Hamor. [19]And the young man[33] did not hesitate to do the thing because he delighted in the daughter of Jacob and he was the most honored[34] of all his father's house. [20]And Hamor came, and Shechem, his son, to the gate of their city. And they spoke to the men of their city, saying, [21]"These men, they are peaceful with us. Let them dwell in the land and trade it. And look! The land is spacious enough[35] before them—let us take their daughters for ourselves as wives and let us give our daughters to them. [22]Only by this will the men agree to dwell with us to become as one people: by circumcising ourselves—every male—just as they are circumcised. [23]Their livestock and their property and all their animals—will they not be ours? Only let's agree with them so they will dwell[36] with us."

[24]And everyone who went out of the gate of his city listened to Hamor and his son Shechem, and they were circumcised—every male—everyone who went out of the gate of his city.

---

there is no parley between the parties and no deceptive speech; Hamor asks, and Jacob and the rest of his sons hold a conference to decide what to do and come to no conclusions. The characterization of Simeon and Levi in *Aseneth*, however, may rely on their agency as expressed in the LXX, or on other traditions, such as that of Jubilees, that herald these two men as primary.

31. The "you" is plural here and throughout the brothers' speech to Shechem and Hamor.

32. LXX καὶ ἀπὸ τῶν θυγατέρων ὑμῶν λημψόμεθα ἡμῖν γυναῖκας, "and from your daughters we will take wives for ourselves."

33. Heb. הנער, LXX ὁ νεανίσκος. The narrator's designation of Shechem as a נער and Dinah as נערה (34:3–4) suggests a correspondence in the identification of them as youths. The pairing of νεανίσκος and παρθένος in the Greek functions in a similar way.

34. Heb. והוא נכבד מכל בית אביו. *Niphal* of כבד used adjectivally here in a comparative construction. LXX uses the superlative form of the adjective ἔνδοξος, "honorable," which is a regular OG gloss for נכבד (See 1 Sam 9:6, 22:14, Isa 23:8). See further discussion below.

35. The Hebrew phrase רחבת ידים gives the sense of hands spread out wide in demonstration of the vastness of the land (also found in Judg 18:10, Is 22:18). This is similarly reflected in LXX 34:10 (see note 29 above).

36. Here, the verb ישב has the connotation of remaining and assumes the brothers' threats to leave in 34:17.

2. Dinah Decides

^{25}And it was on the third day when they were in pain that two sons of Jacob, Simeon and Levi, the brothers of Dinah, each took his sword and came on the city securely, and they killed every male. ^{26}Hamor[37] and Shechem his son they killed by the edge of the sword, and they took Dinah from Shechem's house[38] and left.

^{27}The sons of Jacob came on the slain, and they plundered the city because they[39] had defiled their sister. ^{28}Their sheep and their cattle and their donkeys and what was in the city and what was in the field they took.[40] ^{29}And all their wealth[41] and their little ones[42] and their women they captured and plundered, that is, all that was in the house.[43]

^{30}And Jacob said to Simeon and to Levi, "You have ruined me by making me stink among the inhabitants of the land,[44] among the

---

37. This sentence (ואת חמור ואת שכם בנו הרגו לפי חרב) begins with Hamor and Shechem as direct objects and emphatically specifies two very notable members included in the previous sentence's "every male." The initial *vav* may be operating epexegetically (see note 11 above), since the more literal translation is poetically emphatic in Hebrew but somewhat illogical in English: "And they killed every male. And Hamor and Shechem they killed by the edge of the sword." Nevertheless, here is a point of temporal ambiguity. For this same construction could also be read as indicative of sequence, with 34:25 indicating that they killed every (other) male, and *then* they killed Hamor and Shechem. I have chosen to leave the *vav* untranslated here in an effort to convey the poetic emphasis of the Hebrew. LXX Τόν τε Εμμωρ καὶ Συχεμ τὸν υἱὸν αὐτοῦ ἀπέκτειναν, "Both Hamor and Shechem they killed."

38. This is the first mention of Dinah's whereabouts since the beginning of the story.

39. Heb. אשר טמאו אחותם. The usage of אשר to begin a causal clause is also found in 34:13. The LXX, perhaps following the usage of אשר as a relative pronoun, renders this ἐν ᾗ ἐμίαναν Διναν τὴν ἀδελφὴν αὐτῶν, "in which they defiled Dinah, their sister." Both the Hebrew and Greek, however, have the plural active verb, as Westermann maintains ("because they defiled their sister" [*Genesis 12–36*, 534]). However, the NRSV and JPS rendering of the verb as a singular passive, "because their sister had been defiled," is not supported by any manuscript tradition. See further discussion below.

40. Note the echoes of Hamor's speech to his countrymen in 34:23. With a twist of irony, all that Hamor claimed the Shechemites would have from the Israelites, the sons of Jacob take from the Shechemites.

41. LXX πάντα τὰ σώματα αὐτῶν, "all their bodies," which may indicate servants or slaves here, as in Gen 36:6, Tob 10:10.

42. The SP, Syr., Vulg., and Targumim also reflect this. LXX πᾶσαν τὴν ἀποσκευὴν αὐτῶν, "all their baggage" or "all their portable property."

43. Hebrew is singular, but perhaps with a collective sense.

44. The Greek is less odious, "You have made me hated so that I am an evil to all the inhabitants of the land!" The minimization of Hebrew olfactory sensory idioms is

Canaanites and the Perizzites! And I am few in number, so if they gather against me and attack me, then I will be destroyed—I and my house!" ³¹But they said, "Should he use⁴⁵ our sister like a prostitute?"

3. The Kernel Event: Genesis 34:2

A reader's understanding of what the string of transitive verbs in Gen 34:2 depicts is essential to one's reading of this story, as verse 2 constitutes its kernel event—the event that sparks all of the dramatic unfoldings that follow. Yet there has been heated debate over the past forty years in biblical scholarship over what kind of sexual encounter is intended by the Hebrew text. The debate has centered heavily on the translation of the string of transitive verbs in Gen 34:2, ויקח אתה וישכב אתה ויענה.⁴⁶ Scholars have questioned whether the text indicates that Shechem assaulted Dinah and whether we can responsibly label a sexual assault in ancient Israelite culture "rape."⁴⁷ Grammatically, Shechem is the subject of each verb, and Dinah either the direct object or potentially a companion in the

---

a well-known feature of the LXX and OG. See Ian D. Richie, "The Nose Knows: Bodily Knowing in Isaiah 11:3," *JSOT* 87 (2000): 71.

45. Heb. הכזונה יעשה את אחותנו, in the most literal rendering, "Should he make our sister like a prostitute?" LXX Ἀλλ ὡσεὶ πόρνῃ χρήσωνται τῇ ἀδελφῇ ἡμῶν; "But should they use/treat our sister like a prostitute?" Here Simeon and Levi give voice to their perspective that multiple men are to blame. The "they" *may* be Shechem and Hamor, who had been attempting to deal with them in money and gifts *after* Shechem had been with Dinah sexually, unlike the typical ancient marriage deal, in which agreements and gifts were exchanged before the union of the couple. Even if their plural verb choice only included Shechem and Hamor in its scope, it was "every male" who felt their swords of vengeance (34:25). See further discussion in §5 below.

46. "And he took her, and he laid [with] her, and he debased her."

47. Throughout this book, I use the terms *rape* or *sexual assault* interchangeably, to indicate "a forced sexual encounter that occurs without the consent of the victim." This definition, however, does not assume an implicit binary between rape and consensual sex but acknowledges that there are "edges of consent" that our language regarding sexual coercion and violence often fails to account for (Graybill, *Texts after Terror*, 30–39). This definition is also broader than others that specify the genders of the rapist and victim or include various psychological diagnostics of the rapist. See Linda B. Bouque, *Defining Rape* (Durham, NC: Duke University Press, 1989), 15. Furthermore, this definition does not reference the psychological damage inflicted on the victim (see Bechtel, "What if Dinah Is Not Raped?," 20–21)—certainly a major feature of the understanding of rape in modern, individualist cultures—but it does not preclude the presence of psychological damage either. Thus broadly defined, one

case of ישכב אתה. Aided by the linguistic research of Lyn Bechtel, Alison Joseph, and Ellen van Wolde, I argue in agreement with them that the verb choice of Gen 34:2 is ambivalent with regard to whether this encounter was forced. Rather, what is clearly depicted is the resulting social implications for Dinah.

The first verb in question in Gen 34:2 is a *Leitwort* appearing ten times throughout the narrative. The root for "take," לקח, appears in the *qal* stem[48] instead of a verb that invariably depicts force, such as חזק. When humans are the object of לקח in Genesis, it is sometimes in situations of force (e.g., 14:12, 34:29, and possibly 16:3). In other situations it indicates "to bring along with," as Abraham does with his family (12:5), or as Jacob asks Joseph to bring Manasseh and Ephraim along with him so that he may bless them (48:9).[49] It is also used idiomatically to depict marriage, as in "taking a wife" (4:19, 11:29, 21:21). Alison Joseph, agreeing that the use of לקח is somewhat ambiguous in this verse, suggests that the semantic implications could be marital in 34:2.[50] Its range of semantic meaning is employed and explored throughout the Gen 34 narrative,[51] found in the speech of Hamor to describe intermarriage, "Give your daughters to us, and our daughters you may take for yourselves" (34:9), as well as in the narrator's description of Jacob's sons' seizure of people and property in 34:29. Outside Genesis, לקח is also found carrying the connotation of calling or summoning (e.g.,

---

can speak of rape in the collectivist culture of ancient Israel, which I argue in detail further below.

48. The LXX uses λαμβάνω throughout the narrative and here as an aorist active participle. The semantic range of λαμβάνω is similar to that of the Hebrew לקח. It can be used in situations of force as well as to depict gentler actions (bearing or bringing along with), and in idioms of marriage.

49. קחם־נא אלי ואברכם, "Bring them to me so that I may bless them" (Gen 48:9). Outside Genesis, לקח is also used in this sense, for example, in Balak's invitation to Balaam to come to yet another mountain to curse the Israelites ("Come now, and I will take you to another place. And Balak took Balaam," Num 23:27–28).

50. Alison L. Joseph, "Understanding Genesis 34:2: ʿInnâ," *VT* 66 (2016): 664.

51. In Esth 2, as in Gen 34, the semantic range of לקח is explored and poetically exploited. In Esth 2:7, Mordecai's adoption of his orphaned cousin Esther is described this way: לקחה מרדכי לו לבת, literally rendered: "Mordecai took her for himself as a daughter." This taking, a rescue from the dangers of orphanhood, is contrasted with the more fearsome and forceful taking that follows shortly after: Esther is "taken" to the house of the Persian king, who has been introduced as a quick-tempered man who does away with any woman who would deign to disobey him (Esth 2:8) to take place in his beauty contest.

Num 23:11, Judg 11:5, 1 Sam 16:11) and could therefore possibly indicate seduction in Gen 34:2.[52] The quality and semantic emphasis of Shechem's taking of Dinah is therefore ambiguous, and the verb supports a range of interpretations.

Similarly, שכב, which literally means "to lay down," is used idiomatically to depict sex within the Hebrew Bible. When used idiomatically, שכב depicts situations of mutual, forced, and ambiguous sexual relations, taking the prepositions עם or את ("with"), or את (direct object marker) interchangeably.[53] The interchangeability of these prepositions is also evinced in the fluidity found in other textual witnesses. The Samaritan Pentateuch, LXX,[54] Targums Pseudo-Jonathan, and Neofiti all attest to the use of את, "with," or more fully, אתה, "with her." While much has been made over the MT's choice to use the direct object marker here in Gen 34:2 and in the description of Amnon's assault on Tamar in 2 Sam 13:14,[55] the direct object marker with שכב is used in other MT passages that do not imply force. For example, שכב with the direct object marker is found in the Levitical laws regarding emissions in Lev 15:18 and menstrual impurity in Lev 15:24, and in laws regarding consensual adulterous relations in Num 5:13, 19. This, together with the fluidity found in other ancient witnesses, leaves open the question of what type of sexual encounter is indicated in Gen 34:2.[56]

Finally, the word most central to the recent scholarly discussion of this text is the *piel* verb ענה. Though rendered as "rape" or adverbially as "by force"[57] by such prominent English translations as the NRSV and JPS, by appealing to semantic linguistics Bechtel, van Wolde, and Joseph argue

---

52. See below.

53. עם: e.g., Gen 19:32, 35; 30:15. Also, in the invitations of Potiphar's wife to Joseph (Gen 39:12, 14), and Amnon's plea to Tamar (2 Sam 13:11). את ("with"): e.g., Gen 19:33, 26:10, 34:7, 35:22, 1 Sam 2:22. את (direct object marker): e.g., Lev 15:18, 24; Num 5:13, 19; 2 Sam 13:14; Ezek 23:8.

54. Which reads ἐκοιμήθη μετ' αὐτῆς, "he laid with her."

55. E.g., Sternberg, *Poetics of Biblical Narrative*, 446; Shimon Bar-Efrat, *Narrative Art in the Bible* (Sheffield: Sheffield Academic, 1989), 265; Bader, *Sexual Violation*, 13.

56. See also Abraham Tal, "Introduction and Commentaries on Genesis," in *BHQ Gen*, 162.

57. In the JPS translation, the verb ענה is rendered as an adverbial description of שכב, "he lay with her by force." The Anchor Bible commentary by E. A. Speiser also opts for this adverbial rendering. See Speiser, *Genesis*, 2nd ed., AB 1 (Garden City, NY: Doubleday, 1964), 262.

2. Dinah Decides

that these are mistranslations.[58] Rather, a survey of the use of the term throughout the Hebrew Bible suggests that ענה indicates a downward shift in social status, brought about by a number of causes, some of which are related to sex and others not. Its semantic range is similar to those of the English verbs *debase*, *degrade*, or *lower*.[59] This is reflected in Gerhard von Rad's rendering, "[he] humbled her," and Claus Westermann's translation, "[he] dishonored her."[60] Throughout the Hebrew Bible, ענה is used in a variety of cases in which no sexual transgression is involved. In Gen 15:13, when God proclaims to Abraham that his children will be afflicted in a foreign land for four hundred years, the word employed is ענה. The opening narrative of Exodus depicts how in the span of a few generations, the people descend from a politically favored and prosperous משפחה living in the lush land of Goshen to Pharaoh's slaves, forced to make an oppressively high daily quota of mudbrick and threatened with an imperial edict to murder their children.[61] Another example may be found in Gen 16; after Hagar becomes pregnant by her master, Abraham, with the effect that her mistress, Sarah, "became small in her eyes" (16:4), Sarah "humbles" Hagar, her slave (Gen 16:6). The verb ענה is not indicative of sexual assault in these situations but rather a demotion of status socially. The people of Israel, who had previously enjoyed a generation of favor and freedom under the rule of Egypt, were forced into slavery. Hagar, who had been elevated to the status of mother of Abraham's potential heir, was cast out from the בית אב.[62] It is also the verb used for humbling one's soul in prayer or fasting on the day of atonement (Lev 16:29, 31) or in other times of lamentation (Isa 58:3, Ps 35:13). Thus, ענה cannot be definitively translated as "rape" or "by

---

58. Bechtel, "What if Dinah Is Not Raped?"; Ellen van Wolde, "Does ʿinnâ Denote Rape? A Semantic Analysis of a Controversial Word," *VT* 52 (2002): 528–44; Joseph, "Understanding Genesis 34:2," 663–68.

59. Van Wolde, "Does ʿinnâ Denote Rape?," 542.

60. Gerhard von Rad, *Genesis: A Commentary*, trans. John H. Marks (Philadelphia: Westminster, 1972), 329; Westermann, *Genesis 12–36*, 533. Von Rad's proffered title for Gen 34 is "The Rape of Dinah," following the traditional interpretation of the event. Nonetheless, he notes (in accordance with Bechtel, van Wolde, and Joseph) that "the verb which is usually translated 'humble' (ʿinnâ) indicates the moral and social degrading and debasing by which a girl loses the expectancy of a fully valid marriage" (von Rad, *Genesis*, 331).

61. משפחה means "clan based on kinship."

62. Literally "father's house," the basic family unit of ancient Israelite society.

force," for it indicates neither a sexual act nor an adverb of coercion but a demotion in social status.

A survey of the many usages of ענה shows, however, that the majority of the cases in which it is used in the Hebrew Bible *are* in a sexual context.[63] This verb is used when Laban makes Jacob swear to take no other wives so his daughters may not be debased (Gen 31:50), and in the case of a divorced wife in Deut 21:14. To the man who chooses to divorce a wife who was once a captive of war, the law of Deut 21:14 states: "And it may be, if you do not delight in her, that you may let her go free. But you must certainly not sell her for money. You may not enslave her, because you have debased her [תחת אשר עניתה]." Here a husband who divorces his wife debases her. These examples help to demonstrate that "it is not the sex act itself that causes '*innâ*," as Alison Joseph argues. Though sex is involved in such cases (both of the above examples concern marriage), it is only when a sex act violates social, cultural, legal, or economic standards that it results in social debasement.[64] Even in the case of the 2 Sam 13 account of Amnon and Tamar, where Tamar's agonizing protestations are unquestionably present and the situation is undoubtedly one of rape, the use of ענה still depicts the *social* consequences that Tamar faces as a result of Amnon's actions. Without Amnon agreeing to marry her (to fulfill the laws of Deut 22:29, discussed below), she becomes socially marginalized and lives desolate (שממה) in the house of her brother Absalom (2 Sam 13:20). Thus, what the use of ענה indicates in Gen 34:2 is the social, societal consequences for Dinah from the sexual encounter with Shechem, whatever its nature. In conclusion, the MT most often used today and all extant forms of Gen 34:2 in antiquity support several scenarios: that yes, this was rape; that no, this was something like seduction; or that it was a mutual affair. What *is* clear in the text is that through the use of ambiguous terminology,[65] the event itself is somewhat shrouded.

3.1. Disclaimer: An Excursus

It is important to note at this point that this argument does not seek to discredit intentionally ideological readings that leverage Dinah's story for

---

63. Joseph, "Understanding Genesis 34:2," 664.
64. Joseph, "Understanding Genesis 34:2," 664–65.
65. "Take" and "lay with," rather than, say, "seize" (Deut 22:25) or "overpower" (2 Sam 13:14).

the service of liberation and healing for victims of sexual assault and for polemics against rape culture and victim blaming.[66] Such work of theologians and interpreters is valiant and viable to these noble aims. I honor such work and the public-facing work of others, such as Monica Coleman's *Dinah Project*,[67] that employ Dinah's story in service of starting important conversations about the appalling prevalence of rape today and the damaging effects of rape culture, including victim blaming and silencing, and the marginalizing effects of shame. There is something healing in reading one's own story in the pages of one's sacred Scriptures, and I do not seek to deny that salve to anyone. I share with these interpreters and theologians a concern for the well-being, safety, and flourishing of women and especially abused and silenced women. We also agree that the way the narrative of Gen 34 is read to the question of whether Shechem raped Dinah shapes the discussion of the ethical issues involved within it. We also share a vested interest that the narratives of the Hebrew Bible, and Dinah's in particular, be engaged with by modern readers in an ethically responsible way, in a way that does good and not harm.

3.2. Consent in Ancient Israel

I posit that it is the inherent linguistic ambiguity of the encounter between Shechem and Dinah that allows for various readings in answer to the question, "Was Dinah raped?"[68] or, better phrased, "Did Shechem rape

---

66. E.g., Susanne Scholz, "What Really Happened to Dinah: A Feminist Interpretation of Genesis 34," *LD* (2001): 1–15; Bader, *Sexual Violation*; Graybill, *Texts after Terror*; Yael Shemesh, "Rape Is Rape Is Rape: The Story of Dinah and Shechem (Genesis 34)," *ZAW* 119 (2007): 2–21; Frances Klopper, "Rape and the Case of Dinah: Ethical Responsibilities for Reading Genesis 34," *OTE* 23 (2010): 652–65. Scholz argues, "Even though we cannot say for sure what 'really' happened to Dinah," it is essential to the value of the story in today's world to understand that Dinah *is* raped (Scholz, "What Really Happened," 2). Only this way, Scholz argues, can Gen 34 be leveraged "to address the prevalence of rape.... Then the story becomes our own, and we will know what 'really' happened to Dinah" (14). While Bader and Graybill find that Gen 34:2 allows for semantic ambiguity regarding whether Dinah was raped, Shemesh and Klopper side with Scholtz's assertion that the only viable interpretation is that Shechem raped Dinah.
67. Monica A. Coleman, *The Dinah Project: A Handbook for Congregational Response to Sexual Violence* (Eugene, OR: Wipf & Stock, 2010).
68. See note 47 above.

Dinah?" The text itself does not definitively answer the question, but its answer has often been considered essential to a reader's assessment of the characters and their actions that follow, especially for modern readers. By broad, modern definition, rape is coerced sexual intercourse performed without the consent of the victim.[69] It follows, therefore, that consent is essential in the determination of whether a sexual encounter may be considered rape. Yet things are not so simple. Even in modernity, the complex reality of sexual relations can hold far more uncertain gray areas between a convenient binary between consensual sex and rape.[70] Nonetheless, here I make the case that the relevance of Dinah's consent in the evaluation of the characters and the events that follow is not only a modern concern; the laws of the Hebrew Bible indicate that a woman's consent was important in ancient Israel as well.

While the Hebrew Bible attests to a culture in which a woman's sexuality was governed by men, a woman's consent, or lack thereof, still plays a role in several of those laws (Deut 22:23–24 vs. 22:25–27, 25:5–10), stories (Gen 24:58; 38; 2 Sam 13), and poems (Song of Songs). Modern historians have often claimed that the question of a woman's consent is an irrelevant one in a society where women were the sexual property of men, and therefore it is also irrelevant within this narrative that arose from such a society. Alison Joseph, for example, asserts that the "offstage" nature of the encounter between Shechem and Dinah and the fact that "we know nothing of her attempt to refuse or submit" is "irrelevant to the function of the story." She holds that the text is not concerned with consent.[71] Based on the distinctions made within the biblical legal corpus, however, it is inaccurate to assert that rape was not a reality distinct from mutual relations in ancient Israel, and that whether Dinah was a consensual party was irrelevant in ancient readings of this text. Deuteronomy 22:20–21 declares that the penalty for a young woman found to have had illicit sex before marriage is

---

69. See note 47 above.

70. In *Texts after Terror*, Graybill argues for destabilizing the oft-assumed categorization of sexual experiences within a consensual sex/rape binary. Drawing from modern psychological studies and memoirs, she demonstrates that the stories of many modern sexual experiences describe a "complex gray area" or "fuzziness" between mutually consenting sex and rape/coercion (12–13). Graybill also holds that the narrative logic within Dinah's story—that in ancient Israel, a daughter's male relatives could hold the power of consent with regards to her marriage—serves to draw attention to the "problematic logic of consent" in general (41).

71. Joseph, "'Is Dinah Raped?,'" 28–29, 32–33.

death: "You shall stone her to death with stones, because she has done an outrageous thing [נבלה][72] in Israel by fornicating in her father's house." If one aims to contextualize the characters and actions of the story in light of its ancient Israelite culture, knowledge of Dinah's consent would certainly influence ancient assessments of the kernel event and its aftermath.

The contrasting legal rulings found in Deut 22:23–24 and 22:25–27 also support the claim that a woman's consent mattered when assessing cases of sexual transgression. In the first case (22:23–24), if a man "finds" a betrothed woman—a woman legally bound for marriage to another man—within a city and "he lies with her,"[73] they are both considered guilty of adultery and sentenced to death. The location matters to the sentencing of the woman because "she did not cry out in the city" (22:24), and the absence of her protest is assumed to be her complicity. Though a modern reader may find this problematic in many ways, it is somewhat beside the point, which is that the laws of ancient Israel *do* reflect a consideration for a woman's consent in situations involving sexual transgression.

This is made clear with the following case, in which "a man finds a betrothed young woman in a field, and he seizes her [והחזיק־בה] and lays with her [ושכב עמה], then only the man who laid with her shall die" (Deut 22:25). In this situation, the force of the encounter is made clear by the verb choice, "he seizes her," and in the explanatory statement that follows the rapist's indictment: "But to the young woman you shall not do anything; the young woman has committed no offense punishable by death. For this case is likened to when a man rises up against his neighbor and murders him, because he met her in the field. The betrothed young woman cried out, but there was no one to save her" (Deut 22:26–27). Thus, when the encounter is understood to be forced, the woman is free from blame. These ancient laws, arising from the same society that produced Gen 34, make a distinction between consensual sex and an unwelcome sexual assault or, in modern terms, rape.[74]

Perhaps it is more fitting to amend our view of women's sexual consent in ancient Israel. While the stark binary of consensual sex versus rape is not applicable to a culture in which the sexual activities of women were wholly governed by the men of their family, the extant laws attest that a woman's consent was still a concept important to the people of

---

72. The use of this term in Gen 34 is discussed below.
73. Heb. ושכב עמה.
74. See note 47 above.

that culture. The laws and policies governing sex may have been different from modern, individualistic cultures in which sexual assault is a heinous offense even *within* legally viable relationships such as an engagement or marriage. Perhaps it is more accurate to think of a continuum of consent in ancient Israel, with much undeterminable middle ground.[75] Most or all of this middle ground many modern feminists automatically consider rape, such as arranged marriages and other situations considered legal in ancient Israel, such as levirate marriages. They remain undeterminable, however, in all situations for which we have no knowledge of the woman's will. It is possible that consensuality in these cases was as diverse as the individuals within them, *depending on the woman's perspective*, as is true even today. In each unique circumstance, truth lies in the perspective and voice of the woman involved, not of outside analysts. This positioning of truth, I argue below in section 6, is highlighted by the narrative structure of Gen 34.

4. The Narrator and the Placement of Highly Charged Terms and Familial Epithets

Contrary to popular assumptions that the narrator of Gen 34 has an implicit evaluation of the characters and their actions to impose on the readers through subtle clues,[76] I propose that the narrator withholds evaluation of the characters and their actions. The narrator of Gen 34 is, in biblical narratologist Simon Bar-Efrat's terminology, more "silent and self-

---

75. This suggestion overlaps the modern critique against binarized consent discourse, which fails to account for the complexity of sexual realities (see Graybill, *Texts after Terror*, 30–39). Graybill applies this critique to her reading of the Hebrew Bible, arguing from the evidence of several narratives that consent is just as complex in the world of the biblical texts (39–57).

76. Bar-Efrat, *Narrative Art in the Bible*, 16; Sternberg, *Poetics of Biblical Narrative*, 445–46. Sternberg, for example, argues strongly for the "foolproof composition" of Gen 34, asserting that while readers may bring to the text their own assumptions and "counterread" it, to the detriment of themselves and others, the rhetoric and art of the Hebrew Bible's narratives *always* point the reader to the emotional and moral sympathy of the "right" characters and the "moral point" made by the narrative (55, 194). The assumption is not unlike that of Dietrich Ritschl, who argues that every biblical narrative has an "implicit axiom" underlying it. See Ritschl, *Zur Logik der Theologie: Kurze Darstellung der Zusammenhänge Theologischer Grundgedanken* (Munich: Kaiser, 1984).

effacing" than intruding—in a word, covert.[77] Rather than dominating the story with his voice, the narrator presents the events of the story by alternating between the different characters' points of view, in other words, by focalizing the events through their differing perspectives. Although some make the case that certain highly charged terms or familial epithets in Gen 34 are meant to either provide evaluation or sway the reader in the direction of the narrator's sympathies, I argue below that they function rather to intimate certain characters' perspectives and to heighten dramatic tension. The overall effect is that the role of evaluation is placed on the reader.

With the exception of some first-person narration, such as that in Ezra, Nehemiah, and Daniel, the biblical narrators rarely mention themselves but at times will indicate their temporal distance from the stratum of events with editorial asides, including phrases such as "to this day" (e.g., Gen 26:33, 2 Kgs 2:22) or "in those days" (e.g., Judg 17:6). The narrator of Gen 34, in contrast to these examples, is a covert narrator. This is seen in part through the minimal use of explanations. When explanations for actions are offered, as in verses 13 and 27, they are provided from the perspectives of the characters whose actions are described. Both of these verses contain causal phrases that offer the volition of the characters doing the action: "And the sons of Jacob answered Shechem and his father Hamor with deceit, *because he had defiled Dinah*, their sister" (Gen 34:13), and "they plundered the city *because they had defiled their sister*" (34:27). These explanations of motive are a manifestation of the narrator's omniscience and characterization techniques, rather than an evaluation or forefronting of the narrator's point of view. There are few asides or explanations from the narrator's point of view, allowing him to slip into the background as the events and characters are forefronted. This covert presence of the narrator gives the illusion of immediacy; the reader is brought straight into the action through the perspectives, words, and emotions of the various characters in their turn.

The narrator of Gen 34 withholds evaluation of the characters and their actions, and even refrains from offering the standards for evaluation, thus enhancing ambiguity at every turn. What I mean by this is not

---

77. Bar-Efrat, *Narrative Art in the Bible*, 23–34. Bar-Efrat posits a continuum of manifestations of the narrator that spans between the extremes of overt and covert. Overt narrators make their presence known by referring to themselves regularly, which enhances and creates a "double structure within the narrative: the stratum of events ... and the stratum of the narrator" (24).

that the author was a completely objective party with no ethical convictions or ideas about justice and right practice. It is *the narrator* through whom the story is continually mediated, long after the author or redactor has disappeared into history. While the narrator subtly shapes the story to forefront the ethics and perspectives in tension in the narrative, he refrains from explicit evaluation of the characters and their actions. For contrast, one may consider the presentation of Israelite and Judean history by the Deuteronomistic Historian(s). While the narrator of the Deuteronomistic History readily offers his own evaluation of events and rulers in Samuel and Kings through explicit theological assessments (e.g., "Indeed, there was no one like Ahab, who sold himself to do what was evil in the sight of YHWH," 1 Kgs 21:25), the narrator of Gen 34 in his presentation of the characters and events withholds criteria for ethical conduct and evaluations.

The lack of the narrator's evaluation in Gen 34 combined with the presentation of the narrative's events through the characters' perspectives—whose desires, social positions, ideologies, and actions are in conflict—enhances the complexity of the ethical conundrum he presents. Modern interpreters who assume that an implicit evaluation is readily available to the keen reader sometimes appeal to affective semantics. For example, Bar-Efrat suggests that when words with "a powerful positive or negative charge" are used, they "essentially convey the evaluative attitude of the narrator."[78] The examples he gives from the Deuteronomistic History[79] display that this indeed is a way in which a biblical narrator can color the characters and events of a narrative with evaluation. I suggest that something different is happening in Gen 34. Although there are terms present in Gen 34 that are heavily hued with negative and positive connotations, a survey of their usage within the story shows that these highly charged terms and relational epithets are presented through the lens of the various characters' own perspectives, not that of the narrator, whose terminologies are neutrally descriptive.

Let us begin with the use of ענה in Gen 34:2, the nuances of which I discussed above. Here the perspective is that of the narrator, who presents the impact of Shechem's actions on Dinah with this sociolegal term. The connotations of this verb in the *piel*, when it takes an external object,[80] are

---

78. Bar-Efrat, *Narrative Art in the Bible*, 36.
79. Bar-Efrat, *Narrative Art in the Bible*, 34–35.
80. As opposed to the humiliation of oneself or one's soul before God, for instance,

wholly negative, just like the transitive verbs *afflict*, *humble*, and *debase* in English. Through the use of this term the narrator highlights the result of Shechem's lying with Dinah on Dinah's social status and marriageability. Ancient Israelite women were legally subordinate to the men of the בית אב in which they operated, and while mothers were to be held in honor (e.g., Exod 20:12, Lev 19:3, Prov 1:8), unwed daughters and wives were considered the legal property of their fathers or husbands. Lying with another man's wife or betrothed was punishable by death (Deut 22:22–27), and lying with an unbetrothed virgin debased her. Because of this debasement, the laws declare that the male perpetrator, even in the case of rape, should be made to pay the bride-price as restitution, and either the perpetrator is forced to marry her (Deut 22:28–29), or her father is allowed to decide whether to enforce the marriage requirement (Exod 22:16–17).[81] The forced marriage in this ancient patriarchal context would prevent a rape victim (Deut 22:28–29) or seduced woman (Exod 22:16–17) from living in destitution as debased, with a status equal to or beneath that of widowhood, outside the protection that positionality within a בית אב provided her. A narrative example of this is provided by David's daughter Tamar, who proclaimed in anguish when her rapist and half-brother Amnon dismissed her, "No! Because by sending me away, this evil is greater than the other thing that you have done to me!" (2 Sam 13:16). Here in Gen 34:2, however, the reader does not know Dinah's level of complicity, her desires, or her thoughts after verse 1. There is no explicit moral evaluation of the narrator with regard to their intertribal sexual union or whether it was forced or consensual, but the narrator does communicate the precarious position Dinah is put in legally and socially by the use of the term ענה.

One of the central features of the narrator's presentation of the events of Gen 34 is that, with the exception of brief increments of external narration, they are relayed for the most part through the point of view or perspective[82] of the various characters. In *The Craft of Fiction*, literary critic Percy Lubbock theorizes four types of point of view observed in nar-

---

as in Lev 16:29, Num 30:14.

81. These laws pertain to the people of ancient Israel, however, and do not map onto the Gen 34 narrative directly, as Shechem is a non-Israelite.

82. European literary criticism favors the term *perspective*, while *point of view* is more common in Anglo-American parlance. I use both terms interchangeably to refer to the same phenomenon: "the way the representation of [a] story is influenced by the position, personality, and values of the narrator and the characters." See Burkard

ration.⁸³ While he was remarking on works of modern fiction, the same methods of perspectival presentation are witnessed in the Hebrew Bible. Lubbock's third type of narration is that of third-person narration *from the perspective of a character*.⁸⁴ The narrative style of Gen 34 most closely maps onto Lubbock's third type, in which the narration is presented in the third person but most prevalently through the perspectives of the story actors. Indeed, the narrative tension and suspense relies on its play of multiple perspectives. Through this type of narration, the reader is made to know that Shechem, his father Hamor, Jacob, and his sons Simeon and Levi all perceive the stakes of the moment and the actions of the story through their own situated positions, emotions, and desires. Many modern interpreters have implicitly sensed this feature of multiperspectivity as they assess and evaluate the positions and perspectives of the various characters in the narrative. Few, however, have explicitly reflected on the effects of this multiperspectivity as a formal feature of the narrative presentation. By attending to the story's many perspectival shifts, it becomes more apparent that the terms טמא (which in the *piel* stem means "to defile, to make unclean") and נבלה ("outrageous offense")⁸⁵ are employed when the narrative progresses through the perspectives of Jacob or his sons.

Twice in the narrative, טמא is used to describe the actions of Shechem to Dinah, intimating the impact of what he has done to her. The term is prevalent in priestly codes and prophetic indictments but is absent elsewhere in Genesis.⁸⁶ In Gen 34, טמא is employed through the perceptual

---

Niederhoff, "Perspective—Point of View," in Hühn, Meister, and Schmid, *Handbook of Narratology*, 692.

83. The first type of narration is third-person narration from the perspective of the primary narrator, in which the narrator's voice and presence is more overt; the second is first-person narration (which is not present here in Genesis but found in books such as Daniel and Nehemiah); the fourth is the "dramatic method" of third-person narration "without comment or inside views" (Niederhoff, "Perspective—Point of View," 694).

84. Niederhoff, "Perspective—Point of View," 694. This is also sometimes called "the reflector mode," following the terminology of Henry James.

85. Alternatively, "heinous offense," "foolish thing" (Bader, *Sexual Violation*, 38).

86. Throughout the Hebrew Bible, defilement is depicted as a state of either physical, ritual, or moral contamination. See L. E. Toombs, "Clean and Unclean," *IDB* 1:641. Normal, socially acceptable acts or states such as burying one's dead family member (Num 6:9), having a menstrual period (Lev 15:25), giving birth (Lev 12:1–8), or engaging in legally sanctioned marital relations could render one unclean (Lev 22:4),

viewpoints of either Jacob or his sons. With Jacob, this is achieved through the use of a verb of aural perception (שמע, "to hear"). In the case of the sons, it occurs through descriptions of volition, indicating the reason behind their actions with causal phrases. Verse 5 says, "Jacob heard that he [Shechem] had defiled [טמא] Dinah his daughter." This is a description of Jacob's perception of what he heard. The narrator focuses on Jacob's hearing rather than on a messenger or perhaps Dinah herself, who may have brought the news. The reader also is not told the full contents of this message, though it might offer answers to many questions. Either a messenger has told Jacob, "Shechem defiled Dinah your daughter," or they told him something else, something about their sexual encounter, and Jacob's perception is that it was a defilement. As for the verb's second occurrence in verse 13, it supplies the motive behind Jacob's sons' falsehood: "The sons of Jacob answered Shechem and Hamor his father with deceit ... because he had defiled Dinah their sister [אשר טמא את דינה אחתם]." It is not because Shechem debased Dinah but because, in the view of her brothers, he *defiled* her—rendered her defiled or unclean by having sex with her—and committed נבלה (see below) that they set into motion their plan for revenge.

The final usage of the term טמא comes at the end of the story, in a causal phrase indicating the motive for the sons of Jacob's raid and plunder on the city of Shechem: "They plundered the city because they had defiled their sister [טמאו אחותם]" (34:27). The verb is shockingly plural yet explains why, *in the minds of the sons of Jacob*, their thirst for vengeance is not satisfied with the death of Shechem alone (34:26); the whole city must pay because "they" are all to blame for the defilement of their sister. Some interpreters, both ancient and modern, have assumed that the narrator's sympathies are with the brothers, concluding that what the brothers call defilement was in line with the narrator's own point of view.[87] Yet in this narrative, in which the play of perspective is a

---

as well as eating certain animals (Lev 11). In regard to sexual practice, the unacceptable offense of adultery is depicted as a woman "defiling herself" or a man "defiling his neighbor's wife" (Num 5:13, Ezek 18:6, 33:26). Such defilement is transgressive; they have crossed the bounds of what is acceptable in sexual practice. Uncleanness or defilement is also associated with idolatry or worship of gods other than YHWH, which is connected metaphorically to the concept of defilement by adultery in the prophets (Hos 5:3, Jer 2:23, Ezek 20:30, Zech 13:2).

87. E.g., Jubilees and the Testament of Levi in their ancient recountings of the tale, and both Meir Sternberg and Alison Joseph in their modern assessments. Chapter 3 will address one such interpretation, that of Jub. 30.

central feature of its dramatic effect,⁸⁸ the points of view that regard what Shechem has done to Dinah as defilement are of Jacob or his sons. The narrator uses the term ענה to describe the social consequences for Dinah in his own voice (Gen 34:2) but depicts Jacob and his sons thinking in terms of טמא.

Another highly charged term, נבלה, meaning "foolish thing" or, more severely here, "outrageous offense," is also offered through the perspective of the brothers. For the brothers, not only has Shechem defiled Dinah, but the reason for their anger and intense grief is that "he did an outrageous thing [נבלה] in [or 'against'] Israel [בישראל] by sleeping with a daughter of Jacob—it is not done this way" (Gen 34:7). Whether Jacob shares this intimation is unknown, or rather unnarrated. Through the causal phrase (כי נבלה עשה בישראל), the narrator connects this term to the viewpoint of Jacob's sons. Of the twelve times this word is used in the Hebrew Bible, there are six instances where it occurs in the phrase "an outrageous offense in Israel," and of those six, five refer to some sort of sexual transgression.⁸⁹ In her assessment of the use of נבלה in the Hebrew Bible, Mary Anna Bader concludes, "The infractions described by the word נבלה" often resulted in the death of the offenders, whether "prescribed by law [or] death resulting from family members who sought revenge/justice."⁹⁰ Thus, by using this term to describe how the brothers viewed Shechem's "sleeping with a daughter of Jacob," the narrator may have been suggesting to the original audience at this point what sort of restitution they would seek.

Through the narrator's use of the highly charged term נבלה to indicate the perspective of the sons, he signals that the rift between Jacob and his sons has begun with their differing perceptions of what has happened. This term is offered only through the viewpoint of Jacob's sons, not Jacob. As previously explored, they both considered the sex act to be "defiling" to Dinah, but only the brothers are attributed with considering it נבלה. As before with טמא, whether the narrator shares the views of Jacob's sons is not conveyed.⁹¹ The covert narrator does not indicate his position on the

---

88. See below for further discussion.

89. Here in Gen 34:7 but also Deut 22:21, Judg 20:6, 2 Sam 13:12, Jer 29:23. The remainder of the twelve times are in Josh 7:15, Judg 19:23–24, 20:10, 1 Sam 15:15, Isa 9:16, 32:6, Job 42:8.

90. Bader, *Sexual Transgression*, 46–47.

91. In regard to this verse, Sternberg writes, "We have here, in short, the kind of perspectival ambiguity traditionally thought to be peculiar to the age of the novel.

side of one perspective or another but allows the audience to view the event through the internal perception of Shechem (v. 3), Jacob (v. 5), and Jacob's sons (vv. 7, 13, 27) in turn. The effect is a highlighting of the complexity of the situation and heightening of the tension between the various characters, who each perceive the situation differently. The employment of נבלה heightens the tensions between Jacob's sons and Shechem, as the reader now knows that they perceive his offense to be deserving of death. Also, at this point (34:7) in the story, both the reported emotional responses (or lack thereof, in the case of Jacob) and adjectives used (or not used, in the case of Jacob) distinguish the response of Jacob's sons from the report that Shechem had been with Dinah sexually.

The final highly charged term has a positive connotation: נכבד, meaning "honored." It is found in 34:19, "and the young man [Shechem] did not hesitate to do the thing [i.e., be circumcised] because he delighted in the daughter of Jacob and he was the most honored [נכבד] of all his father's house." Rather than a narrator-endorsed evaluation of Shechem's character, however, this comparative adjectival construction functions as an explanation of Shechem's social status and possibly his motivation. In this verse, we have both the description of Shechem's volition ("because he delighted in the daughter of Jacob") and what some have read to be a word of evaluative characterization from the narrator's point of view.[92] As the exploration of perspective and characterization in Gen 34 below highlights, this conspicuous description of character *is* unusual. Nowhere do we get adjectives describing any of the other characters. We are privy to their actions, their words, and sometimes their intentions and emotions,

---

Where does the insider view end, or where does the narrator's voice begin? What is the narrator's standing in and attitude to the explanatory statement? Its weight crucially depends on the answer" (*Poetics of Biblical Narrative*, 454). Interpreting this *ki*-clause to be an explanatory note from the narrator rather than a description of the cause of the brother's emotional response adds fodder to Sternberg's argument that the narrator favors the brothers' perspective and actions above those of Jacob throughout this narrative. Certainly, the ambiguity of the construction can lend support to such a reading, but I do not find it convincing in light of all of the other evidence stacked toward the objectivity of the narrator. Such a reading is viable only if one assumes, as Sternberg and many readers throughout the ages have, that there is an implicit evaluation to dig for through the evidence of minute clues.

92. For instance, Bechtel reads this adjective as emphatically informative regarding the character of Shechem *and* Hamor: "the text stresses that these are honorable men" ("What if Dinah Is Not Raped?," 29).

but the reader is left to piece together such snippets of character and evaluate both what kind of person is being depicted and whether their actions are honorable. Here the narrator tells the reader outright that Shechem was "the most honored of all his father's house." By comparing this usage of כבד in the *niphal* participle with other similar constructions in the Hebrew Bible,[93] however, one can see that it provides comment about social status, not nobility of character. Similar comparative constructions are found in Num 22:15 and in the descriptions of David's mighty men in 2 Sam 23:19, 23[94] (and their parallel passages in 1 Chr 11:21, 25). In each of these examples, what is being indicated by the construction is the person's status or social weight among other men. As noted in the annotated translation of Gen 34 above, connected by a simple *vav*, the phrase used to describe Shechem has an ambiguous connection to what precedes it. It could technically be a narrator's aside that precedes the causal clause before it, as the NRSV renders it: "And the young man did not delay to do the thing because he was delighted with Jacob's daughter. Now, he was the most honored of all his [father's house]" (Gen 34:19). Conversely, it could be a second explanation of cause for Shechem's quick action, joined to the first by a *vav*. Thus translated, it reads as a continuation of the explanation for why Shechem does not hesitate to be circumcised: "And the young man did not hesitate to do the thing because he delighted in the daughter of Jacob and he was the most honored of all his father's house."

In the context of the story, Shechem's acquisition of the woman he longs for rests on the agreement that every male in the city be circumcised (or so he thinks, unaware that the agreement was proposed by Jacob's sons with guile). Here the information that Shechem is the most honored among his father's house is provided as a framework for his action and perhaps as a second reason for why he does not hesitate to circumcise himself. He has social weight in the community, the community that Shechem is hoping will follow in his actions. What may be

---

93. כבד is a stative verb meaning "to be weighty, to be honored."
94. Numbers 22:15: ויסף עוד בלק שלח שרים רבים ונכבדים מאלה, "And Balak again sent princes, more numerable and distinguished than these." Second Samuel 23:19: of Abishai, מן השלשה הכי נכבד, "Out of the [Thirty], is it that he was honored?" (The rhetorical question implies a positive answer; the following sentence declares that "and he became their chief" (2 Sam 23:19). Second Samuel 23:23: of Benaiah, מן השלשים נכבד, "Out of the Thirty, he was distinguished." The latter half of the verse offers a concession, "but he did not attain to the Three" (2 Sam 23:23).

taken to be the narrator's one evaluative claim on the characters and their actions when studied against the backdrop of similar grammatical constructions throughout the Hebrew Bible is actually an explanatory note.[95]

Although some argue that familial epithets serve an evaluative function in this narrative, betraying the narrator's sympathies,[96] I suggest that the familial epithets and relational terms that pervade this narrative serve to signal perspectival changes as well as emphasize the connectedness of the characters. Modern interpreters often note that in biblical narrative, where descriptive detail is rare and therefore all the more valuable, the naming practices of characters indicate subtle messages.

In certain places in Gen 34, for instance, the shift in the relational designation of a character indicates a shift in perspective, which others have observed. As Meir Sternberg notes, "A change in viewpoint (from character to character, narrator to character, external to internal report) [may be] signaled by nothing but its variation."[97] Thus, when the designation of Dinah as "daughter of Jacob" shifts to "their sister" in verse 13, it is indicative of the shift in point of view that occurs in that verse to that of the brothers. Similarly, in the causal clause of verse 27 that tells of the young men's motivation for plundering the city, their perspective is indicated with the use of the sororal epithet "because they had defiled their sister." A subtle difference in appellation is also witnessed in the narratorial preface before the words of Hamor and Shechem to the Israelites.

---

95. I concede that the ambiguity of the phrase could support and has supported other readings. I offer this concession because not every reader in antiquity or modernity has read the story referencing other comparative usages of the *niphal* participle of כבד. The present argument is concerned with the character of the narrator in the text as it stands.

96. E.g., Sternberg, *Poetics of Biblical Narrative*, 450. Sternberg and Bar-Efrat both argue that the naming practices of characters, in particular that of assigning them familial epithets, are a covert way in which narrators convey subtle evaluation. For example, in Sternberg's reading, which argues for the narrator's sympathy toward the brothers, Dinah's designation as "daughter of Leah" and the juxtaposition of Jacob's silence with the reference to Dinah as "his daughter" (34:5) has the effect of casting a negative light on Jacob (*Poetics of Biblical Narrative*, 451). Yet this is not readily apparent to all readers, and the same juxtaposition has indicated to others the wisdom and strength of Jacob to maintain his composure (e.g., Bechtel, "What if Dinah Is Not Raped?," 34–35).

97. Sternberg, *Poetics of Biblical Narrative*, 450.

When Hamor speaks to Jacob and his sons, his speech is prefaced with, "Hamor spoke with them" (34:8). "They" are one group, with whom he is about to propose a deal. Hamor does not simply ask for Dinah's hand, as Shechem had requested (34:4), but proposes a social contract between the groups including intermarriage, sharing of land, and trade. In contrast, when Shechem speaks, he pleads to "her father and her brothers" (34:11). This subtly emphasizes the singleness of his desire—to have Dinah as wife—and his awareness that the men he speaks to hold the authority for her marital rights. It is all his speech is concerned with.

Perspectival shifts, however, cannot account for every use of familial epithets and relational ties, which abound in Gen 34. The overwhelming prevalence of familial epithets draws attention to the connectedness of each character, enmeshed as they are in their kinship groups. Rather than being very subtle clues about the narrator's evaluatory inclinations, together they serve to remind the audience that what happens to each individual, and each individual's choices of action, directly affect the others they are tied to by kinship. The narrative of Gen 33:18–34:31 contains sixteen instances in which a character is presented by the narrator with a name followed by an epithet indicating a familial relationship. Seven times a familial epithet stands in place of a name. Additionally, the men's speeches are peppered with acknowledgment of the familial ties they have with one another. Hamor begins his speech with, "Shechem, my son, his whole being longs for your[98] daughter" (34:8). The sons of Jacob alternately call Dinah "our sister" and "our daughter" in their (deceitful) proposition to the Hivites (34:14, 17). Later, the full brothers of Dinah defend their actions to Jacob with the cry, "Should he use our sister like a prostitute?" (34:31).

Furthermore, the relational epithets in Gen 34 serve to highlight specific kinship ties and invoke the social roles associated with those ties. The introductory designation of Dinah as "daughter of Leah, whom she bore to Jacob" (Gen 34:1), and the designation of Simeon and Levi as "Dinah's brothers" (34:25) emphasize their connection as uterine siblings, children of the same mother.[99] As Cynthia Chapman argues, several biblical narratives attest to the roles of uterine siblings within maternal subunits (a "house of the mother" or בית אם) of a larger, polygynous house of the

---

98. The Hebrew is plural.
99. Cynthia Chapman, *The House of the Mother: The Social Roles of Maternal Kin in Biblical Hebrew Narrative and Poetry* (New Haven: Yale University Press, 2016), 65.

father (בית אב).¹⁰⁰ She lists Gen 34 as one of several biblical narratives in which "uterine siblings are presented as those honor bound to avenge wrongs committed to one another."¹⁰¹ The relationship of uterine siblings in the Bible "is characterized by heightened emotional ties, public displays of physical affection, mutual loyalty, and a perceived duty to enact revenge on one another's behalf."¹⁰² It is this tie of maternal kinship that is evoked in Gen 34:25, when "Simeon and Levi, *Dinah's brothers*, took their swords" to enact their revenge. By signaling the maternal connection between Dinah and her brothers, Simeon and Levi, a layer of kinship-based complexity is added to the tension between father and sons, whose final debate may be undergirded with the tension between loyalty to one's בית אם and concern for the larger בית אב.¹⁰³

While shifts in relational epithets serve in places to indicate perspectival shifts and emphasize kinship roles and the tensions they provoke, the *overall* effect of the copious use of relational designations is the constant reminder throughout the narrative's events and the character's choices that no one stands alone in this story. What befalls one affects them all, and their actions affect one another. Dinah is introduced as "the daughter of Leah whom she bore to Jacob" (Gen 34:1) and is frequently identified as either Jacob's daughter (34:3, 5, 7, 19) or, when the perspective shifts to that of the young men, a sister (34:13, 27).¹⁰⁴ When Shechem's נפש clings to Dinah, when he delights in her, she is not just a young woman but a daughter: "the daughter of Jacob" (34:3, 19). Whatever happens to Dinah inevitably has an impact on Jacob and the other men of her family, to whom we are constantly reminded that she is tied through kinship. The narrator often reminds the reader that Shechem is the "son of Hamor" (34:2, 18, 20, 24, 26), and Hamor is repetitively "the father of Shechem" (33:19; 34:4, 6, 13). Though reference to being the son of one's father is a common appellation in the Hebrew Bible, the designation of a man as

---

100. Chapman, *House of the Mother*, 96–109.
101. Chapman, *House of the Mother*, 96.
102. Chapman, *House of the Mother*, 109.
103. Chapman, *House of the Mother*, 66.
104. When the sons of Jacob answer Hamor and Shechem, they refer to Dinah alternatively as "our sister" (34:14) and "our daughter" (34:17). Chapman argues that in the brothers' designation of Dinah as "our daughter," they signal their role over the marriage-negotiation process for their sister, a role also played by Laban in Rebekah's marriage to Isaac (Gen 24; Chapman, *House of the Mother*, 67).

"father of so-and-so" is less so. Nevertheless, the repetition in Gen 34 is nearly excessive. Only once the reader is told that Hamor is "the Hivite, the prince of the land" (34:2), and only once such an introduction is necessary to cement this information for the audience. Yet almost every time that Hamor or Shechem is mentioned, it is in connection with each other. The reader therefore is reminded at every turn of the plot that their fates are tied; though at first both Jacob and his sons view Shechem as a "defiler" (34:5, 13), Hamor will also meet the blade in Simeon and Levi's final revenge.

Similarly, Jacob's sons are throughout the narrative identified with reference to their relationship to Jacob. The group of young men is collectively labeled "the sons of Jacob" (34:5–6, 13, 25, 27), and they speak and act as one. Thus, these relational designations consistently signal to the reader that the words and actions of "the sons of Jacob" will inevitably affect their father, who has been the focal figure of the Genesis narrative for seven chapters spanning roughly thirty years up to this point. When Simeon and Levi are identified as leaders of the brothers' raid on the city (34:25), the narrator indicates their positionality with two epithets; they are both the "sons of Jacob" *and* "the brothers of Dinah." Here, the tension of their actions is represented in the tension of their familial relations. In acting as Dinah's uterine brothers by seeking to avenge her honor (and/or perhaps the honor of their בית אם),[105] they have further jeopardized the honor and safety of their father, Jacob, to whom they owe allegiance as the head of their בית אב. The relational epithets and familial designations of the characters in this narrative heighten awareness of the tension in perspectives and the ethical impact of words and choices of the individual actors on the other members of their family.

5. Multiperspectivity and Reticence in Characterization

In addition to the absence of the narrator's explicit evaluation, multiperspectivity and ambiguity in characterization function together to place the weight of the ethical evaluation of the characters and their actions on the

---

105. So Chapman, *House of the Mother*, 66. Chapman reads the final argument between Jacob and the duo, Simeon and Levi, as an argument about kinship alliances. Jacob speaks with concern about his בית, whereas "the two uterine brothers, on the other hand, seem more concerned for their mother's house, which they feel has suffered an assault."

2. Dinah Decides

reader. Yet the questions of who is in the right and who is in the wrong, and what should or should not have been done, are complicated by the fact that each character's actions are potentially justifiable from the character's own interests and perspective.[106] The presentation of a narrative's events through the perspective of multiple characters is a well-known feature of biblical narratives, even those that have a more heavy-handed and ideologically driven narrator.[107] Tension and suspense increase in Gen 34 as the divergence of perspectives is revealed, and it is not altogether certain who is to blame, who is in the right, or who is wildly out of line. Adele Berlin asserts, "The reader of such narrative is not a passive recipient of a story, but an active participant in trying to understand it. Because [the reader] is given different points of view, sees things from different perspectives, [they] must struggle to establish [their] own."[108] This responsibility is put to the reader by the multiperspectival structure of the text.

The multiperspectivity crafted by the narrator of Gen 34 reaches beyond the aforementioned instances of highly charged terms and relational epithets. On the one hand, with an omniscient, third-person narrator, everything in a narrative is relayed through the narrator's perspective. On the other hand, through narration, the perspective of the omniscient, covert narrator offers access to the characters' perspectives. The narrator can see the inner world of the character and describes it to the reader, and in so doing the reader gets a view of the world from the character's spatial, temporal, or psychological perspective.[109] In Gen 34, we enter a character's

---

106. Adele Berlin's assessment of point of view in the Hebrew Bible informs my engagement with it in this narrative. Playing off Erich Auerbach's famous statement that biblical narrative is "fraught with background," Berlin reads Gen 37 as "fraught with ambiguity" for similar reasons: "Because it is told from several perspectives, Gen 37 is fraught with ambiguity. There is no clear right and wrong. Each character's actions are justified from their point of view." See Berlin, *Poetics and Interpretation of Biblical Narrative* (Winona Lake, IN: Eisenbrauns, 1994), 50. The various perspectives in Gen 37 are those of the many sons of Jacob. As my somewhat parallel words above indicate, something very, very similar is at work in *this* narrative.

107. Berlin notes that this multiperspectival storytelling results in a narrative that has "depth and sophistication; one in which conflicting viewpoints may vie for validity. It is this that gives biblical narrative interest and ambiguity" (*Poetics and Interpretation*, 82).

108. Berlin, *Poetics and Interpretation*, 82.

109. While some narrative theorists have categorized perspective into distinct categories, I find that importing these distinctions from narratological studies of modern

point of view through any combination of four formal devices: (1) verbs of perception or insights into the inner world (of cognition, emotion)[110] of a character; (2) explanations of motivation or volition, typically rendered in purpose clauses; (3) direct speech; and (4) familial or relational epithets used to describe other characters, as discussed above. Throughout the narrative, events are presented through the various discordant perspectives of the characters.

One effect of such multiperspectivity—of presenting the story through various characters' perspectives in tension—is the creation of friction in the narrative's drama. It is through the perspectives of the characters, relayed through verbs of perception, purpose clauses indicating motivation, direct speech, and familial epithets, that the reader discovers all that is at stake in the narrative and what ethics are in conflict. At points, this tension is a strand that weaves Gen 34 into the other family stories of the patriarchs and matriarchs of Genesis through essential thematic motifs of deceit and disharmony. On the whole, the multiperspectivity in this narrative relativizes the perspectives of the characters, constructing the complexity of the predicament that the men have found themselves in in the wake of the kernel event of Gen 34:2 and resulting in ambiguity with which the readers must grapple.

These complicating effects of multiperspectivity are further compounded by the ambiguity that results from the narrator's strategies of characterization. One way of evaluating the perspectives present in a multiperspectival narrative is to evaluate the characters themselves, but the characters of Gen 34 are drawn in ways that support equivocal interpretations. The complexity of Gen 34 and the way it presents its events and characters with such artful reticence has allowed for hundreds of generations of interpreters to dissent on the requisite questions, "What exactly *are* the perspectives of the characters (including the narrator)?"

---

fiction does not map on well to the more laconic form of the Hebrew Bible's narratives. Yes, it is helpful to think about the overlapping possibilities of indicating a character's spatial/temporal perspective and their psychological perspective (which, in my usage of the term, includes the entire "inner world" of the character, emotions, thoughts, ideologies, and sensory perception). These I call "overlapping possibilities," because while a narrator's choice of words may depict one or the other, a character's spatial/temporal perspective and psychological perspective can also be conveyed simultaneously. For this reason, I only note distinctions between the two types of perspectives when they are found to be significant in the narrative.

110. Bar-Efrat, *Narrative Art in the Bible*, 20–21.

and "What are the issues in tension in this text?"[111] Many readers have come away with different understandings, even claims of certainty, of what is at stake in the narrative and what ideologies and perspectives are being pitted against one another within it. The sparsely sketched foreground of the biblical narrative here in Gen 34 facilitates ambiguity, while the openness of the narrative's gaps and silences allow for multiple "possibilities of interpretation."[112] Even though the omniscient narrator is privy to the perceptions, volition, and emotions of his characters, when the narrator chooses to disclose such information, it is brief and laconic, often raising more questions than it answers. This narrator characterizes by clearly describing some details while leaving others tantalizingly opaque. This reticence has an effect on the reader, who must become an active participant

---

111. This most puzzling effect of Gen 34's narration is the highlighting of the audience's limitations. Genesis 34 is a prime example of Sternberg's assertion that in reading a narrative thus constructed, "The only knowledge perfectly acquired is the knowledge of our limitations. It is by a sustained effort alone that the reader can attain at the end to something of the vision that God has possessed all along: to make sense of the discourse is to gain a sense of being human" (*Poetics of Biblical Narrative*, 47).

112. Alter, *Art of Biblical Narrative*, 143. The phrase "sparsely sketched foreground" is Alter's. Here he is referencing Erich Auerbach's famous essay, "Odysseus' Scar," in which Auerbach elaborates on Gen 22's omission of definite descriptions and details in "the foreground," or narrated material. In Auerbach's terms, "so much of the phenomena as is necessary for the purpose of the narrative" is externalized, whereas "all else is left in obscurity," rendering the narration as "mysterious and fraught with background." See Auerbach, "Odysseus' Scar," in *Mimesis: The Representation of Reality in Western Literature*, trans. Willard R. Trask (Princeton: Princeton University Press, 1968), 12. Here I agree with Alter that it is not only suspense or mimesis that Gen 34's minimalism constructs but ambiguity and an openness to interpretive engagement. Auerbach also asserts that the "merely touched upon" and "fraught with background" elements of the biblical narrative not only "require subtle investigation and interpretation," but "they demand them" (15). In Auerbach's reading, however, the narrative construction that demands investigation serves a purpose of subjugation; it is but "a means" to the narrator's true end: subjecting his readers to absolute claims of truth (13–15). Rather than a means of subjecting the reader to a certain doctrinal outlook (15), I am proposing that the minimal narration of Gen 34 invites its readers to grapple with the ethical complexity of the events and agents through the presentation of multiple perspectives and the narrator's withholding of evaluation. As mentioned above and as this section explores below, not even the standards of evaluation are made clear by the narrator of Gen 34, fostering debate and diverse engagement rather than doctrinal domination.

in the story, filling out the characters, as it were, from the few lines that the narrator offers.[113]

To better evaluate those few lines, I incorporate the insights of Alter's assessment of biblical characterization techniques, or how "the Bible's artful selectivity produces both sharply defined surfaces and a sense of ambiguous depths in character." He describes a "scale of means, in ascending order of explicitness and certainty, for conveying information about the motives, the attitudes, and the moral nature of characters." On the lowest spectrum of this scale are (1) the narrator's report of a character's actions and any descriptions of appearance, gestures, posture, and dress. External details such as these leave the reader in the "realm of inference" when it comes to characterization.[114] Jacob's silence in verse 5 is a prime example of this from Gen 34.[115] Slightly more substantial in weight are (2) one character's comments about another or direct speech by a character, though this sort of speech has its limitations. At times, a character's own words may give us a direct glimpse into their inner world, while other times, especially when the setting of the speech is a public one, the inner world of the character may remain opaque. In the middle of this scale, I add the technique of characterization through comparison, in which the actions, descriptions, or words of a character are presented as a foil against another's. The certainty or uncertainty that this technique provides to characterization is dependent on how well the contrasted characters are defined. The next step on Alter's scale is that of (3) inward speech. With this, Alter asserts, "we enter the realm of certainty … there is certainty, in any case, about the character's conscious intentions, though we may still feel free to question the motive behind the intention."[116] In Gen 34, there is no such inner speech that would offer certainty to the audience seeking to understand and assess the characters.

Finally, (4) there are statements by the reliable, omniscient narrator about the attitudes and intentions of the narrative agents. Even here, how-

---

113. "In many cases, a minimal description of character, especially of one outstanding trait, is that magic line of suggestion around which the reader fills in the picture" (Berlin, *Poetics and Interpretation*, 137). It stands to reason that different readers, approaching the story from their own subjective perspectives and contexts, may fill in that picture in different ways.

114. Alter, *Art of Biblical Narrative*, 144, 146.

115. See below.

116. Alter, *Art of Biblical Narrative*, 147.

ever, there is still room for inference and uncertainty. Alter writes, "At the top of the ascending scale we have the reliable narrator's explicit statement of what the characters feel, intend, desire; here we are accorded certainty, though biblical narrative … may choose for its own good purposes either to explain the ascription of attitude or to state it baldly and thus leave its cause as an enigma for us to ponder."[117] In this story, there are both explanations (e.g., Gen 34:13, 18) and enigmatic statements of motivation (e.g., 34:27) that raise more questions than they answer. Through this framework, we are able to see that the techniques used by the narrator to characterize in Gen 34 requires the reader or audience to finish the brushstrokes that the narrator begins. Thus, the text pulls its audience into an active role—whether the audience is aware of it or not—while supporting equivocal readings of each of its characters. The following paragraphs explore Gen 34's multiperspectivity and its characterization of Dinah, Shechem, Hamor, Jacob, Jacob's sons as a collective, and Simeon and Levi, while demonstrating the resulting ambiguity that readers have interacted with in various ways over the centuries.

5.1. Dinah

In the first verse of Gen 34, the narrator introduces Dinah with reference to her maternal lineage and a brief description of her action and intention. After a short exposition from the narrator's point of view (Gen 33:18–20), he states, "And Dinah, the daughter of Leah whom she bore to Jacob, went out to see the daughters of the land" (Gen 34:1). As noted above, the signal to Dinah's position in Leah's בית אם becomes an important connection between her and Simeon and Levi, invoking the unique kinship ties and associated roles of these uterine siblings. Even this brief maternal appellation, however, has been fleshed out by interpreters to indicate either a negative evaluation of Dinah's character or a reason for why Jacob remains silent in Gen 34:5. For example, Gen. Rab. 80 preserves a rabbinic tradition prompted by the text's description of Dinah as "daughter of Leah." In Gen. Rab. 80, Leah is negatively evaluated for "going out" to meet Jacob in Gen 30:16, as tradition held that she "went out dressed like a prostitute" (יצאת מקשטת כזונה). Genesis Rabbah quotes the proverb found in Ezek 16:44 ("like mother, like daughter") to conclude that Dinah also went out dressed as a prostitute in

---

117. Alter, *Art of Biblical Narrative*, 147.

Gen 34:1. The rest of the parashah repeatedly blames Dinah's going out for all that transpires. In Sternberg's interpretation, however, this same detail is taken not as a negative pronouncement against Dinah but as a coded hint toward Jacob's motivation for his silence and inaction: "The twofold identification of the poor girl accounts of Jacob's attitude in terms of her being the daughter of his hated wife, whose suffering and strife for her husband's love loomed so large in the previous chapters [Gen 30]."[118] Likewise, the presence of the brief phrase "to see the daughters of the land," while offering a volitional detail, has inspired more questions, and interpreters have offered various settings to account for Dinah's intention. Theodotus and Josephus, for example, suggest that a festival was going on at the time. *Judean Antiquities* 1.337 narrates that Dinah went out not only to see or perhaps meet with the native women but to view their "adornment" (κόσμος), indicating Dinah's curiosity in their festal garb.[119]

Functioning as a technique of characterization, the purpose clause of Gen 34:1 also emphasizes that Dinah is a person with action and volition, with a perspective all her own—making it all the more curious, and this gap all the more gaping, when the critical element of her perspective is withheld for the rest of the narrative. I explore the effect of the absence of Dinah's perspective throughout the bulk of the narrative below in section 6.

5.2. Shechem

The next perspective offered by the narrator comes through a description of Shechem's emotional attachment to Dinah that follows the narrator's description of his actions in Gen 34:2. It offers a glimpse into his inner world, overflowing with passion: "And his whole being[120] clung to Dinah, daughter of Jacob. And he loved the young woman" (34:3). Shechem's perspective is also brought to bear later in the narrative through his direct speech in verses 11–12 and through a purpose clause in verse 19. Carrying over the information of Shechem's brimming emotional state from 34:3, the reader then encounters Shechem's speech to Dinah's father and brothers as genuinely flowing from his passions: "Let me find favor in your eyes—and whatever you say to me I will give! Exceedingly increase on me the bride-price and

---

118. Sternberg, *Poetics of Biblical Narrative*, 462.
119. Josephus does not introduce Dinah in connection to Leah but as "Dinah, who was Jacob's only daughter" (*A.J.* 1.337).
120. See note in translation above.

gift and I will give just what you say to me, just give me the young woman as my wife!" (34:11–12). Hamor's words about Shechem testify to his intense desire: "Shechem, my son, his whole being longs for your daughter" (34:8), and Shechem's own direct speech emphasizes his desperate state, as he offers to give anything to have Dinah as his wife. While his father speaks of economic benefit and a joining of the peoples through many intermarriages (34:8–10), Shechem's emotional state and his candid speech reveal that he is focused on one thing: acquiring Dinah to be his wife.

Readers throughout the ages have drawn different pictures of Shechem based on these few lines. Through explicit statements by the narrator, Shechem is depicted with a fair degree of certainty as desperate, emotional, and willing to do anything to have Dinah as his own. Yet this comes just after the report of his actions, offered in verse 2 *without* explanation or motive: seeing, taking, lying with, and in effect socially debasing Dinah. The combined certainty of his inner passion coupled with the laconic description of his actions (which leaves much room for inference) supports readings of Shechem as an entitled rapist or a desperate young Romeo in love.[121] The description of Shechem "speaking to the heart" of Dinah has been associated with "terms of courtship and marriage," leading some to assume that Dinah must have shared in the affections.[122] Others, however, counter this claim by appealing to texts in the Hebrew Bible in which the phrase is used by an actor who has certainly done harm or victimized the addressee.[123] Some conclude that sympathy is being accumulated for the

---

121. If so, perhaps the first Romeo of the world's extant prose literature. On Shechem as an entitled rapist: Suzanne Scholz argues that the string of verbs in 34:3 by no means acquits Shechem of his rapist character or depicts a change of heart from sexual attacker to compassionate lover ("What Really Happened," 6–11). On Shechem as young: Gen 34:19 refers to Shechem as הנער.

122. Fewell and Gunn, "Tipping the Balance," 196. "These verbs [in Gen 34:3] form a powerful sequence in language that is strongly affective and with almost uniformly positive overtones.... Moreover, the last expression—'to speak to the heart of'—may move us beyond the account of Shechem's affection to those of Dinah.... In our present context, therefore, the expression, 'he spoke to [her] heart,' indicates both Shechem's action and Dinah's positive response." Bechtel similarly reads that Shechem has not only spoken to Dinah's heart but "touched" it ("What if Dinah Is Not Raped," 25).

123. Sternberg, drawing from the use of "speak upon the heart" [rendering על as "upon" rather than "to"] in Gen 50:21, Ruth 2:13, 2 Sam 19:7, Isa 40:1–2, 2 Chr 32:6–8, asserts that the idiom does not "have any special romantic bearing" ("Biblical Poetics and Sexual Politics," 477). Although implying words that are "designed to move

young Shechem, while others claim that his self-centered desires are morally reprehensible and indicative of reckless avarice that led him to the act that cost Dinah her undefiled maiden status and cost the city of Shechem their lives.[124]

Interpreters also differ regarding the effect of Shechem's display of desperation and willingness to endure pain and sacrifice to obtain his beloved—or his victim. When the sons of Jacob order Shechem and all of the Hivite men of the city to be circumcised, "the young man did not hesitate to do the thing, because he delighted in the daughter of Jacob" (34:19). There are two laws in the ancient Israelite corpus, Exod 22:16–17 and Deut 22:28–29, often brought in to assess Shechem's actions and speech due to the parallels found between the laws and this narrative.[125] Both involve sex between a man and a virgin (בתולה) not betrothed to another man. Exodus 22:16–17[126] presents a case of seduction: "If a man persuades [וכי יפתה איש] a virgin who is not betrothed and he lies with her [ושכב עמה], he must pay her bride-price to become his wife. If her father utterly refuses to give her to him, he must weigh out money equal to the bride-price for virgins." In Deut 22:28–29, the case more clearly involves a rape: "If a man finds a young woman, a virgin who is not betrothed, and he seizes her and lies with her,[127] and they are found, then the man who laid with her must give fifty pieces of silver to the father of the young woman, and she will

---

the addressee's heart," Sternberg argues that the phrase does not indicate that such "movement" is achieved (477). Scholz notes that the phrase "speak upon the heart" is found in situations of consolation or comfort, but notably in Judg 19:3, 2 Sam 19:7, Isa 40:2, Hos 2:16, where the one who speaks upon the heart is one who has been responsible for some action that created the need for consolation (the Levite, David, God, and God, respectively; Scholz, "What Really Happened," 6–11). Interestingly, the LXX has εἰς τὴν καρδίαν in those passages, while in Gen 34:3 it is καὶ ἐλάλησεν κατὰ τὴν διάνοιαν τῆς παρθένου αὐτῇ. Rather than render the phrase literally as it does elsewhere, the Greek uses a different expression. It is possible that "and he spoke with her according to the young woman's mind [διάνοια, meaning 'thought, intention, or understanding']" may have conveyed to Greek-speaking readers a dialogical exchange about intentions and desires, nuancing the event as a conversation rather than a consolation.

124. For the former, see Fewell and Gunn, "Tipping the Balance," 197. For the latter, see Sternberg, "Biblical Poetics and Sexual Politics," 475–476.

125. Heb. Exod 22:15–16. E.g., Fewell and Gunn, "Tipping the Balance," 210; Bechtel, "What if Dinah Is Not Raped?," 25–27.

126. Heb. Exod 22:15–16.

127. Heb. ותפשה ושכב עמה. The first verb, תפש, is clearly indicative of a violent

become his wife, because he has debased her [ענה]. He is not permitted to divorce her all his days." In the former case, the father of the woman gets to decide the fate of his seduced daughter, and in the latter, the rapist must marry the woman. One could make the argument that the "persuasion" in Exod 22:16 could surely encompass the use of violence, and in this case, both consensual sex and rape would lie within the scope of this law. In both cases, monetary compensation is required of the man who lies with an unbetrothed young woman—either her bride-price (Exod 22:17) or the more specified fifty pieces of silver (Deut 22:29)—and Deut 22:29 goes further to describe why: "he has debased her." As argued above, the term ענה describes a downward shift in social status. Here debasement is the social result of *any* type of premarital sex for a young woman in ancient Israel, one the rapist must compensate for monetarily and by securing for her a future in this society where the sexual activities of women were heavily guarded by their fathers, brothers, and husbands.[128] Thus, they are brought to bear on the narrative both by interpreters who hold that Shechem did rape Dinah and by interpreters who suggest that the affair was mutual.

Feminist literary critics Danna Nolan Fewell and David Gunn conclude, "[Dinah's] best interest within the narrow limits of this society is to marry Shechem," in light of "her rights" under the law.[129] Bader, however, argues against Fewell and Gunn's claim "that Deut 22:28–29 provided for

---

action, found frequently in descriptions of war (e.g., Deut 20:19, Josh 8:23, 1 Kgs 13:4) and is often rendered "to seize," "to take possession of," or "to capture."

128. Tamar's cries to her rapist Amnon in 2 Sam 13:16 help illuminate this concept that was operative in ancient Israelite culture. After overpowering her and thus debasing her (2 Sam 13:14), he commands her to get out. She responds, "No! For this evil—to send me out—is greater than the other that you have done to me!" Though we do not know how Dinah felt after her debasement, Tamar, it seems, hoped that Amnon would fulfill the custom reflected in Deut 22:28–29 and make the appropriate recompense. When he did not, she was forced to live as a desolate woman in the house of her brother, Absalom (2 Sam 13:20).

129. Fewell and Gunn, "Tipping the Balance," 210. While these laws help us to understand the politics governing sex within the historical society of ancient Israel that produced the Gen 34 narrative, and though Shechem certainly seems at pains to act in ways that parallel the stipulations of these laws, it is not altogether certain that a law as such is active within the narrative setting itself. There are Middle Assyrian laws, however, that require a rapist to pay the bride-price for virgins, and, like Exod 22:15–16, allow the victim's father to decide whether the offender should marry her. See Chaim Potok, *The JPS Torah Commentary: Genesis* (Philadelphia: The Jewish Publication Society, 1989), 235.

'Dinah's right' to be married to Shechem," countering it with an appeal to semantics: "Fewell and Gunn obviously concluded that Shechem had raped Dinah; that stance has been refuted by the study of the verb עִנָּה. Connecting Deut 22:28–29 with Genesis 34 is plausible only if one concludes that Shechem raped Dinah."[130] Thus, due to the inherent ambiguity of the text, interpreters who read the narrative of Gen 34 in light of the legal materials can still emerge with different pictures and evaluations of Shechem. He may be read as unforgivably self-seeking—adding insult to injury by not leaving poor Dinah alone—or as a "mediating figure," attempting to do the right thing after his offense, as "honorable" as his בית אב held him to be.[131] The speech and narrative descriptions of Shechem sketch a solid but partial line, while his unqualified actions in verse 2 allow for various possible shadings to be considered by the reader.[132]

5.3. Hamor

Known only through a minimal report of his actions and public speech, Hamor similarly can be read in different ways. The Hivite prince speaks more than any other characters in the narrative, but his words are public and opaque; thus, even though his perspective is presented, its authenticity is obscured, unknowable. His speeches to both the Israelites and the Shechemites aim at rhetorical persuasion (Gen 34:8–10, 20–23). He presents the offer of intermarriage to the Israelites as beneficial to them, that they will be able to "dwell and trade" in the land and have a hold in it (34:10). In contrast to Shechem's usage of first-person pronouns in his desperate request (34:11–12), Hamor speaks in the second-person plural while offering intermarriage between the communities, and the benefits of sharing the land and trade for all: "Intermarry with us—give your daughters to us, and our daughters you may take for yourselves" (34:9). Interpreters differ over whether his intentions are honorable because this rhetoric of unity and economic advantage is spoken by a character whose

---

130. Bader, "Sexual Violation," 63. In response to Bader, I find that her objection is somewhat mitigated by the law of Exod 22:16–17, which has similar restitution demanded of the man but encompasses sex that is not certainly rape.
131. Bechtel, "What if Dinah Is Not Raped?," 35–36 (see Gen 34:19).
132. Yet almost all of these potential evaluations hinge on the unprovided perspective of Dinah. The importance of her perspective as a peg on which all other evaluations hang is discussed below.

inner world is withheld from the reader. Direct speech, while potentially vocalizing a character's perspective, is hardly a transparent indicator of character or perspective. As Alter notes, "Although a [biblical] character's own statements might seem a straightforward enough revelation of who he or she is and what he or she makes of things, in fact the biblical writers are quite as aware as any James or Proust that speech may reflect the occasion more than the speaker, may be more a drawn shutter than an open window."[133] Nowhere in this narrative is this more true than with the character of Hamor. We know nothing of his inner world, nor whether he knows anything of what has transpired between Shechem and Dinah, only that Shechem has asked his father to negotiate their betrothal (34:4), and Hamor's immediate response is to go out to speak to Jacob about an intertribal arrangement (34:5).

From his proposition for multiple intermarriages and mutual economic benefits, we know that Hamor is concerned about more than just the happiness of his son. Yet here is a drawn shutter rather than an open window, for it is unclear why Hamor proposes such an offer. Hamor may be read as acting in accordance with what is to be expected of a leader of an ancient Canaanite city, making decisions for the welfare of his community as a whole. He is in a higher position of power, he owns the land, and his offer to Jacob and family can be read as a benevolent one, willing to make negotiations and even undergo circumcision to honor the wishes of Dinah's family.[134] The proposal of intermarriage that is contingent on his community being circumcised is "good in the eyes of Hamor" (34:18). While it is more easily inferred why it is good "in the eyes of Shechem," Hamor's mind is more open to interpretation.[135] Thus, when "Hamor and

---

133. Robert Alter, *The Art of Biblical Narrative*, rev. and updated ed. (New York: Basic Books, 2011), 146.

134. So Bechtel, "What if Dinah Is Not Raped?," 29.

135. It is good "in the eyes of Shechem" likely "because he delighted in the daughter of Jacob" (34:19). Though connected regularly by epithets, Shechem "son of Hamor" and Hamor "father of Shechem" are linked through perspective at two points in the narrative: in their response to the sons' of Jacob's proposition and in their collective speech to the men of their city. At both times, a fine line of difference remains between them. Hamor and Shechem's perspectives are indicated through a common Hebrew idiom of perception, "And their words were good in the eyes of Hamor and in the eyes of Shechem, son of Hamor" (34:18). In Shechem and Hamor's speech of 34:20–23, they re-present the pain-promising proposition of the sons of Jacob in palatable terms, sandwiching the condition of circumcision between "These men are peaceful with us

Shechem his son" speak to persuade the Shechemites to be circumcised and "become one people" with the Israelites, the added phrase, "their livestock and their property and all their animals—will they not be ours?" opens up a spectrum of possible readings. These words in the mouth of Hamor, however, since he is more sparsely defined, for some, have relayed a greedy opportunist, craftily utilizing the vulnerable social position of Dinah to his own gain.[136] For others, Hamor is "peace-loving and conciliatory," attempting to make the best of a bad situation.[137] Whether his motivations were for the collective good or for personal gain (or both) and whether he did anything deserving of the death he was dealt similarly remain unresolved and left for the reader to determine.

5.4. Jacob

Jacob's perspective is offered in brief glimpses, though for the majority of the narrative he remains utterly opaque. When news comes to Jacob, the narrator briefly positions the reader in his mind. There is no description of messenger or message, only the narration of hearing and how Jacob perceives what he has heard: "And Jacob heard that he had defiled Dinah his daughter" (Gen 34:5). This verb of perception, שמע, is a cue that Jacob's perspective is being relayed. As noted above, this is the reader's only clue as to how Jacob perceives what has happened: Dinah, his daughter, has been defiled, and Shechem—the implicit subject of the verb טמה—has done the defiling. Other than Dinah, Jacob is the most enigmatic and impenetrable

---

… the land is spacious enough!" and "Their livestock and their property and all their animals—will they not be ours?" (34:23). For all of its power in convincing the men of Shechem to circumcise themselves, it hides Shechem's previously exposed perspective—that of his passionate desire to have Dinah as his wife. Because Shechem is so well drawn as desiring Dinah elsewhere (34:3, 11–13, 19), anything he says to the men may be read through this filter. Alternatively, this speech given by both of the Hivite leaders hides the central element of Shechem's personal desire for Dinah and thus may relay that they too are operating with some degree of deceit.

136. If so, he would not be unlike Jacob in Gen 25, who exploits Esau's hunger, or Laban in Gen 29, who takes advantage of Jacob's desire for his younger daughter and the darkness of their wedding night. The themes of deceitful tactics and gain by trickery flow throughout the Jacob narratives and are richly present here, potentially in the character of Hamor and certainly in the sons of Jacob.

137. Speiser, *Genesis*, 268.

of the characters in this narrative, known only through a description of his perception and his choice to stay silent (34:5).

Jacob's silence and lack of narrated emotion or cognition, being in the "realm of inference," support radically different character evaluations. For some, the lack of description of any emotion or activity indicates that he is a passive "do-nothing," letting Dinah and the reader down with his indifference and inaction.[138] For others, Jacob makes the most difficult response by maintaining composure and engaging in negotiations to pursue the next best step for his daughter's welfare.[139] Until the very end of the story, the perspective of Jacob, after that one clear moment, is shrouded with silence. It is therefore not explicitly indicated whether he agrees to the marriage-and-economic propositions of Hamor and Shechem or whether he is aware that his sons were speaking deceitfully (34:13), leaving open many possibilities of interpretation.[140]

It is not until the very end of the narrative that the audience is afforded another glimpse into Jacob's mind. From the start of the negotiations, the narrator does not relay any of Jacob's speech or actions, and no insight is given into his perception of Hamor and Shechem's words or those of his own sons. He "kept silent until [his sons] came" (34:5), but even after they do arrive, Jacob remains silent, disappearing until the end of the narrative apart from regular epithets that describe his children, the "sons of Jacob" and the "daughter of Jacob." When he finally does speak, seemingly provoked by his surprise and outrage at the destruction that his sons have wrought on the city, Jacob's final words to Simeon and Levi indicate his disagreement with their plan and action of violent retribution on the Shechemites. His speech indicates fear for himself and his family's well-being as a small, seminomadic group in foreign territory: "You have ruined me by making me stink among the inhabitants of the land, among the Canaanites and Perizzites! And I am few in number, so if they gather against me and attack me, then I will be destroyed—I and my house!" (34:30). Previously, Jacob had narrowly escaped potential annihilation at the hands of angry kinsmen several times (Gen 27:41–45, 31:22–24, 32:6–8),[141] suggesting the possibility that anxiety about his family's safety has

---

138. Sternberg, *Poetics of Biblical Narrative*, 448.
139. Fewell and Gunn, "Tipping the Balance," 198.
140. E.g., in Jub. 30, Jacob shares in the anger of his sons and takes part in the deception of the Shechemites with full approval.
141. In each of those previous scenarios, salvation came about through a mix of

been on his mind all along. Jacob, as head of the clan and its namesake, speaks here on behalf of all of his dependents. According to Jacob, Simeon and Levi's rash actions have put them all in danger.

As with his silence, Jacob's words engender different readings of his character. Some read Jacob's concerns as lesser in the eyes of the authoritative narrator, since they are followed by the "last word," given to Simeon and Levi.[142] This is often supported by interpreting the subsequent "terror from God" that falls on the surrounding cities (Gen 35:5) as negating the concerns of Jacob and validating the brothers' actions.[143] Alternatively, others read Jacob's outlook as indicative of "proper group-oriented behavior" valued in collectivist cultures and therefore also valued in this narrative.[144] That Jacob is the more validated party is supported with reference to God's continued revelations (35:1, 9–13), blessing (35:9), and promises (35:11–12) to Jacob in the wake of the argument. Due to the reticence in his characterization, the evaluation of Jacob's silence, lack of action, and final words is ultimately allocated to the reader.

5.5. The Sons of Jacob

The sons of Jacob are presented first as a collective with one mind, before Simeon and Levi become distinct leaders in 34:25, and events are relayed through their unified perspective many times in this narrative.[145] The narrator describes their emotional responses and provides an internal rationale for them: "They were deeply grieved and greatly angered because [Shechem] did an outrageous thing in Israel by sleeping with a daughter of Jacob—it is not done this way" (34:7). From their perspective, Shechem did an outrageous thing, נבלה, in (or against) Israel,[146] something—as dis-

---

fleeing and divine intervention. Similarly, immediately following the closing debate of Gen 34, God appears to Jacob and urges him to move on (Gen 35:1). Jacob obeys, and "the terror of God was upon the cities that were around them, so that they did not pursue the sons of Jacob" (35:5).

142. Sternberg, *Poetics of Biblical Narrative*, 475.

143. Sternberg, *Poetics of Biblical Narrative*, 475; Westermann, *Genesis 12–36*, 545.

144. Bechtel, "What if Dinah Is Not Raped?," 35.

145. Early LXX manuscripts have Simeon and Levi as the speakers of 34:14. Thus, readers of the LXX would have understood all of the sons to share the emotions and perspectives relayed in 34:7, 13, but Simeon and Levi to be their spokesmen.

146. While some modern interpreters claim this terminology being used by the family to describe their people is "anachronistic," that need not be the case.

cussed above—often punishable by death. This is the first time in Genesis[147] where the family is referred to as "Israel," and it reflects a collective identity that the sons of Jacob hold. Use of this term from the perspective of the brothers reflects their perception that the grave offense has been done against them *as a people*. After Hamor and Shechem make their propositions, the narrator allows the audience to know that the sons speak במרמה, "with deceit" (34:13). What is deceitful about their speech, however, is not fully clear. It could be that their sentiments about marrying their sister to "a man with a foreskin" are truthful, but their offer to intermarry after the Shechemites' circumcision is false. Alternatively, perhaps their words alone were their plan A, in that they never intended to "become one people"; rather, they expected the men to refuse the painful offer and hoped to scare Hamor and Shechem off—to "take our daughter and go." Due to narrative reticence, there is room for either of these interpretations and more. What *is* made clear is one reason *why* they speak with deceit, the volition behind it that reveals their perspective: "because he had defiled Dinah, their sister" (34:13). With their intentions withheld, the audience must assess the sons' actions alone, weighing various possibilities in light of what is revealed about their character(s).

5.5.1. Circumcision and Intermarriage: An Excursus

The brothers' deceitful proposal of union through circumcision inevitably brings the idea of covenant inclusion to the forefront of this narrative. Before turning to other characterization techniques at work for the sons of Jacob, I will first address the content of their speech in 34:14–17:

> We are not able to do this thing, to give our daughter to a man who has a foreskin, for it is a disgrace to us. Only by this will we agree with you:[148] If you become like us by circumcising yourselves—every male—then we will give our daughters to you and your daughters we will take for our-

---

147. At this point in Genesis, Jacob has received his new name (32:22–32), and a significant amount of time has passed, enough time for the children to grow from youths small enough to convince Esau that the family caravan had to move at a slow pace (33:12–14) to men who not only care for Jacob's flocks (34:5), which even older children could be responsible for, but are also welcomed to play an instrumental role in the marriage negotiations of their sister (34:8, 11, 13–17).

148. The "you" is plural here and throughout the brothers' speech to Shechem and Hamor.

selves, and we will dwell with you and become one people. But if you do
not obey us by being circumcised, then we will take our daughter and go.

When circumcision is introduced in Gen 17, it is in connection with God's
covenant with Abraham and his descendants:

> Behold, my covenant is with you, and you shall become the father of a
> multitude of nations. Your name will no longer be called Abram, but your
> name will be Abraham, because I am making you as the father of a multitude of nations. And I will make you very, very fruitful and I will make
> you into nations, and kings shall come forth from you. And I will establish my covenant between me and you and between your descendants[149]
> after you for their generations, as an everlasting covenant: to be God for
> you and for your descendants after you. And I will give to you and to your
> descendants after you the land of your sojourning, all the land of Canaan,
> as an everlasting possession. And I will be their God. (Gen 17:4–8)

Circumcision serves as a marker or sign (אות) that the male human recipients of this covenant make on their bodies to mark inclusion into this covenant. It is the condition of circumcision that makes the covenant effective: "As for any uncircumcised male who is not circumcised in the flesh of his foreskin, his life will be cut off from its people; he has broken my covenant" (Gen 17:14). While the promise is given to Abraham and his descendants (and later narrowed to Isaac and then Jacob and his descendants through the course of the Genesis narrative), there is opportunity for other male household members to be included: "Every male among you shall be circumcised.… Every male throughout your generations, the one born in your house and the one bought with money from any son of a foreigner who is not of your seed. The one born in your house and the one bought with your money shall surely be circumcised" (17:10, 12–13). With circumcision, inclusion in this covenant relationship with God, which includes the promised inheritance of the land of Canaan, is on the line. The covenant stipulates two groups explicitly: biological descendants of Abraham and enslaved males of other lineages. In connection with Gen 34, interpreters have grappled with whether others could also be included if they were willing to be circumcised and thus marked as

---

149. Heb. and LXX: lit. "seed," here and throughout Gen 17. The promise to Abraham's seed was an important element through which the author(s) of Jubilees interpreted Gen 34 (see ch. 3).

covenant observers. Taken at face value and not as a deceptive tactic, the brothers' words in 34:14–17 offer such a possibility, yet there is no talk of covenant or inheritance, only that of becoming "one people." While readers have reason to believe that the proposal is not all that it seems, and they later discover that the brothers violently prohibit the uniting of the clans, the possibility lingers as an issue for audiences to consider.

Later generations of readers contemplated and answered such questions of whether non-Israelites may enter into the covenant or become one with Israelites through circumcision in their own times,[150] but here in Gen 34, it is an unresolved issue set forth, undecided in the narrative. Some suppose that Jacob's silence and later outrage could suggest that he was in favor of the idea, just as Hamor and Shechem, and indeed all of the male Shechemites, undoubtedly were.[151] It is never certain what the brothers would have permitted under different circumstances—that is, if Shechem had not debased their sister.[152]

Although exogamous relations with Canaanites are a regular aversion for the protagonists of Genesis (e.g., Abraham in Gen 24, Rebekah in Gen 27:46, Isaac in Gen 28:1), and Jacob's sons say that they consider giving their daughter "to a man with a foreskin" to be a disgrace (חרפה), whether this is a *law* operative within the world of the story depends on the interpretation of the reader. Interpreters ancient and modern have brought in the proscriptions of Deut 7 as informing the assessment of these issues in the narrative (Jub. 30; Josephus, *A.J.* 1.338).[153] Deuteronomy 7:1 lists the Hivites as one of the seven nations of Canaan with

---

150. See, e.g., chapter 3's discussion on circumcision and covenant in Jubilees and *Judean Antiquities*.

151. For instance, Bechtel asserts, "Jacob is also willing to include outsiders who honor the group values, customs, and ideals" ("What if Dinah Is Not Raped?," 35).

152. Adding to the complexity, both Judah and Simeon married Canaanite women (Gen 38; 46:10, respectively), and Joseph married Asenath the Egyptian (Gen 42:45). In the case of Simeon and Joseph, this is presented as unproblematic. When the promise is to the descendants/seed of Abraham, Genesis does not indicate how its transfer is affected by gender. Thus, the question of whether intermarriage with foreign women is different from marrying one's daughters off to foreign men was taken up by later generations and resolved in very different ways. See Christine Hayes, *Gentile Impurities and Jewish Identities: Intermarriage and Conversion from the Bible to the Talmud* (Oxford: Oxford University Press, 2002).

153. Sternberg, "Biblical Poetics and Sexual Politics," 481–83; Bader, "Sexual Violation," 65.

which Israel is not permitted to intermarry with or have dealings with: "You shall make no covenant with them and show no mercy to them. You shall not intermarry with them, giving your daughters to their sons or taking their daughters for your sons" (Deut 7:2–3). The author(s) of Jubilees present this law as binding in the case of Gen 34 and even extend the law to forbid intermarriage with *any* foreigner (Jub. 30.11–16). Modern readers also take Deut 7 (and its comparable text, Exod 34:11–16) as binding within the narrative world of Genesis and thus undergirding this account,[154] while others read the Mosaic laws as not applicable in the pre-exodus narratives. The ethics of circumcision, covenant, and intermarriage are thus set before the audience like a smorgasbord of unresolved issues and questions on which to ruminate.

5.5.2. The Sons of Jacob: Characterization

The sons of Jacob, including the named Simeon and Levi, are as carefully drawn and as open to interpretation as Shechem. Like the young man with whom they find grave offense, the brothers of Dinah are defined by descriptions of their emotions (Gen 34:6–7), actions (34:25–29), motivations (34:7, 13, 27), and direct speech, with varying degrees of transparency (more opaque in 34:14–17 and clearer in 34:31). While the narrator reports their emotions, their speech, the deceitful quality of their speech, and their violent actions, he does not evaluate them explicitly, crafting characters that have been read either as the honorable heroes of this narrative or as devilish in their tactics and murderously excessive in their exaction of justice.[155] They are presented by the narrator as highly emotive, like Shechem, and with a hidden agenda behind their speech, possibly like Hamor. Thus, their foil in the story is their father Jacob.

Unlike Jacob, the brothers are described as bursting with emotion when they hear what has happened to their sister. The first word used to describe their reaction, the *hithpael* form of עצב, is found only one other time in the Hebrew Bible. It is used to depict the emotions of YHWH in Gen 6:6 that precede his decision to "blot out" all life and everything he

---

154. Sternberg, "Biblical Poetics and Sexual Politics," 481–83.
155. For the former, see Jub. 30. While Sternberg does not assert that the brothers are heroes to him, he claims that the text of Gen 34 upholds them as such (Sternberg, *Poetics of Biblical Narrative*, 472). For the latter, see Fewell and Gunn, "Tipping the Balance," 205; Bechtel, "What if Dinah Is Not Raped?," 34–36.

has made with the flood.[156] The word indicates great emotional distress, sorrow, and outrage. Perhaps it is due to this that some ancient interpreters read the sons as acting in accord with the divine character, celebrated with heaven's full approval (Jub. 30.17–20). Some suggest that this emotional response, a mixture of grief and rage, is meant to "soften our judgment" of their later actions, while others suggest that their inability to restrain their emotions is what leads to the reckless bloodshed that follows.[157]

5.5.3. The Sons of Jacob: Simeon and Levi

As with each of the other characters, the reader must not only color in what the narrator sketches of Simeon and Levi but weigh the ethics of their actions accordingly. Simeon and Levi "took" their swords, enter the city, and kill all the males along with Hamor and Shechem (Gen 34:25–26), and "the sons of Jacob" "took" all the livestock, property, women, and children from the city. Some understand this taking of life, property, and freedom as indicating righteous retribution on Shechem, who first "took" Dinah (34:2).[158] Others, however, find this violent response egregiously disproportionate to the offense.[159]

Various interpreters turn to other biblical texts to evaluate Simeon and Levi's actions, to drastically different effects. First, the laws of Deut 7:1–4, mentioned above, are brought to bear on Simeon and Levi's slaughter of the Shechemites. Deuteronomy 7:2 proclaims to the Israelites, "When YHWH your God gives [the Canaanite nations, including the Hivites] over to you, and you defeat them, you must devote them to destruction. You shall make no covenant with them and show no mercy to them." When interpreters read this law as comprising an evaluative criteria implicitly undergirding the Gen 34 narrative, they understand the narrator to be approving

---

156. This connection is only made in the Hebrew text. In the LXX, the verb used to depict the brothers' emotions is κατανύσσομαι in the aorist passive, and the LXX Gen 6:6 passage is void of *any* indication of God's emotional state.

157. For the former, see Sternberg, *Poetics of Biblical Narrative*, 453. For the latter, see Bechtel, "What if Dinah Is Not Raped?," 33–34. Reading Gen 34 in light of a "group-oriented" perspective, Bechtel interprets the description of the sons' emotions in terms of shame: "The shame and threat have made them feel vulnerable, inferior, and without control," and they respond with cunning and violent retaliation in an effort to "save face" (33–34).

158. Sternberg, *Poetics of Biblical Narrative*, 469–70.

159. Fewell and Gunn, "Tipping the Balance," 205.

of Simeon and Levi in their actions (Jub. 30).[160] Others look within the context of Genesis for evaluative criteria and claim to find it in Jacob's pronouncements against Simeon and Levi in Gen 49. On his deathbed, Jacob prophetically declares to his sons "what shall meet [them] in days to come," relaying his words to each son in regards to their birth order.[161] In Gen 49:5–7, Simeon and Levi receive their pronouncement together, which is full of negative evaluation:

> Simeon and Levi are brothers;
>   their knives are instruments of violence.
> Let my being never come into their council,
>   let my honor never be joined with their company—For in their anger they killed a man,
>   and in their pleasure,[162] they hamstrung an ox.
> Cursed is their anger, for it is mighty, and their wrath, for it is cruel.
> I shall divide them in Jacob
>   and scatter them in Israel.

Jacob's displeasure in these two sons is reflected in his desire to not be associated with them, his cursing of their anger, and the declaration that he will "scatter them." Later in the biblical narrative, the tribe of Simeon inherits a portion of land that is surrounded on all sides by Judah's much larger territory, and the Levites, as the priestly tribe, have no allotted inheritance but are indeed scattered throughout the tribal holdings of Israel. Jacob does not pair any other siblings in Gen 49, and the pairing of Simeon and Levi, together with the negative pronouncement of their violence, naturally leads interpreters to connect this with Gen 34. For those who hold that Gen 49 exerts a stronger evaluative claim over Gen 34 than Deut 7, Simeon and Levi's actions are taken as condemnable.[163]

---

160. Sternberg, "Biblical Poetics and Sexual Politics," 481–83; Steven Geller, *Sacred Enigmas: Literary Religion in the Hebrew Bible* (New York: Routledge, 1996), 145.

161. That is, according to the birth orders provided in the narrative of Gen 30. Technically, Jacob first blesses the sons of Leah in their birth order; then he blesses the firstborn sons, Gad and Dan, of Bilhah and Zilpah; then their second-born sons, Naphtali and Asher; and concludes by blessing the youngest sons, born from his favorite wife, Rachel, Joseph and Benjamin. Dinah is not mentioned in Gen 49. For how *Aseneth* may have implicitly addressed this beatific lacunae, see ch. 4, §2.

162. Or "with their intention." Heb. ברצנם.

163. Genesis 49, though not fully recounted in the *Judean Antiquities*, may undergird Josephus's presentation of Gen 34 in Josephus, *A.J.* 1.337–341. See ch. 3.

In other attempts to evaluate the actions of Simeon and Levi, interpreters turn to biblical texts pertaining to vengeance. Although YHWH poetically declares in Deut 32:35 that "vengeance is mine, I will repay," the law against taking vengeance in Lev 19:18 is followed by the qualification "[against] a son of your people." There is no law against taking vengeance against a foreign offender, but the wisdom tradition advocates for refraining from vengeance and trusting in the Lord. Proverbs 20:22 instructs, "Do not say, 'I will repay a wrong.' Wait upon YHWH so he may rescue you." Proverbs 24:29 echoes, "Do not say, 'I will do to him just as he has done to me. I shall repay the man in accordance with his deed.'" When the exhortations of Prov 20:22 and Prov 24:29 are brought to bear on Gen 34, evaluation of Simeon and Levi's choices takes on an altogether negative tone.[164] Alternatively, taking God's injunction in Deut 25:19 as a comparable guide for action yields a different assessment. In that passage, YHWH impresses on the Israelites to "never forget" the wrongs of Amalek but to "blot out the memory of Amalek from under heaven." If this is read as a template for dealing with the wrongs of foreigners, then Simeon and Levi come off as righteous.

Finally, the narrative is capped by the rhetorical question of Simeon and Levi, spoken in defense of their actions, "Should he use our sister like a prostitute?" (Gen 34:31). Having had sex with Dinah, *then* offering to pay, Shechem has treated their sister like a prostitute rather than a potential bride in the eyes of Simeon and Levi. With a word, the brothers are revealed to be unyielding, that even after confronted with the danger they have put their family in through their actions (34:30), they consider themselves in the right. Some read the position of their speech in the last lines of the narrative as indicative of the exaltation of their viewpoint over that of Jacob, while others claim that their unrepentant response to their father's protests further characterizes them as irreverent toward their father's status as the head of the clan.[165] The reader is left to grapple

---

164. MS F of *Aseneth* presents Simeon and Levi's slaughter at Shechem as "repaying evil for evil" and representing an ethic that they are instructed by Aseneth to turn from. See ch. 4, §4.

165. Josephus does not allow Simeon and Levi to have the last word in *A.J.* 1.337–341 and negatively evaluates that Simeon and Levi acted "without the knowledge of their father." See ch. 3 for further discussion. For their speech in as indicative of the exaltation of their viewpoint over that of Jacob, see Sternberg, *Poetics of Biblical Narrative*, 475.

with—or provide—the unspoken intentions of the brothers, with various possibilities. They have been painted as concerned for Dinah's honor and well-being, making them her only true champions in this story, or as self-concerned and insecure, avenging their own pride.[166] The techniques used to characterize Simeon and Levi define them as deeply offended and vengeful, but a reader's evaluation of them is contingent on how that reader fills in the gaps left by the narrator.

5.6. Multiperspectivity and Thematic Connections

This story, told through contrasting perspectives, ends without resolution and is connected to other Genesis narratives through the shared motifs of familial discord and deception. The final words between Jacob and his sons hang in the air, unresolved, in the aftermath of all that has transpired. The motif of family tension and disagreement is prevalent throughout the Genesis narrative, and especially through the parts of Genesis commonly called the Jacob cycle, in which Gen 34 is embedded, and the Joseph novella that follows it. In Gen 34, it has the effect of introducing the brothers as untrustworthy and violent, and establishing a rift between Jacob and the next generation. Although deception and discord are family traits that in one tale or another mark every patriarch and matriarch since Abraham and Sarah,[167] these traits are particularly prevalent in Jacob's life. He tricks his older brother Esau out of his birthright (Gen 25) and deceives his blind father, coming to him במרמה, "in deceit," to receive the blessing of the firstborn son (Gen 27:35). Isaac shakes and Esau weeps over what Jacob has done to them (27:33–34), and the rift between brothers grows when Esau vows revenge (27:41). The family trickery continues in Haran with Uncle Laban, though this time it is Jacob who is deceived (Gen 29). When Jacob makes for a sneak escape from his overbearing uncle, it almost costs him his life (Gen 31:21–33).

By the dawn of Gen 34, amends have been made and covenants cut between Jacob and the enemies he had procured among his family mem-

---

166. For the former, see Fewell and Gunn, "Tipping the Balance," 205–7. For the latter, see Bechtel, "What if Dinah Is Not Raped?," 33.

167. Abraham and Sarah made it a practice of pretending to be unwed siblings and making off with royal treasures (Gen 12, 20), and they fought about Ishmael (Gen 16, 21). Isaac and Rebekah followed suit when they pretended to be siblings to avoid a Philistine attack (Gen 26:6–9) and were divided in their parental favoritism (25:28).

bers. Jacob's autonomy is somewhat secure as he moves into the land of Canaan, the promised land, and finds a place for himself and his many dependents, out from under the authority of father, uncle, and older brother. Yet deception and discord erupt from the next generation. His own sons succeed in deceiving not only their Hivite landlords but Jacob himself, who flares with objection after their deceit and its consequences have been made known to him (34:30). As the metanarrative of Genesis goes on, there is antagonism and discord among the brothers, and Jacob is again deceived by his sons, made to think that his beloved Joseph has died (Gen 37). Then Judah, who took part in the paternal deception, slights his daughter-in-law and is subsequently deceived by her into conferring the marital rights he had withheld (Gen 38). After Joseph's turn at deceiving his terrified brothers (Gen 42–43), there is somewhat of a tentative restoration, of honesty and unity that closes the story of this generation (Gen 47:11–12).[168] Embedded in the intergenerational family narrative, Gen 34 introduces the sons of Jacob as deceptive and insolent as young Jacob had been to his father and as threatening and violent as a scorned Esau. A new fracture has split the family, yet these tactics and traits of deceit and discord are unevaluated by the Genesis narrator throughout. In every case, the reader is invited to assess them and their consequences in their unique contexts.

5.7. Conclusions on Multiperspectivity and Reticent Characterization

Woven with reticent characterization, the narrative of Gen 34 progresses through the contrasting perspectives of the various characters within it, producing narrative tension and complexity. Narratologist Mark Hartner argues that while, like any formal feature of narrative, "the perspectival arrangements in multiperspective narratives may fulfill a variety of functions, mostly, however, they highlight the perceptually, epistemologically, or ideologically restricted nature of individual perspectives."[169] Here in Gen 34, the ideologically restricted nature of the perspectives of Shechem,

---

168. Yet after Jacob's death, Joseph's brothers sent word to him that Jacob on his deathbed commanded that Joseph forgive them (Gen 50:15–16). The narrator informs that this message was inspired by their fear of Joseph's retribution (50:15) and was likely fabricated. If so, in the brothers' final scene their speech is still tinged with deceit.

169. Marcus Hartner, "Multiperspectivity," in Hühn, Meister, and Schmid, *Handbook of Narratology*, 353.

Hamor, Jacob, and his sons is highlighted. As Berlin notes, this feature of multiperspectivity, which she calls "multiplicity of viewpoints," is "one of the best vehicles for conveying a subjective presentation of one viewpoint."[170] Each character's actions can thus be understood through their perspectives, conveying their subjectivity. Jacob perceives his daughter to be "defiled," and while his sons agree, they also consider what Shechem has done as נבלה, an outrageous offense considered deserving of death.[171] The reader knows what the desperate Shechem and his opportunistic father do not yet know: the outrage that the sons of Jacob feel and that there is deceit in their speech. Having access to these perspectives, all in tension with one another, builds the dramatic tension and suspense of the narrative. This multiperspectival narration continues to the end, where the tensions between perspectives grow and eventually lead to violence, followed by a heated argument within the family of Israel. Yet in addition to this tension produced by multiperspectivity, the narrator's reticence regarding characterization forms a complex web of relations in which the interpretation of one character affects the reading or understanding of another.[172]

Artful parallels between characters and plays of perspective provide a brilliantly complex ethical conundrum for the contemplation of the audience. In addition to highlighting subjectivity of viewpoints, multiperspectivity also "draw[s] attention to various kinds of differences and similarities between the points of view presented."[173] Although some characters' perspectives are more transparent than others, the reader is invited to view them all in turn. At the point of the negotiations, the reader has been exposed to the minds and intentions of each of the male characters in the story to some degree, with Jacob and Hamor remaining somewhat opaque. This exposure reveals a generational divide; the younger generation is more transparent and marked by passion, the older generation by

---

170. Berlin, *Poetics and Interpretation*, 67.

171. See discussion above.

172. Interpretations of Simeon and Levi, for example, hinge on the conclusions that readers make regarding Shechem or assumed codes of conduct. Either the brothers rescued their sister from the hand of her rapist, or they left her bereft of her beloved (as in Anita Diamant's novelization of Gen 34). See Diamant, *The Red Tent* (New York: St. Martin's, 1997). Either Simeon and Levi deprived Dinah of the only stable future available to her in that society (Fewell and Gunn, "Tipping the Balance," 200), or there was no future for her at all among the Hivites, who were doomed to destruction (Jub. 30).

173. Hartner, "Multiperspectivity," 353.

emotional reservedness—until the very end, at least, when Jacob's alarm is exposed. Shechem and the Israelite sons are all brimming with either love or rage, and they act without concern for the safety of their communities, while the older men, as leaders of their clans, are portrayed with little emotion yet with great concern for their communities (34:4–24).[174] Readers are entrusted with weighing the various perspectives and ethics at play: debasement versus defilement versus נבלה, communal loyalty versus individual passions, age versus youth, inclusion versus separatism, resignation versus revenge, compromise versus violence.[175]

6. Permanent Withholding of Information and Dinah's Silence

Narratorial reticence in Gen 34 not only functions as a characterization technique, but it also creates two significant informational gaps, which form a narrative parallel. The informational gaps are created by the permanent withholding of both Dinah's perspective and the evaluation of the male characters. Based on insights from information theory as applied to narrative, the meaning of Dinah's name, and a comparison with other female figures of Genesis, I posit that Dinah's voice and perspective is centralized by its absence and highlighted as one of crucial importance.

Leona Toker's study of information withholding in modern novels sheds light on the function and effect that permanently withheld information in any narrative has on a reader. I find her insights generative in the study of Gen 34, which is peppered with informational gaps of great conse-

---

174. While Jacob is exasperatingly silent, Hamor is hardly without speech. Rather than a single marriage that his son Shechem asked for (34:4), Hamor proposes the possibility of multiple intermarriages among them, as well as settlement in the land. God had promised this very thing to Jacob so many years before his sojourn in Padan-Aram, in the vision known to most English speakers as "Jacob's ladder" (38:13). Though not mentioned in the narrative, it remains an underlying possibility at this point that this negotiation may be the means through which part of that promise is received, just as Abraham secured a portion of the land in his lifetime through negotiations (Gen 23).

175. Speiser has a different list of what is in tension in this narrative. He suggests "pastoral simplicity and grim violence, love and revenge, candor and duplicity" (*Genesis*, 268). Each of his pairings relies on the interpretations of its characters that he offers. While I am inclined to include "candor and duplicity" in the list above, some readings of Hamor and Shechem (explored above) hold that they too speak with duplicity, to the Israelites or/and their own countrymen.

quence. In addition to having a magnetizing effect on the reader, drawing them in to ponder what is missing, the withholding of information acts as a mirror to the audience; the conjectures, expectations, and evaluations of the audience are exposed though these silences as the audience grapples with what is left unsaid.[176] The audience meets the informational gaps in a process of dialogical engagement that is active and exploratory, in which "the process of reading … becomes a play in which the text and the audience read each other."[177] In certain stories, there may be a *diffusion of information*, in which the information withheld (in a mystery, for example, the answer to "Who is the culprit?") is gradually offered to the reader in scattered clues as the narrative progresses. With a *temporary suspension of information*, reader expectations and conjectures are "either fulfilled or thwarted by subsequent portions of the text."[178] For example, at the very end of Gen 34, Jacob finally breaks his silence, and there is a glimpse, albeit a partial one, into his thoughts and concerns that had been previously concealed. Most of the other informational gaps in Gen 34, however, fall under Toker's category of *permanent suspension of information*, when "what seems to be a crucially important separate piece of information is suppressed and never revealed."[179] These significant informational gaps engage the reader in a kind of moral-intellectual experience in which they become both coauthors and judges. To make sense of the silences in this "complicated ethical situation,"[180] the audience must not only supply what is lacking in the construction of the characters but also evaluate their perspectives and actions.

The brilliance of this narrative in providing such an ethical-intellectual challenge to its readers is highlighted in the name of its silent heroine, Dinah. *Dînāh*, דינה, is a feminine name derived from the Hebrew verb with ethical and judicial connotations, דין, meaning "to execute judgment," or "decide a legal case," or from the related noun דין, meaning "legal judgment," "plea," "cause," or "condemnation." Rendered verbally, דינה is an infinitive construct form of the verb דין, with a feminine singular suffix. The infinitive construct form is notoriously ambiguous, and rendering its meaning is largely dependent on the context in which one finds it, which

---

176. Toker, *Eloquent Reticence*, 5–6.
177. Toker, *Eloquent Reticence*, 7–8.
178. Toker, *Eloquent Reticence*, 7.
179. Toker, *Eloquent Reticence*, 15–16.
180. Fewell and Gunn, "Tipping the Balance," 197.

is why it is difficult to attest a precise meaning to Dinah's name. I suggest, however, that דינה may be faithfully rendered "she decides," or "her decision." The absence of Dinah's voice, perspective, and even location in this story parallels the absence of ethical evaluation of the characters and their actions in the narrative. Above I argued that Gen 34's artful use of ambiguity and multiperspectivity presents a complex ethical case to the audience, while formal reticence places the audience in the role of coauthor and judge. Although the perspective of "her decision" is permanently withheld, the semantic connotation of Dinah's name suggests that *it would make all the difference*. Thus, the narrative is structured in a way that heightens the value and ethical impact of the voice of Dinah.

The absence of Dinah's perspective qualifies as a *significant* informational gap. There is a distinction between the regular *in*significant silences of narrative that readers naturally fill in to imagine the story-world and those of greater significance that the audience is invited to engage with more deeply. Toker asserts that any narrative text is "characterized by a degree of indeterminacy, but when it presents a sufficient number of features … to cause instant pattern recognition, the missing details are supplied for the reader's imagination."[181] Every reader knows this instinctively, for a short phrase such as "while the sun was setting" can cast a backdrop of lighting, shadows, and mood to the narrated action that the reader instantaneously fills in. Yet when "the content of the missing information" is "of some consequence,"[182] it qualifies as an informational gap. Such gaps may include those discussed above, such as character motives, manner of action, and other elements that are central to the plot.[183] As previously mentioned, the evaluation of the characters in Gen 34, especially regarding the retributive violence of Simeon and Levi, has been a felt informational gap in the narrative from ancient times, as interpreters have sought to fill this gap by bringing in other texts, contexts, and ideologies to supply evaluative criteria lacking in the story itself. I suggest that the lack of Dinah's perspective in Gen 34 also qualifies as a significant informational gap.

The absence of Dinah's voice and perspective is conspicuous and a weighty feature of this narrative. Genesis 34:1 opens with a blend of narrative exposition and an insight into the volition of Dinah, "And

---

181. Toker, *Eloquent Reticence*, 6.
182. Toker, *Eloquent Reticence*, 6.
183. Toker, *Eloquent Reticence*, 6.

Dinah, the daughter of Leah whom she bore to Jacob, went out to see the daughters of the land." The narrator, whose focus was on Jacob before (Gen 33:18–20), has now shifted to Dinah, and we get a glimpse of her inner world, the intention behind her action of going out. From this point forward, Dinah's perception, emotion, volition, actions, and even her location are withheld from the reader. She is completely opaque to us, even, for much of the narrative, not visible. From the explorations above, we know that the narrator is an omniscient narrator, privy to the emotions, volition, and perspectives of each of his characters. While the narrator *could* have offered the reader an insider's view into Dinah's perspective at any point in this narrative, *he does not*. Rather, Dinah is so thoroughly absent from the deliberations about her future that one is surprised to find mention of her again in verse 26, when Simeon and Levi take her from the house of Shechem. When and how she came to the house of Shechem, the narrator does not say. Whether she was there all along[184] or whether she was permitted to go after the brothers' deceitful proposition was accepted by the Shechemites, the reader will never know. This does not indicate a lack of omniscience on the narrator's part but a choice to withhold such vital information.

Drawing from the insights of the ways in which narrative reticence functions, I propose that the artful and selective use of silences and gaps in Gen 34 serves to highlight, not diminish, the importance of Dinah's perspective to the reader in evaluating the issues in tension set forth by the narrative, the perspectives of the characters, and their actions. As noted above, another one of the major perceived informational gaps of Gen 34 by modern interpreters is the question of whether Shechem raped Dinah. The above exploration of the verbs describing the kernel event (Gen 34:2) concluded that, due to their semantic ranges and implications, the answer is indeterminable. While it is viable for theologians and interpreters to argue that the less dangerous reading for feminist concerns is one in which Dinah *is* raped, as Alison Joseph argues in her article, "'Is Dinah Raped?' Isn't the Right Question: Genesis 34 and Feminist Historiography," historiography's hands are tied: "There is ambiguity concerning the acts of Shechem in Gen 34:2.... So what do we

---

184. Sternberg reads 34:26, "[Simeon and Levi] took Dinah from Shechem's house and left," as indicative of her location throughout the entire story. In this reading, Dinah is essentially held hostage, and "the Hivite negotiation technique has included blackmail" (*Poetics of Biblical Narrative*, 467).

make of the linguistic evidence?... We cannot properly translate *'innâ* as rape.... In denying Dinah's 'rape,' do we silence her and other victims?"[185] While Joseph's article goes on to propose other questions through which feminist historiographers may explore the Gen 34 narrative to hopefully more ethical ends, I argue that the silence of Dinah in this narrative is its most crucial feature. It is unavoidable. The only character who could offer the information of whether Shechem raped Dinah is Dinah, whose perspective is withheld from the narrative.

The lack of depiction of Dinah's voice and volition is not simply, as some have suggested, an unfortunate quality of a story originating from an ancient culture where patriarchy dominated over the affairs of women. Many modern feminists have assumed, ironically not unlike the patriarchy-upholding interpreters before them, that beneath this narrative was an implicit evaluation, a narrator's judgment of the characters' actions. Along with this, they have assumed that the narrator and ancient (male) readers simply must have not cared about Dinah's perspective. Furthermore, some assume that the silence of the narrator indicates approval for the excessively violent retribution of Simeon and Levi and the other sons of Jacob, a "silent endorsement of their actions."[186] Surely, the text has been read this way. Throughout the ancestral narratives of Genesis, however, linked to Gen 34 by both characters and thematic motifs, women's perspectives and words are valued alongside those of the male characters. In Gen 16:4, we view the scene through Hagar's perspective, "And she saw that she was pregnant, and her mistress [Sarai] became diminished in her eyes." Hagar also features as the human protagonist of two divine encounters involving rescue and promise in the desert (Gen 16, 21). In some stories, Sarai/Sarah indeed plays a silent role, a backdrop to the foregrounded Abram/Abraham; Gen 12 offers no indication of her response to departing for "the land that [YHWH] will show" or her feelings about her husband's deceptive plan and being taken into Pharaoh's house. In other tales, however, such as Gen 16, 18, and 21, Sarai/Sarah is active, speaking, and shaping the plot. While she is alone and listening to Abraham's conversation with his three mysterious

---

185. Joseph, "'Is Dinah Raped?,'" 30, 32. Feminist interpreter Suzanne Scholz argues that any interpretation that marginalizes Dinah and "the rape" is dangerous: "Many contemporary interpretations of Genesis 34 are dangerous in a culture that some define as a 'rape culture'" ("What Really Happened," 2).

186. Joseph, "'Is Dinah Raped?,'" 34.

guests in Gen 18, the narrator allows the reader access to Sarah's secret thoughts. In response to hearing that she would bear a child in her old age, "Sarah laughed in her heart, saying, 'After my wearing out, will there be pleasure for me? But my lord is old!'" (18:12). Additionally, Rebekah is a strong, active, and vocal foil to her more passive husband, Isaac. She is instrumental in the account of her own betrothal, and ascribed agency and choice (Gen 24, especially vv. 57–58). It is Rebekah who receives the divine oracle regarding her unborn twins, the eponymous ancestors of "two nations" in her womb, Esau/Edom and Jacob/Israel (25:23). Loving the younger (25:28), she instructs him to take bold measures to secure his father's blessing (27:5–13). Thus, it is through the actions and words of Rebekah that God's oracle is fulfilled and Jacob's destiny is established. Furthermore, although Bilhah and Zilpah are presented as little more than pawns in their mistresses' rivalry, Rachel and Leah are central narrative agents in Gen 29–30. While operating within a culture in which men were legally dominant, Genesis presents its cast of women as speakers and agents; they are complex characters with their own unique motives and desires.

Dinah's voice is not withheld from this narrative because it does not matter. Rather, the meaning of her name and the withholding of her voice emphasize how essential her perspective is. The other significant informational gaps of the narrative—the question of whether Dinah was raped and the evaluation of the characters and their actions—hinge on the perspective of "she decides." The question of what happened between Shechem and Dinah is a central concern to modern interpreters when grappling with the fallout of the event and, as argued above, would have been a concern in ancient Israel as well. Even so, only Dinah can answer the truth of what happened, of how *she* perceived their encounter. Highlighted by this artful shaping of the story is the central tragedy that Dinah's voice is *not* asked for, either by the one who reportedly loves her or her family members. Dinah is thus not allowed a chance to share her perspective or her desires. Either struck with silence after the horror that has befallen her or silenced by the forces of gendered power that govern her world, her voice is withheld. Jacob's initial silence is narrated as a choice, an action (Gen 34:5), but Dinah's voice and perspective are simply absent, paralleling that of God in this narrative, another central figure of whom no one inquires. While God, being God, continues to speak and act in the aftermath of the slaughter at Shechem, directing and protecting Jacob and his family (35:1–5), Dinah is never heard from again but only briefly appears in a genealogical list of the Israelites who descended into Egypt (Gen 46:15).[187]

The assumption that the lack of Dinah's narrated perspective is indicative of a lack of its importance fails to acknowledge the artful and ethical role that reticence plays in this story. The permanent withholding of Dinah's voice is in parallel to the permanent withholding of the ethical evaluation of the actions and words of Shechem, of Hamor, of Jacob, and of Simeon and Levi and their brothers. These are central narrative gaps. There is no valid reason to assume that the one gap (the ethical evaluation) is more valuable than the other (the voice of Dinah). Rather, they are inextricably tied to each other. Dinah's silence is not simply an unavoidable feature of a textual relic from an ancient androcentric culture, as some suggest, but an artistic choice with ethical implications. What is withheld from the reader is therefore exalted as of central importance in evaluating the actions and choices of the characters within it.

7. Conclusion

As mentioned in chapter 1, modern literary scholarship on Gen 34 has focused heavily on the question of what happened between Shechem and Dinah and on the evaluation of the male characters and their actions. I have argued that the text is ambiguous in regard to both of these concerns. Rather than provide the answer to these questions, the formal features that weave together to form this narrative—an omniscient, covert narrator; multiperspectivity; degrees of reticence in characterization; and the permanent withholding of evaluation and the perspective of Dinah—put forth a complex ethical conundrum for the audience to take up and dialogically engage with. Readers both ancient and modern have brought

---

187. This comes shortly after the description of the sons of Simeon, one of whom was born of a Canaanite woman (Gen 46:10). Concern for Dinah's fate is not new to feminist modernity, but ancient stories and traditions have suggested various outcomes for her redemption and future. Tragically, Jubilees offers her no future but an untimely death. An ancient rabbinic tradition, however, held that Dinah became the mother of Asenath, Joseph's wife, and thus grandmother to the great northern tribes of Ephraim and Manasseh. The Testament of Job, written during the Second Temple period, portrays Dinah as the second wife of Job, who gets to share in the redeeming abundance of the latter part of his life. For a discussion of the rich parabiblical traditions of Dinah's life after Gen 34, see Michael Legaspi, "Job's Wives in the *Testament of Job*: A Note on the Synthesis of Two Traditions," *JBL* 127 (2008): 71–79.

their own unique perspectives, values, contexts, and cotexts—consciously or unconsciously—to their encounter with the rich ambiguity of the Gen 34 narrative and its silence regarding the evaluation of its characters' actions and perspectives. That readers have felt the need to look elsewhere for clues and guides for the ethical or legal values with which to assess the narrative's characters and their actions undergirds my argument that the narrative itself does not provide such evaluations. The narrator's withholding of the perspective of Dinah, whose name holds connotations of evaluative and legal judgment, is paralleled with the withholding of evaluation, suggesting that her perspective is of central evaluative importance. Yet Dinah's perspective is forever absent from the text. Instead, though the artful use of reticence, Gen 34 demands its audience's active engagement to puzzle over what was done and what should have been done.

3
The Ethics of Representation in Jubilees 30 and Josephus's *Judean Antiquities* 1.337–341

> Want a different ethic? Tell a different story.
> —Thomas King, *The Truth about Stories*

1. Introduction

The ancient Judean narratives of Jubilees and Josephus's *Judean Antiquities* are two of the earliest witnesses to narrative encounter with Gen 34. Each of them re-presents Gen 34 in ways that demonstrate their unique engagement with the biblical story's ambiguities and reticences. I argued in the previous chapter that Gen 34 is structured in a way that demands active engagement from its readers, especially by withholding evaluation of the characters and their actions. By including their re-presentations of the biblical tale as a formative historical event in their larger narrative compositions of Israel's history, Jubilees and *Judean Antiquities* each provide evaluations of the characters and of Simeon and Levi's retributive violence that are lacking in Genesis. In Jub. 30, the voice of evaluation resounds from heaven through its overt and authoritative narrator, eliminating space for dialogical engagement or debate. In *A.J.* 1.337–341, the narrator allows more room for the audience to assess the characters and their actions but subtly parallels this episode of the ancient past with narratives of first-century CE conflicts and peoples in which the narrator's evaluation is explicit.

In this chapter I consider both Jubilees and Josephus's *Judean Antiquities* as authoritative national histories—narratives that tell "the story of a single political community over an extended period of time"[1] while self-presenting as reliable. Jubilees and *Judean Antiquities* were written for their second-century BCE and first-century CE audiences, respectively; as national histories self-presenting as true and authoritative, they functioned to emplot their contemporary generation of Judeans in an ongoing story. Through the narration of shared origins and experiences, and through the representation of Israelite/Judean selves and their cultural others, these histories worked to shape their audiences' conception of their present temporal landscape[2] as well as their corporate identity and ethics. Each history uses its unique representations of the Israelites and their cultural other(s) to construct Judean identity, draw boundaries, and promote a relational ethic toward outsiders. Through the lens of socionarratological theory about narrative representation, I also assess the ethical potentials and dangers of the representations of Israelites and Shechemites in Jub. 30 and *A.J.* 1.337–341 in a way that contributes to representational ethics in modern history writing.[3]

2. A Proposition of Genre: Jubilees and *Judean Antiquities* as Authoritative National Histories

With the support of developments in genre theory, I argue that although the scope, form, and cultural audience of Jubilees and *Judean Antiquities* differ, they may both productively be considered national histories. As

---

1. Jeremy Popkin, *From Herodotus to H-Net: The Story of Historiography*, 2nd ed. (Oxford: Oxford University Press, 2021), 33.

2. See introduction, §1. By temporally mapping a nation's collective history, a nation's "stories serve as meaning-generating interpretive devices which frame the present within a hypothetical past and an anticipated future" (Bruner, "Introduction," 18). As numerous anthropological and sociological studies have shown in the past half-century, this functionality has real consequences for the lives of the peoples shaped by their histories (see Somers, "Narrative Constitution of Identity").

3. In an article aptly titled, "Why We Need an Ethics of History Writing," Dom Birch laments the "dearth of discussion about what ethical history could look like" and calls on historians to, with their work, generate "a productive discussion that could expand the idea of an ethics of history." See Birch, "Why We Need an Ethics of History Writing," Doing History in Public, December 6, 2016, https://tinyurl.com/SBL6710a. Representation is among the four categories of ethics that Birch proposes as constituting an "ethical framework for history writing." The other categories are explanation, understanding, and empathy.

national histories, both texts functioned to inform the collective identity and ethics of their contemporary Judeans by temporally emplotting the present generation in an ongoing story. The claims to authority and reliability made by their narrators also qualify them as *authoritative* national histories, thus adding to the force of their ethical evaluations and representations of Judeans and their cultural others.

2.1. Genre Theory: The Function of National Histories

Genre not only affects what types of representations are operable and valid within a particular narrative and what roles are available for characters to play; it also affects the *force* of those representations on the audience. In his study of twentieth-century European and American public narratives regarding international conflict, Philip Smith argues that the generic distinction of public narratives—which differs from country to country and conflict to conflict—shapes the representation of national agents.[4] This representation, informed by genre, forms a causal arrow going from narrative to action, in this case military action.[5] Genre choices shape the representational modes available to a given narrative and thus shape the perception of available and viable actions for the characters within those narratives. Thus, when the narratives are public and living people are emplotted within them, "genre choices shape the way that we make history."[6] For instance, within a romance, a genre that features the optimistic storyline of a hero's triumph over adversity, the villain is allowed a certain degree of dynamism; the villain may take a turn toward the good in a conversion of sorts; negotiations may win the day.[7] Whereas the same villain, cast into an "apocalyptic" tale, depicting "a struggle between radical evil and the forces of fundamental good," is irredeemably and absolutely bad, and the only available option for dealing with them is through war.[8] Smith found

---

4. Smith, *Why War?*
5. Smith, *Why War?*, 208.
6. Smith, *Why War?*, 227. In the cultures Smith studied, he found that events and actors were cast into stories spanning four genres, which he labeled "low memesis," "tragedy," "romance," and "apocalyptic."
7. Smith, *Why War?*, 26–27.
8. Smith, *Why War?*, 27. Smith defines the apocalyptic genre found in modern American and Western European social discourse as depicting "events as a struggle between radical evil and the forces of fundamental good in a supernatural setting,"

that in these twentieth-century European and American public narratives, "genre choices align with war in ways that are regular and predictable over a large number of cases."[9] It stands to reason that the genre choices available to any given culture are culturally determined. The genres available in modern Western Europe and the United States differ from those of ancient Israel and Judea (although through biblical literature, there is a degree of influence from Judean antiquity to Western modernity). It is widely agreed among scholars of antique Judean/Jewish literature that the narrative modes of Jubilees and *Judean Antiquities* differ and may be considered as belonging to different genres. In order to bring them productively into conversation with representational ethics, however, I argue for considering them *both* as authoritative national histories.

It is necessary to clarify my operative conceptualization of generic labels in general and what I mean when I use the term "national history." Informed by recent trends in genre studies, I consider genre to be a grouping of related texts, often with fuzzy or fluid boundaries, rather than a rigid pigeonhole in which to classify texts.[10] Literary genres can be defined by a variety of features, which are sometimes formal (e.g., letter, curriculum vitae, sonnet) but not always. Texts within a genre may share aim and style rather than any formal features.[11] Genres can overlap with other genres, depending on the features that compose the group, and texts can participate in multiple genres simultaneously.[12] I am making the case that

---

and notes that "secularized equivalents where our very salvation is at stake can be found from time to time in civil discourse" (27).

9. Smith, *Why War?*, 205. He continues, "When successfully institutionalized and widely shared, the apocalyptic frame encourages war," while "realist [low mimetic] and tragic frames are associated with low levels of legitimacy and military intervention."

10. Alastair Fowler, *Kinds of Literature: An Introduction to the Theory of Genres and Modes* (Cambridge: Harvard University Press, 1982), 37.

11. Molly Zahn, *Genres of Rewriting in Second Temple Judaism* (Cambridge: Cambridge University Press, 2020), 60. Zahn offers the example of satire as this kind of genre grouped by aim and style, noting that texts of very different forms may be included (e.g., an article from the satirical newspaper *The Onion*, or a novel such as *Gulliver's Travels*).

12. Zahn, *Genres of Rewriting*, 60–61. Zahn describes potential overlapping schemes in two ways. First, as a series of concentric circles, in which broader genres (e.g., prose) contain more narrowly defined genres (e.g., article or novel), which in turn contain even more narrowly defined genres (e.g., op-ed article or romance novel, respectively). Alternatively, as a series of overlapping but distinct circles, as in a Venn

both Jubilees and Josephus's *Judean Antiquities* participate in the broad genre of national history. By national history, I mean a narrative that tells the "story of a single political community over an extended period of time,"[13] regardless of author or audience. There are formal features of this genre (narrative), features of content (story of a single political community), and scope (over an extended period of time). Within each of those generic requirements, there is of course much room for diversity. Even the "narrative" requirement allows for a range of media and participation within other genres to be operative within any given national history. A diversity of aim, style, and cultural expectations can be found among the genre participants because the requisite features of national history are so broadly defined. Cultural expectations, for example, may include a certain view toward what qualifies as reliable source material or what role (if any) divine agents are understood to play in the causality of depicted events.

This broad generic category, with its room for diversity, allows for histories across culture and time to be grouped and analyzed in conversation with one another. Both Jubilees and the *Judean Antiquities* belong in the genre of national history, even though they may also participate in a number of other genres simultaneously. This generic distinction does not preclude these works from belonging to other genres, such as ancient Jewish apocalypse (for Jubilees) or Roman constitutional discourse (for *Judean Antiquities*), or "rewritten Scripture" (for both).[14] By considering them both as national histories, however, the analysis of representational ethics within these ancient Judean narratives can be brought into fruitful conversation with discussions of representational ethics in national histories across time and culture.

---

diagram. Thus, an article from *The Onion* can be located within the overlapping genre circles of satire and news article, participating in the aim and style of the first genre and in the form of the latter. Though Zahn does not focus on this in her article, the places of overlap between genres can also be considered as their own genres. Thus, we have the genre of nineteenth-century British romance novel, arising from the intersection of the broader genres of novel, nineteenth-century British literature, and romance, all genres in which works such as *Jane Eyre* and *Pride and Prejudice* arguably belong.

13. Popkin, *From Herodotus to H-Net*, 33.

14. Molly Zahn, "Genre and Rewritten Scripture: A Reassessment," *JBL* 131 (2012): 271–88; Sidnie White Crawford, *Rewriting Scripture in Second Temple Times* (Grand Rapids: Eerdmans, 2008); Teppei Kato, "Ancient Chronography on Abraham's Departure from Haran: Qumran, Josephus, Rabbinic Literature, and Jerome," *JSJ* (2019): 178–96.

Although the genre of national history is defined in part by its form (narrative), the functional aspect of this genre is highly pertinent to this study. Inherent to genre is the aspect of function, or what kind of "work" or "action" the members of particular genres accomplish.[15] In the words of Molly Zahn, "Differences in genre imply differences in what a text is intended to do and how it is used by or impacts its audience."[16] Within any given genre, especially more broadly defined genres, there may be several purposes operative in the diverse collection of its members. Yet each genre has its own distinguishing function, and genre may be thus assigned on the basis of function alone.[17] Due to the overlapping nature of genre and the propensity for works to participate in multiple genres, any given work may have a number of functions. For the texts in question, I will consider the functions they share as national histories.

National histories function to emplot a generation in a temporal landscape and to shape the collective identity of a nation. These works often narrate the shared beginnings of a group, a political entity, defining who they are by who they have been and what they have been through together. In this sense, they are predominantly narratives that function to "connect people into collectives."[18] This collective identity inevitably comes with ethical expectations; "who we are" is often defined by "what we have done" and "what we do." By temporally mapping a group's collective history, these "stories serve as meaning-generating interpretive devices which frame the present within a hypothetical past and an anticipated future."[19] Thus, national histories, though they may only recount the past, consequentially function to shape the perspective of the present and inform possibilities for the future. As anthropological and sociological studies have shown, this functionality has real consequences for the lives of the peoples shaped by their histories.[20]

The function of national history to shape collective identity, frame the present, and inform possibilities for the future is dramatically

---

15. Zahn, *Genres of Rewriting*, 62, 64.

16. Zahn, *Genres of Rewriting*, 71.

17. Carolyn Miller, "Genre as Social Action," *QJS* 70 (1984): 151.

18. Which is one of the two main functions of story in general, as proposed by Frank in *Letting Stories Breathe*, 15.

19. Bruner, "Introduction," 18.

20. See Somers, "Narrative Constitution of Identity"; Polletta, "Contending Stories"; Bruner, "Ethnography as Narrative."

evinced by the twentieth-century shift in the dominant historical narratives about Native Americans told by ethnographers and indigenous Americans alike. Though "Native America" is not one nation or political entity but rather a collective identity of many indigenous nations, their shared historical experiences of forced removals and political and social oppression, and the stories told about those experiences, have helped to knit them together in identity and action. In "Ethnography as Narrative," anthropologist Edward Bruner reports a relatively sudden shift (within a decade)[21] in the dominant historical narrative about Native American culture that coincided with a shift in the perceived social roles of both indigenous peoples and anthropologists who were shaped by this narrative reframing:

> In the 1930s and 1940s the dominant story constructed about Native American culture change saw the present as disorganization, the past as glorious, and the future as assimilation. Now [after the shift that occurred in the 1970s],[22] however, we have a new narrative: the present is viewed as a resistance movement, the past as exploitation, and the future as ethnic resurgence.[23]

With this shift in national history-telling came a shift in collective identity and ethic, and new assignments of social roles. "In the 1970s story … the golden age is in the future, as the indigenous people struggle against exploitation and oppression to preserve their ethnic identity." In Bruner's work among the Navajo in 1948 and the Mandan Hidatsa in 1951, he found that most people were "eager to provide information about the glorious past," but after the shift in the seventies, "now we meet many Indian activists fighting for a better future."[24] Here we see the force of historical narratives to inform power structures and political actions:

---

21. Bruner, "Ethnography as Narrative," 139.
22. Bruner attributes this shift to the change in discursive practice shared across the world in the wake of World War II and the dismantling of the colonial system. The post–World War II and postcolonial story of "exploitation, resistance, and resurgence" is thus "an international story" told not only in native America but in Sumatra, in India, and is "retold almost daily in debates at the United Nations" ("Ethnography as Narrative," 149).
23. Bruner, "Ethnography as Narrative," 149.
24. Bruner, "Ethnography as Narrative," 140.

> The assimilation story has been a mask for oppression; the resistance story is a justification for claims of redress for past exploitation. Both carry policy and political implications. The reasoning in the assimilation narrative is that if Indians are going to disappear anyway, then their land can be leased or sold to whites; in the ethnic resurgence narrative we are told that if Indians are here to stay, tribal resources must be built up. Assimilation is a program for redemption; resistance, for self- and ethnic fulfillment.[25]

In this example, national history is shown to function to emplot the people of the present in an ongoing story—in this case, one of two ongoing stories. Emplotment shapes the national interpretation of the present, informing the roles and requirements—the identity and ethic—of the present generations as agents, as characters, in the chosen story.

2.2. Jubilees and *Judean Antiquities* as National Histories

One may question whether Jubilees' author(s) and Josephus understood and composed their works as national histories, or whether this matters to the analysis of their works as participants in that genre. Generic distinctions can be made at an emic level, that is, intrinsic to the culture or society in question, and at an etic level, determined and applied by scholars studying a body of literature. The broad genre of national history that I employ is primarily an etic one, but many of its participants across time and culture may very well have been composed by people, individuals or collectives, who were consciously composing national history in accordance with the standards of their time and cultures. In those cases, national history operates as an emic genre as well. The expectations for inclusion in the emic genre(s) of national history, however, may vary over time and culture in ways that hinder cross-cultural and interchronological comparisons. Modern American and European academic national history, with its expectation of critical interpretation of primary source materials and its strict requirement that claims for causation be atheistic, would not include historical narratives that take primary sources at their word or claim divine providence as a causal agent.[26] Modern academic histo-

---

25. Bruner, "Ethnography as Narrative," 144.
26. E.g., the primary sources of the American Revolution include the personal correspondences of George Washington, Benjamin Franklin, and other such founda-

rians would likely categorize such a religiously informed history as myth, or even propaganda, depending on its contents. *Both* such narratives—the academic and the religious—however, can be included in the *etic* category of national history.[27] Thus they may be productively brought into conversation with one another as stories in competition among the general public (or accepted by certain distinct segments of the general public), both claiming to present a reliable account of a nation's history. Jubilees and Josephus's *Judean Antiquities* strongly differ from the cultural expectations of modern academic history, and Jubilees differs strongly from the tradition of Greek and Roman history writing in which Josephus embedded his *Judean Antiquities*, but both of these works participate in the broad etic genre of national history that spans time and cultural expectations.

While it is well accepted that Josephus's *Judean Antiquities* is the written history of a nation, composed in the style of and in conversation with other ancient Greek and Roman histories of the Roman republic and early imperial period,[28] the designation of Jubilees as a national history is perhaps less obvious, even questionable. With regard to scope, *Judean Antiquities* proudly boasts of covering five thousand years of Judean history, from the creation of the world and humanity to the dawn of the failed Judean revolt against Roman imperial rule in 66–70 CE (*A.J.* 20.259–262).[29] Jubilees, on the other hand, re-presents ancient Israel's traditional history from cre-

---

tional American figures, who regularly attributed victories or other circumstances to God. See John C. Fitzpatrick, ed., *The Writings of George Washington from the Original Manuscript Sources, 1745–1799* (Washington, DC: U.S. Government Printing Office, 1931), 12:343, 20:95; and Albert H. Smyth, ed., *Writings of Benjamin Franklin* (New York: Macmillan, 1905–1907), 9:702.

27. It is through understanding history as a broad, etic genre that historiographers may study the "the history of history itself," that is, "understanding how historians of the past conceived of their projects and the method they used" (Popkin, *From Herodotus to H-Net*, 3). Examples of such projects include Ernst Breisach's *Historiography: Ancient, Medieval, and Modern* (Chicago: University of Chicago Press, 1993) and Donald R. Kelley's *Faces of History: Historical Inquiry from Herodotus to Herder* (New Haven: Yale University Press, 1998).

28. Steve Mason, "Introduction to the *Judean Antiquities*," in *Flavius Josephus: Judean Antiquities 1–4* (Leiden: Brill, 2004), xiii–xxxvi; Popkin, *From Herodotus to H-Net*, 38.

29. Flavius Josephus had written an extensive account of that war, and the centuries preceding it, fittingly titled *The Judean War*, before publishing the *Antiquities* volume by volume, which he references at the open and close of *Antiquities* in a way that assumed his audience's familiarity with his previous work.

ation to the reception of the Torah at Sinai, covering roughly the same narrative scope of Gen 1 to Exod 24. While significantly shorter, the narrative of Jubilees still claims to cover a period of almost twenty-five hundred years. Instead of events being narrated by a historian from the perspective of the present, an optional but common—and typically expected—formal literary feature of historical narration,[30] Jubilees is written in the voice of a divine messenger, the angel of the presence, who relates the history of the world and the ancestors of the emergent Israelite nation directly to Moses, the internal audience of the work.

For this reason alone, scholars of Second Temple Judaism have typically referred to Jubilees as an apocalyptic text, fitting the now-traditional generic description as "revelatory literature with a narrative framework, in which a revelation is mediated by an otherworldly being to a human recipient."[31] Jubilees in all of its uniqueness is known for being an atypical participant in *that* genre as well.[32] Genres may have prototypical expectations, but atypical members may still participate. To draw a parallel from nature, the prototypical bird, from a North American perspective, at least, is something like a robin or sparrow.[33] While it may be the flamingo

---

30. The origins of such narration stretch back to Herodotus, Thucydides, and Sima Qian. Sima Qian (ca. 145–86 BCE) is acknowledged as the first chronicler of Chinese history. Like Herodotus, he included many aspects of human life, not just political leaders and military excursions, in his history, which spanned a period of two thousand years. Like Josephus, he peppered his narrative with explicit moral or ethical lessons to be learned from the various historical episodes included (Popkin, *From Herodotus to H-Net*, 36–37).

31. Though the designation of the generic category of apocalypse has recently been under review by scholars of ancient Judaism, the traditional definition of the genre makes reference to features both formal and content related: "a genre of revelatory literature with a narrative framework, in which a revelation is mediated by an otherworldly being to a human recipient, disclosing a transcendent reality which is both temporal, insofar as it envisages eschatological salvation, and spatial insofar as it involves another, supernatural world." See John J. Collins, "Introduction: Towards the Morphology of a Genre," *Semeia* 14 (1979): 9. On the review of the generic category of apocalypse, see Collins, "The Genre Apocalypse Reconsidered," *ZAC* 20 (2016): 21–40.

32. Collins, "Genre Apocalypse Reconsidered," 38. Collins argues with the use of genre prototype theory that Jubilees does not fit the prototypical expectations of the apocalyptic genre but resides on "the fuzzy fringes" instead, while participating in other genres such as rewritten Bible/Scripture.

33. Zahn, "Genre and Rewritten Scripture," 278.

among a host of sparrows, I posit that Jubilees still participates in the genre of national history through its form, content, and, most importantly, its function. It is a narrative that self-presents as a true account of the history of a political entity (Israel) over an extended period of time (from the prophecy of Israel's special status at creation through the ancestral origins to the birth of the nation), and moreover, it functions to temporally emplot every subsequent generation of Israel in the metaphysical reality it constructs by shaping their collective identity through its foundational story.

Although the operative category of national history is primarily an etic distinction, from a modern viewpoint, Jubilees' dramatic framing, its regular concern with angels and other heavenly beings, its meticulous attention to and instruction for the proper observance of the times and seasons and festivals, and its enfolding of legal material throughout the historical narrative may lead some to disqualify it from consideration as history all together. At some point, some may think that its uniqueness lends it to pterodactyl-like status; it may fly, but this is no bird. Yet in its second-century BCE Judean context, it was widely believed as historical fact that the writings of the Torah, with its ancestral narratives and its legal decrees, were revealed to Moses at Sinai.[34] That Jubilees re-presents the entire ancestral history as a dramatic unfolding of this revelatory moment, story and law entwined together, is reasonable when one considers that this was an event commonly accepted as historical. Thus, Jubilees' presentation is not as far-fetched as a modern may think. Second Temple period literature is rife with heavenly beings, angelic and demonic, and it is reasonable to conclude that their existence and influence in daily human life was a widely held perception of reality.[35] Though the generic category of national history at use in this book is an etic one, it stands to reason that Jubilees may also have been participating in an emic conceptualization of history writing, in addition to participating in other emic genres.[36]

---

34. Kugel, *Traditions of the Bible*, 658–62.

35. Though the belief in divine beings was prevalent, it was not necessarily ubiquitous. The author of the Acts of the Apostles distinguished between the Sadducees and Pharisees with reference to their belief in angelic and demonic beings (Acts 23:7–8).

36. In ancient Judean literature, there remains no evidence of systematic reflection on genre types like that witnessed among their Greek neighbors, such as in Aristotle's *Poetics* or Polybius's reflections on history writing in his *Histories* (Collins, "Genre Apocalypse Reconsidered," 23). Emic generic labels such as testament, *mizmor* (a certain type of song), or apocalypse, however, are evinced in the extant biblical and Second Temple period literature.

Josephus wrote the *Judean Antiquities* for a Roman aristocratic audience in accordance with the emic expectations for first-century Greek and Roman history writing. He argued for the reliability of his written sources, appealed to the works of other, more ancient historians to bolster the veracity of his account, and regularly referenced the utility of the past for the philosophical and political considerations of the present.[37] If one of the primary functions of national history is to emplot its national audience into an ongoing story, one may question whether *Antiquities* can be understood to participate in this work since it was not written for—and potentially never read by—other first-century Judeans. There is no extant evidence that points to the *Judean Antiquities* being circulated among a Judean readership, though Josephus concedes that a fellow Judean may happen to encounter his text and critique his arrangement of the laws (*A.J.* 4.197).[38] As Steve Mason notes, this one reference to a potential Judean reader is contrasted with the regular and persistent signals to a non-Judean readership that frame (*A.J.* 1.5, 9; 20.262) and pervade (e.g., *A.J.* 1.128–129; 3.317; 14.1–3, 186–187; 16.175; 17.254; *Vita* 1, 12) the narrative.[39] Being a history composed by a Judean for a non-Judean audience of primarily Roman aristocrats, however, does not disqualify *Antiquities* as a functioning participant in the operative *etic* national history genre. Although Josephus's narrative may not have been taken up by any number

---

37. Mason, "Introduction to the *Judean Antiquities*," xxiv.

38. "There is a real question as to how much impact [Philo and Josephus, the only two major surviving Jewish writers in Greek] had upon their fellow Jews." See Louis Feldman, "The Reshaping of Biblical Narrative in the Hellenistic Period: A Review Essay," *IJCT* 8 (2001): 79. This is in contrast to Josephus's account of the *War*, which he claims he wrote first in his native language (τῇ πατρίῳ) and sent to "the upper Barbarians," including Judeans living "beyond the Euphrates" (*B.J.* 1.3, 6). No copies of that account are extant, though it is reasonable to assume that it may have differed in various aspects from his extant Greek "translation" of it "for those throughout the dominion of the Romans" (*B.J.* 1.2). "The arrangement of each law in accordance to its kind has been innovated by us. For having been written by [Moses], they were left scattered and as he may have learned it from God. I considered it necessary to premise this beforehand, lest anyone among my countrymen who happen upon the document fault us as having utterly failed" (*A.J.* 4.198).

39. Mason, "Introduction to the *Judean Antiquities*," xix. In addition to the *Antiquities*' explicit claim to be written for interested non-Judeans in the prologue (*A.J.* 1.5, 9), Mason draws attention to Josephus's "frequent explanations of even the most basic items of Judean culture" and the posture he assumes throughout the work as "an insider relating his story to outsiders."

of Judeans of his time, its historical mapping and representations proved to be influential among other later communities, notably the Greek- and Latin-speaking Christian church.[40]

It is with these important considerations of the original and later audience(s) that I maintain that *Antiquities does* do the work of identity construction of Judeans and their cultural others through their representation in narrative. Though the force of that representation for other first-century Judeans is somewhat mitigated due to their likely exclusion from Josephus's readership, one can still assess what work such representations do for those who would take up this history—Roman, Judean, or otherwise.

2.3. Implications for Jubilees and *Judean Antiquities* as National Histories

The narrativizing of human history, and thus the representation of people as characters in a story, has inherently ethical implications.[41] The people about whom a national history is told are inevitably cast as the protagonists of that story. This is natural; they are the people the story is about. They are not, however, the only characters. Any history that functions to collectively identify a group will do so by drawing and negotiating boundaries with others. In national histories, this boundary negotiation is often accomplished through narrative representation of others as more or less peripheral characters in the protagonist group's story. Others may be cast into a number of roles, depending on culture and context, including supportive friend, estranged brother, or antagonist. These are simple examples of what is often a more complex phenomenon of representation, as characterization can be dynamic as well as static. Also, just as groups are composed of individuals, so too may they be represented with inherent diversity. What is essential to note about the representation of the corpo-

---

40. Josephus's own history was taken up as an authoritative source and quoted by fourth-century Christian historian Eusebius to enforce an anti-Jewish message, and Eusebius's history was widely received as an authoritative source of history for well over a hundred centuries. See Gohei Hata, "The Abuse and Misuse of Josephus in Eusebius' Ecclesiastical History, Books 2 and 3," in *Studies in Josephus and the Varieties of Ancient Judaism: Louis H. Feldman Jubilee Volume*, ed. Shaye J. D. Cohen and Joshua J. Schwartz, AJEC 67 (Leiden: Brill, 2006), 91–102.

41. See Adam Zachary Newton, *Narrative Ethics* (Cambridge: Harvard University Press, 1995), 11.

rate self (or selves) and other(s) in national history-telling is that the force of such representation is extremely potent due to the truth claims inherent to this genre. Newton, in postulating representational ethics, suggests, "Narrative ethics [including representational ethics] is often a matter of force.... Texts tax readers with ethical duties which increase in proportion to the measure with which they are taken up."[42]

While it stands to reason that any given national history need not be taken up by a population but may be resisted or retold as a new narrative (as among Native Americans in the latter half of the twentieth century, mentioned above), the self-presentation of national histories *as reliable accounts* brings an ethical weight to their representations. The potential for national histories to be taken up and thus have a shaping effect on great numbers of people adds to their ethical force. This is why critical study of representation in national histories is so important. My analysis of Jubilees and *Judean Antiquities* below centers on their representations of Israelites/Judeans in contrast to Shechemites, Canaanites, and Samaritans, the othered peoples of their histories.

2.4. Authoritative Narration

Jubilees and *Judean Antiquities* each self-present as reliable accounts of the history of Israel, as *authoritative* national histories. This is in part achieved through the characterization of their narrators. Just as the omniscient and objective narration in Gen 34 shapes the engagement of the audience and the ethical role into which they were placed, the styles of narration and the authority of the narrators uniquely act to shape the roles of the audiences of these texts. The authority claimed by both of these narrators, and their self-presentation as reliable, also adds to the force of the representations they employ.

2.4.1. Endowed with Divine Authority: The Narrator of Jubilees

Through the mediating voice of Jubilees' narrator,[43] stories of the Israelite past are relayed monologically, and the overt evaluations they contain are

---

42. Newton, *Narrative Ethics*, 290, 292.
43. Some scholars argue that there are essentially two authors of Jubilees, the "original" narrator and the "interpolator," a second author to whom some of the legal or "eschatological" material that is deemed to have their own "distinct terminology"

backed with heaven's authority. Indeed, it is the Lord God who instructs this narrator to "dictate to Moses from the beginning of the creation until the time when my temple is built among them throughout the ages of eternity" (Jub. 1.27).[44] In Jubilees, the narrator of the bulk of the book (chs. 2–50) is identified as the "angel of the presence" (Jub. 1.27).[45] This divine messenger conveys Israel's past as revelation to the internal audience, Moses, with overt evaluation and regular pronouncements of the meaning and import of narrated events for every generation of Israel "forever" (e.g., Jub. 30.10). The narrator of Jubilees is overt; the angel's first-person voice interjects at regular intervals in direct address to Moses (e.g., "Now you, Moses, write for the people so that they keep it and do not act like this," Jub. 33.18).

In this way the narrator of Jubilees differs greatly from that of Gen 34. As demonstrated in chapter 2, in Gen 34 there is subtle storytelling from multiple perspectives, the withholding of evaluation, and the relative objectivity of the covert narrator, who is never personified but is hidden behind the third-person exposition. In contrast, the angel of the presence is at times present and active *in* the narrative, relating events in the first person (e.g., Jub. 16.1, 48.13). Yet when recounting all that happened before the life of Moses,[46] even when the first person is being used, the dictation is not presented as a spontaneous report of the angel's own recollections;

---

is attributed (e.g., Kugel, "Jubilees," 278–80). Others, finding such arguments unconvincing, hold that Jubilees is an "authorial unity." See James C. VanderKam, *Jubilees: A Commentary on the Book of Jubilees* (Minneapolis: Fortress, 2018), 28. This book follows the latter view. Yet whether one supposes Jubilees to be a composite or a unified text, the final form has one narrator, who relates story and legal material in a continuous voice.

44. Unless otherwise noted, translations of Jubilees follow VanderKam, *Jubilees*.

45. This angel of the presence is identified with the angel mentioned in Exod 14, who is "going along in front of the Israelite camp" as they flee Egypt (Jub. 1.29; cf. Exod 14:19).

46. Beginning in chapter 47, as the angel dictates to Moses concerning the events that happened in his own lifetime, the second-person address naturally becomes more frequent (if, however, awkward). Just in case Moses did not know, or perhaps may have thought to write his own witness of his life and the exodus events from his own perspective, the angel tells him the account from heaven's perspective: "You remained in the [Egyptian] court for three weeks of years until the time when you went from the royal court and saw the Egyptian beating your kinsman who was one of the Israelites. You killed him and hid him in the sand" (Jub. 47.10). While I cannot help but wonder about the Jubilean Moses's emotional reaction at having his life thus dictated to him,

rather, the angel "took the tablets of the divisions of the years from the time the law and the testimony were created" (Jub. 1.29) and read them to Moses. Thus, Moses receives the *heavenly* record of creation, of the deluge, of the ordering of the times and seasons and festivals, and of the lives of the ancestors who came before him, and the laws and ordinances that are related to their lives. Backed by the authority of his identity, his God-given commission, and the validity of the heavenly tablets from which he reads,[47] the narrator of Jubilees freely identifies with unquestionable authority who is righteous and who is not, who is holy and who is profane. All judgments, declarations, prophecies, and evaluations of the narrator are thus backed with divine authority. This is a monological account, and all other perspectives are structured far below that of the voice that speaks from heaven.

2.4.2. An Exceptionally Reliable Tradent: The Narrator of *Judean Antiquities*

The narrator of *Judean Antiquities*[48] uses at least four authorizing strategies that the following paragraphs will demonstrate: (1) the claim that the sources used are God-given revelations, (2) regular references to the works of other historians to verify the account, (3) repeated claims to the truth and accuracy of the account, and (4) the author's identity as a learned and politically honored Judean of a prominent priestly lineage. Then, in

---

Jubilees does not disclose this information. What is essential is that heaven's record is revealed to Moses, so that he may write it down for the Israelite people.

47. For argumentation about the role of the heavenly tablets in Jubilees, see Hindy Najman, "Interpretation as Primordial Writing: Jubilees and Its Authority Conferring Strategies," in *Past Renewals: Interpretive Authority, Renewed Revelation, and the Quest for Perfection in Jewish Antiquity* (Leiden: Brill, 2010), 39–72.

48. Josephus's narrator speaks in his own voice, albeit a constructed literary voice for the purposes of his history. It is easy to conflate the two figures, the man Josephus and the narrator of his history, for he regularly uses the first person in direct address to his audience and self-references (e.g., *A.J.* 1.15–29, 10.281, 20.259–268). Surely there is a degree of overlap between author and narrator, yet all that we know of the first-century Judean Flavius Josephus is through his published works, which are rhetorically constructed. That being said, it is common in scholarship to refer to the narrator of *Antiquities* as Josephus, for that is precisely who the narrator of the history purports to be. In this book, I likewise alternate between referring to the narrator as "the narrator" and as "Josephus." When a distinction between Josephus the narrator and Josephus the author needs to be made, it is made explicit.

a paragraph that follows, I will turn to the type of narration that Josephus employs, which is overt and heavily evaluative. The narrator's authorization strategies serve to add weight to his representations of character and his evaluative claims, although his tendency to "moralize the story" makes it all the more curious when he refrains from offering his explicit judgment of people and events, as in *A.J.* 1.337–341, which re-presents the events and characters of Gen 34.

By indicating the source of the Hebrew writings as divine revelation, and the tradents of those writings as reliable, the narrator substantiates the authority of his account, which he claims to be set forth from "the precise matters from what is in the records" (τὰ ... ἀκριβῆ τῶν ἐν ταῖς ἀναγραφαῖς, *A.J.* 1.17).[49] Furthermore, he promises "neither to have added nor, moreover, to have omitted anything" (*A.J.* 1.17, 10.218; cf. Deut 4:2, 12:32).[50] While the claims of divine revelation are especially applicable for the Judean laws or the political constitution (διάταξις τοῦ πολιτεύματος, *A.J.* 1.5), they also bolster the validity of the ancestral accounts traditionally attributed to Moses. The early narratives and laws, the narrator claims—and the historical Josephus likely believed—came from heavenly revelation to Moses, the ancient and divinely appointed leader of the people. Moses the lawgiver received them at Sinai and arranged or composed the constitution and the laws (ἡ πολιτεία καὶ νόμοι) "in accordance with the counsel of God" (3.213). Not only is the source of the Judean

---

49. Unless otherwise noted, all translations from Josephus's *Judean Antiquities* are my own.

50. Many scholars have honed in on this phrase, which was a common claim of accuracy, also used by Dionysius of Halicarnassus (*Thuc.* 5, 8), Lucian (*Hist.* 47), Berossus, Manetho, Philo of Byblos, Ctesias, and Hecataeus of Abdera (Feldman, *Judean Antiquities 1–4*, 8 n. 22). In comparison with both the MT and LXX, Josephus has both added and omitted much, freely altering episodes and adding his own narratorial framing and contents. Josephus even admits to such changes in his later books, when he fears that certain contents may seem disorganized or "tiresome" to his readers (*A.J.* 4.197, 9.242). Feldman draws attention to the fact that the words Josephus uses for "translate" "are all ambiguous and seem to include paraphrasing and amplifying" (*Judean Antiquities 1–4*, 8 n. 22). These words, μεθερμηνεύω (*A.J.* 1.5), μεταφράζω (10.218), and ἑρμηνεύω (6.230), all carry with them connotations of interpretation, signifying, describing, or explaining, rather than the more static μεταγράφω, which means "to transcribe" or "to translate" (see Feldman, *Judean Antiquities 1–4*, 3 n. 4). Thus, Josephus promises his readers much more than a literal rendering of the Hebrew sources into Greek, and much more is precisely what he delivers.

constitution and laws heavenly, but the conduit through which those laws came was exemplary in virtue, wisdom, courage, temperance, and piety.[51] Moses is presented as a wholly righteous and virtuous figure in *Antiquities*; the dubious account of his murder of an Egyptian foreman from Exod 2:11–15 is omitted, as well as the striking of the rock against God's instructions to speak to it (Num 20:8–11).[52] He is lauded as being a master of his passions, a prophet without peer, and his words were like the very words of God (*A.J.* 3.328–329).[53] Furthermore, the data Josephus gleans from the Hebrew writings is presented as passed down with meticulous accuracy: "The time has been recorded in the holy books, the births and deaths of the notable men having been signified with great accuracy by those of that time" (1.83).[54] The narrator of *Judean Antiquities* thus self-presents as reliable by asserting the reliability and superiority of his primary sources.

Although Josephus presents the most ancient history (books 1–4, corresponding to Genesis–Deuteronomy) as a recounting of Moses's writings, he also regularly appeals to works of other historians to validate the events and figures mentioned in his own. For example, after relating the biblical account of Noah[55] and the flood, he states, "All those who have recorded the barbarian histories have remembered this deluge and the ark, among whom is Berosus the Chaldean" (*A.J.* 1.93). According to Tatian's *Oratio ad*

---

51. Louis Feldman, "Josephus' Portrait of Moses," *JQR* 82 (1992): 285–328.

52. Furthermore, while in Deut 32:51–52 the reason given to Moses for being barred from entering the promised land is the striking of the rock, no mention of this is made in *Antiquities*.

53. Thus the narrator exalts the laws as being aligned with the will of God, not only for the Judeans but for all of humanity (*A.J.* 1.14).

54. While more explicit claims to the divine nature of all "twenty-two books" of the Hebrew Scriptures are found in Josephus's openly apologetic work *Against Apion* (1.38–40), the argument of this section is concerned with the construction of narratorial authority in *Judean Antiquities*, which predated *Apion*. For the purposes of *Antiquities*, which included the presentation of the Judean constitution and laws to an interested non-Judean audience for consideration, the nature of the *politeia* in question is highlighted as divine. In *Antiquities*, Josephus also presents the Hebrew prophets as accurate foretellers of historical realities. For example, Jeremiah's prophecy about the date of return from Babylonian exile is relayed as accurate (11.1); the prophecy about the Persian conquering king Cyrus in Isa 45:1 is relayed as God's discourse to the eighth-century Isaiah of Jerusalem "in secret," fulfilled and read to Cyrus himself (*A.J.* 11.5); and Josephus includes a long excursus on the prophecies of Daniel and their fulfillment in the times of Antiochus IV (10.269–281).

55. Greek Νῶχος.

Graecos, Berosus was a third-century BCE Babylonian priest who translated the traditions of Babylonian astronomy and astrology into Greek, and who wrote a history of Chaldea/Babylonia around 281 BCE.[56] Josephus quotes a detail from this history—that the boat surviving the flood still rests on a mountain in Armenia—as verifying the Hebrew story, failing to make mention of the many other discrepancies between the accounts.[57] To demonstrate the veracity of *Antiquities*' account, the corroborating details of Berosus's history are cited as an ancient history of still more ancient things.[58] Berosus is also cited to validate the ages of the ancestors (1.107), the existence and expertise of Abraham (1.158), the campaigns of King Sennacherib (10.20), and the sack of Jerusalem and exile of the prisoners of war by Nebuchadnezzar (10.219–226). Excerpts from the universal history by Nicolaus of Damascus, a philosopher and rhetorician who lived from about 64 BCE to the beginning of the first century CE,[59] are also regularly cited by Josephus to validate the flood account (1.94–95), the ages of the ancients (1.108), the venerated status of Abraham (1.159–160), and King David's military expeditions (7.101–103). The ancient history of Hieronymus the Egyptian is likewise referred to as evidence to support the reliability of Josephus's *Judean Antiquities*, though the need to introduce him (1.94) may reflect his audience's unfamiliarity with the source.[60] The Sibylline Oracles and the otherwise unknown Phoenician historian Hestaios are cited as supporting evidence to the story of the tower of Babel (1.118–119), and Hecataeus of Abdera (ca. 300 BCE) is reported to have composed a work about the great ancestor Abraham (1.159).[61] By making

---

56. Feldman, *Judean Antiquities 1–4*, 34 n. 235.

57. The works of Berosus only survive in fragments and through the citations or abridgement of other ancient writers, such as Alexander Polyhistor, whom Eusebius used in his *Chronica*. These discrepancies, that the hero's name was Xisuthros, or that Xisuthros and his wife and daughter were granted life with the gods after their survival (Syncellus, *Chron.* 55), may not have been common knowledge to Josephus's audience, as the popularity of Berosus during Roman times may have been slight (Feldman, *Judean Antiquities 1–4*, 34 n. 235).

58. Thus Josephus harmonizes what is in Berosus and what Moses wrote (*A.J.* 1.158). For Josephus, the author/compiler of the narratives and laws of the Pentateuch was Moses (*A.J.* 1.16–23).

59. Feldman, *Judean Antiquities 1–4*, 34 n. 240.

60. Unfamiliarity with Hieronymus continues, for to date this particular author remains unknown (Feldman, *Judean Antiquities 1–4*, 34 n. 238).

61. On Hestaios, see Feldman, *Judean Antiquities 1–4*, 34 n. 264, 42 n. 304. There

regular mention of the corroboration of the *Judean Antiquities* with works of other authors concerned with "barbarian histories" (1.93), the narrator seeks to firmly ground his own account in a bedrock of accuracy.

The narrator of *Antiquities* further authorizes his account by explicitly claiming that what is being presented is true and accurate. This begins from the prologue and is repeatedly stated through the work. Josephus references his previous history on the war between the Judeans and the Romans and states that he was "forced to tell it in detail, because of those who ruin the truth in their writing" (*A.J.* 1.4). Thus, making mention of the value this historian places on truth in past works and that he is so compelled by it, the narrator bolsters his authority as a writer of truth. At the start of book 14, the narrator pauses to expound on his aims of presenting an eloquent and accurate account of history:

> Having made clear the things concerning Queen Alexandria and her death in the previous book, I will now speak of what followed and was connected, not taking care for anything else, nor omitting anything of the events, either through ignorance or trouble of memory. For concerning the history and the explication of events that many are ignorant of because of their ancientness, it is necessary that also the beauty of the account is considered, indeed, as much as this is from proper words[62] and the harmony of these, and as much as toward these things the adornment of the message is considered to have for the readers, so they may take the experience with some favor and delight. But above all it is necessary that the historians endeavor after accuracy [τῆς ἀκριβείας ... στοχάζεσθαι] and to speak nothing untruthfully, showing honorable preference to those about to trust them concerning things they have not known. (*A.J.* 14.1–3)

Josephus bolsters the presentation of his own account as accurate and true with such rhetoric. With his explicit value of "accuracy above all" and promise to "omit nothing," he presents himself as a conscientious historian,

---

has been much debate about Hecataeus of Abdera and this source's authenticity (59 n. 510). What matters for the purposes of this argument is that the narrator of the *Judean Antiquities* presents this source as authentic and not a pseudepigraphical Jewish apologetic work, as Hans Lewy argues it to be and John Gager maintains. See Lewy, "Hekataios von Abdera περὶ Ἰουδαίων," *ZNW* 31 (1932): 117–32; Gager, "Pseudo-Hecataeus Again," *ZNW* 60 (1969): 130–39. How Josephus the author understood its provenance is unknowable.

62. Or "names."

honoring his audience with accuracy and truthfulness. Should any doubt the accuracy of Josephus's history, after enduring the sixty thousand lines of *Antiquities*' twenty books (*A.J.* 20.267), he completes the account with a final declaration of their reliability: "From the first creation of man" to the harsh treatment the Judeans faced under the Romans, Josephus professes in the present tense that "I intend to organize everything with accuracy [μετ' ἀκριβείας]" (*A.J.* 20.260); in essence this is a statement of his continual concern throughout the history. In the lines that follow (*A.J.* 20.261), the narrator affirms that he attempted to preserve and report the lineage and deeds of priests and kings "without error" (ἀπλανῆ). These explicit claims are only reliable, however, if they come from a reliable speaker. Which is why, at the end of the twenty books detailing the thousands of years of the history and political constitution of the Judean people, Josephus offers his own biography as an affirmation of his character.

The twenty books of the *Judean Antiquities* are backed with the validating evidence of the author's expertise and character. Though often read as a separate work from the *Antiquities*, Josephus's *Life* originated as an appendix to his magnum opus. Josephus's appedicized autobiography is a demonstration of his worthiness to write *Antiquities* and be considered an authority,[63] and he says as much in the conclusion to book 20:

> Indeed, I say now, emboldened because of the completion of what was proposed, that no one else who desired, either Judean or foreigner, would have been able to carry out this treatise in this way—accurately— to the Greeks. For in this I have agreement from my fellow nationals to far exceed them according to our native instruction, and also I have labored to partake of the Greek letters by taking up the scholarly craft. (*A.J.* 20.263)

Further noting that the acquisition of Greek learning is not encouraged by his fellow Judeans, he insists that only "two or three" wise men through strenuous training come to know the Judean laws clearly and are able to interpret the sacred things (20.264). No outsider knows the full trove of the Judean treasures, and only a handful of men from his own nation have such expertise that is necessary for the accurate presentation of the Judean

---

63. Steve Mason, "'Should Any Wish to Enquire Further' (*A.J.* 1.25): The Aim and Audience of Josephus' *Judean Antiquities/Life*," in *Understanding Josephus: Seven Perspectives*, ed. Steve Mason (Sheffield: Sheffield Academic, 1998), 102–3.

laws and sacred things. Furthermore, since the others, according to Josephus, devalue Greek learning, they are ill-equipped to communicate these things to Greek-speaking populations. Josephus, then, self-presents as a rare gem. He also proposes to briefly relate his own lineage and the deeds of his life (περὶ γένους τοῦ μοῦ καὶ περὶ τῶν κατὰ τὸν βίον πράξεων βραχέα διεξελθεῖν, A.J. 20.266), which serve to demonstrate the preeminence of his family line (*Vita* 3–7), his exemplary education and intellect (8–12), his political and military prowess among his people (throughout), the proof of his trustworthiness and character (80, 430), and his favor with God through revelation and protection (208–211, 425). Not only is he a trustworthy narrator and purveyor of history, but the *Vita* conveys that "he is a living, breathing representative of the πολιτεία and φιλοσοφία that he has offered to his readers [through the *Antiquities*]."[64]

In support of his initial claim that what is being offered in this work is something "useful" (A.J. 1.9) and "for the common advantage" (1.3), Josephus regularly expounds on the virtues and vices of the forebears of the nations and Israel.[65] The narrator has a heavy evaluative hand on the re-presentation of most figures and events. Moral reflections often take the form of character evaluation, explicit commentary on the deeds of historical figures, and one positively appraised character speaking ethical exhortations to the other.[66] For example, Josephus heavily moralizes the story of Cain and Abel. Though such assessments are absent in Gen 4, and it is never clearly stated *why* Abel's sacrifice was pleasing to God,[67] Abel is introduced in *Antiquities* as being concerned with righteousness, and "in all the things that were done by him, considering God to be pres-

---

64. Mason, "'Should Any Wish,'" 103.
65. For a detailed study on virtues and vices according to *Antiquities*, see Harold Attridge, *The Interpretation of Biblical History in the "Antiquitates Judaicae" of Flavius Josephus* (Missoula, MT: Scholars Press, 1990), 109–44.
66. Attridge, *Interpretation of Biblical History*, 110, 119–20.
67. The nature of the sacrifices that Cain and Abel offer raised a rich debate in rabbinic tradition (see Gen. Rab. 22:5). Philo presents Abel as virtuous (*Sacr.* 4.14) and holy (3.10; see Feldman, *Judean Antiquities 1–4*, 19 n. 112). The righteousness of Abel is also an assessment present in the New Testament (Matt 23:35, Heb 11:4, 1 John 3:12), but in each of these occasions it is mentioned as a result of or displayed through his acceptable sacrifice, not as an assessment of his character before his actions. Rabbinic traditions preserved in Targum Pseudo-Jonathan and Fragmentary Targum on Gen 4:8 and Tanhuma Balak also celebrate Abel's virtue or righteousness (Feldman, *Judean Antiquities 1–4*, 19 n. 112).

ent, he took thought for virtue [ἀρετή]" (*A.J.* 1.53). Cain, his elder brother and character foil, was "most wicked [πονηρότατος] and only looked to make a profit" (1.53), something not indicated in Genesis.⁶⁸ Josephus thus provides his reader with a reflection on destructive desires and behavior as well as the good.⁶⁹ The speech of the righteous characters of *Antiquities* also serves to edify the audience. Characterized openly and unswervingly⁷⁰ as a man of wisdom, virtue, and piety, Abraham, for example, instructs his contemporaries in the orderliness of creation and honor due to creation's divine commander (1.156–157). Though the Chaldeans and Mesopotamians reject Abraham's teachings, they are meant to be accepted by the audience of *Antiquities*. This narrative technique continues throughout the *Judean Antiquities* as the narrator provides moralizing evaluations through the descriptions of character and action and through the speech of figures who are openly labeled as virtuous.⁷¹ It is a regular and well-acknowledged feature of Josephus's historiography, and one also employed by other historians of the time.⁷²

2.5. A Proposition of Genre: Conclusions

In conclusion, although the ancient Judean narratives of Jubilees and *Judean Antiquities* differ in style, scope, content, original audience, and aim(s), they may both be considered authoritative national histories. As

---

68. Though perhaps a characterization fittingly derived from the meaning of his Hebrew name, related to the verb קנה, "to acquire."

69. The wickedness of Cain is revisited and intensified after his exile: "He did not take the punishment as an occasion for chastisement, but for the increase of wickedness, providing every pleasure for his body, even if it was necessary to obtain this with the violence [μεθ' ὕβρεως] of his companions" (*A.J.* 1.60). Continuing to gain property through "robbery and force" (ἐξ ἁρπαγῆς καὶ βίας), Cain becomes a "teacher of wicked pursuits" to other men (*A.J.* 1.61). This obvious villainous behavior is contrasted with the aforementioned glimpse into Abel's mind. Cain thought only of gain, which led to violence and wicked deeds, while Abel considered God present at all times and was compelled to act virtuously (1.53). Feldman notes that here Josephus's "language is highly reminiscent of Greek and Roman descriptions of the decline of man from the age of primitive simplicity. The ancients generally, starting with Hesiod, agreed that the chief cause of human decline was greed and selfishness" (*Judean Antiquities 1–4*, 19–20 n. 131).

70. See Feldman, *Josephus's Interpretation of the Bible*, 223–89.

71. See Attridge, *Interpretation of Biblical History*, 110–44.

72. Attridge, *Interpretation of Biblical History*, 110–44.

national histories, they each re-presented the Judean past to their contemporary audiences, shaping their historical content to address contemporary concerns.[73] Through the authorizing strategies of their narrators, they self-present as reliable and authoritative accounts of the events and figures they describe. In Jubilees, the angel of the presence speaks with all the majestic clout of God himself, allowing no room for human challenges to the ultimately omniscient and righteous perspective regarding characters and events offered in his account. In *Antiquities*, Josephus constructs the authority of his history by asserting the reliability of his sources and the accuracy of his account, while supporting those claims with a lengthy autobiography intended to display his trustworthiness. Both histories thus self-present as reliable accounts of events, with narrators who are trustworthy evaluators of character. It is their claims—either implicit or explicit—of veracity that heighten the ethical force of their moral perspectives and their representations of Judeans and cultural others.

3. The Texts

3.1. Jubilees 30

In Jub. 30, the angel of the presence narrates the events of Gen 34 to Moses, but for a reader familiar with Genesis's version, the story is much abridged. All human dialogue is absent from the story; it is a monovocal account told from heaven's perspective. The narration is brief, yet much space is given to the multiple exhortations and admonitions to the people of Israel that this tale occasions. Below is a translation of the narration (vv. 1–4, 23–26), followed by a structural outline demonstrating the series of heavenly pronouncements that the narrative frames.

> ¹During the first year of the sixth week [2143] he went up safely to Salem, which is on the east side of Shechem, in the fourth month. ²There, they snatched [Eth. *mašaṭawa*, Lat. *rapuerunt*] Dinah, daughter of Jacob, away to the house of Shechem,[74] the son of Hamor the Hivite, the ruler of the

---

73. See below.

74. VanderKam has the passive construction, "There Jacob's daughter Dinah was taken by force to the house of Shechem," though he notes in his translation that in both Ethiopic and Latin, the texts themselves say otherwise. See VanderKam, *The Book of Jubilees*, 2 vols., CSCO 510–511 (Leuven: Peeters, 1989), 190. Indeed, the Ethi-

land. He lay with her and defiled her.[75] Now she was a small girl, twelve years of age.[76]

³He begged her father and her brothers that she become his wife. Jacob and his sons were angry with the Shechemites because they had defiled their sister Dinah. They spoke deceptively with them, acted in a crafty way toward them, and deceived them. ⁴Simeon and Levi entered Shechem unexpectedly and effected a punishment on all the Shechemites. They killed every man whom they found in it. They left absolutely no one in it. They killed everyone in a painful way[77] because they had defiled[78] their sister Dinah....

²³On the day that Jacob's sons killed Shechem, a written notice was entered in heaven for them [to the effect] that they had carried out what

---

opic verb *mašaṭawa* is a perfect form of the verb *mašaṭa*, "to carry off, carry away, grab, seize and carry off by force, snatch away, kidnap," with a third masculine plural marker for subject. See Wolf Leslau, *Comparative Dictionary of Geʿez* (Wiesbaden: Harrassowitz, 2006), 369. Dinah, and her accompanying qualifier "daughter of Jacob," is marked by the paraphasic accusative marker *la*. Similarly, Dinah (*dinam*) is the accusative subject of *rapuerunt* in the Latin. This is an important element of this story. In Jubilees, not only Shechem but a grouped "they" of Shechemites are to blame for the taking of Dinah, which is described with verbs of force. I have indicated this with the translation above.

75. Eth. *wasakaba məṣəleha waʾarəskʷasa*. Lat. *et polluit eam quia dormiuit*, "he defiled her because he slept with her." The two versions have the same verbs but in reverse order, and where Latin joins them with *quia* ("because"), Ethiopic has a simple conjunction. Notably, in all the extant manuscripts of this chapter (in Latin and Ethiopic), the narrator uses "defile" to describe what Shechem did to Dinah. The Ethiopic syntax is closer to Gen 34:2. See R. H. Charles, *The Ethiopic Version of the Hebrew Book of Jubilees* (Oxford: Clarendon, 1895), 109 n. 12 to Lat. In both languages, the words "with her" agree with the reading of the LXX tradition, where MT has the unusual אֹתָהּ. Even so, context indicates that the encounter in Jubilees was forced.

76. Dinah was born to Leah on the seventh day of the seventh month of the sixth year of the fourth week (Jub. 28.24). So, by the seventh day of the seventh month of the seventh year of that week, she would be one year old. Jubilees 30:1 notes Jacob's arrival in the fourth month of the first year of the sixth week of this Jubilee. By the last year of the fifth week, Dinah would be eight and about to turn nine when they arrived in Shechem. So, Jubilees has them (implicitly) living near Shechem for about three years before Dinah is taken.

77. Lat. *in iudicio*, "in judgment."

78. VanderKam's translation reads, "because they had violated their sister Dinah." Latin maintains the plural verb *polluerant* from 30:2. The verb used here in Ethiopic is the third masculine plural perfect form of *gammana*, which is rightly translated "violated"; however, it carries connotations of pollution and profanation. I have tried to indicate these connotations with my translation.

was right—justice and revenge against the sinners. It was recorded as a blessing.

²⁴They led their sister Dinah from Shechem's house and captured[79] everything that was in Shechem—their sheep, cattle, and donkeys; all their property and all their flocks—and brought everything to their father Jacob. ²⁵He spoke with them about the fact that they had killed a city because he was afraid of the people who were living in the land—of the Canaanites and Perizzites. ²⁶A fear of the Lord was in all the cities which were around Shechem. They did not set out to pursue Jacob's sons[80] because terror had fallen on them.

3.1.1. Structure of Jubilees 30

A. Narration of Events at Shechem (30.1–4)
   30.1: Exposition: Jacob moves to Salem, near Shechem, date
   30.2: Kernel event: "They" snatch away Dinah to Shechem's house. He lays with her and defiles her
   Aside: She was a small girl, twelve years old
   30.3: Dialogue-less discussions and deceit: Shechem begs her father and brothers to have Dinah as a wife. Jacob and sons are angry with all the Shechemites because they had defiled Dinah. "They" (Jacob and his sons) speak deceptively and deceive them

---

79. Lat. *captiuauerunt*. Eth. *waḍewawu*, a third masculine plural form of *ḍewawa*, "to take prisoner, capture," or "seize (goods)" (Leslau, *Comparative Dictionary*, 153). As VanderKam indicates with his word choice, though indicative of similar actions, the verb is a different one from the one used in 30:2 to describe what the Shechemites did to Dinah (Lat. *rapuerunt*, Eth. *mašaṭawa*, "they snatched away" or "they carried off"; see note above). Where Gen 34 poignantly repeats the same verb לקח at these narrative moments and in the dialogues, it is interesting that Jubilees chooses to distinguish between the types of action that the groups take.

80. Lat. *Iacob*. "The Eth. reading [translated above] agrees with MT SP LXX OL [i.e., Vulg.] Gen 35:5; Syr. Gen 35:5, like Lat., lacks 'sons' here but adds 'and his sons' after Jacob's name. Using the name 'Jacob' aligns Jubilees with MT SP Syr.; the LXX tradition reads '[the sons of] Israel'" (VanderKam, *Book of Jubilees*, 817). Though there is slight variation in the manuscripts regarding this phrase, I find that little changes in the meaning. The unmitigated praise for Jacob's sons is still present, as well as the alignment of Jacob with his sons (argued below). They are so unified in their characterization that it matters little whether the surrounding cities did not pursue the man "Jacob" or "Israel," the group "Israel" or "Jacob and his sons," or the smaller group "Jacob's sons." In a way, the multiple extant renderings support chapter 30's overall depiction of the men as a single entity.

30.4: Destruction: Simeon and Levi enter the city and kill everyone
B. Legal pronouncements, exhortations, and warnings (30.5–22)
   30.5–10: Laws against intermarriage with any foreigner, or any sexual impurity. These laws have "no temporal end" (v. 10)
   30.11–22: Series of instructions to Moses, "Tell the Israelites …." It is a disgraceful thing to marry a foreigner
   30.17–20: Simeon and Levi performed a just act. Levi is praised.
   30.21–22: Do not sin, or else you will be enemies and uprooted
C. Narration Resumes (30.23–26)
   30.23: Heavenly notice records the vengeance as a blessing
   30.24: Leading Dinah from Shechem's house, plunder of the city
   30.25: Narrated report of Jacob speaking about his fear of retaliation
   30.26: Fear of God is on all the land, and the Canaanites do not retaliate

3.2. *Judean Antiquities* 1.337–341

Josephus's account is also much abbreviated when compared to Gen 34.[81] Although, like many Greek and Roman historians of his day, he often inserted dialogue and speeches into his narration of the past (e.g., *A.J.* 1.223–236, 2.21–31),[82] here there is no dialogue; rather, everything is indirectly mediated through the narrator. Contextual details are added, such as the mention of a festival setting for both Shechem's attack and the brothers' retaliation. The plot in *Antiquities* also features unique elements; Shechem never speaks to the Israelites, only Hamor, who leaves Jacob and sons to discuss a course of action together, though no consen-

---

81. In my translations of Josephus's *Judean Antiquities* I use Benedict Niese's critical edition as the source text, with consultation of Étienne Nodet's critical edition. Though a critical text, by nature, cannot faultlessly produce the illustrious and elusive original, it gives witness to the dominant strains of the Josephan narrative as transmitted through the past two millennia. Nodet provides a new critical edition of the first eleven books of the *Antiquities*, and work continues on the latter nine, making use of more manuscripts that Niese did not work with. The differences between Niese's and Nodet's editions are primarily found in the apparatus, where Nodet makes extensive notations of spelling variations of place names and persons to serve his primary goal of determining "l'identification de la Bible utilisée par Josèphe." See Flavius Josephus et al., *Les Antiquités Juives: Introduction et text, Livres I à III* (Paris: Cerf, 1990), xiii.

82. In Josephus's account of the Aqedah (Gen 22), Abraham and Isaac dialogue with one another extensively. In *A.J.* 2.21–31 is a lengthy speech by Reuben to his brothers against fratricide, something not found in the parallel narrative of Gen 37.

sus is reached. There are no negotiations, deceptions, or agreements, only Simeon and Levi's violent attack on the city, clearly done in secret.

> [337]Jacob reached what is still now called "Tents," from which he came to Shechem [Σίκιμον]—the city is of the Canaanites. While the Shechemites were celebrating a festival [ἑορτή],[83] Dinah [Δεῖνα], who was Jacob's only daughter, passed by toward the city to see[84] the adornment [τὸν κόσμον] of the local women. But Shechem son of Hamor the king, having seen her, ruined [her] by force [φθείρει δι' ἁρπαγῆς], and being amorously disposed, he begged his father to take the girl for him to marry [πρὸς γάμον].
>
> [338]And he, being persuaded, came to Jacob asking to join Dinah to his son Shechem according to law.[85] But Jacob, neither having a response because of the rank of the one entreating him, nor considering it lawful

---

83. According to Eusebius's *Praeparatio Evangelica*, Theodotus's poetic rendering of the events at Shechem also featured a festival setting (*Praep. ev.* 9.22.4), though the word used by Theodotus is πανήγυρις. Theodotus's identity and precise dating is elusive, but the fact that Eusebius accesses his poem through the writings of Alexander Polyhistor of the first century BCE leads some to conclude that Theodotus's poem may date to the second century BCE. See James Charlesworth, *The Pseudepigrapha and Modern Research*, SCS 7 (Atlanta: Scholars Press, 1981), 210. Whether a first- or second-century composition, the tradition of a festival setting predates *Antiquities*. It is also found in late rabbinic sources Sefer Hayashar and Sekel Tov (Feldman, *Judean Antiquities 1–4*, 123 n. 954). These sources indicate that a festival setting was a common tradition associated with the story in Jewish antiquity. Even so, I argue below that Josephus employs it to make a unique connection between Judean/Samaritan clashes in his own day.

84. The verb ὁράω is found here in the future participle, conveying Dinah's intention or purpose.

85. The laws of Exod 22:16–17 and Deut 22:28–29 that demand for a rapist to wed his victim and pay for her bride price are presented as one ruling by Josephus in *A.J.* 4.252: "For the one who ruins [ὁ φθείρας] a virgin not yet betrothed—he must marry her. But if it does appeal to the father of the girl for her to dwell with him, he must pay fifty shekels, the price of the offense." Unlike both Exod 22:16–17 and Deut 22:28–29, in Josephus's related law, a price is seemingly paid only when the victim is not wed by the rapist (though payment of a bride price on marriage may be implied). In this ruling, the rapist is dubbed ὁ φθείρας, "the ruiner," further connecting Shechem to this law. Whether to wed "according to law" here indicates *this* law, however, is uncertain, since Josephus does not expect his non-Judean readers unfamiliar with the traditions and laws of the Judeans to have knowledge of it at this point in the narrative. Instead, Hamor's request for the young people to be wed "according to law" may simply indicate a proposition of a legally binding marriage.

to give his daughter in marriage to a foreigner [ἀλλοφύλῳ συνοικίζειν], requested him to allow the gathering of a council concerning what he was entreating.

³³⁹While the king therefore departed hoping for Jacob to grant the marriage, Jacob, after revealing to his children both the ruin of their sister [τὴν φθορὰν τῆς ἀδελφῆς] and the request of Hamor, asked to deliberate what it was necessary to do. While most were silent, being in want of a resolution, Simeon and Levi, brothers of the girl by the same mother, agreed between themselves on this kind of action:

³⁴⁰The festival was going on, and the Shechemites were turning to relaxation and feasting. At night, falling first on the guards, they killed them as they slept, and passing into the city, they did away with every male, also the king with them and his son, but they spared the women. And having done these things without the knowledge of their father [δίχα τῆς τοῦ πατρὸς γνώμης], they brought back their sister.

³⁴¹Now, while Jacob was astonished at the magnitude of what happened and was angry at his sons, God stood by and commanded him to have courage, and after purifying his tents, to offer the sacrifices he had vowed upon seeing the dream when he first went away to Mesopotamia.

4. Reshaping the Past

The re-presentations of Gen 34's characters and events in Jubilees and *Judean Antiquities* shape traditions about the collective Judean past to speak to contemporary concerns.[86] Both of these histories frame the clash at Shechem as a historical event in which the Judean ancestors, the Israelites, were involved.[87] Although these texts offer to their audiences an account of their national past, backed with claims to authority,[88] the way they are written belies their chief concern: addressing issues of their respective presents. Jubilees 30 shapes its account of ancient history to

---

86. This is fitting, as history telling and history writing are always shaped by the perspectives, the concerns, and the questions of the present generation for which they are being written. As historian Jeremy Popkin writes, "Although history is concerned with the past, it is conducted in the present" (*From Herodotus to H-Net*, 12).

87. At this point in their narratives, both histories emplot the events at Shechem after Jacob's return to the land of Canaan and encounter with his brother, Esau, events also found in Gen 33. Each history contains a very unique telling of those events; however, an analysis of Jubilees' and *Antiquities*' re-presentations of Gen 33 is beyond the scope of this study.

88. See above.

address a second-century BCE audience in the land of Judea facing the pervasive influence of Hellenism. Through the crafting of plot elements and providing Jacob with an internal dialogue, *A.J.* 1.337–341 parallels the plight of the ancient Israelite patriarch with that of first-century Judean leadership under Roman rule.

4.1. Reshaping the Past: A Key Difference and Some Similarities

Both Jubilees and the *Judean Antiquities* present a unique kernel event in their accounts. In Jub. 30.2, it is not Shechem who takes Dinah but a collective of Shechemites, "they." "They" snatch Dinah away, then Shechem alone lies with her and defiles her. As explored below, this accords with Jubilees' affirmation that the Shechemites are collectively guilty of defiling Dinah. In *Antiquities*, the kernel event is similarly unambiguous, but Shechem alone is the guilty agent; Dinah is not defiled but ruined, a verb likely used to indicate the spoiling of her virginal status but decidedly not indicating ritual, moral, or biological purity as operable concepts in this event.[89]

Although written for audiences nearly three centuries apart, it is worth noting at this point that both Jub. 30 and *A.J.* 1.337–341 re-present the characters and events of Gen 34 in some similar ways. In both of these histories, verb choices clearly indicate that Shechem raped Dinah. In chapter 2, I argued that in Gen 34:2, the narrator's verb choice shrouds Dinah's encounter with Shechem in ambiguity. In Jub. 30.2, there is no ambiguity. Rather, a collective of Shechemites "snatch her away" to Shechem's house, described with a verb that clearly indicates force (Eth. *maśata*, Lat. *rapio*). Details from the Genesis account that may have led readers to consider Dinah and Shechem's relationship a mutual affair, such as Dinah's

---

89. Josephus uses φθείρω in a range of contexts, many of which involve destruction/death of people, lands, or property, often in connection with war, plague, or famine (*A.J.* 1.70; 2.34, 208, 307; 3.17; 4.56, 155; 5.12, 157; 7.294, 326; 9.70, 289; 13.5, 391; 15.122, 310; 17.276, 20.29, 51). It is also used to indicate a corruption of character in connection to bribery or deceit (18.100, 20.127) and the decay of fruit (5.296, 15.302) or governments (19.249). It is also the verb that Josephus uses to describe sexual violation, including Abimelech's intention toward Sarah (1.207), Shechem's actions toward Dinah (1.337), a promiscuous woman's actions toward herself for "not preserving her virginity" (4.248), and what a man does to a consenting woman who is betrothed to another man or to a not-consenting woman who is not betrothed (4.251–252), and what the rapist Amnon does to his victim Tamar (7.172).

"going out" of her father's house to see the women of the land (Gen 34:1) or Shechem's love for Dinah and speaking to her heart (34:3),[90] are not found in Jubilees' terse account. Her innocence and the tragedy of the deed are emphasized by the addition of her stature and age following the abduction;[91] she is "a small girl, 12 years old" (Jub. 30.2). In *Antiquities*, Shechem "ruins" or "injures" Dinah by seizing her (φθείρει δι' ἁρπαγῆς, *A.J.* 1.337). There is no ambiguity in these acts; Dinah is a victim of forced sexual violence in both accounts.

Unlike in Gen 34, where the circumcision of the Shechemites features prominently in the dialogue and plot of the story, there is no mention of circumcision in either of these accounts. Circumcision is an issue of importance for both histories, however, as indicated in Jub. 15 and *A.J.* 1.192 and 20.34–48, 139, 145–146,[92] though arguably in quite different ways. What is noteworthy at this point, however, is that for both of these re-presentations of history, circumcision is not an issue present in *this* event. Each history shapes the story to highlight other matters of importance.

4.2. A Story for the Second Century BCE: Jubilees 30

Jubilees 30 features unique plot elements and direct addresses from the narrator that display a strong concern for the maintenance and bolstering of Judean identity against the strong tide of Hellenistic influence in the second century BCE. After the kernel event in Jubilees, Shechem begs Jacob and his sons to have Dinah as a wife, then "Jacob and his sons" speak craftily and deceptively to the Shechemites before the attack on the city by Simeon and Levi. The content of any of these speeches, however, is not given. What is highlighted as essential in this event is the central concept of purity and

---

90. A discussion on the range of interpretations of these moments is found in ch. 2 of this book.

91. Kugel notes that this detail "increas[es] the pathos of the incident" ("Jubilees," 394).

92. In these latter two examples, found in descriptions of intermarriages between two elite Judean women, Drusilla and Bernice, and the foreign kings Azizus king of Emesa and Polemo king of Cicilia, respectively, the men were required to be circumcised before marriage to the Judean women. Jubilees 15 asserts and intensifies the command to Abraham in Gen 15, insisting on eighth-day circumcision as the only authorized observance of the requirement. In *A.J.* 20.34–48, about King Izates, circumcision is presented as an essential element of male observance of the Judean law that God rewards.

defilement, also evinced through the *Leitwort* found eleven times in this chapter, *defile* (Lat. *polluo*, Eth. [ʾa]rkʷasa). Furthermore, the brief narration of events serves as a springboard for the lengthy pronouncement of heavenly decrees against intermarriage between Israelites and any foreigners, which constitutes defilement, a grievous sin to be repaid with death (Jub. 30.7–10). These decrees align with and expand the laws of Exod 34:11–16 and Deut 7:1–7 that prohibit intermarriage with Canaanite nations. Thus, the clash between Shechemites and Israelites becomes an arena to directly address the issue of exogamy. Jubilees 30:18 singles out Levi and blesses him for his eagerness to "carry out justice, punishment, and revenge for all who rise against Israel," serving the Jubilean agenda of promoting the Levitical priesthood "for all time," including its second-century BCE context. On the whole, the events at Shechem are re-presented in a way that undergirds the central messages of Jubilees to its contemporary audience regarding covenant observance, the holy status of Israel, and the authority of the Levitical priesthood, as discussed in detail below.

4.2.1. The Historical Context of Jubilees

Although the precise date of the composition or compilation of Jubilees is debated, scholars generally agree that it was composed in Hebrew in the second century BCE.[93] Many have assumed that dating the text with accuracy would help us to understand the political situation of its Judean audience, and perhaps more fully understand its purpose or the intended impact of its messages. Early Jubilees scholar R. H. Charles proposed that it was composed quite late in the century, sometime between 109 and 105 BCE, claiming that the celebration of the destruction at Shechem in Jub. 30 acts as a celebratory parallel to John Hyrcanus's conquest of Samaria in 110 BCE.[94] This designation was the dominant view of scholarship until

---

93. James VanderKam, "Recent Scholarship on the Book of Jubilees," *CurBR* 6 (2008): 407. Kugel holds to a theory of the redactional layering of Jubilees that attributes to an "interpolator" all mentions of heavenly tablets and many legal injunctions that he reads as contradicting the narrative. See Kugel, "On the Interpolations in the Book of Jubilees," *RevQ* 94 (2009): 215–72. I follow VanderKam in considering the text of Jubilees as an "authorial unity" (VanderKam, *Jubilees: A Commentary*, 25–28, esp. 28).

94. R. H. Charles, *The Book of Jubilees or Little Genesis: Translated from the Ethiopic Text and Edited, with Introduction, Notes, and Indices* (London: Black, 1902), lxiii–lxvi.

the late twentieth century.⁹⁵ Dating Jubilees on internal evidence and narrative details is fraught with problems, however, as the whole of the book presents itself as an ancient, Mosaic document. Charles's date was conjectural based on a somewhat allegorical reading of one portion of the text and was proposed before the discovery of the fragmentary Hebrew copies of Jubilees and the treasure trove of other sectarian documents at Qumran in 1947, which dramatically affected the modern world's understanding of the landscape of ancient Judaism and the role that Jubilees played in it. Through paleographical analysis of Qumran's Jubilees fragments, James VanderKam and Józef Milik determined that the book likely dated to the mid-second century BCE, since the oldest extant copy could be dated to somewhere between 125 and 100 BCE.⁹⁶ This manuscript evidence, together with Jubilees' awareness of the Enochic Book of Dreams (ca. 164 BCE), led them to conclude that Jubilees is a mid- to late second-century BCE composition.

Curious to some scholars is Jubilees' lack of discernible reference to the political upheavals of that time period.⁹⁷ The oppressive policies and persecutions under Seleucid ruler Antiochus IV are not mentioned, not even as coded into the apocalyptic forecast of chapters 1 and 23,⁹⁸ and

---

95. VanderKam, "Recent Scholarship on the Book," 407.

96. Contra arguments that posited a first-century date, such as that of Hermann Rönsch, who argued that Jubilees was a narrative polemic against the teachings of the Christian apostle Paul. See Rönsch, *Das Buch der Jubiläen oder die Kleine Genesis* (repr., Amsterdam: Editions Rodopi, 1910), 518–29. Wilhelm Singer proposed that Jubilees was a Jewish-Christian document familiar with Paul's writings. See Singer, *Das Buch der Jubiläen oder die Leptogenesis* (Stuhlweissenburg, Hungary: Singer'sche Buchhandlung, 1898), 264–322. James VanderKam and Józef Milik studied the scribal handwriting of the oldest surviving copy (4Q216 [4QJubᵃ]), which has both original text and a copied segment sewn into the original manuscript as a repair. See VanderKam and Milik, "Jubilees," in *Qumran Cave 4 VIII Parabiblical Texts, Part 1*, ed. James VanderKam (Oxford: Clarendon, 1994), 2.

97. George Nickelsburg, *Jewish Literature between the Bible and the Mishnah: A Historical and Literary Introduction*, 2nd ed. (Minneapolis: Fortress, 2005); Jonathan Goldstein, "The Date of the Book of Jubilees," *PAAJR* 50 (1983): 63–86; Liora Ravid, "Issues in the Book of Jubilees" (PhD diss., Bar Ilan University, 2001); VanderKam, "Recent Scholarship on the Book," 408.

98. Which, I posit, operates less like an apocalypse in the manner of Dan 6–12 or Enoch's visions but rather foretells the exile and return of ancient Israel/Judah. In this way, it parallels or re-presents Deut 28 and 30 rather than pointing to an era after the second century BCE. This is supported by the use of language from Deuteronomy,

neither is the Maccabean revolution or the establishment of the new Hasmonean dynasty of priest-kings, nor the various military campaigns that followed the establishment of the autonomous state of Judea. This absence of direct reference to contemporary events is easily explainable: the entire narrative presents itself as very ancient, written by the hand of Moses himself. While the dating of Jubilees' composition is unable to be determined with exactitude, it is sufficient to acknowledge the many upheavals in the political and religious policies and leadership of Judea that were taking place in the mid- to late second century BCE, and situate the emphatic messages of Jubilees accordingly. The rhetorical exhortations of Jubilees, presented as applicable to Israel's descendants "forever," in effect address second-century challenges facing the Judean populace, such as the growing influence of Hellenistic culture, frequent political upheavals, and various Judean factions vying for political and religious authority.

4.2.2. Major Themes of Jubilees in Their Historical Context

With this general context in mind, we can read the major themes and central concerns of Jubilees as aimed at a mid-second-century Judean audience. The following paragraphs will address three of these themes and concerns: (1) the emphasis and regular exhortations to the descendants of Israel to keep the covenant as defined in Jubilees, including the observation of divinely ordained festivals in accordance with the correct calendrical system; (2) the chosen and holy status of Israel, and the requirements of cultural and sexual separation that are required to maintain that status; and (3) the authority of the Levitical priesthood as divinely ordained preservers and interpreters of the oral and written legal codes and historical traditions of Israel. Each of these emphases may be read as a direct address to the controversies and challenges facing second-century Judeans.

---

that repentance and return will make them "a blessing instead of a curse, the head and not the tail" (Jub. 1.16). Chapter 23 similarly prophesies a future "evil generation" and the "sword, judgment, captivity, plundering, and devouring" (Jub. 23.22) that will befall them, followed by their repentance (involving "begin[ning] to study the laws, seek[ing] out the commands, and return[ing] to the right way," Jub. 23.26), and restoration in which the Lord "will dispel his enemies" (Jub. 23.30). While some have argued that chapter 23 is a coded reference to the rule of Antiochus IV and Maccabean revolt, I agree with VanderKam's statement that "the language is pliable enough to be read in more than one way" (*Jubilees: A Commentary*, 33).

Throughout the book of Jubilees, the angel of the presence exhorts the descendants of Israel through Moses, the internal audience, to keep the commandments and festivals of God. This regular rhetorical feature functions as a direct address to the external audience, second-century Judeans who identify as the descendants of Israel. At the start, the angel of the presence indicates the purpose of the book; for a future backslidden generation,[99] it will serve as a reminder of God's faithfulness to uphold the covenant, including his faithfulness to enforce judgment when they fail to keep its stipulations and his faithfulness to adhere to the promises of restoration on their repentance. The angel addresses Moses in Jub. 1.5–17,

> [5]Pay attention to all the words that I tell you on this mountain. Write them in a book so that their generations may know that I have not abandoned them because of all the evil they have done in breaking[100] the covenant between me and your children that I am making today on Mount Sinai for their offspring. [6]So it will be that when all of these things befall them they will recognize that I have been more faithful than they in all their judgments and in all their curses. They will recognize that I have indeed been with them....
> [9]They will turn after other gods.... [13]Then I will hide my face from them. I will deliver them into the control of the nations for captivity, for devastation, and for devouring. I will remove them from the land and disperse them among all the nations. [14]They will forget all my laws, all my commandments, and all my verdicts. They will forget beginning(s) of the month, Sabbath, festival, jubilee, and covenant.
> [15]After this, they will return to me from among the nations with all their minds, all their souls, and all their strength. Then I will gather them from among all the nations.... [16]I will plant them as a righteous plant....
> [17]I will be their God and they will be my true and righteous people.

Thus, the revelatory writings of Jubilees are internally presented as a message to future generations who have gone astray from covenant observance and have suffered the loss of land and political autonomy as a result (Jub. 1.13). Throughout the narrative, stipulations of covenant observance are interwoven as revealed through the lives of the righteous ancestors. The angel often demands that Moses write them so that the Israelites

---

99. That is, a future generation with respect to the time of Moses.
100. Slight alteration yields "neglecting" (VanderKam, *Jubilees: A Commentary*, 133 n. 5i).

may forever observe them faithfully. For example, the story of the seven-day creation concludes in this way: "Now you command the Israelites to observe this [Sabbath] day so that they may sanctify it" (Jub. 2.26). A similar conclusion is found after the story of the primeval flood: "Now you command the Israelites not to eat any blood so that their name and their descendants may continue to exist before the Lord our God for all time. This law has no temporal limits because it is forever" (Jub. 6.13–14). Following the brief description of events from Gen 34, the exhortation of God's messenger is three times as long as the narrative account that occasions it (Jub. 30.5–22).[101] It also features the now-familiar direct address to Moses and admonitions for second-century BCE Judeans: "Now you, Moses, order the Israelites and testify to them that they are not to give any of their daughters to foreigners and that they are not to marry any foreign women because it is despicable to the Lord" (Jub. 30.11).

A second way that exhortation to the external audience is rhetorically accomplished is through the frequent testimonies—or admonitory addresses—of the ancestors to their children and grandchildren within the narrative. Noah (Jub. 7.20–39), Abraham (20.1–10; to Isaac, 21.1–25; to Jacob 22.10–24), Rebekah (35.18–27), and Isaac (36.1–11) each have long speeches delivered to their descendants with admonitions to keep the ways of the Lord,[102] properly observing festivals and sacrificial offerings, while keeping away from the Canaanites and all sexual transgressions. Frequently spoken with reference to "forever," these exhortations are not only for the internal audience but are to be kept by Israel's descendants in every subsequent generation.

Calendrical observance is a pervasive central concern for Jubilees, which was written in a century in which differing views concerning the ritual year were vying for preeminence. In this arena, Jubilees vehemently promotes the observance of a 364-day solar calendar (Jub. 6.32).[103] The

---

101. See outline above.

102. Jacob, unlike the major figures before him, does not deliver a farewell speech but hands over "all of his books and his fathers' books" to Levi (Jub. 45.15).

103. This calendar is initiated at creation. The sun alone is made to demarcate the times and seasons: "On the fourth day the Lord made the sun, the moon, and the stars. He placed them in the heavenly firmament to shine on the whole earth, to rule over day and night, and to separate between light and darkness. The Lord appointed the sun as a great sign above the earth for days, Sabbaths, months, festivals, years, Sabbaths of years, jubilees, and all cycles of the years" (Jub. 2.8–9).

whole of the composition is prefaced with, "These are the words regarding the divisions of the times for the law and for the testimony, for the events of the years, for the weeks of their jubilees throughout all the years of eternity" (Jub. prologue). This title reflects Jubilees' concern to present the events and figures of Gen 1 to Exod 24 according to their precise times and seasons.[104] Creation and human history are presented as unfolding on a divinely ordained timeline, made up of units of seven-year blocks, or "weeks of years," which combine together in larger units of seven "weeks." Seven "weeks" of seven years, or forty-nine years, equates to a jubilee. There is hardly an episode narrated in Jubilees that is not assigned its precise place on this temporal map.[105]

---

104. Often the timing associated with special events serves to explain a law or festival that, in the narrative plot of the biblical Torah, is revealed at Sinai. For example, Noah is not just randomly drinking the fruit of his vineyard in Jubilees but rather celebrating one of four yearly memorial festivals to the Lord, one that has been ordained and recorded on heaven's tablets (Jub. 6.23–28). The purification laws for women after childbirth, found seemingly without justification or reason in Lev 12:1–5, are interwoven with the birth of the first humans in Jub. 3.8: "In the first week Adam and his wife—the rib—were created, and in the second week [God] showed her to him. Therefore, a commandment was given to keep (women) in their defilement seven days for a male (child) and for a female two (units) of seven days" (see VanderKam, *Jubilees: A Commentary*, 214). Similarly, the following verses (Jub. 3.9–14) more elaborately connect the times of entrance for Adam and Eve into the garden with the time-bound Levitical laws for women entering the sanctuary after the birth of a male or female child. Thus, there are multiple levels of revelation in play in Jubilees: Moses simultaneously is receiving heaven's view of human history (which roughly corresponds with the biblical Genesis) and the law "written in the heavenly tablets," corresponding with various Torah laws. What is separated in Torah is an integrated revelation in Jubilees. Narrative interprets, explains, justifies, or foreshadows law. At times, law, especially Sabbath law or festival legislation, is revealed to the patriarchs in Jubilees' account of history. Thus, some revelations of heavenly ordinances precede Sinai and are transmitted by the patriarchs, even as they are freshly revealed to Moses by the angel of the presence. As Jubilees frames all of its contents as the very same contents of the revelation Moses received at Sinai, and it was traditional that Moses was the author of Genesis as well as Exodus–Deuteronomy, this is fitting exegesis on the one hand. On the other hand, the law and narrative according to Jubilees are mutually interpreting and thus mutually serve to legitimize both Jubilees' account of ancestral history and its interpretation of the law.

105. In Gen 9, Noah seemingly plants a vineyard and gets drunk from its wine a breath later, due to the brevity with which his actions are expressed: "And Noah began to be a man of the ground. And he planted a vineyard. And he drank from the

Preeminent Jubilees scholar James VanderKam suggests, on the evidence of Dan 7:25 and the calendrical concerns reflected in the documents of the Qumran community, that debates about the festal calendar were a key feature of second-century Judean discourse.[106] In Dan 7:25, it is foretold in a vision to Daniel that a king will arise who will "speak words against the Most High," "wear out the saints of the Most High," and "will think to change the times and the law." This verse is understood by VanderKam to be a coded discourse in reference to the Seleucid ruler Antiochus IV, whose reforms likely included a change of calendar on the Judean populace.[107] Such a reading is supported by the statements in 1 Macc 1:43–45 lamenting the acceptance of Antiochus's λατρεία, or ways of worship, which included the profaning (βεβηλῶσαι) of Sabbaths and festivals by "many from Israel."[108] The writings of the separatist community at Qumran, whose founding is now dated to the late second century BCE,[109] also indicate that calendrical concerns were common at the time. It is understood that the sectarians held Jubilees to be an authoritative document, since fourteen fragmentary copies have been found among the caves, and there are several "points of contact" between

---

wine, and he became drunk" (Gen 9:20–21). In Jubilees, however, the time between his actions and the date of his drinking is demarcated on the divine timeline. "During the seventh week, in its first year, in this jubilee [1317], Noah planted a vineyard.... It produced fruit in the fourth year [1320]. He guarded its fruit and picked it in the seventh month. He made wine from it, put it in a container, and kept it until the fifth year [1321]—until the first day at the beginning of the first month. He joyfully celebrated the day of this festival.... When evening came, he went into his tent. He lay down drunk and fell asleep" (Jub. 7.1–3, 7). Similarly, Adam and Eve, who exist in Gen 2–4 in a mysterious and uncharted ancient landscape and time, are plotted precisely by Jubilees: "During six days of the second week we [angelic beings] brought to Adam, on the Lord's orders, all animals, all cattle, all birds, everything that moves" (Jub. 3.1).

106. James VanderKam, "The Origins and Purposes of the *Book of Jubilees*," in *Studies in the Book of Jubilees*. ed. Matthias Albani, Jörg Frey, and Armin Lange (Tübingen: Mohr Siebeck, 1997), 22.

107. VanderKam, "Origins and Purposes," 22.

108. "And many from Israel [πολλοὶ ἀπὸ Ισραηλ] approved of [Antiochus IV's] religious service [τῇ λατρείᾳ αὐτοῦ] and sacrificed to the idols and profaned the sabbath. And the King sent letters by the hand of messengers to Jerusalem and the cities of Judah [saying that they were] to go after laws strange to the land [νομίμων ἀλλοτρίων τῆς γῆς] ... and to profane sabbaths and festivals [βεβηλῶσαι σάββατα καὶ ἑορτὰς]" (1 Macc 1:43–45).

109. VanderKam, "Origins and Purposes," 19–20.

the material in Jubilees and the Qumran sectarian literature.[110] Although the community did not adhere to the purely solar calendar that Jubilees advocates,[111] the writings of Qumran reveal a shared concern in the dating of the times of the patriarchs and the calendrical order. For example, 4QCommentary on Genesis^a (4Q252) preserves reflections on the precise dating of the flood events and the age of Abraham. The priestly calendars 4Q320–330 and 4Q337 also reveal a meticulous concern for the calculation of solar *and* lunar months and the precise dating of the New Moon and annual festivals.

In Jubilees, Moses is told to command the people to observe the 364-day calendar so that they may "neither omit a day nor disturb a festival" (Jub. 6.32). There is a deep concern expressed for the loss of divine temporal orientation and the observance of the wrong (lunar) calendar (Jub. 6.32–38), which would result in future generations not being able to find "the way of the years" after forgetting it (Jub. 6.34). Such disturbance and forgetting is expected to come about through the influence of "the festivals of the nations, after their error and after their ignorance" (Jub. 6.35). In second-century BCE Judea, such an external cultural influence came first through subjugation to Greek rule and then continued cultural exchange with other nations now steeped for decades in the far-reaching waters of Hellenism. It is against this backdrop that we can read the angel's announcement that he is revealing "the divisions of the times ... ordained on the heavenly tablets"—heaven's own record—for the descendants of Israel to return to after they have strayed (Jub. 6.35). For Jubilees, much is at stake in the proper ordering of the calendar, as well as in continued covenant observance, for it is only through proper observance that Israel can maintain their holy status and avoid the destruction that awaits all other nations (e.g., Jub. 21.21–25).

The special status of Israel as elected and holy is a foundational concept throughout the body of Jubilees; it is the marrow fueling every exhortation ascribed to heaven or Israel's ancestors. Such a special status is *granted* at the moment of creation as an unmerited identity (Jub. 2.19–20), but the burden of *maintaining* this privileged status is on the people. They are responsible for keeping separate from the nations in regard to conduct and copulation. Abraham instructs Jacob to "separate from the nations,

---

110. VanderKam, *Jubilees: A Commentary*, 104.
111. Geza Vermes, *The Complete Dead Sea Scrolls in English*, rev. ed. (London: Penguin Books, 2011), 347.

and do not eat with them. Do not act as they do, and do not become their companion, for their actions are something that is impure, and all their ways are defiled and something abominable and detestable," for all who worship idols as they do "will descend to Sheol and will go to the place of judgment" (22.16, 22). Any unlawful sexual relations (33.15–20), including intermarriage with those not of the "holy seed" of Israel (e.g., 2.19–20, 16.17), is a defiling act, one that automatically profanes the offender and thus renders them common. Like the rest of the unholy nations, they will perish: "If they transgress and act in all the ways of defilement, they will be recorded in the heavenly tablets as enemies. And they will be blotted out of the book of life and written in the book of those who will be destroyed and with those who will be rooted out from the land" (30.23).

Several scholars have suggested reading these warnings as an argument against the segment of Judeans represented by 1 Macc 1:11–15.[112] Although depicted with disdain by the Maccabean historian, who calls them "lawless sons," this second-century Judean group was interested in adopting Greek customs and assimilating by mitigating their observance of the Torah laws, including circumcision, and intermarrying.[113] The reason this party gives that is so persuasive to the populace is that "from the time we separated from [the nations], we have encountered many disasters" (1 Macc 1:11). This suggests that they perceived there was a time in history when their people did not live separately from the nations but coexisted without legal stipulations that demanded otherwise, and that life was better for Israel back then. The way forward, for this influential group, was assimilation and participation in the wider culture.[114] Jubilees' presentation of even the most ancient ancestors as covenant-observing and separation-promoting

---

112. John C. Endres, *Biblical Interpretation in the Book of Jubilees*, CBQMS 18 (Washington, DC: Catholic Biblical Association of America, 1987); Klaus Berger, *Das Buch der Jubiläen*, JSHRZ 2.3 (Gütersloh: Gütersloher Verlagshaus Gerd Mohn, 1981); VanderKam, "Origins and Purposes," 22.

113. "In those days, lawless sons came out of Israel and persuaded many, saying 'Let's go and make a covenant with the nations around us, because from the time we separated from them, we have encountered many disasters.' And the word was pleasing in their eyes. And some from the people were eagerly willing, and went to the king and he gave them authority to do the ordinances of the nations. And they built a gymnasium in Jerusalem according to the customs of the nations, and they made foreskins for themselves and opposed the holy covenant and they were yoked with the nations and sold themselves to do wickedness" (1 Macc 1:11–15).

114. VanderKam, "Origins and Purposes," 22.

in addition to the Mosaic law as an eternally binding expectation for the nation directly contests such arguments. Indeed, the law of circumcision as given in Jub. 15 seems to presuppose these practices,

> Now you [Moses] command the Israelites to keep the sign of this covenant throughout their history as an eternal ordinance so that they may not be uprooted from the earth.[115]... I am telling you now that the Israelites will prove false to this ordinance. They will not circumcise their sons in accord with this entire law because they will leave some of the flesh of their circumcision when they circumcise their sons. All the people of Belial will leave their sons uncircumcised just as they were born. (15.28, 33–34)

Like the laws of circumcision, Sabbath keeping and the holy status of Israel are depicted as most ancient and eternally binding (Jub. 2). To a second-century BCE audience, Jubilees promotes the idea that for holiness to be maintained, and for Israel to have any hope, they must reject the pervasive influence of the nations in all their conduct and adhere to the everlasting commands of the covenant.

In addition to this, there is a strong emphasis in Jubilees on the appointment of Levi and his sons "to the priesthood of God Most High forever" (Jub. 32.1), while curiously, there is no mention in the book of the role of Levi's descendant Aaron and his sons as high priests.[116] Levi is depicted as the heir of the oral and written traditions of the patriarchs (45.16), especially Noah (7.38–39), Abraham, (12.25–26) and Isaac (21.1–26), who are also presented as fulfilling priestly roles in their generations. Levi's zeal in demolishing the city of Shechem is the occasion for heaven's declaration that he and his descendants are appointed for the priesthood and Levitical roles forever (30.18–20).[117] This is subsequently emphasized by a prophetic dream that Levi has (32.1) and the ordination ceremony Jacob performs for him (32.3–9). Some have suggested that this emphasis on Levitical authority serves a Hasmonean agenda, since the Hasmonean high priests claimed to be descendants of Levi, though they were not "sons

---

115. Or "land."

116. In the biblical books, Aaron and his sons (descendants) are set apart for the role of priest (Exod 29:44; Lev 8), while other descendants of Levi are appointed to supportive roles as servants of the priest and of the cult (Num 3:5–51).

117. Simeon's later marriage to a Canaanite woman perhaps disqualified him from such an honor in the reading of the author of Jubilees.

of Aaron."[118] This may be so; however, there is reason to believe that the Levi tradition represented in Jubilees predates 152 BCE, when the Hasmoneans took office, by over a century, perhaps even extending to Ezran times.[119] Alternatively, it may be independently promoting the Mosaic blessing over the tribe of Levi in Deut 33:10: "They shall teach your judgments to Jacob and your *torah* to Israel."

Promotions of Levitical legitimacy need not be connected to Hasmonean legitimacy. In a second-century BCE backdrop, they can also be read as a polemic against the growing influence of the non-Levitical Pharisaic (or proto-Pharisaic)[120] interpreters of the law. In a century when various groups claimed authority to guide the nation into the correct practice of its laws and interpretation of its traditions, Jubilees stresses that it is Levi alone who received all of Jacob's books "and the books of his fathers," containing revelatory material and priestly stipulations, "so that he could preserve them and renew them for his sons until today" (45.16). This preservation and renewal, copying and interpreting or teaching, as "the most reliable tradent"[121] of the oral and written ancestral traditions is the divinely ordained role of Levi's descendants only. This role is arguably demonstrated by Jubilees itself, which preserves and renews the "testimony" of Gen 1–Exod 24, by retelling it infused with concepts and excerpts from Israel's legal, prophetic, and poetic literature.[122]

4.2.3. Jubilees 30 Shaping Genesis 34 for the Second Century BCE

Each of the second-century BCE concerns noted above is reflected in Jub. 30. While the story functions in part, as mentioned above, to legitimize Levitical authority, it especially emphasizes the concerns for covenant observance and the maintenance of holiness through avoiding exogamy.

---

118. Such a position was argued by R. Meyer in 1938 (VanderKam, *Jubilees: A Commentary*, 874).

119. VanderKam, *Jubilees: A Commentary*, 874.

120. Solomon Zeitlin, "The Origin of the Pharisees Reaffirmed," *JQR* 59 (1969): 255–67.

121. VanderKam, *Jubilees: A Commentary*, 1116.

122. VanderKam, *Jubilees*, 39. For this reason, it is generally concluded that the author of Jubilees was a second-century Levite himself. See Charles, *Jubilees*, 244; Friedemann Schubert, *Tradition und Erneuerung: Studien zum Jubiläenbuch und seinem Trägerkreis*, EHGIH 771 (Frankfurt: Lang, 1998), 177–266.

The narrator of Jubilees makes explicit the purpose of this event and the reasons it was mandated to record it in the annals of Israelite history. First, the commentary of the angel suggests that it was all allowed to happen in the first place to prevent something like it ever happening again:

> Nothing like this is to be done anymore from now on—to defile an Israelite virgin.... The Lord delivered them [the Shechemites] into the hand of Jacob's sons *so that* they may uproot them with the sword and *so that* they may enact punishment against them *and so that* there should not again be something like this within Israel—to defile an Israelite virgin. (Jub. 30.5-6, emphasis added)[123]

Within Genesis, the tale implicitly raises unanswered questions with regard to intermarriage with outsiders.[124] Yet in Jubilees, the potential for the merging of peoples is taken off the table as a choice of action for the Israelites; indeed, in the words of the narrator, that is why this event was revealed to Moses: "Now you, Moses, order the Israelites and testify to them that they are not to give any of their daughters to foreigners and that they are not to marry any foreign women because it is despicable before the Lord. *For this reason*[125] I have written for you in the words of the law everything that the Shechemites did to Dinah" (Jub. 30.11-12, emphasis added). Not only does this account of the ancestors demonstrate what is not to be done, but the narrator emphasizes why. Much is at stake, for the individual and for the nation. For the one who gives his daughter or sister

---

123. This is my translation. It differs only slightly from VanderKam's but draws more attention to the purpose clauses in this verse (three in Ge'ez and two in Latin). In Ge'ez, this sentence is composed of a main clause and three purpose clauses, each headed by the conjunction *kama*. The first two are positive purpose clauses "so that they may," and the last one is negative, *kama 'i* + the verb *kwn*, rendered "lest there be," or here, "so that ... not." In Latin, however, the final phrase stands alone grammatically (*et non amplius erit in Istrahel ut polluatur uirgo Istrahel*, "And it shall no longer be in Israel that a virgin of Israel be defiled"). While not technically a result clause, the sense of this pronouncement in its context is similar to that of the Ge'ez.

124. See ch. 2, §5.5.1. In Gen 34, the possibility of merging with other people groups through circumcision and intermarriage is something that undergirds the damage-control marriage deliberations between the leaders of the Shechemites and Israelites. In the narrative arc of Genesis to Exodus, intermarriage with Canaanite peoples is not banned until the exodus generation leaves Egypt (Exod 23:32, 34:11-16).

125. Eth. *ba'əntazə*, Lat. *propter hoc*.

to *any* foreigner, or for the woman who marries any foreigner, death is their sentence by the ordinance of heaven (Jub. 30.7–10). If left unpunished, their actions have consequences for the nation: "Israel will not become clean from this impurity while it has one of the foreign women or if anyone has given one of his daughters to any foreign man.... The entire nation will be condemned together because of all this impurity and this contamination" (Jub. 30.14–15). Thus, the story serves as a point of ethical reflection for the Israelites (or, rather, their second-century BCE descendants); they are called to choose with their actions between two futures: obedience, leading to friendship with God, or disobedience, leading to annihilation.

> I have written this entire message for you and have ordered you [Moses] to tell the Israelites not to sin or transgress the statutes or violate the covenant that was established for them so that they should perform it and be recorded as friends. But if they transgress and behave in any impure ways, they will be recorded on the heavenly tablets as enemies. They will be erased from the book of the living and will be recorded in the book of those who will be destroyed and with those who will be uprooted from the earth. (Jub. 30.21–22)

While leaving the second-century BCE Judean audience with a choice, it is barely a choice at all for those who accept the authority of Jubilees.

4.3. Ancient Israel with First-Century CE Issues: *Antiquities* 1.337–341

As in Jubilees, *Antiquities* shapes the inherited past—the characters and events of Gen 34—to reflect contemporary issues and concerns. After the offense of Shechem in *Antiquities*, Jacob is placed into a pressurized state of conflicting loyalties, a condition that also marks Josephus's depictions of first-century CE Judean leaders under Roman rule. In this telling, which takes place during a festival, Shechem has certainly wronged Dinah. In *Antiquities*, there are no marriage negotiations, no deceitful speeches, no agreements made, and, in strong contrast to Jub. 30, no mention of defilement at all. When Hamor "the king" approaches Jacob to ask that Dinah may be given in marriage to his son, Shechem, Jacob asks to hold a council with his sons privately, and they are all at a loss as to what to do. By narrating Jacob's inner thoughts, *Antiquities* highlights the precarious position in which Jacob has been placed by Hamor's request, locked in an internal debate between adhering to what he considers lawful and honoring the request of his non-Israelite overlord. The central problem caused by Shechem's actions thus lies in the predicament *Jacob* is put in as a result of them, caught in the tension between honoring Israelite law and a foreign king (ὁ βασιλεὺς, A.J. 1.337, 339): "Jacob, neither having a response because of the rank of the one entreating him, nor considering it lawful to give his daughter in marriage to a foreigner [ἀλλοφύλῳ συνοικίζειν], requested him [Hamor] to allow the gathering of a council concerning what he was entreating" (1.338). This is the central predicament into which the ruler of the nascent clan of Israel is put when members of their own have been wronged by ruling foreign landowners and are caught between their inability to refuse (οὔτ' ἀντιλέγειν ἔχων) the requests of their ruler and their loyalty to what they consider to be lawful. Jacob's inner struggles, opaque in the laconic narration of Gen 34, are presented in A.J. 1.338 as the struggles of the "most reasonable" (20.201) of Josephus's Judean contemporaries under Roman rule, as seen in book 20 of *Judean Antiquities*. Those first-century Judeans who were concerned with "the accurate [observance] of the laws" bore offenses against them "with difficulty" (20.201), yet they are depicted as regularly seeking to respond with respect to the authority of their Roman overlords (e.g., 20.116, 121, 193–194, 202–203), with varying degrees of success. Like Jacob, they seem pressed between a rock and a hard place in their strained political position as a people in their land of promise occupied by others in authority. Navigating the system, however, was not the only choice of response taken. As the section on representation below further demonstrates, the divide among the Israelites in A.J. 1.337–341 mirrors the divide among first-century CE Judeans as represented by Josephus in A.J. 20.

Although the episode at Shechem is shaped to reflect internal issues that faced the Judeans during Josephus's lifetime,[126] *Antiquities* as a whole is addressed to an external audience. As with Jubilees, historically contextualizing this massive work of literature is important to

---

126. Everything we know about the author comes from the autobiographical information that he wrote in the *War* and his authorizing autobiographical appendix to the *Antiquities*, the *Life*. Claiming a priestly heritage and elite education, Josephus was a general in Galilee during the revolt. He was captured as a prisoner of war after the siege of Jotapata and gained the support of the Flavian dynasty when he reportedly prophesied to the Roman general Vespasian that he would be the next Roman emperor. When Vespasian rose to the throne, Josephus received his freedom and a degree of support for a new life in the capital.

understanding its contents and function. This study takes Josephus's first-century Roman context into consideration while taking seriously the rhetorically constructed self-presentation of *Antiquities*. In other words, it attends to how the narrator indicates the function and audience of his work.[127] Mason argues for taking the prologue of *Antiquities*

---

127. Traditionally, throughout much of Josephan scholarship, it has either been assumed or argued that what is being presented is an "apologetic history," that Josephus was writing to a hostile Roman world after the collapse of his nation during the Judean War of 66–70 CE, presenting his ancestral history in a radiantly positive light. This view was promoted by Laqueur and Thackeray in the early twentieth century, and it has been a prevailing interpretation of the *Judean Antiquities* ever since. See Richard Laqueur, *Der jüdische Historiker Flavius Josephus* (Darmstadt: Wissenschaftliche Buchgesellschaft, 1920); Henry St. John Thackeray, *Josephus: The Man and the Historian* (New York: Ktav, 1929); Mason, "Should Any Wish," 65–66. There is certainly evidence within *Antiquities* that points to an implicit preclusion of "the widespread slander and misinformation about Judean origins" that circulated widely in the first century CE (Mason, "Should Any Wish," 68). This is done implicitly, however, not as open confrontation, as in *Against Apion* (Mason, "Should Any Wish," 69). When this assumption—that Josephus's primary goal in writing is to confront slanders through an apologetic history—is brought to the reading of every episode within the text, however, every detail perceived as added or omitted to the biblical account is read as having been done for "apologetic reasons," even when the conclusions are contradictory. An example may be found in Feldman's commentary on *A.J.* 1.277: "In stating that Isaac and his family were not well disposed to Esau's marriages with Canaanite women, Josephus uses restrained language, for apologetic reasons, since the Jews in Josephus' day had been accused by writers such as Juvenal and Tacitus of hating non-Jews" (*Judean Antiquities 1–4*, 109 n. 824). Two sentences later, Josephus declares that the reason Jacob slept outside, lodging with no one on his travels through Canaan, was "because of his hatred [μῖσος] toward the inhabitants." Clearly, Josephus has no problem depicting the ancestors at enmity with the Canaanites. Yet this too is explained away: "Josephus here supplies a reason why Jacob slept in the open air (Gen 28:11). One may wonder why Josephus speaks of Jacob's hatred (*misos*) toward the Canaanites, since this would lend credence to the charge of Jewish misanthropy. Perhaps the answer is that his hatred is directed solely at the Canaanites, in view of their inexcusable violence to the wells that Isaac had dug (Gen 26:18–21; *A.J.* 1.260–261)" (109 n. 828). This seems to be stretching the text to fit the theory. First, it is not altogether certain that Abimelech of Gerar, Isaac's rival, was understood to be "Canaanite" at all, by either Genesis or Josephus. Genesis labels his territory as "the land of the Philistines" (Gen 21:32), and the inhabitants, the opponents in the Isaac well incident, are termed "Philistines" (Gen 26:18); Josephus likewise calls the land of Abimelech "Palestine," a region seemingly distinct from Canaan (*A.J.* 1.207). Second, this, and many similar arguments, is stuffing the rich and nuanced material

seriously in the effort to understand the purpose behind Josephus's work. Mason's conclusions form the starting point of this study for understanding the *Judean Antiquities*:

> Given the tone of this prologue as well as the very demanding size and scope of the work, we cannot avoid the conclusion that [Josephus] was writing for a group of Gentiles who were keenly interested in Judean culture. What did he hope to tell them? ... He offers Judaism as an alternative political constitution and as an alternative philosophical system.[128]

The prologue presents the work as a response to interested non-Judeans, and one Epaphroditus by name, who loved "every form of learning." In short, the text is for non-Judean Greek-speakers ("Greeks") who "labor to know things about us [Judeans]" (*A.J.* 1.9). Josephus likens his audience to Ptolemais II Philadelphus and the Greek Egyptians of old behind the legend of the translation of the LXX, who were "lovers of learning" (φιλομαθεῖς, 1.12) and who asked the third-century BCE high priest Eleazar to share with them a copy of the Judean law and to have it translated. Josephus thus claims to write for an interested audience, not defensively against a hostile one.[129] The chief content of his history is stated as the "the entire ancient history" (ἅπασαν τὴν παρ' ἡμῖν ἀρχαιολογίαν) concerning the Judeans and "the constitution of the state" (διάταξιν τοῦ πολιτεύματος) from the Hebrew writings (1.5). What is presented is labeled as both "useful" and "beautiful" (1.9), a perspective that the narrator indicates that his audience shares.[130]

---

of Josephus's narrative into a narrow niche, and it does not quite fit. Each textual detail must be turned and squeezed to suit the demands of the restrictions of the "apologetic" label *when* apologetic assumes the requirement of an only-ever-positive presentation of one's ancestors and history. This apologetic definition is too narrow to account for the diversity of material, the richness of the characterizations present in Josephus's telling of ancient history. The apologetic label thus skews the evidence. Every instance of Josephus making the ancestors more appealing or mitigating the more explicit (potential) faults from the biblical sources is interpreted as aiding in his apologetics or done for apologetic reasons. Every instance of blatant deception, murderous behaviors, attempts at fratricide, and so on that remains from the biblical sources in Josephus is seemingly ignored.

128. Mason, "Should Any Wish," 80.
129. Mason, "Should Any Wish," 79. One version of this tradition is preserved in the Letter of Aristeas.
130. Mason, "Should Any Wish," 79. Especially Epaphroditus, who may have

There was good reason for late first-century Romans to be interested in alternative political constitutions. After the extreme political instability preceding the reign of the Flavian dynasty and Flavian Emperor Domitian's direction away from the republican senate and toward a monarchial court, "whether they dared to speak openly of it or not, every educated person in Rome must have been thinking about issues of political constitution."[131] The constitution, or πολιτεία, of the Judeans, presented as a priestly ἀριστοκρατία,[132] is a central theme of the twenty volumes. Books 1–3 build up to the revelation of the constitution and laws, books 3–4 describe them in detail, and the rest of Judean history is presented in light of obedience to or divergence from the constitution and laws.[133] In the twentieth and final volume, the story of the Adiabenian king Izates is exemplary of this central purpose of the *Antiquities*. It tells how Izates, by adopting the Judean constitution—including undergoing circumcision to obey the full law—experienced the protection of God through many trials (*A.J.* 20.17–96). Thus, in *Antiquities*' final chapter, Izates is put forth as a paragon for the audience: the outsider who responds to instruction in the most supreme law by adopting and adhering to it, who is rewarded with divine assistance and blessing (see *A.J.* 1.14). Furthermore, by paralleling the twenty-volume *Judean Antiquities* to the twenty-volume work *Roman Antiquities* by Dionysius of Halicarnassus (ca. 60 BCE–7 BCE) and by implicitly using rhetorical constructions from Cicero's *On the Republic* and *On the Laws*, Josephus enters the Judean constitution into the Roman political arena for consideration as an "appealing alternative."[134]

---

been one of the patrons of his work.

131. Mason, "Introduction to the *Judean Antiquities*," xxvi. After Emperor Nero's suicide in 68 CE, Rome was thrown into turmoil with a rapid succession of leaders; 69 CE was known as "the year of four emperors," at the end of which Vespasian took the role and ushered in a new dynasty (Mason, "Introduction to the *Judean Antiquities*," xxvi).

132. Mason, "Should Any Wish," 82. See also *A.J.* 4.304, *C. Ap.* 2.185.

133. "At the end of *Against Apion*, Josephus recalls that his purpose in writing the earlier *Antiquities* was to give 'an exact account of our laws and constitution' (*Apion* 2.287). In Josephus's view, the *Antiquities/Life* was from start to finish about the Judean constitution" (Mason, "Should Any Wish," 81).

134. Mason, "Introduction to the *Judean Antiquities*," xxix. See Mason's detailed elaboration of this argument on xxiv–xxviii. On the paralleling to Dionysius of Hali-

Honoring the Judean law, and thus honoring the will of the God who gave it, is simultaneously presented by *Antiquities* as an alternative philosophical system. Many of the important figures of Judean history, especially Abraham, Moses, Solomon, and Daniel, are presented as philosophers, and the sects of the Pharisees, Sadducees, Essenes, and Zealots/Sicarii are presented as Judean philosophical schools (*A.J.* 13.171–173, 18.12–18). In accordance with the philosophical discourse of the day, this "Judean philosophy" is one to which outsiders are welcome to convert to by rethinking (μετάνοια) and choosing a new way of life.[135] Mason calls attention to the prologue of *Antiquities* being "replete with philosophical language," which is fitting, as discourse about the optimal constitution was most frequently conducted in the realm of philosophy.[136] "Showing the way to *eudaimonia* was understood to be the goal of philosophy in Josephus's day," and Josephus repeatedly asserts in his prologue that following the Judean law alone brings one εὐδαιμονία or "happiness" (1.14, 20).[137] Louis Feldman calls εὐδαιμονία a "key word" in the *Antiquities*, and though it is absent in the OG Bible, it is found forty-seven times in Josephus's narrative.[138]

Similarly, God's providential care of the universe, or πρόνοια, is a major theme that recurs throughout the *Antiquities*, and many biblical stories are shaped to emphasize this principle.[139] Πρόνοια was a common theme within the discourse of Stoic philosophy, the most influential school among the old republican oppositions to the principate.[140] Josephus's presentation of God's universal πρόνοια takes on a decidedly Judean character, however, as he establishes it on the law revealed to Moses and displays how all of Judean history reflects the activity of God in upholding his "excellent legislations" (*A.J.* 1.14). As Mason notes, "Josephus claims that the code of Moses reflects the very laws of the universe, and so anyone wishing to

---

carnassus's *Roman Antiquities*, see Attridge, *Interpretation of Biblical History*, 43–44, 54, 64–65.

135. Mason, "Should Any Wish," 88.
136. Mason, "Should Any Wish," 87–88; Mason, "Introduction to the Judean Antiquities," xxix.
137. Mason, "Should Any Wish," 87. This Greek term, meaning "well-being" or "happiness," was a central topic of ancient Greek and Roman philosophy.
138. Louis H. Feldman, "Josephus as a Biblical Interpreter: The 'Aqedah,'" *JQR* 75 (1984–1985): 241 n. 79. See Mason, "Should Any Wish," 87.
139. Attridge, *Interpretation of Biblical History*, 67–92.
140. Mason, "Introduction to the *Judean Antiquities*," xxx–xxxi; Mason, "Should Any Wish," 87.

enquire more deeply about the reasons for the laws would find the exercise rich and 'highly philosophical' (1.25)."[141] Thus, all—or more specifically, the Greco-Roman aristocratic audience of the *Antiquities*—are welcome to contemplate this universal and most excellent order in accordance with the character of God (1.15). Furthermore, they are encouraged to adopt it as their own.

A crucial implication of the presentation of Judaism as both peerless law and most excellent philosophy is that, according to Josephus, the answer to both political wellness and personal εὐδαιμονία rests in aligning both national and individual ethics to the commandments set out in the Mosaic law. The common overlap between Josephus's presentation of Judaism as both the most excellent constitutional law and the truest philosophy is that these two arenas of discourse accentuate the ethical conduct required for the best life, both national and personal. The national well-being of any nation is dependent on the willingness of individual people to submit to its laws, albeit when they are good. For that reason, the fundamental goodness of the Judean law is a central argument of the *Antiquities*. Josephus praises Moses for his wisdom in understanding that the willingness for obedience to such a good national law comes from "raising the thoughts" of people "on God and the construction of the universe," and accepting their identity as the "noblest of God's works" (A.J. 1.21). This philosophical elevation of the mind to the contemplation of God inspires the submission to a life of piety (εὐσέβεια); Josephus claims that Moses the lawgiver thought that all people ought to try to participate (πειρᾶσθαι μεταλαμβάνειν) in the pure virtue (ἀρετή ἀκραιφνής) of God, thus motivating obedience to his perfect law (1.23). For the *Antiquities*, right ethics thus follow right philosophy, and subsequently fuels personal and national εὐδαιμονία. These central claims undergird all of the stories of *Antiquities*, including Josephus's re-presentation of Gen 34. Although Josephus's exposition of the Judean law comes after A.J. 1.337–341, it retrospectively informs the ethical content of that account in ways that are explored below.

---

141. Mason, "Should Any Wish," 87.

5. Representational Ethics of Jubilees and *Judean Antiquities*

As authoritative national histories, Jubilees and *Judean Antiquities* worked to shape collective conceptions of the roles and requirements—or the identity and ethics—of their primary audiences.[142] This shaping work is in part advanced by the subtle yet powerful craft of representation, that is, the narrativization of individuals and groups as characters in an ongoing story.[143] Below, I analyze Jub. 30 and *A.J.* 1.337–341 dialogically with each other and with their shared source material, Gen 34, which describes the nascent clan of Israel's first collective encounter and clash with another people group, the Shechemites. First, I argue that undifferentiated national representations in Jubilees promote an impermeable boundary between Judeans and others, with violence as a legitimized and valorized ethos of cross-cultural engagement. Second, in light of the pervasive influence of Jubilees' representational effects in late Second Temple times,[144] I posit that Josephus's renarrativization of Judean history offers a corrective to the representations in Jubilees. His work, the *Judean Antiquities*, imagines a new future of more permeable boundaries and diplomatic negotiation for first-century CE Judeans (and to some extent his primary audience, elite Romans) through diversified corporate representations.

5.1. Irrefutable Holy Heroes: Israelite Representation in Jubilees

The ethical imperatives of Jub. 30 rest on the representation of Israel as a holy and chosen nation, which is established from the beginning of Jubilees and regularly reiterated. This identity is asserted from heaven as a nonnegotiable truth. Unlike in Genesis, where the chosenness of Abram (and by extension his descendants) seems abrupt and barely rationalized,[145]

---

142. Arguably, as the section on Jubilees' influence below addresses, Jubilees' shaping work on its Judean contemporaries was more powerful than *Antiquities*' work on its Judean contemporaries, as *Antiquities* was not "taken up" by Judeans as authoritative based on the current evidence. Although Josephus wrote for Roman elites rather than Judeans, both histories sought to shape the ethical outlook of their primary audiences, in part through the representation of Israelites and others in their narratives.

143. Richter, "Review of *Narrative Ethics*," 249.

144. I discuss the influence of Jub. 30 on Second Temple period thought and literature below.

145. In Genesis, there is no explanation before the Lord says to Abram, "Go from your land and your kindred and your father's house and go to the land that I will

in Jubilees, the chosenness of the people of Israel who descend from Abraham is preordained and declared at creation. Just after the Sabbath day is established, the Lord says to his angels, "I will now separate a people for myself among the nations. They, too, will keep the Sabbath. I will sanctify a people for myself and I will bless them.... They will be my people and I will be their God. I have chosen the seed of Jacob as a treasured people out of all the nations" (Jub. 2.19–20). Thus, the declarations of the nation's holy status made in Exod 19:5–6 or Deut 7:6 as part of the postliberation giving of the covenant were declared first, according to Jubilees, at creation.[146] Belonging to Israel is represented as an identity with a very clear boundary drawn by familial descendancy. The descendants, or "seed," of Jacob are holy, set apart for God, right from the start.[147]

In Jubilees, this concept of genealogical purity applies to not only the priests and Levites but for all Israel.[148] As the declaration at creation and

---

show you" (Gen 12:1). His call is seemingly random, and there is no backstory for Abram before the age of seventy-five, other than his inclusion in the genealogy from Shem to Terah and the matter of settling in Haran under the leadership of his father (Gen 11:31). However, in Gen 26:4–5 YHWH tells Isaac, "I will multiply your seed/offspring like the stars of the heavens, and to your seed/offspring I will give all these lands. And all the nations of the earth will bless themselves by/through your seed/offspring *because* Abraham obeyed [עקר אשר־שמע] my voice and he observed by charge, my commandments, my statutes, and my instructions." Though this does not give a reason for the initial choosing of Abram (yet it could be read as such), it announces that Abraham and his offspring through Isaac will be so blessed *because of* the obedience of Abraham.

146. Exod 19:5–6: "Now, if you surely obey my voice and keep my covenant, you will be my treasured possession among all the peoples, for all the earth is mine. And you shall be for me a kingdom of priests and a holy nation." Deut 7:6: "For you are a holy people of YHWH your God. YHWH your God has chosen you to become a people for his treasured possession from all the peoples that are upon the face of the earth." This idea of being chosen for holiness before the foundation of the world is also found in Eph 1:1–3.

147. The idea of a holy seed is first attested in Isa 6:13 to describe God's faithful remnant that survives judgment and developed in postexilic times as a literal, biological concept of genealogical purity. For the Ezran development and concept of holy seed and genealogical purity in other Second Temple period literature, see Christine Hayes, "Impurity, Intermarriage, and Conversion in Second Temple Sources," in *Gentile Impurities and Jewish Identities: Intermarriage and Conversion from the Bible to the Talmud* (Oxford: Oxford University Press, 2002), 68–91.

148. As in Ezra 9:2, 10:5. Leviticus 21:6–15 contains instructions on the marriage requirements of members of the priesthood. Only a virgin from among the people is

various exhortations throughout the work (e.g., Jub. 16.24–29, 22.10–18, 25.2–18, 32.19) make clear, this "holy seed" is Jacob and his descendants. Jubilees records a heavenly announcement to Abraham while Sarah is pregnant with Isaac: "We blessed him and told him everything that had been commanded for him.... One of Isaac's sons would become a holy seed and would not be counted among the nations, for he would become the portion of the Most High" (Jub. 16.16–18).[149] The holiness of Jacob and his seed is God-given in Jubilees but tentative, which supplies tension and imperative force to the events and pronouncements of chapter 30. As noted, this holiness involves election and chosenness, arbitrarily announced at creation. Yet holiness also contains an element of sharing in the covenant, the character, and the conduct[150] of God: "For [Abraham] knew and ascertained that from him there would come a righteous plant for the history of eternity and (that) from him there would be holy seed *so that they should be like the one who had made everything*" (Jub. 16.26, emphasis added). Yet it is also a conditional position. Holy things can become common. One way in which this happens is through defilement.[151]

The threat of the loss of holiness and the consequences (destruction) are ubiquitous in Jubilees. Throughout the narratives, and in the several blessings and exhortations of the patriarchs—and matriarch, in the case of Rebekah—what defiles the holy people or the holy seed is made explicit. According to Jubilees, defilement chiefly happens as a result of sexual sin.[152] Indeed, other than in regards to Sabbath keeping (in Jub. 2) or childbirth

---

acceptable for a priest to marry, lest he "profane his seed" (Lev 21:16) with a widow, a divorcée, a defiled woman, or a prostitute. These injunctions are given in the context of concern for keeping the sanctuary holy, and ritual purity is likely the issue here. For other male Israelites would not be defiled and their seed would not be profaned if they married a widow from among their own people; indeed, the injunction to do so is found in the laws of levirate marriage (Deut 25:5–10).

149. This is my translation of the Ethiopic text.

150. This conduct includes the keeping of the holy days and festivals ordained in heaven, including the keeping of Sabbath. God and the angels keep Sabbath, and part of Israel's set-apartness is that they might keep the Sabbath with God (Jub. 2.19–22).

151. Christine Hayes, "Intermarriage and Impurity in Ancient Jewish Sources," *HTR* 92 (1999): 5–6.

152. Working on or defiling the Sabbath results in death (2:25–28), and the one who keeps Sabbath remains holy (2:28), though there is no explicit implication that Sabbath defilement also defiles the defiler.

purity laws (Jub. 3), every other mention of defilement in Jubilees is in regard to sexual transgression.[153] Defilement by sexual transgression is found in the account of the prediluvian Watchers (Jub. 4.22) and the transgressions of Sodom, Gomorrah, and Zeboim (16.5), both of which result in God-given judgment.

Defilement by sexual sin is also found in Reuben's unlawful taking of Bilhah (Jub. 33.7–9).[154] The event is clearly depicted as an unsolicited sexual assault—the woman was asleep (33.4)! Sadly, it is the victim, Bilhah, who is "defiled" by Reuben's transgression, though "the man" who commits such a sin (sleeping with his father's wife, not rape necessarily) is also declared "despicable and impure" (33.14). Indeed, the angel of the presence says the transgression is so severe that it has been written *twice* in the "heavenly tablets" that correspond to Lev 21:11 and Deut 27:20: "It is written and ordained ... that a man is not to sleep with his father's wife and that he is not to uncover the covering of his father because it is impure" (Jub. 33.10).[155] Discussion of defiling acts and defilement finds its richest concentration in Jub. 30.[156] The interaction with the Shechemites becomes the occasion for the expounding of the laws of sexual transgression through

---

153. One exception may be found in the ambiguous phrase of Jub. 23.21, "They will defile the holy things [or holy ones] of the holy one with the impure corruption of their contamination." This may point to the defilement of the temple in preexilic or even postexilic times, depending on the reading. However, when read in light of Jub. 30.15, this too likely refers to exogamy; Jub. 30.15 equates the intermarriage with foreigners as defilement of "the Lord's sanctuary," and "the entire nation will be condemned together because of all this impurity and contamination."

154. In Gen 35:22, "Reuben went and lay with Bilhah, his father's concubine," and Jacob reprimands him in 49:4, declaring, "You went up from your father's couch, then you profaned it—he went up on my bed!"

155. This impurity, Jubilees' heavenly messenger declares, is imputed to the man and woman involved, and they are sentenced to death (Jub. 33.10). Concession is made for both Reuben and Bilhah in this tragic case, however. Apparently, Reuben did not know better because the law was not yet given (33.15), though any other man "who commits it in Israel will not be allowed to live a single day on the earth because he is despicable and impure" (33.14). Bilhah's victimhood is not explicitly dealt with in the chapter, but she carries no guilt, even though she is forced to carry the burden of impurity. She is "defiled" by Reuben's act, and thus Jacob refrains from sexual relations with her for the rest of their lives so as not to be rendered impure as well (33.9), yet she is allowed to live.

156. "Defilement" or "defiling" is mentioned twice in chapter 2 (Sabbath), once in chapter 3 (childbearing purity laws), once in chapter 4 (the Watchers), once in chapter

sex or intermarriage with non-Israelites and the consequential defilement of the holy seed of Israel.

While Jub. 30 mentions exogamy to be for an Israelite the equivalent of "giving one of his seed to Molech," a Canaanite deity, the chief issue is the defilement of the holy seed of Israel. As Christine Hayes states, "In Jubilees, the holy seed is not only made profane by mixing with the seed of the Gentile but also is defiled by the immoral act of [illicit] sexual union. Intermarriage is *zenut*, a sin that generates a moral impurity that defiles the holy seed of Israel and indeed the entire house of Israel."[157] Jubilees' injunctions against intermarriage are founded on the biblical laws banning intermarriage with the seven Canaanite nations in Exod 34:15–16, Deut 7:16, and 20:18, where the chief concern is practicing "abominations" and worshiping other gods.[158] Jubilees heightens the biblical mandates found in these Torah laws and in Ezra's extension of them (Ezra 9:1 adds Ammonites, Moabites, and Egyptians to the list of banned nations) by banning intermarriage with people from *any* other nation.

In contrast to their divided representation in Gen 34, Israel in Jub. 30 is represented as a unified group, in emotion and perception. In Gen. 34:5, Jacob keeps silent and his thoughts are unknown to the reader when he hears that "[Shechem] had defiled Dinah his daughter," but when his sons hear, "They were deeply grieved and it angered them greatly, because

---

21 (holy things, sanctuary), three times in chapter 33 (Reuben/Bilhah incident), and ten times in chapter 30.

157. Hayes, "Intermarriage and Impurity," 21.

158. Leviticus 18 lists unlawful sexual relations that the Canaanites partake in (Lev 18:24) and instructs Israel to refrain from them. In the injunctions against these practices, purity and defilement are presented as a central concern, and the consequences are severe: "Do not become defiled with all these things, for with all these things the nations that I am driving out before you have become defiled.... For anyone who does any of these abominations, those who do them will be cut off from among their people" (Lev 18:24–29). Louis Epstein argues that the biblical concern for purity here is of a moral rather than a ritual kind. See Epstein, *Marriage Laws in the Bible and Talmud* (Cambridge: Harvard University Press, 1942). Hayes makes the compelling case that "an alleged Gentile ritual impurity communicated by physical contact to the Israelite partner is not the rationale for restrictions on intermarriage in the biblical, Second Temple, and rabbinic periods," but the contamination comes from the moral impurity or contamination from the sin of זנות, any illegal sexual union (Hayes, "Intermarriage and Impurity," 5). These sources differ, however, on what defines זנות. For Jubilees, any Israelite sexual union with a non-Israelite (or non-Judean, by temporal extension) is illicit and defiling.

he did an outrageous thing in Israel by sleeping with a daughter of Jacob" (Gen 34:7). The narrator of Jubilees collapses this difference, and *both* Jacob and his sons are angry at the offense. After Shechem comes to beg Jacob and his sons to allow him to marry Dinah, "Jacob and his sons were angry with the Shechemites because they had defiled their sister Dinah" (Jub. 30.3). In Genesis, Jacob keeps his silence until the very end, and it is "the sons of Jacob" who engage in negotiations "with deceit" (Gen 34:13); they alone are responsible for the plan to weaken and annihilate the men of the city. In contrast, Jub. 30.3 describes the collective action of "Jacob and his sons": "*They* spoke deceptively with [the Shechemites], acted in a crafty way toward them, and deceived them" (emphasis added). While it is still only Simeon and Levi who do the slaying, everyone is unified in their choice to deceive the Shechemites. Jacob's final rebuke to Simeon and Levi in Gen 34:30 indicates his displeasure with their choice of action:[159] "You have ruined me by making me stink among the inhabitants of the land, among the Canaanites and Perizzites!"

It is coupled with a concern for the entirety of his family clan: "I am few in number and they will gather against me and attack me and I will be destroyed, I and my house" (Gen 34:30). In Jubilees, this outrage is mitigated by the narrator's presentation of the content of his speech: "He spoke with them about the fact that they had killed a city because he was afraid of the people who were living in the land—of the Canaanites and Perizzites" (Jub. 30.25).

By removing the force of the outrage expressed though Jacob's direct speech and by eliminating Jacob's testament of displeasure found in Gen 49:5–7,[160] Jubilees erases any indication that he is in disagreement with

---

159. This is further supported by his later curse of their anger in Gen 49:5–7 (see ch. 2, §5.5.3).

160. Jubilees 45.13–16 contains an account of Jacob's death and last testament to his sons: "Israel lived for 17 years in the land of Egypt. All of the time that he lived was three jubilees—147 years. He died during the fourth year of the fifth week of the forty-fifth jubilee. Israel blessed his sons before he died. He told them everything that would happen to them in the land of Egypt; and he informed them (about) what would happen to them at the end of time. He blessed them and gave Joseph two shares in the land. He slept with his fathers and was buried near his father Abraham in the double cave in the land of Canaan—in the grave that he had dug for himself in the double cave in the land of Hebron. He gave all his books and the books of his fathers to his son Levi so that he could preserve them and renew them for his sons until today." Every major patriarch from Noah to Isaac, and even Rebekah the matriarch, has a lengthy

his sons about their violent retribution. All that is conveyed is that he is afraid of potential backlash from their neighbors.[161] Although it is Simeon and Levi who draw their swords, Jacob plays a part in the deception of all the Shechemites that leads to their destruction. Thus, in Jub. 30, Jacob and sons are represented as being of one mind regarding Dinah's defilement and in their choice of action against the Shechemites.

By representing a unified Israel in a way that removes the generational divide of Gen 34 and by lauding the collective Israelite responses with the voice of heaven, Jub. 30 eliminates any room for dialogue or dissension while casting Israel in the role of God's agents of retribution. There is no arguing with a heavenly decree in the world that Jubilees constructs, and heaven praises the violence done by Jacob's sons as carrying out the Lord's will: "The punishment had been decreed against them in heaven that they were to annihilate all the Shechemites with the sword, since they had done something shameful in Israel. The Lord delivered them [the Shechemites] into the hand of Jacob's sons so that they may uproot them with the sword and so that they may enact punishment against them" (Jub. 30.5–6).[162] Furthermore, the one voice in Genesis that argues against the course of violence is, as shown above, brought into agreement with the narrator's monological interpretation of this event.

Here we see the danger of this story as an authoritative origin story of Israel, for it not only "calls the nation to violence toward other groups of people"[163] but also eliminates both the presence and the validity of any other points of view. Howard Brody and Mark Clark in "Narrative Ethics: A Narrative" raise caution against these kinds of dangerous stories: "Stories that call us to violence towards other groups of people and simultaneously make it seem disloyal to seek other points of view are extreme examples of bad stories that are commonly used to justify war and genocide."[164] Brody and Clark write in terms of "good" or "bad" stories here, but I prefer Frank's

---

testamental speech delivered to their children. Jacob's specific words, however, are hidden behind the narrator's presentation of this moment like they are in chapter 30.

161. This fear is immediately dismissed as unnecessary, for "a fear of the Lord was in all the cities which were around Shechem. They did not set out to pursue Jacob's sons because terror had fallen on them" (Jub. 30.26; cf. Gen 35:5).

162. This is a composite translation of VanderKam's (30.5) and my own (30.6).

163. Howard Brody and Mark Clark, "Narrative Ethics: A Narrative," HCRSR 44 (2014): S9.

164. Brody and Clark, "Narrative Ethics," s9.

terminology of *danger*, as it implies potentiality of threat rather than communicating an absolute binary. Frank writes in terms of a continuum of more- or less-dangerous stories:

> Some fairly obvious qualities of less-dangerous stories includ[e] openness to more stories; depiction of characters who acknowledge mistakes and work to set things right; making heroes of characters who cooperate; and giving antagonists names, faces, and purposes that cannot be immediately dismissed. Less-dangerous stories make the world and actions *more* complicated.[165]

Genesis 34 is thus comparatively a *less* dangerous story. It ends in dialogue, in an unanswered question that beckons the reader to deliberate and evaluate between the perspectives and actions presented by the diverse cast of characters. Jubilees 30, however, has all the answers, backed by heavenly authority, and the reader's role is to accept the indoctrination. To dissent is to disobey God. This becomes a dangerous story, then, for those who accept its authority and for those who reject it. For those who accept, acts of war and genocide are justified for those who identify as Israel, justified as doing the will of God. For those who dissent, who would want to find a compromise or seek punishment only for the individual offender, there is no room in Israel or heaven for such opinions.

5.2. Irredeemable Villains: Shechemite Representation in Jubilees

It is not only Israel who is chiseled into a monolithic entity; the Shechemites are condensed into a faceless mob of evildoers. Jubilees 30 removes the diversity represented among the mostly male cast of Shechemites in Gen 34, representing the whole city—men, women, and children—as equally guilty of sin and deserving of capital punishment. In Genesis, the Shechemites are composed of differing individuals and groups. Shechem, the son of Hamor, is a distinct figure in Gen 34, acting alone in his seeing, taking, lying with, and thus debasing Dinah (34:2). His desires and pas-

---

165. Frank, *Letting Stories Breathe*, 159. Hanna Meretoja echoes this destabilization of the assessment of narratives in binary terms: "The ethically crucial question is not whether narratives are 'good' or 'bad,' but rather how individuals and communities use, perpetuate, and transform cultural narrative practices to construct their identities, interpret their experiences, and engage with those of others" (*Ethics of Storytelling*, 143–44).

sions are made known to the audience; he longs for Dinah and desperately wants to marry her, whatever the cost (34:3, 12–13). Hamor, his father, through acts of speech, is presented as obliging to his son's demands, while (selfishly or otherwise) making the economic best of the situation for everyone, Israelite and Shechemite, at least as his words would have them believe (34:8–10, 20–23). The Shechemite men, having nothing to do with the young Shechem's actions—indeed, it is unclear whether they are aware of what transpired at all—agree to undergo circumcision in the hopes of intermarriage and economic gain (34:20–24). In Genesis, the women and children of the town have no role in the deliberations. In Jub. 30, however, these distinct persons and groups are distilled into one mass of "sinners" (Jub. 30.23). The young Shechem is not alone in his crime against Dinah, but all of the Shechemites are to blame, since "they snatched Dinah, daughter of Jacob, away to the house of Shechem" (Jub. 30.2).[166]

This representation of the Shechemites as a collective unified in both malice and guilt garners support for their ultimate annihilation. In Gen 34, Simeon and Levi kill Shechem, Hamor, and all the male Shechemites who had undergone circumcision but leave the women and children to be captured by their brothers. In Jubilees, no survivors are left; rather, "Simeon and Levi entered Shechem unexpectedly and effected a punishment on all the Shechemites. They killed every man whom they found in it. They left absolutely no one in it. They killed everyone in a painful way because they had defiled[167] their sister Dinah" (Jub. 30.4). Jubilees allows for no conception of an innocent Shechemite, no matter the age, station, or gender. This indeed is a central instruction of "the testimony" in the words of the angel: "Observe how it turned out for the Shechemites and their children, how they were handed over to Jacob's two sons. They killed them in a painful way. It was a just act for them and was recorded as a just act for them" (30.17). The even *more* exorbitant violence of Jacob's sons in Jubilees is presented as following heaven's own decree: "The punishment had been decreed against them in heaven that they were to annihilate all the Shechemites with the sword, since they had done something shameful in Israel" (30.5).

---

166. See notes in the translation above. Thus, following the pattern mentioned above, the perspective of the sons of Jacob in Gen 34 is affirmed by the angelic narrator of Jubilees; Gen 34:27 states the motive for the Jacob's sons' plundering of the city, "because *they* had defiled their sister."

167. See notes in the translation above.

Whether Simeon and Levi's choice to annihilate the entire city was the right course of action is not in question. The angel of the presence makes it repeatedly clear (30.6, 17–20, 23) that God approved their actions and that all of heaven celebrates them "at all times of the year" (30.20). Any suspicion of excess is denied by the declaration, "On the day that Jacob's sons killed Shechem, a written notice was entered in heaven for them that they had carried out what was right, justice, and revenge, against the sinners. It was recorded as a blessing" (30.23). In this re-presentation of Gen 34, the offense of the one is transferred to the many. Shechem in Jubilees is no longer an individual but a conglomerate of "sinners." The entire people group is represented as collectively responsible for Dinah's rape and defilement, and violence against them all is not only justifiable but praised.

The Shechemites are further vilified by their familial association with Canaan, son of Ham, their direct ancestor in the genealogy of Gen 10:15–18 (and implicitly understood in Jubilees). In Jubilees, the peoples descended from Canaan (including the Shechemites, who are Hivites; see Gen 10:17[168]) are especially singled out as inherently worthy of destruction due to the curse on them "and their ways" (Jub. 22.21–22). All of "Canaan's seed," and thus every person from among his descendants, is "destined for uprooting from the earth" because of the curse that Canaan received (22.20–21). Canaan's curse in Jubilees is far less arbitrary than the one Noah pronounces on him in Gen 9, where it is seemingly punishment for the offense of his father, Ham.[169] In Jub. 8–9, a backstory is given that justifies and intensifies the curse on Canaan and all his descendants: When the earth was divided in the presence of an authorizing angel, an account of the division was written and thus deemed authoritative and binding by heaven. In addition, a declaration went out, a curse on any who would violate the boundaries set for them:

---

168. This connection is not explicitly found in Jubilees but assumed, as all the inhabitants of Canaan are supposed to be descendants of Canaan who stole the land allotted to Seth (Jub. 10.29–34).

169. See Justin Reed, "The Injustice of Noah's Curse and the Presumption of Canaanite Guilt" (paper presented at the Annual Meeting of the Society of Biblical Literature, November 2020). See also Reed, "The Injustice of Noah's Curse and the Presumption of Canaanite Guilt: A New Reading of Genesis 9:18–29" (PhD diss., Princeton University, 2020).

In this way Noah's sons divided (the earth) for their sons before their father, Noah. He made (them) swear by oath to curse each and every one who wanted to occupy the share that did not emerge by his lot. All of them said, "so be it." So be it for them and their children until eternity during their generations until the day of judgment on which the Lord God will punish them with the sword and fire because of all the evil impurity of their errors by which they have filled the earth with wickedness, impurity, fornication, and sin. (Jub. 9.14–15)

Despite this deadly warning, Canaan transgresses.[170] Rather than traveling out to occupy his allotted land in northwest Africa, he stops on Shem's plot, spanning from Lebanon to Egypt, and, finding it "very beautiful," he decides to settle in it (10.29). Although his father and brothers warn him, reminding him of the curse he is choosing to receive by this action of illegitimate occupation,[171] "he did not listen to them" (10.33). As a result of this curse, every Canaanite descendant throughout all of history is doomed to destruction. The Shechemites, therefore, were condemned to destruction whether or not they chose to attack, rape, or defile. They are

---

170. The account in Jub. 10.35–36 of the negotiations between Madai, son of Japheth, and Elam, Asshur, and Arpachshad, the sons of Shem, serves as a foil to Canaan's actions. Here Madai was displeased with his own lot and entered into negotiations with his kinsmen to acquire some of their land as his own inheritance. No curse results, for the taking happened as a result of negotiations between two willing parties. Canaan did not negotiate with Shem but rather took the land illegally. This contrast further taints Canaan as being unreasonable and deserving of punishment.

171. "His father Ham and his brothers, Cush and Mizraim said to him, 'You have settled in a land that was not yours and did not emerge for us by lot. Do not act this way, for if you act this way both you and your children will fall in the land and be cursed with dissension and in dissension your children will fall and be uprooted forever. Do not settle in Shem's residence because it emerged by their lot for Shem and his sons. You are cursed and will be cursed more than all of Noah's children through the curse by which we obligated ourselves with an oath before the Holy Judge and before your father Noah'" (Jub. 10.30–32). This story also, of course, serves to justify the Israelite claim to the land of Canaan. As per this tradition recorded in Jubilees, it was allotted to them by Noah and by God from ancient times. The land was Shem's territory, and thus the declarations for their extermination and disinheritance in Joshua's generation are justified. Canaan knew full well what he was doing, what he did was wrong, and the punishment on his descendants and the later Israelite occupation of the land is therefore just. As in the indictment of Lot and thus all Ammonites and Moabites, unproblematic to Jubilees is the cursing and damnation of a whole people group for the sins of just one of their ancestors.

depicted as inherently guilty from birth, guilty *of being Canaanite*, a crime punishable by death.

This collective representation of the Shechemites as impermeably other, defiled and defiling, and inherently guilty on account of their genealogical descent has dangerous consequences for the audience who accepts the authority of such a representation and is willing to have their perceptions shaped by it. A cultural group is cast into a role in which they are bad and do bad; they are emplotted as irredeemable villains from birth. The postexilic narrative of Ezra shows the dangers of casting one's contemporary neighboring cultures into the roles offered to them by one's history. Both biblical and extrabiblical sources suggest that the mid-fourth-century BCE inhabitants were either descendants of exiled Judeans who had returned to the land, descendants of the motley collection of conquered peoples who were settled in the land by Assyria after Northern Israel's fall in 722 BCE, or were descendants of the poorest of Judeans, left behind by the Babylonian king Nebuchadnezzar.[172] Yet Ezra and his contemporaries cast their neighbors into the roles that the Book of the Law of Moses offered, calling them "the Canaanites, the Hittites, the Perizzites, the Jebusites … and the Amorites" (Ezra 9:1–2), all peoples with whom nascent Israel was forbidden to intermarry in Exodus and Deuteronomy.[173] The result was a mass divorce ceremony and banishment of a hundred or more women and children from the nascent postexilic community (Ezra 10:18–44). This is but one example of how representation in historical narrative has the power to shape collective identity and action. When the dominant public narrative represents

---

172. Second Kings 17:24–41 depicts the repopulation of the Northern Kingdom by Assyria after the deportation of tens of thousands of its Israelite citizens, which is paralleled in the annals of Assyrian King Sargon II (*ANET*, 284–85). Second Kings 24:12 suggests that the only people left in the conquered land of Judah after Nebuchadnezzar's destruction of Jerusalem and death or deportation of the nobility were "the poorest people of the land."

173. For a study of how the Ezran community may have arrived at their policies of familial expulsion through legal exegesis, see Michael Fishbane, *Biblical Interpretation in Ancient Israel* (Oxford: Clarendon, 1988), 114–21. Fishbane mentions but does not theorize on "the parallelism" that Ezra "draws … between the impurities of the autochthonous Canaanites and those of the contemporary 'peoples of the land'" (119). He does, however, explore the exegetical moves that likely led the Ezran community to associate Ammonites and Moabites with the seven Canaanite nations with whom Deut 7 prohibits intermarriage (114–21).

other nations or people groups as inherently villainous or irredeemably bad—as are the Canaanites in Deuteronomy and the Shechemites in Jub. 30—lines for deliberation or compromise with all who become associated with those identities are broken. Consequently, violence or warfare becomes the only justifiable course of action.[174] The whole group or nation can be blamed for any offense of the individual or the few, and retributive violence paid out to any who share the identity of the offending other is legitimized by this logic.[175]

Furthermore, the strong line drawn between holy, pure Israel and profane, impure others would naturally have negative implications for children of mixed descent among second- and first-century BCE Judeans who accepted the authority of Jubilees. The issue of intermarriage with Canaanites in particular is one of such momentous severity that to intermarry with the Canaanites is to bind oneself to a ship on fire and destined for utter destruction. Abraham warns Jacob, "Do not marry from the seed of Canaan, because all of his seed is destined for uprooting from the earth!" (Jub. 22.20). As noted above, Jub. 30 extends this imperative to include a ban from marrying *any*one of *any* other nation, for similar reasons; they will defile the holy seed, and thus all who engage in sexual relations with foreigners, or allow their children to do so, are accused with defiling the seed and are sentenced to death, and "there is no remission or any forgiveness" (Jub. 30.7–10). This labels any children ("seed") born of such unions as defiled, a threat to the community of Israel, and destined for destruction, since "Israel will not become clean from this impurity while it has one of the foreign women or if anyone has given one of his daughters to

---

174. In studying twentieth-century public narratives about conflict, Philip Smith discovered that there was a strong correspondence between villainizing, "apocalyptic" depictions of other nations or groups and war: "When radical evil is afoot in the world there can be no compromise, no negotiated solution, no prudent efforts to effect sanctions or to maintain a balance of power. This evil is so absolute that there is no possibility for trust or for upward conversion of the bad … in consequence that evil must be destroyed" (*Why War?*, 27). He uses the term *apocalyptic* in a modern sense to depict a genre that features "radical evil vs. fundamental good in a supernatural setting" (26).

175. Middle Eastern and south Asian citizens and immigrants dwelling in America after the September 11, 2001, attacks knew this all too well, as American neighbors turned against them and hate crimes were rampant in 2001. FBI statistics on hate crimes report that although anti-Muslim hate crimes have decreased since 2001, their frequency has never returned to pre-2001 levels. See "Muslims in America after 9/11, Part II," 9/11 Memorial and Museum, https://tinyurl.com/SBL6710b.

any foreign man.... The entire nation will be condemned together because of all this impurity and this contamination" (Jub. 30.14–15). As the heavenly sentence for such unions is death by stoning (Jub. 30.8–9), violence against children of exogamous unions could thus be legitimized.

Though Jub. 30 is a story of Israel's past, reshaped and re-presented to a mid-second-century BCE audience, it explicitly promotes the validity of the representations it presents, authorizing them with heaven's voice, and offers models of behavior through the actions of its heroes. Simeon and Levi are the unquestionable heroes of this narrative and the ethical exemplars for the audience. Pitilessness and genocide are authorized actions, praised by the heavenly narrator. A narrative so cast can be read to validate any exaction of "justice" through means of violence. Indeed, to kill the other, whether their offense is legitimate or they are guilty by association, is to do the will of God. Like Ezra cast his contemporary other into the role of the Canaanite that his history offered, Jubilees' second-century BCE Judean audience is primed by *this* narrative to cast any people or group of people from other nations living in their promised land into the role of Shechemite. The injunctions of Jub. 30 already paint all of the non-Israelite nations with the same color; they are foreigners, people of the nations, and relations with them are forbidden. This collective othering of all people groups perpetuates a strong boundary between the Israelite self and all others.

5.3. Revising History: Josephus's Awareness of Jubilees 30

Josephus's retelling of this story was likely made in awareness of Jubilean traditions about the ancient clash at Shechem, and thus it offers his contemporaries a new, corrective reading of the past. Unfortunately, nothing can be known for certain about the reception of Jub. 30 when it comes to direct textual influence, yet it remains possible that Jubilees' version of Gen. 34 became authoritative in the Second Temple period. Extant literature shows that Jubilees was known and influential among Second Temple period Judean communities.[176] Furthermore, Kugel's careful sleuthing on the "exegetical motifs" that circulated in Jewish antiquity reveals that motifs found in Jub. 30 are peppered throughout the extant literature. These include the ideas that "the whole city was guilty" and that "God

---

176. See VanderKam, *Jubilees: A Commentary*, 98–113.

ordered the destruction."[177] Interestingly, Jubilees' telling is the common denominator of *many* ancient Jewish exegetical motifs that were associated with the story of Dinah and Shechem. The diagram below demonstrates this. Each outer circle contains a heading representing a shared exegetical motif that Kugel has found and the literature in which it is represented. Jubilees 30 is located in the middle, overlapping with the rest, because it depicts every one of these popular motifs.[178] Kugel demonstrates that each of these motifs is reconstructable by bringing together other scriptures with Gen 34,[179] and therefore each of them could be arrived at indepen-

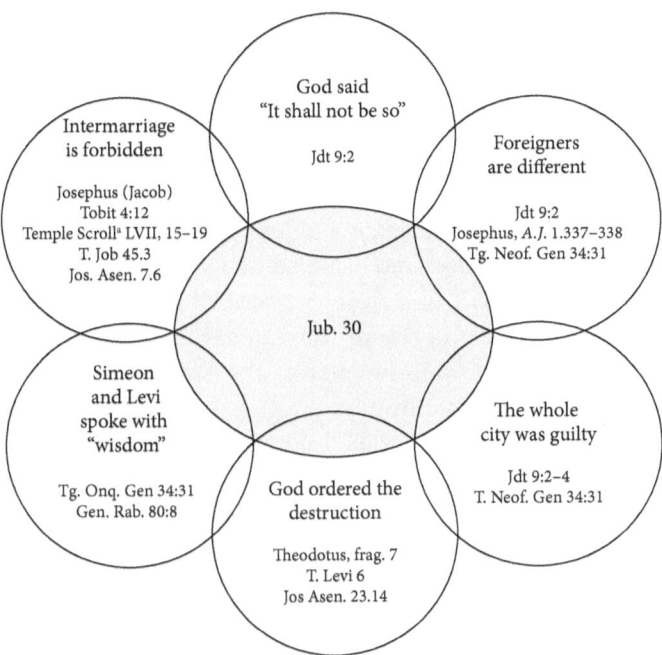

---

177. Kugel, *Traditions of the Bible*. Exegetical motifs of Gen 34 not found in Jubilees but extant in other texts include uncontrolled anger (4 Macc 2:19–20, which relies on Gen 49), Dinah married Job (Testament of Job; Pseudo-Philo; Job Targum; Gen. Rab. 57:4; y. B. Bat. 15:2), Simeon and Levi killed one [man] each (T. Levi 6.4–5; Theodotus, frag. 8; likely a literal reading of Gen 49:6), a sincere proposal (Theodotus, frag. 4; T. Levi 6.3–6), Shechem the nonpeople (T. Levi 7; Sir 50:25–26; likely origins of 2 Kgs 17:24–31), Simeon and Levi were given swords from heaven (Jdt 9:2, T. Levi 5.3, Jos. Asen. 23.14).

178. There are also several places of overlap between Jdt 9 and Tg. Neof. Gen 34.

179. Kugel, *Traditions of the Bible*, 404–35.

dently through an intertextual exegesis of the Torah. Jubilees 30, however, is home to *every one* of these prevailing exegetical motifs. It is highly possible that this re-presentation of Israel's ancestral past had a pervasive influence on its second-century BCE audience and the generations that followed, including that of Josephus.

There is also strong literary evidence suggesting Josephus was aware of the book of Jubilees and even used its contents as source material for his own historical narrative in volumes 1 and 2 of *Judean Antiquities*. Betsy Halpern-Amaru has uncovered "forty-eight instances of parallel exegesis" in the two works' retelling of Genesis, "twenty-eight of which appear in no other known, extant work from the Second Temple period."[180] Some of these parallels, however, can be explained as stemming from shared traditions or sources, either oral or literary. For example, the assertion that all creatures spoke a common language before the exile from Eden is present in Jub. 3.28 and *A.J.* 1.41, 50 as an explanation of the serpent's ability to speak to Eve. This legend of primordial animal speech does not necessitate a direct connection between Jubilees and *Antiquities*, for it was a widespread ancient tradition and can also be found in rabbinic literature, Plato's *Statesman*, the *Iliad*, and Aesop's fables.[181] A similar example is the explicit identification of the site of the Aqedah as the site of the future temple, a common tradition found among the Targumim.

A few striking parallels, however, suggest that Jubilees may have been among Josephus's source material, influencing his presentation of the past. Jubilees is well known for assigning names to many of the unnamed women and wives of Genesis and Exodus; it identifies Pharaoh's daughter and Moses's foster mother as Tarmuth/Thermuthis (Jub. 47.5), an appellation also used by Josephus in *A.J.* 2.224 but found nowhere else.[182] Both texts condense Jacob's final blessing to his sons into a "double-tiered set of predictions" about their descendants in general (Jub. 45.14; *A.J.* 2.194).[183] Both neglect to narrate Jacob's offering of a special piece of clothing to his favored son Joseph, neither mentions matriarchal barrenness, and both

---

180. Betsy Halpern-Amaru, "Flavius Josephus and the Book of Jubilees: A Question of Source," *HUCA* 72 (2001): 15.

181. Louis Ginzberg, *Legends of the Jews* (Philadelphia: Jewish Publication Society, 1969), 5:94 n. 58; Halpern-Amaru, "Flavius Josephus," 27.

182. Halpern-Amaru, "Flavius Josephus," 23.

183. Halpern-Amaru, "Flavius Josephus," 30. Also noted in Kugel, *Traditions of the Bible*, 468–69.

share a series of narrative additions and exegetical harmonizations. Halpern-Amaru admits that the "number and variety" of affinities between the two works can be explained by other shared sources, no longer extant, or by a "common pool or store of traditions" that both authors drew from. "However, the simplest, and by Ockham's razor the most credible, explanation for the affinities is that Josephus, like his contemporaries, the sectarians at Qumran, was familiar with the *Book of Jubilees*."[184] Whether or not Josephus had a copy in hand while writing his history, due to its prevalent influence,[185] it is safe to say that Josephus was aware of Jubilees, or at least aware of the Jubilean presentation of Gen 34, and the impact of its shaping power on his fellow Judeans. In the following sections, I posit that the representation of the Israelites and Shechemites in *A.J.* 1.337–341 in some ways offers a corrective to their representations in Jubilees.

5.4. History Repeating Itself: Representation of Israelites in *Judean Antiquities*

In *A.J.* 1.337–341, the family members of Israel are the collective protagonists under threat, but unlike in Jubilees, they are a house divided. First, I suggest that Josephus's representation of the Israelites at Shechem serves less of an apologetic function and instead serves to shape the ethical content of this narrative. Second, the representation of the nascent clan of Israel as divided acts as a corrective to Jubilees' undifferentiated and monological depiction of it. Furthermore, the internal divisions of the Israelites in this ancient episode are paralleled by Josephus with the internal divisions among Judeans in the first century CE. By crafting the depiction of the ancient ancestors in book 1 to parallel his contemporary countrymen in book 20, the event of the past becomes a mirror through which to view the present (or very recent past) and reflect on pressing internal conflicts that, in Josephus's depiction of them, the ancients also shared. Two of these central conflicts were (1) the precarious balance sought by the elders of Galilee and Judea between maintaining peaceful relations with their foreign overlords and adhering to what they considered lawful before God, and (2) the factioning of the populace after an offense by others who shared the land into two camps: those striving to keep the peace and those

---

184. Halpern-Amaru, "Flavius Josephus," 44.
185. "The book of Jubilees is arguably the most important and influential of all the books written by Jews in the closing centuries BCE" (Kugel, "Jubilees," 272).

in favor of violent retribution. Finally, I propose that A.J. 20.118–136, Josephus's account of first-century conflicts between Samarians and Judeans, evinces an influence of Gen 34 in Josephus's re-presentation of events and people from his own time.

5.4.1. Representation as Shaping the Ethical Content of A.J. 1.337–341

Interpreters often note that the element of deceit is lacking in *Judean Antiquities*' representation of the Israelites in Gen 34. Although others argue that Josephus made this omission for apologetic purposes, when we set aside the focus of whatever hidden agenda the historical Josephus may have harbored, the effects of this omission on the content of the story become more apparent. The Israelites as a whole, including the faction of Simeon and Levi, are not depicted as speaking deceitfully to their Shechemite neighbors. In fact, there are no marriage negotiations here, true or feigned, and no voluntary circumcision among the Shechemite males, simply a request of the king and a period of internal deliberation. The omission of these elements, of course, would be known only to those familiar with the Genesis account. Josephus, however, frames his *Antiquities* as being aimed at an audience curious about "the Hebrew writings" but not necessarily having access to them on their own, an audience in need of a worthy transmitter of Judean tradition (A.J. 1.8–13, 17).

Modern interpreters, honing in on Josephus's seemingly empty promise to "neither add nor omit anything" from the Hebrew Scriptures (A.J. 1.17), argue that the omission of deceit in the re-presentation of Gen 34 is centrally a tactic of apologetics. Christopher Begg, for example, considers the omission of Jacob's sons' "fraudulent demand" (that the Shechemite males be circumcised) to be primarily buffering the public image of the ancestors. Begg lists this as one of several omissions in A.J. 1.27–2.200 that eliminates "problematic" or "unedifying" behavior, or the "failings of the ancestors."[186] Feldman similarly highlights changed details of Jacob's deceit of his father Isaac (A.J. 1.267–275; cf. Gen 27), claiming that "the deception practiced on Isaac is minimized" because "it is only Jacob's arm that is covered by a goat skin, and he is not dressed in Esau's choice garments [as in Gen 27:15]."[187] Granted, details are changed, yet the event is not; Jacob still deceives his

---

186. Begg, "Genesis in Josephus," 312–13.
187. Feldman, *Judean Antiquities 1–4*, 106 n. 810.

blind father, Isaac, and receives the blessing of Esau, the firstborn.[188] If depicting the ancestors as deceitful was a regular aversion of Josephus, why is it not omitted in Abraham's dealings with Pharaoh (*A.J.* 1.162), or when Jacob's sons deceive him with the bloody clothing of their little brother Joseph, whom they have just sold into slavery (*A.J.* 2.35)?

Elsewhere, Josephus has no qualms about depicting the failings of the premonarchical ancestors. While certain figures, such as Joseph and Moses, are admittedly cloaked with perfection as moral exemplars (*A.J.* 2.40–260, 4.324–331),[189] the ancestors as a whole are hardly perfect. They engage in plans of fratricide (2.18, 33), rebellion against God and against their God-ordained leaders (e.g., 3.295–299, 317), and religious apostasy (5.198). These representations, for better *and* for worse, rather than presenting a flawless ancestry, serve to demonstrate the central thesis of *Judean Antiquities*, that those who attend to God's will will prosper, while those who transgress his laws will face calamity (1.14). So rather than asking, "To what apologetic purpose has the deceit from Gen 34 been removed?" it is more fitting to ask, Without the element of deceit in *Antiquities*' representation of Gen 34, *what is this story about*?

With a minimal plotline and elimination of dialogue, this story centers on the division among the ranks of the Israelites after a family member has been wronged by a foreigner with political power. In *Antiquities*' brief treatment of this story, there are few elements of plot: the attack on and ruining of Dinah by the son of the king, the proposal of the king, the troubled position Jacob finds himself in as a result, the Israelites' stagnant council, the citywide massacre that Simeon and Levi perform alone, and Jacob's shock and anger at their deeds. In strong contrast to their depiction in Jubilees, Josephus represents the nascent clan of Israel as divided. Their leader, Jacob, is in favor of collective deliberation, while a minority group, Simeon and Levi, choose to act on their own with swift violence. The majority of the sons

---

188. Feldman also points to *A.J.* 2.173, where God tells Jacob, "For when you were deprived of the preeminent authority [ἡ ἀρχή] by your father, I granted you this," seemingly indicating God's orchestration behind the deception, thereby providing justification for it (*Judean Antiquities 1–4*, 106 n. 810). That the deception happened, and that it caused grief to Isaac and Esau and problems for Jacob, who had to flee the wrath of his brother, however, is not erased from the narrative.

189. While Moses's killing of the Egyptian in Exod 2 and disobediently striking the rock in the wilderness in Num 20 are omitted in *Antiquities*, the Israelite people's faults receive no such treatment.

follow the leadership of their father, Jacob, who is depicted as torn between what he considers lawful (not marrying foreigners) and the request of the local reigning king. The majority of the sons seemingly share this tension, for when they take counsel together to "deliberate what it was necessary to do," "most were silent, in want of a resolution" (*A.J.* 1.239). As a contrast, in Genesis, although Simeon and Levi are identified as ringleaders, killing the males of the city and arguing with Jacob about it afterward (Gen 34:25, 30–31), *all* the sons of Jacob take part in the deceit[190] and the plundering of Shechem (34:13, 27). In *Antiquities*, the violence is carried out secretly by Simeon and Levi alone. They are a rebellious minority, who did "these things without the consent of their father" (*A.J.* 1.340). After being wronged by a foreign ruler, the leadership and majority are in favor of diplomacy and deliberation, though they arrive at no resolution. A rebellious few take matters into their own hands and respond with violence against not only the criminal offender but his entire city. The righteous leader of Israel, Israel himself, is "astonished at the magnitude" of his sons' actions and "angry" with them (1.341). The horror of the massacre is made known to him when "they brought back their sister." Jacob's shock and anger at this point, however, is not stated in connection to the newfound vulnerability of the clan as a result of Simeon and Levi's actions (a concern expressed in both Gen 34:30 and Jub. 30:25), but Jacob is upset "at the magnitude of what happened" (τὸ μέγεθος τῶν γεγονότων, *A.J.* 1.341). The narrator of *Antiquities* permits Simeon and Levi no words in their defense, yet the divide in the family, as in Gen 34, remains unresolved.

In *A.J.* 1.337–341, Israelite representation serves to shape the identity of the Judean people as composed of diverse perspectives, thus mitigating the dangers of Jubilees' undifferentiated representation. In this way, Josephus keeps the diversity inherent in the source material of Gen 34, though the details of the perspectives and actions of the Israelite protagonists are changed in his telling. Multiple perspectives are acknowledged rather than erased or blended monologically to promote one authorized (and dangerous!) point of view, as Jubilees does. Violent backlash on an entire populace for the offense of one or a few is not the only action or option chosen by the ancients, and it is not heralded as "right—justice and vengeance against the

---

190. Some LXX manuscripts have only "Simeon and Levi" named as the sons who speak deceitfully to Hamor and Shechem. See translation notes in ch. 2.

sinners" as it is by Jubilees' authoritative narrator (Jub. 30.23). Rather, it is the *un*authorized minority that chooses such paths of action.

5.4.2. Past and Present Paralleled: *Antiquities* 1.337-341 and 20.118-136

Josephus parallels the ancient violence at Shechem with a conflict between Judeans and Samarians that happened within his own lifetime. This parallel follows a structural pattern that Mason notes among *Antiquties*'s twenty volumes. Mason argues convincingly that *Antiquities* is organized in a concentric "ring composition," with the conclusion of volume 10 serving as the "central panel" or "fulcrum."[191] Per Bilde had noted before him that the depiction of King Saul in volume 6 parallels that of King Herod in volumes 14-17.[192] Mason found that this was but one of several parallels extant between the first ten and the latter ten volumes of the *Antiquities*, while conceding that these parallelisms are not "strictly ordered," nor do "they necessarily constitut[e] Josephus's chief structuring principle."[193] Nevertheless, they are easily distinguishable through content, style, and vocabulary.

There are several examples in which Josephus links the events of the Second Temple period to preexilic history: The destruction of the temple in volume 10 is paralleled with its rebuilding in volume 11.[194] The "conflicts with various enemies" in volume 9 contrastingly parallels the "peaceful coexistence and the support of foreigners" in the postexilic period of volume 12.[195] The reign of David as the "zenith of the first monarchy" in 7.290-291 is paralleled to the reign of John Hyrcanus as the "zenith of the Hasmonean

---

191. Steve Mason, "Introduction to the *Life* of Josephus," in *Life of Josephus*, FJTC 9 (Leiden: Brill, 2001), xiv; Mason, "Introduction to the *Judean Antiquities*," in *Judean Antiquities, Books 1-4*, FJTC 3 (Leiden, Brill: 2004), xxi. Mason notes that this type of composition has been recognized in other ancient Greek, Roman, and Mesopotamian literature. For example, such ring structure has been employed in each volume of Herodotus's *Histories*. See John L. Myres, *Herodotus: Father of History* (Oxford: Clarendon, 1953), 89-117; Henry Wood, *The Histories of Herodotus: An Analysis of the Formal Structure* (The Hague: Mouton, 1972).

192. Per Bilde, *Flavius Josephus between Jerusalem and Rome: His Life, His Works, and Their Importance* (Sheffield: JSOT Press, 1988), 88.

193. Mason, "Introduction to the *Judean Antiquities*," xxi.
194. Mason, "Introduction to the *Judean Antiquities*," xxi.
195. Mason, "Introduction to the *Judean Antiquities*," xxi.

dynasty" in 13.299–300.[196] Likewise, the presentation of the Judean constitution in volumes 3–4 (including Josephus's claims to its excellence in *A.J.* 3.322; 4.196, 319) is contrastingly paralleled with the Roman constitutional crisis and political turmoil described in *A.J.* 19.221–278.[197]

Volumes 1 and 20 are also paralleled in several ways. In addition to those Mason notes, I posit that this also includes the thematic parallels of strife with other people groups in the land and resulting divisions within the Israelite/Judean populace over what to do in times of conflict. The prologue of 1.1–26 is reiterated in 20.259–268 through Josephus's closing remarks, the two passages serving as the bookends of the composition. Furthermore, certain narratives of volume 1 and volume 20 parallel each other. For example, Mason details the parallels between the conversion of the royal house of Abiadene in 20.17–96 and the "conversion" of Abraham in 1.148 in Chaldea.[198] Both Mesopotamian settings feature the persecution of these protagonists by other Mesopotamians for their divergence of thought and practice from their countrymen (*A.J.* 1.154–157; 20.39, 48) and their miraculous preservation and blessing by God. Both protagonists are also marked by circumcision as a central aspect of their obedience to God. In addition to this close narrative parallel, volumes 1 and 20 also share themes of circumcision and intermarriage between Israelites/non-Israelites and Judeans/non-Judeans (1.192, 277–278, 299, 337–339; 20.34–48, 139, 145–146).[199]

---

196. Mason, "Introduction to the *Life* of Josephus," xxiv.

197. Mason, "Introduction to the *Life* of Josephus," xxiv.

198. This parallel works on several levels of overlap with the ancestors of Genesis. Izates's narrative parallels that of Joseph as well. The Adiabene ruler, the favorite of his father, flees from his murderous brothers, much like Joseph of Genesis (and of *A.J.* 2.2–10), and is blessed and favored in a foreign court (2.91, 20.22–23; see Mason, "Introduction to the *Judean Antiquities*," xxi).

199. These latter two examples (*A.J.* 20.139, 145–146) come from descriptions of intermarriages between two elite Judean women, Drusilla and Bernice, and the foreign kings Azizus King of Emesa and Polemo King of Cicilia, respectively. Josephus reports that the men were required to be circumcised before marriage to the Judean women. *A.J.* 1.192 contains the commandment to Abraham to be circumcised, and Josephus's comment that he aims to explain circumcision in a later work (which eventually took shape as *Against Apion*). *A.J.* 1.277–278 references Isaac and Rebecca's desire that their sons not marry Canaanites (for undisclosed reasons, as in Genesis), and the report that Esau already had. *A.J.* 1.299 contains Laban's lament that his sister Rebecca had gone off to Canaan to be married to Isaac and his resistance to let his

3. The Ethics of Representation

I posit that one of the most dominant thematic parallels between these volumes is that of strife with other inhabitants of the land. In book 1, this is found repeatedly in the ancestors' clashes with Abimelech (1.207–212, 259–262), the Assyrians (1.171–179), and the Shechemites (1.337–341), and in book 20 there are multiple incidents of conflict between Judeans and other peoples also inhabiting or ruling the land—the Philadelphians (20.2-4), Samari(t)ans (20.118-136), Syrians (20.173-178), and Romans (20.252-258 and throughout). In volume 20, Josephus highlights the disagreements that arise between various factions of the Judean populace in regards to what sort of actions to take in response to wrongs and injustices done to them by these various groups. In these highlights, we hear echoes of Josephus's depiction of the Israelites in *A.J.* 1.337–341 as a nation split between leaders in favor of peaceful relations and a faction of men who prefer to take vengeance on their neighboring enemies. For example, in the quarrel with the Philadelphians, the "Judeans of Perea took up arms and destroyed many of the Philadelphians without the consent of their leaders [χωρὶς γνώμης τῆς τῶν πρώτων]" (20.2), just as Simeon and Levi acted, in Josephus's phrasing, "without the consent of their father [δίχα τῆς τοῦ πατρὸς γνώμης]" (1.340). Similarly, when "the Syrians" of Cesarea hurled insults at their Judean neighbors, stone-throwing violence broke out (20.176), sparking a *more* violent response from the Roman occupiers to quell the fighting (20.178). Yet Josephus reports that not all the Judeans took part in the vengeful stone-throwing, for there were "those more forbearing of the Judeans and prominent in dignity," who, like Jacob in Gen 34, "feared for their lives" (*A.J.* 20.178). This "more dignified" faction, instead of resorting to violence, was in favor of forbearance, peace, and a diplomatic solution; they urged the Roman procurator Felix to call off his army and were successful (20.178).

Although factional disagreement among the Judean populace is a thematic feature throughout book 20, Josephus's brief account of Gen 34's events in *A.J.* 1.337–341 is especially paralleled with 20.118–136, which contains his depiction of a violent clash between Samarians[200] and Judeans under the Roman procurator Ventidius Cumanus around 50 CE. As the following paragraphs demonstrate, this parallel is accomplished through

---

daughters leave for that land. In *A.J.* 20.34–48, about King Izates, circumcision is presented as an essential element of male observance of the Judean law that God rewards.

200. Josephus uses *Samaritan* and *Samarian* interchangeably, but in this account in chapter 20, it is most often rendered "Samarian."

key words and elements of plot in addition to the roles played by Judean factions. Previously, I noted the festival setting of Josephus's re-presentation of Gen 34, a somewhat unique element of his depiction of those events (ἑορτή in 1.337, 340). A festival setting is the first link between *A.J.* 1.337–341 and 20.118–136. According to Josephus, Galilean Jews were traveling through a town of Samaria during the time of a festival (ἑορτή): "When they were going down a road of the village called Ginea ... some [Samarians], having joined together for battle, killed many of them" (20.118). This is the first half of the kernel event of the story: an attack on a group of Judeans by a group of Samari(t)ans.[201] Like Shechem's actions in book 1, this attack is the first part of their offense; the second is described as "corruption."

Josephus's use of the verb φθείρω, meaning "to corrupt, to ruin,"[202] in 20.127 and 1.337 links this first-century CE event to the ancient tale of Shechem and Dinah. In *A.J.* 20.119, this offense of corruption is quickly discovered when the leaders of the Galileans choose to operate with respect to Roman authority and take the matter to the procurator Cumanus: "The principal men of the Galileans, having learned of what had been done, went to Cumanus and were urging him to investigate the murder of the ones killed. But he, having been persuaded with money from the Samarians, made little of it" (20.119). Later the Judeans recount this moment by accusing Cumanus of being "corrupted by gifts," using a passive form of φθείρω (20.127). Galilean Jews were harmed while passing through the same region in which Shechem was located, and the attack was coupled with the offense of corruption. The parallels continue beyond the kernel event, for just as in *A.J.* 1.337–341, where the Israelites are depicted as divided about what course of action to take in response to an act of violence from a neighboring people group, so too are the Galileans/Judeans of the first century. Note the contrast between the leaders, or "principal men" (οἱ πρῶτοι), and the indignant who lead others to arms:

> The Galileans, being indignant about this, were persuading the multitude of the Judeans to grasp weapons and cling to freedom, for they were saying slavery was bitter by itself, but this added insult was altogether

---

201. In Josephus's first account of this clash in Samaria, found in *B.J.* 2.232–246, it is one Galilean who is killed (ἀναιρεῖταί τις Γαλιλαῖος, 2.232), sparking the outrage and actions of "many more from Galilee" (2.233).

202. φθείρω can also mean "to destroy" in other contexts.

intolerable. The principal men were trying to pacify them by promising to persuade Cumanus to do justice for the ones killed, but they [the indignant] did not pay attention to them. (*A.J.* 20.120–121)

Undeterred, the angry masses take up weaponry, but not before seeking the aid of a local revolutionary, Eleazar son of Deinaius. Though there is no good reason *not* to give Josephus the benefit of the doubt in recording this man's name truthfully, apart from Dinah of Genesis (spelled *Deina* in every Greek manuscript of *Antiquities*), this is the only other mention of anyone by the name of "Deina" or something containing it in all of *Antiquities*.[203] Whether by bizarre serendipity or authorial intent, the echo of *A.J.* 1.337–341 is heard by the mere mention of this name. Eleazar ben Deinaius joins the vengeful populace and, like Simeon and Levi over a millennium before them, deals out violence to the many for the offense of the few: "Having taken up weapons ... they plundered many villages of the Samarians by lighting them on fire" (20.121). Unlike Simeon and Levi, however, they do not get away with it; the land is no longer ruled by Iron Age Canaanite city-states but dominated by imperial Rome. Cumanus draws up his own force, cavalry from nearby Sebaste and four units of footmen, and after arming the Samarians, he slaughters many Judeans and takes many more captive (20.122).

5.4.3. The Shaping Power of History: Genesis 34 in *Antiquities* 20.118–136

Not only is Josephus's re-presentation of the clash at Shechem shaped to parallel his account of this first-century event in Samaria, but the characterization of Judean groups in 20.118–136 belies the possibility that Gen 34 influenced Josephus's re-presentation of contemporary events and divisions among his fellow Judeans. The evidence for this is the parallels that exist between Josephus's account of the "disturbance" (20.129) in Samaria and the representational elements of Gen 34 not included in *A.J.* 1.337–341. The small group of offended Galileans are paralleled with Simeon and Levi in Gen 34, and the "multitude of Judeans" with their brothers. When the Galileans hear that the Samarians have bribed Cumanus to

---

203. The capture of the same Eleazar ben Deinaius by Felix is later reported in *A.J.* 20.161. The man's name is also found in the parallel account of *B.J.* 2.232–246. In *B.J.* 2.235, Eleazar and his men are described as going throughout Samarian villages, "killing them without sparing any age."

indifference regarding their attack of the travelers, they, like Simeon and Levi in Gen 34:7 (but *not A.J.* 1), are exceedingly outraged. In response, they incite "the multitude" to join them in a retribution against the many for the crimes of the few, just as Simeon and Levi led the charge against the entire Shechemite city for its young prince's offense against their sister but were followed by their brothers, who plundered the city (Gen 34:27–29). The principal men of Jerusalem are likewise paralleled with Jacob in Gen 34. Their fears and pleas to their violent countrymen are echoes of Jacob's concerns voiced in Gen 34:30 (but not in *A.J.* 1.341). Jacob spoke to Simeon and Levi after their massacre at Shechem, "You have ruined me by making me stink among the inhabitants of the land, among the Canaanites and Perizzites! And I am few in number, so if they gather against me and attack me, then I will be destroyed—I and my house!" (Gen 34:30). The leaders from first-century Jerusalem respond to the Galileans and Judeans who rampaged through Samarian towns with a cry that evinces a similar concern for their nation, which they now perceive to be under dire threat (*A.J.* 20.122):

> Now, the principal men by rank and birth of the Jerusalemites, upon seeing what great evils had happened, having put on sackcloth and covered their heads with ashes, believing they [the rebels] were setting the destruction of their fatherland before their eyes, and the temple would be in flames, and the enslavement of themselves and their wives and children, they were urging the rebels in every way to change their thinking and throw down their weapons, to be quiet from now on and depart to their own homes. (*A.J.* 20.123)

The leaders of Jerusalem, like Jacob in Gen 34, are depicted as fearful for the continuance of their nation because of the violence of those lesser in "rank and birth." Their fears are well founded, since the Romans, unlike the Canaanites and Perizzites in Genesis, *did* respond with war. As Jacob had "kept quiet" (Gen 34:5; Heb. החרש, LXX παρεσιώπησεν) as a first response to hearing about Shechem's offense, the leaders of Jerusalem urge their fellow Judeans to "be quiet" (ἠρεμεῖν) and go home. With access only to Josephus's rhetorically constructed narrator, we can never know for certain, but it is possible that he was reading the events and peoples of *his* present in light of Genesis's account of the past. What is determinable is that through his narration in *A.J.* 20.118–136, Josephus parallels the schisms among his contemporary Judeans in the wake of the attack by the Gineans with the ancient Gen 34 schism between father and sons that resulted from Shechem's offense.

5.4.4. Some Conclusions on Israelite Representation in *Antiquities* 1.337–341

Josephus's representation of the Israelites in *A.J.* 1.337–341 served to shape perceptions of Judean identity as essentially divided from the start. Jacob's entrance into Canaan with his children[204] marks the first time any entity called Israel, indeed any*one* called Israel, had entered the land. At this moment, the nascent group finds itself wronged by another dwelling in the land, and their response is divided. The leadership is hard pressed to find a diplomatic solution, while a few renegades decide on their own to respond with violence. This essential identity as a divided nation between a careful leadership and a rash or disobedient populace is further developed in the exodus and wilderness wanderings of books 2–4, when the explicitly virtuous Moses (*A.J.* 4.324–331) must navigate obedience to God and the management of a wayward crowd (2.327–329, 3.11–13). This divide of the people in times of strife with other people groups *in* the land, however, is most richly manifest throughout the turmoil of the first century CE, as depicted in *A.J.* 20. The ways *A.J.* 1.337–341 re-presents the ancient tale from Gen 34 in parallel with the account of clashes between first-century CE Judeans and Samarians in *A.J.* 20.118–136 supports the thesis that Josephus was reshaping the past to reflect the issues and schisms among Judeans in his own time.

5.5. Corrective History? Josephus's Representation of the Shechemites in *Antiquities* 1.337–341

As in Jubilees, the Shechemites depicted in Josephus's history operate as other to the Israelites, but *Antiquities*' differentiation between individuals and groups among the Shechemite others in 1.337–341 seems a welcome corrective to the dangers of Jubilees' representation of them noted above. In *Antiquities*, there is diversity allowed between the rapist offender Shechem, the seemingly benevolent ruler Hamor, and the unwitting, innocent citizens of the city who unexpectedly meet their end. The scope of the

---

204. Jacob's children, in Genesis and *Antiquities*, with the exception of Benjamin, the youngest, were born in Padan-Aram.

analysis below is limited to the representation of Shechemites, including their identification as Canaanites, in book 1 of *Antiquities*. Josephus's representation of Canaanites in the postexodus period, including the divine mandate for their extermination (*A.J.* 4.300) and the conquest narratives in which they meet their end (*A.J.* 5), is worthy of careful attention. Such an extensive project, however, lies beyond the scope of this present investigation. I argue that Josephus allows a range of diversity of character among the Shechemite others that somewhat restores the difference erased by Jubilees. When viewed in isolated comparison to Jub. 30 and in the context of *A.J.* 1, *Antiquities*' representation of the Shechemites acts as a corrective to the dangerous representation of them as inherently evil and deserving of death. Thus, Simeon and Levi's violence against the whole group in retribution for the crime of one becomes delegitimized and problematic rather than heralded as exemplary.

Before attending to the Shechemites' representation in *A.J.* 1.337–341, an overview of book 1's representation of the Canaanites, the people group to which the Shechemites belong (*A.J.* 1.337), is necessary. In book 1 of Josephus's history, leading up to the incident at Shechem, the Canaanites are mentioned in reference to their position in the land promised to Abraham and his descendants and as the "natives" whom the Hebrews disdain and avoid.[205] The patriarchs' dealings with the Canaanite nations are somewhat

---

205. In the historical narrative of *Antiquities*, as in Josephus's sources of Exodus and Deuteronomy, the Canaanites become marked by God for destruction in the postexodus generation to make way for the Israelites to settle. In Exodus and Deuteronomy, this is justified by their practice of "abominations," including child sacrifice, sexual transgression, and worship of other gods (e.g., Deut 20:13–18). It is not until book 5 of the *Antiquities*, however, midway through Joshua's conquest of the land, that they become associated in any way with "strange gods" and "wicked practices" (5.107), thus providing a retrospective legitimization for God's pronouncement against them and imperative for the Israelites to destroy them.

Abraham and Isaac dealt mostly with the inhabitants of Sodom (for Abraham) and with the "Philistines" in Gerar, not with the Canaanites. While Abraham's friendship and allied position to the people of Sodom is depicted (*A.J.* 1.176), it is unclear whether the Sodomites are to be considered Canaanite. This is also the case in the biblical text, stemming from the uncertainty of the boundaries represented by Gen 10:19, which states, "The territory of the Canaanites was from Sidon toward Gerar as far as Gaza, toward Sodom and Gomorrah and Admah and Zeboiim as far as Lasha." Gerar, located southeast of Gaza, is beyond the borders indicated, and the lands of Abimelech, king of Gerar, are labeled "Philistine" (Gen 20:32). The location of Lasha is unknown (therefore the location of the four cities mentioned in relation to the border at Lasha is

ambivalent. Out of the three major patriarchs, Abraham alone has dealings with the Canaanites, and they are minimal but positive. In *A.J.* 1.180, Abraham meets Melchizedek, king of Solyma (Gk. Σόλυμα; cf. Gen 14:18; Heb. שלם). The king receives Abraham and his army with hospitality and blesses him after returning from war with the Assyrian kings of the north.[206] Though *Antiquities* does not include the detailed transactions of Gen 23 that describe Abraham's public purchase of the cave of Machpelah from the "sons of Heth," *A.J.* 1.237 mentions at Sarah's death that "Abraham buried her in Hebron,[207] for the Canaanites had allowed him her burial ground with public consent [δημοσίᾳ]." This positive interaction with the inhabitants of the land, however, ends with Abraham. Isaac and Jacob are not depicted as engaging with the locals in trade or political affairs, and their attitudes toward Canaanites are presented as wholly negative. Before the encounter at Shechem, Josephus hints toward Isaac and Jacob's avoidance of and disdain for the Canaanites, though the root of such animosity remains unstated. When Esau married Canaanite women without the consent of his father, the reader is notified that "Isaac would not have allowed it if the decision had been up to him. For he would have not gladly joined together in kinship with the natives" (*A.J.* 1.266). When mentioning Esau's third marriage to the Ishmaelite Basemath, the narrator states, "For those associated with Isaac were not well-inclined [οὐ εὐνόουν] toward the Canaanites, so that they were annoyed about his previous marriages" (*A.J.* 1.277).

---

also unknown). See Carl G. Rassmussen, *Zondervan Atlas of the Bible*, rev. ed. (Grand Rapids: Zondervan, 2010), 291. It is likely, however, that they are being used here in a similar relationship indicated between Gaza and Gerar. Gerar is outside the border of Canaan, but reference to it is used directionally. If Sodom, Gomorrah, Admah, and Zeboiim are referenced in the same way, then they are east of the Canaanite territory, which ends at Lasha. The contrast between Sodom and Canaan is strengthened by the description of the separation of Lot and Abraham in Gen 13:11–12: "And Lot chose for himself all the Jordan Valley, and Lot set out east. And so they separated from each other. Abraham dwelled in the land of Canaan, but Lot dwelled among the cities of the Valley, and pitched his tent as far as Sodom." It is most likely, therefore, that Sodom was considered a non-Canaanite city in the patriarchal narratives.

206. Solyma is identified as the site of what would later be called Jerusalem (*A.J.* 1.180), as it is in Ps 76:2 and other rabbinic traditions (Feldman, *Judean Antiquities 1–4*, 68 n. 572). When David overtook this site in 2 Sam 5:1–12, it was inhabited by Jebusites, descendants of Canaan (Gen 10:16; *A.J.* 7.61).

207. Gk. ἐν Νεβρῶνι. "Sons of Heth," is often translated as "Hittites" in English Bibles. In Gen 10:15, Heth is listed second as a son of Canaan.

Shortly afterward, when Jacob goes to Mesopotamia to find a wife from among his mother's relatives, "He proceeded through Canaan, and because of his hatred [μῖσος] toward the natives, considered it best to lodge with no one" (*A.J.* 1.278).[208] Thus, in the generations before the debacle at Shechem, the family of Israelites are depicted as harboring a growing animosity for the inhabitants of the land that has been promised to them. They consider the Canaanites as others to avoid marrying and avoid staying around, though the reason for this is unstated. For two generations, the Israelites did avoid them, traversing through Egypt or staying in Gerar or other areas until the fateful events of *A.J.* 1.337–341. Thus, tensions are high before they ever meet at Shechem, at least from the Israelite point of view.

In the account of the events at Shechem, the Shechemite others of *Antiquities* are represented in a way that allows for their individuality. Although they are somewhat flat characters, with minimal description or insights into their perspectives, the diversity depicted among the Shechemites mitigates some of the dangers inherent in Jubilees' account. The individuals Shechem and Hamor are in positions of power, with Shechem abusing that power and King Hamor showing deference to the autonomy of Jacob. The rest of the Shechemites are depicted as enjoying a festival, seemingly ignorant of Shechem's crime or marriage proposal. In *Antiquities*, there is no relational ground established before the episode, no negotiations between Jacob and the Shechemites, no purchase of land or grazing rights (cf. Gen 33:19). Jacob simply comes to Shechem in his travels, which the narrator notes is a city of the Canaanites (*A.J.* 1.337). The son of King Hamor, also named Shechem, plays the part of an enemy. His actions against Jacob's daughter Dinah are unquestionably criminal, for he "ruined her by force" (1.337).[209] With the narrator's choice of words, there

---

208. Feldman offers a reason for this hatred to be rooted in the kerfuffle over the wells that Jacob's father Isaac experienced with the shepherds of Gerar in *A.J.* 1.260–261, as in Gen 26:18–21 (Feldman, *Judean Antiquities 1–4*, 109 n. 828). However, as stated above, the people of Gerar were labeled Philistines by Josephus and Genesis (*A.J.* 1.136, 207; Gen 20:32).

209. The verb φθείρω ("to ruin, destroy, corrupt"), used idiomatically in cases of sexual seduction or assault with a woman as the object of the verb (*LSJ*, 1928), links this story with what Abimelech of Gerar had intended to do to Sarah in *A.J.* 1.207. Both men are depicted as either loving (Abimelech, "αὐτὸς ἐρασθεὶς τῆς Σάρρας," *A.J.* 1.207) or being amorously disposed (Shechem, "διατεθεὶς ἐρωτικῶς," *A.J.* 1.337) toward their intended prey. Where the king of Gerar is held at bay by divine providence, Shechem experiences no hindrance.

is no question that Shechem has committed a grave crime against Dinah and her family, but the crime is Shechem's alone. His father, Hamor, takes action on behalf of his son: "Having been persuaded [by Shechem's begging], he came to Jacob asking to join Dinah to his son Shechem according to law," hoping that Jacob will grant the marriage (1.338).[210] In contrast to his forceful son, Hamor seems a gracious king by leaving Jacob to debate with his sons about what to do (1.338). The rest of the Shechemites, male or female, are not involved in the marriage offer, nor made aware of it. Hamor comes alone, and only to ask for Dinah as a wife for Shechem, not to propose intermarriage or economic dealings between the peoples, and the council that Jacob convenes between himself and his sons returns no answer to the king or his subjects (1.338–339). Only Shechem is depicted as explicitly in the wrong, but not his other countrymen.

Antiquities' representation of the Shechemites as a mixed group, with differing actions and intentions, and different kinds of interaction with the Israelites, corrects the unified portrait offered by Jubilees, in which the Shechemites are a single, villainous mob. Thus, when the city is attacked by Simeon and Levi, the citizens of Shechem are innocent victims of the brothers' hasty plan; they are either relaxing, sleeping, or feasting, and wholly unprepared for attack (the guards were asleep!). Violence against a group's entire population in response to the offenses of a small number or single member is delegitimized when the other is understood as a diverse group of individuals. As noted above, "Less-dangerous stories make the world and actions *more* complicated," with features that may include "giving antagonists names, faces, and purposes that cannot immediately be dismissed."[211] Because of *Antiquities'* increased complication of the portrait of the Shechemites—as a mosaic of individuals and groups rather than a monolith—this story too becomes less-dangerous.

The *Antiquities* account also offers a corrective to Jubilees' strong boundary between the Israelites and Shechemites, which was established by the authoritative divine narrator, who labeled the former "holy" and the latter both "profane" and condemned to destruction. Such a boundary, drawn with the conceptual lines of purity/impurity and holy/profane, allowed for no mobility or means of peaceful interactions or negotia-

---

210. Here, as in Genesis, the reader remains unaware of what Hamor knows about Shechem's history with Dinah. Josephus's re-presentation of the relevant laws of Exod 22:15 and Deut 22:28–29 comes much later, in *A.J.* 4.252. See note 85.

211. Frank, *Letting Stories Breathe*, 159.

tions at all. Jubilees 30 qualifies as a story that makes "too evident and easy the separation between *us* who have names and faces and *them* who are known only by their unjustified opposition to us and who must therefore be opposed."[212] The more humanized, diversified picture of the Shechemites, some of whom are wholly innocent and nonoppositional, mitigates the us/them—or self/other—divide. There *is* a national boundary drawn in *Antiquities* between the Shechemites as the "natives" of the land (e.g., 1.226, 337) and the Israelites as those traveling through. Though they are national others, whom, as noted above, Isaac and Jacob avoided for undisclosed reasons, the narrator of *Antiquities*, unlike Jubilees, does not validate this perspective with affirmation.

This destabilization of the stark boundary between Israelite and Shechemite—or indeed, Israelite/Judean and *any* other national identity—is further accomplished at the very start of book 1. Where Jubilees had established an impermeable boundary at the moment of creation between the holy nation of Israel and all other common peoples, *Antiquities*' central thesis of God's πρόνοια draws a boundary based on ethics, not *ethnos*. God's providential care of the universe, or πρόνοια, is a major theme that recurs throughout the *Antiquities*, and many biblical stories are shaped to emphasize this principle, which includes the retributive justice of God.[213] In other words, it will go well with those who act in accordance with God's will (as revealed in the Judean law), but for those who do not, calamity ensues. In the prologue, this is made explicit as the most important lesson for the reader of the *Antiquities*:

τὸ σύνολον δὲ μάλιστά τις ἂν ἐκ ταύτης μάθοι τῆς ἱστορίας ἐθελήσας αὐτὴν διελθεῖν, ὅτι τοῖς μὲν θεοῦ γνώμῃ κατακολουθοῦσι καὶ τὰ καλῶς νομοθετηθέντα μὴ τολμῶσι παραβαίνειν πάντα κατορθοῦται πέρα πίστεως καὶ γέρας εὐδαιμονία πρόκειται παρὰ θεοῦ· καθ' ὅσον δ' ἂν ἀποστῶσι τῆς τούτων ἀκριβοῦς ἐπιμελείας, ἄπορα μὲν γίνεται τὰ πόριμα, τρέπεται δὲ εἰς συμφορὰς ἀνηκέστους ὅ τι ποτ' ἂν ὡς ἀγαθὸν δρᾶν σπουδάσωσιν.

On the whole, whoever desires to go through this history, may they especially [μάλιστα] learn from it that those who follow after God's intention [γνώμη] and do not dare to transgress the excellent legislations are to be

---

212. Frank, *Letting Stories Breathe*, 159.
213. Attridge, *Interpretation of Biblical History*, 67–92.

established in everything beyond belief, and happiness [εὐδαιμονία]²¹⁴ is set before them by God as a reward. But, in the same degree, for whoever might depart from the accurate attendance of these [τῆς τούτων ἀκριβοῦς ἐπιμελείας], the practicable things become impracticable, and whatever they may have labored to do as good turns into incurable calamities. (*A.J.* 1.14)

Many of Josephus's narratives about the Judean past regularly reflect back to this foundational principle of his history, on the individual and national level. Such thinking is often labeled "deuteronomic theology";²¹⁵ however, in the biblical Deuteronomy, the exhortations to keep the covenant apply only to the nation of Israel in the land. Though certainly influenced by the rhetoric of Deuteronomy, what Josephus presents is a *universal* law for all peoples, or as Harold Attridge puts it, God's "general mode of relating to the world," of which "God's special care for Israel is seen to be simply a particular case."²¹⁶ Josephus explicitly exhorts "those who will happen upon these books," including the aforementioned "Greeks ... who labor to know things about [Judeans]" (*A.J.* 1.9), "to devote their thoughts to God and assess²¹⁷ our lawgiver" (1.15). By thus presenting the Judean constitution as the operating law of the universe that God himself enforces, Josephus makes an implicit claim on his audience to alter their thinking and change their ways accordingly.²¹⁸

According to *Antiquities*' ordering of the world, this divine system of reward and punishment is not nationally bound. It is not only Israel or Judeans to whom it applies but all peoples at all times. For this reason, non-Israelites such as Abel (*A.J.* 1.52–55) or the Adiabene king Izates (20.17–96) can be exemplary figures to emanate, while certain Israelite

---

214. See above for discussion of Josephus's use of εὐδαιμονία in the *Antiquities*.
215. E.g., Attridge, *Interpretation of Biblical History*, 83–86.
216. Attridge, *Interpretation of Biblical History*, 106–7. In this sense, it is more like the classical wisdom tradition of ancient Israel as represented in Proverbs, in which things go well for those who fear God and keep his commandments, but the wicked or disobedient suffer.
217. Gk. δοκιμάζειν. Here Josephus echoes the rhetoric of Roman history writing and political argumentation. In Polybius's *Hist.* 6.1.4–5, which predates the *Judean Antiquities* by roughly two centuries, the historian invites his readers to assess (δοκιμάζειν) his presentation of the Roman political constitution (Mason, "Introduction to the *Judean Antiquities*," xxiv).
218. Attridge, *Interpretation of Biblical History*, 104.

groups or figures, such as the newly liberated exodus generation (2.327–329, 3.295–299) or Korah and his followers (4.11–56), can operate as examples of what *not* do to. Thus, there is a great degree of individual choice allotted to all peoples, and by extension, none would be wholly doomed to destruction just by being born into the wrong people group. When the events of 1.337–341 are viewed in light of the central ethical message of *Antiquities*, there is no room to validate the violence done to the many citizens of Shechem when only one man among them was guilty. *Antiquities* emplots the peoples of the world into an universe governed by a God of ethics, not ethnic favoritism.

5.6. Preliminary Conclusions on the Representational Ethics of Jubilees and *Judean Antiquities*

Representation in Jubilees and *Judean Antiquities* serves to construct Judean identity, draw boundaries, and promote an ethos of intercultural relations to the contemporary audiences of these histories. Jubilees 30's representations of the Israelite self and Shechemite other dangerously erase diversity among the groups and enforce an impermeable boundary between them, promoting an ethic of violence as the only acceptable means of international engagement. Like the late twentieth-century Native Americans in Bruner's ethnographic study,[219] Josephus retells his national narrative in a way that provides a paradigm shift in self-identity and relational ethics. Within *A.J.* 1, Josephus's diverse representation of those deemed Shechemite and the *Antiquities*' central message of God's πρόνοια work together as a corrective to the strong boundary between Israel and other, holy and profane, elect and doomed, that Jubilees draws with its history, especially in chapter 30. This isolated corrective works to delegitimize violence against whole people groups for the offenses of a few in their midst, while also upholding the importance of an individual's choices over their origins—prioritizing ethos over ethnos. This representational corrective offered by *A.J* 1.337–341, however, is not the end of the story.

---

219. See above and Bruner, "Ethnography as Narrative," 139–55.

6. Caveats and Cautionary Tales

First, an explicit political ethos of the *Judean Antiquities* undermines the interrelational ethos that the representations of corporate self and other promote in *A.J.* 1.337–341. By contextualizing the Israelite representation found in 1.337–341 within *Antiquities*' central message and Josephus's account of the Judean constitution, the ethos promoted by the representation of a divided Israel is not necessarily nonviolence and diplomacy but rather an adherence of a nation's populace to the governance and decisions of their leaders, whatever those decisions may be. Second, based on the explicit parallels made between *A.J.* 1.337–341 and 20.118–36,[220] Samari(t)an representations found throughout the *Antiquities* wholly undermine the corrective that Josephus's diversified Shechemite representation offers. The claims of this section do not negate those above concerning the effect of the diversified representation of Israelites and Shechemites in *A.J.* 1.337–341; rather, they present some caveats and offer a cautionary tale: for all the magnanimity shown to various peoples and nations in the *Antiquities*, the unchecked bias of its author resulted in a dangerous villainization of his present-day other.

6.1. What's Really the Issue Here? *Antiquities*' Shaping of First-Century Judean Ethics

We are on fairly stable ground in assuming that the clash at Shechem in *A.J.* 1.337–341 upholds an ethical message for its readers. *Judean Antiquities* was written in the voice of an authoritative narrator who claimed that the accounts within this history serve explicitly ethical, explicitly useful purposes. Such purposes are highlighted through the narrator's chastisement of certain behaviors or his lauding of others, in the speeches of certain venerated heroes, and through God's judgments or rewards of certain behaviors manifest through the events of the history. The brevity of the Dinah/Shechem account and the narrator's lack of his typical ethical commentary, however, call into question what behavior is being upheld as exemplary and what is disparaged by the narrator. After viewing 1.337–341 in the context of the central message of *Antiquities*, this section will argue that within the small pericope of 1.337–341, the unauthorized violent revenge of Simeon and

---

220. See above.

Levi is being contrasted with Jacob and his other sons' maintenance of the peace by seeking diplomatic solutions in response to an offense by a foreign individual. On this isolated level, the story seems a welcome corrective to the dangers of Jubilees' celebration of violence and vehement disparaging of all other means of international relations. I posit, however, that when viewed within the context of the rest of the *Antiquities*, this supposition falls apart. What is being emphasized here—and in the paralleled account in *A.J.* 20.118–136—is the imperative for the Judean populace—and, by extension, all peoples who would want their nation to succeed under God's blessing—to submit to and obey their aristocratic rulers.

It is first necessary to elaborate on how *A.J.* 1.337–341 operates within the central message of the *Judean Antiquities*. Josephus begins his history by positing that its purpose for being set forth is "for the common advantage" (1.3), but what is advantageous about the account in 1.337–341 is not readily apparent. Josephus claims to aim not only at truth in his writing (1.4) but also what is "useful" (1.9). "Above all,"[221] he hopes that his readers will learn a central lesson of God's πρόνοια, or providential care over all of humanity (1.14). Josephus shapes many of the ancient narratives of Judean tradition from the Hebrew Scriptures to bolster this central message, which affirms God's universal governance and retributive justice. The overt and heavily evaluative narrator of *Antiquities* regularly exalts the virtues and disparages the vices of historical figures, making the stories of the ancient past "useful" for the present. What is curious, though, is that the narrator of *A.J.* 1.337–341 is uncharacteristically reticent to offer an explicit evaluation of the Israelite factions in *A.J.* 1.337–341. The story in 1.337–341 is heavily shaped to highlight Jacob's internal struggles in the wake of Dinah's attack and the marriage request, but the narrator does not assess Simeon and Levi's deeds for the reader, as he so often freely does with others throughout his Judean history, as in describing Noah's sons' disobedience (1.110–112), the Sodomites's misanthropy (1.194–196), and the ill will of Joseph's brothers (2.12, 18–20). Unlike the murderous Cain (1.60–66) or the insolent Nimrodites (1.115–117), no evils befall Jacob or his sons after their divergent actions to prove, as the narrator does in other stories, God's watchful care to bless the virtuous and bring calamities on the wicked. If not through narratorial evaluation or an alternative ending, how is this story rendered useful to Josephus's readers?

---

221. Or "especially" (Gk. μάλιστα).

The narrator of *Antiquities* often uses the speech of venerated ancient characters to evaluate other characters and actions,[222] and it is reasonable that Jacob's outrage and anger at "the magnitude" of what his sons have done (1.341) is an indication of narratorial evaluation through the perspective of a lauded-as-virtuous character. Jacob's virtue, unlike that of Abraham (1.183, 256) and Isaac (1.191, 222) before him, is somewhat tainted by the deceit of his father to obtain the blessing of the firstborn (1.267–275) and his hatred of Canaanites (1.278). Such inhospitality—literally, hating outsiders (εἶναι μισόξενοι)—was considered one of Sodom's unacceptable sins (1.194).[223] At the point of his arrival at Shechem, however, Jacob has developed as a character: God has met and spoken with him, as God had done to the virtuous Abraham and Isaac (1.280–284),[224] and at a time of fear and threat, Jacob entrusted himself to God (1.327), one of the *Antiquities*' key virtues, and he was delivered.

That Jacob's perspective in *A.J.* 1.337–341 offers the key to narratorial evaluation is supported by the parallel account found in 20.118–136. While *A.J.* 1.337–341 is without an explicitly evaluative frame, the divisive picture it paints of Israelite identity in the face of foreign threat serves to offer a reflection of the protagonist nation, as argued above. It is in the parallel episode from the first century in 20.118–136, however, that God's πρόνοια is more fully on display, offering insight into Josephus's promoted ethic for his native people in situations of offense. The group Josephus refers to as "bandits" aroused the populace to a massive slaughter and conflagration of Samarian villages in retribution for the Ginean attack on a group of Galilean Jews passing through. These men are ultimately unsuccessful in their aim: freedom from Roman rule. In the parlance of the prologue, their "labor for good" (political autonomy) "turns into incurable calamities" (1.14); instead of obtaining their freedom, many perished in the Roman backlash, while those left alive by Cumanus were crucified by rule of Quadratus, governor of Syria, for their rebellion (20.129). The "principal men" who implored their countrymen to cease their course of violence, however, succeeded in acquiring justice. The case against Cuma-

---

222. Attridge, *Interpretation of Biblical History*, 110, 119–20.

223. By stating the Sodomites' sins in 1.194, Feldman notes that "Josephus shows that such an attitude is utterly unacceptable" (*Judean Antiquities 1–4*, 74 n. 606).

224. Within these heavenly pronouncements, God promises that he is maintaining his watchful oversight, his πρόνοια, concerning "the things being done for [Jacob] both in the present and much more in the future" (*A.J.* 1.283).

nus and the Samarians was appealed to Claudius Caesar, whose "freedmen and friends" greatly supported Cumanus and the Samarians. According to Josephus, these adversaries "would have prevailed" but for the advantageous providence that Agrippa the Younger "happened to be in Rome" (20.135). His presence turns the tides of the affair, and the principal men of Judea are affirmed "beyond belief":

> [Agrippa] begged Agrippina, the wife of Caesar, many times to persuade her husband holding the hearing to, in his judicial role, properly punish the culprits of the disturbance. And Claudius [Caesar], having been won over by this request, held the hearing. When he discovered the originators of the evils to be the Samarians, he commanded those brought before him to be killed, but he sentenced exile for Cumanus. (20.135–136)

Retrospectively, then, the principal men of Judea acted in a way that was, despite all odds stacked against them, ultimately rewarded with justice, whereas those who took up their weapons faced only death or crucifixion. This paralleled account thus also seems to support the peaceable actions of the principal men over the excessive violence of those who lead the populace to take justice into their own hands.

This partiality toward peaceful diplomacy is significantly bolstered by the narrator's explicit labeling of a violent subset of the populace as "brigands" or "robbers" and his regular denigration of them. In *Antiquities* (and indeed throughout his previous history, the *War*[225]), Josephus relays partiality toward the Judean elders over the "rebels" and "brigands" (Gk. λῃστοί), who "filled the citizenry with uproar and planted the roots of the evils that would overtake us" (*A.J.* 18.9). The narrator freely assesses the faction of Judeans who were in favor of violent retribution against their neighboring peoples and in favor of political revolution against Rome, whom they saw as the greatest offender of them all. These revolutionaries are presented as holding much influence over the general public. His negative evaluation is strong; they "deluded the populace" (*A.J.* 20.160) and filled the land "with all sorts of impiety" (20.167), even murdering and plundering the towns of their own people who refused to cooperate (20.172, 214). In addition to the oppressive rule of Rome under Gessius Florus, who "filled Judea with an abundance of evils" (20.252), it is the

---

225. See Per Bilde, "The Causes of the Jewish War according to Josephus," *JSJ* 10 (1979): 179–202.

unrepentant "brigands" whom Josephus most blames for the war that brought the destruction of Jerusalem and its beloved temple (20.165–166). A former general of the Galilean army, Josephus was by no means a pacifist, and he lays his fair share of blame on certain Roman rulers for the evils that befell his people.[226] Yet he exceedingly condemns the excessive violence of his fellow nationals, claiming "it seemed to be a much lighter thing to be ruined by the Romans" than by his own war-hungry countrymen (*B.J.* 4.128–134). Lamenting the destruction that befell his country, he regularly blames this group for provoking the wrath of Rome and, as he claims, the wrath of God (*A.J.* 20.218, *B.J.* 5.412–415). Thus, the narrator's perspective in book 20 reflects that of the perspective of Jacob in 1.341, "astonished at the magnitude of what had happened and indignant" toward those who chose to retaliate with violence.[227]

Together, these parallel narratives seem to support the ethical choices of the ancient patriarch Jacob and the first-century Judean leadership who were in favor of peaceful, diplomatic ways in response to an attack on a small number of their people over against the choices of Simeon and Levi and the first-century "rebels" with whom they are paralleled. Although in the clash at Shechem (*A.J.* 1.337–341) Simeon and Levi face no consequences for their action other than their father's disapproval, in the paralleled account of first-century CE Samaria, God's behind-the-scenes πρόνοια is demonstrated to be at work. As noted above, *Antiquities*' central message of God's πρόνοια is pervasive; it permeates all twenty volumes of Josephus's history. We can thus safely assume that the key to understanding what ethos is being promoted by the factioned representation of the

---

226. Nodet notes the roles that Josephus claims to have played are somewhat different in *War* and *Life* (the self-biographical appendix to *Antiquities*), but what he deems contradictory can be read as a difference of emphasis. "Sans qu'on discerne clairement comment, Josèphe, âgé de vingt-neuf ans, est chargé peu après par le Sanhédrin d'une importante mission en Galilée; il laisse entendre que ce pourrait être le commandement de la région, mais les contradictions entre les récits de la *Guerre* et de la *Vie* laissent un doute sur sa mission exacte: *organiser la guerre, ou calmer les esprits*" (Josephus et al., *Les Antiquités Juives*, vi, emphasis added). To this I say that *Life*'s emphasis on Josephus's role to stem the rage and thirst for vengeance of his countrymen fits with *Antiquities*' theme favoring careful diplomacy and submission to leadership over rash violence.

227. The repetition of condemnations on this influential group of the populace and their many leaders throughout the account of the *War*, the later books of *Antiquities*, and the *Life* leads one to wonder whether this was Josephus's own perspective.

early Israelites and first-century Judeans is found in light of this claim, which I provide again here:

> On the whole, whoever desires to go through this history, may they especially learn from it that those who follow after God's intention and *do not dare to transgress the excellent legislations* are to be established in everything beyond belief, and happiness is set before them by God as a reward. But, in the same degree, for *whoever might depart from the accurate attendance of these*, the practicable things become impracticable, and whatever they may have labored to do as good turns into incurable calamities. (*A.J.* 1.14, emphasis added)

Questioning "Who is rewarded?" and "For whom do the 'practicable things' become 'impracticable'?" without attending to the importance of what, according to the *Antiquities*, the "excellent legislations" of God *are*, therefore, provides a distorted interpretation. As previously noted, the contrast of behavior between the peace-seeking leaders and the vengeance-minded populace may *seem* to be an indicator of the promoted ethos: seeking a peaceable means for justice through orderly and lawful ways and avoiding rash acts of disproportionately violent revenge. Yet within the greater context of the *Antiquities* and the "most excellent legislations" of God as presented therein, the ethic being contrasted through the representation of the Israelite and Judean factions in *A.J.* 1.337–341 and 20.118–136 is not that of peaceful means versus violent revenge. Rather, the faction between the elite leadership and the populace serves to problematize and disparage disobedience to an aristocratic leadership and whatever directives they may have for the people, peaceable *or* violent. This is supported (1) by the *Antiquities*' explication of the Judean constitution in book 4, which contains no proscriptions against retaliatory violence or warfare, but only against disobedience to leaders; and (2) by episode after episode from the ancient history that validates or even celebrates violent revenge when it is ordered by those "superior by rank [or] birth."

In the *Antiquities*' presentation of the Judean law (*A.J.* 4.196–301), there are no ordinances that directly proscribe taking revenge on an enemy attacker,[228] but there are those that exhort the people to submit to

---

228. The avenging of a man who is murdered in a fight, however, is allowed under the control of the judicial system. The man who strikes and kills his fellow is to be killed in return (*A.J.* 4.277). In a following case, Josephus comments, "The law pronounces it just for a life to be laid down for a life" (4.278). The vengeance in these

their proper authorities, thus maintaining order and securing God's blessing. In Josephus's version of the Judean constitution,[229] it is boldly stated that "aristocracy and the life therein is best. Let not longing for another government take hold of you, but be content with this" (4.223).[230] There is a debate among scholars what Josephus means by this use of *aristocracy*, for he uses it here in contrast to rule by a king but elsewhere to describe the reign of the judges (6.36, 84–85).[231] Formed from a crasis of κρατία ("rule" or "government") and ἄριστος ("noble" or "best"), ἀριστοκρατία is most literally rendered "rule of the best." While in antiquity and later eras, aristocracy implied a rule of the noble or elite classes, Robert Gallant suggests that Josephus means "government by the laws," with the laws being the "most noble" and "best" guides for the πολιτεία of the nation.[232] Feldman suggests that it refers more literally to "a government by the best," with "the best" indicating the revealed laws and God himself, thus a theocracy.[233] While the precise meaning of Josephus's use of ἀριστοκρατία in the

---

cases, the life-for-a-life killing of a killer, is carried out within the context of the judicial system (see Exod 21:12–14, Deut 19:11–13).

229. Josephus's presentation of the Judean constitution in *A.J.* 4.196–301 contains laws pertaining to everything from the ordering of the judicial system to tithing mandates, marriage laws, and provisions for the poor. Josephus openly states that he has provided his own topical arrangement, finding Moses's writings too scattered (*A.J.* 4.197). Josephan scholars have determined that he drew from a range of sources for this re-presentation and interpretation of the Judean laws, harmonizing and interpreting statutes from Leviticus, Exodus, and Deuteronomy, as well as containing traditions found only elsewhere in rabbinic sources, and some found nowhere else (e.g., the ruling found in 4.214 that each city have seven appointed leaders and two Levitical assistants).

230. This quotation is Louis Feldman's translation of Josephus's Ἀριστοκρατία μὲν οὖν κράτιστον καὶ ὁ κατ' αὐτὴν βίος, καὶ μὴ λάβῃ πόθος ὑμᾶς ἄλλης πολιτείας, ἀλλὰ ταύτην στέργοιτε.

231. Feldman, *Judean Antiquities 1–4*, 414 n. 696. The cause for confusion of Josephus's use of the political terms *aristocracy, oligarchy, monarchy*, and *democracy* is that he uses them overlapping in different places to refer to the style of Judean government in the same time period. For example, Feldman notes, "Another apparent contradiction arises in Josephus's designation of the period between the return from Babylonian Captivity until the Hasmoneans as an aristocracy and an oligarchy (*A.J.* 11.111), while elsewhere (*A.J.* 20.234) he refers to the government of this period as a democracy" (414 n. 696).

232. Robert Gallant, "Josephus's Expositions of Biblical Law: An Internal Analysis" (PhD diss., Yale University, 1988), 202.

233. Feldman, *Judean Antiquities 1–4*, 414 n. 696.

different contexts in which it is found is somewhat debated, it is without question that the Judean constitution presented in *Antiquities* adamantly upholds the populace's submission to their appointed leadership. The people are to honor those in the position of judge in every city; reviling is not permitted, but respect is demanded (4.215). To transgress by disrespecting the appointed authorities is "to despise God" (4.215). The laws are framed by two speeches of Moses (4.177–195 and 4.309–319), in which he repeatedly exhorts the people to obey the laws of God. These framing speeches celebrate the excellence of the laws and in places elaborate on them. In the speech of Moses that precedes the ordered laws, he exhorts the people to "obey those[234] that God wishes for you to follow" (4.181) and elaborates on the aforementioned law of 4.215, reminding them that their well-being consists in their obedience to the leadership in place:

> The high priest Eleazar, Joshua, the council of elders, and the heads of the tribes will lead you to the best decisions, which by obeying you will have well-being [εὐδαιμονία]. Listen to them without being difficult, knowing that all who know how to be governed well will also know how to govern, if they come into their own authority. Consider that freedom is not to be indignant toward whatever things the rulers may consider it worthy for you to do … which indeed you will have better conditions [ἄμεινον τὰ πράγματα] if you observe this from now on. (4.186–187)

Viewed in light of these stipulations of the Judean constitution, what is problematic about Simeon and Levi's behavior within the worldview of *Antiquities* is that they acted "without the knowledge" or approval of their father (*A.J.* 1.340). Similarly, the "bandits" and their followers transgress one of God's "most excellent legislations" by attacking the Samarians in opposition to the wishes of their leaders (20.121).

Furthermore, there are a number of episodes in *Antiquities* where the leaders of Israel, explicitly venerated by the narrator, guide the people into violence in response to an offense by a group acting as opponents (foreign or otherwise). The actions are not problematic to the narrator of *Antiquities*; on the contrary, they are often heralded as exemplary and praiseworthy. For example, when his nephew Lot is taken away by the Assyrians, Abraham responds by going after them in a revenge attack. He strikes down his foes, "some of whom were asleep in their beds" (*A.J.* 1.177). His mission

---

234. Gk. τούτοις.

is a rescue mission, and he successfully retrieves those with Lot whom the Assyrians had taken captive (1.179). The narrator renders it an example of zeal and courage (1.178), and "God praised his virtue" and calls Abraham's actions *good* deeds (εὐπραγίας). Similarly, *A.J.* 3.40–61 celebrates the newly liberated Hebrews' violent response to the attack of the Amalekites on their way through the desert. "The actions of the inhabitants caused perplexity and confusion," as Moses did not anticipate their hostility, and the Hebrews are ill-equipped for any sort of warfare (3.43). His response is to lead the people into a counterstrike, exhorting them to take courage and trust in God and "what sort of helper" he has been to them (3.44–46). The Hebrews, despite all odds, are victorious, and God is praised as "the one who gives victory" (3.60). This episode almost encourages violent retaliation of the necessitous few against the more powerful foreign attacker. Everything is carried out, however, through the God-approved leadership of Moses. He encourages the people to trust in God (3.44–47), he instructs younger men to obey their elders and the elders to obey him ("the general," 3.47), and then he begins to station and direct groups of men and appoints Joshua as their captain (3.49). All progresses under the command of Moses, and they prevail.[235]

Another example of retaliatory violence carried out by approved leadership comes from the wilderness narrative of *A.J.* 4.141–164. The episode is complex and extensive, differing in many respects from the more ancient narrative of Num 25, on which it is based, and the offenses of Zimri are intensified. Not only has he married a Midianite, but he has agreed to "render homage to what would bring pleasure to her"[236] rather than to the one God or his leader, Moses (4.141), and he stages a public opposition to the leadership of Moses, whom he accuses of being a "tyrant" (4.145–150). Phinehas is introduced as the son and heir of the high priest, "superior in the dignity of his father," as well as simply "better than the [other] young men" (4.182). This high-ranking youth is incensed and, entering their tent, murders Zimri and his wife Chosbia "to exact judgement on him and to prevent the lawlessness from spreading" (4.152–153). He then leads other

---

235. A similar thing happens with the Amorites after they refuse to allow the Hebrews to peacefully pass through their land (*A.J.* 4.87–94). Such inhospitality is offensive, and Moses "knew that it was not necessary to put up with it" (4.87). This time, "[Moses] asked God whether he permitted him to fight," and God responded with an indication that there would be victory (4.87–88).

236. This is Louis Feldman's translation.

"young men who were aiming after virtue and the love of the good" to "do away with" everyone else who "had been accused of crimes similar to Zimri" (4.154). This massacre is celebrated by the narrator ("through the brave action of these men [ὑπὸ τῆς τούτων ἀνδραγαθίας], many of the lawbreakers were destroyed") and confirmed by a plague sent by God to finish up the job (4.154–155). God and his leaders here, again, work in tandem to put down offenders and their associates.

This example, however, arises from within the nation itself. The life of Samson provides another example of foreign affairs marked with approved acts of vengeance. God's chosen judge, Samson, takes revenge on the Philistines for the offense made on him when his Philistine bride was given to someone else: "Samson, having been provoked by this insult, decided to pursue all the Philistines together with her" (5.295), and proceeds to burn the fields of the Philistines via fiery foxtails. Samson thus burns his former wife and her relatives and goes on to kill many other Philistines in the area (5.295–297). After relating more episodes from Samson's life and his suicide, which brought about the deaths of three thousand Philistines, the *Antiquities*' narrator lists the lessons to be learned from Samson's life: "[Samson] is deserving of admiration for his valor and strength as well as the sublimity of his death and for his wrath against his enemies until the end. His being captivated by women should be ascribed to human nature that easily gives in to offenses; in all other respects, the abundance of his valor is a testimony to him" (5.317).[237]

The supreme importance placed on obedience to the appointed leadership is seen in other instances that do not involve revenge but violence and warfare nonetheless. Like other historians and writers of Josephus's Greek and Roman contemporaries, he venerates fighting courageously and the inventiveness of battle plans while presenting war as an unfortunate inevitability. Josephus champions Moses for "fighting courageously" with "inventive undertakings" in his pre-exodus battles as an Egyptian army officer (2.248, 252), while prefacing the wartime laws[238] of the constitution (4.293–301) with somewhat of a lament that such laws need to exist.

---

237. This is Christopher T. Begg's translation from *Judean Antiquities, Books 5–7*, FJTC 4 (Leiden: Brill, 2005).

238. Such praises of Moses for "fighting courageously" with "inventive undertakings" are not unlike those Josephus expresses for himself in his description of the siege of Jotapata (*B.J.* 3.132–336). According to *Antiquities*, Moses served the Egyptian army by leading them victoriously against the Ethiopians in a defensive war. This role

Although Moses expresses hope for peace and freedom from disturbance (4.292), he claims, "It is inevitable for humankind to fall into troubles and dangers, involuntarily or by choice" (4.293). The laws of war assume that the nation will not seek to go to war with another, unless coerced by a "voluntary enemy" (4.296; cf. Deut 20:10–14). The first rule of warfare is that embassies are to be sent to the enemy to negotiate a peace before any fighting should begin, and fighting is to be considered a last resort (*A.J.* 4.297). This plays out in the narratives differently, however, especially when it comes to the offensive war for the conquest of Canaan, where making peace with the inhabitants is forbidden (5.132–133). What matters instead is obeying the command of the appointed leadership (who are depicted as obeying the commands of God), whether that is to maintain peace or go to war.

This is seen in *A.J.* 4.1–12, in which the people attack the Canaanites without the approval of Moses: "They were intent on going to war with the Canaanites, saying that it was not because God has regard for Moses that he assisted them but that he looked after their nation in general because of their ancestors, whom he had taken under his guardianship" (4.2).[239] These "unruly and disobedient masses" attack without Moses's approval and are utterly defeated (4.7), for they "held God as their general but were not waiting for co-operation from the lawgiver" (4.6). Conversely, when the people follow Joshua's directives and attack the Canaanites, they are met with victory after victory (5.60–61, 65–67, 117–118).[240] Joshua's conquest against the Canaanites cannot be construed as defense or revenge in any sense within *Antiquities*, but it underscores the ideology that violence or war in and of itself is not problematic; what matters more is obedience to God and the appointed leaders. There is a distinction made, then, between *any* acts of violence, including retributive violence, when they

---

is not found in the biblical Exodus. Josephus orders the Judean constitution in two parts: laws pertaining to peacetime (*A.J.* 4.196–292) and laws for war (4.293–301).

239. This is adapted from Louis Feldman's translation.

240. The curse that Noah spoke against Canaan—and Josephus notes that God upheld (*A.J.* 1.142)—is for the offenses of his father, Ham, not his youngest son, Canaan. There is no wrong that they have done against the people of Israel, unlike in Jubilees, where they have wrongfully stolen the land allotted to Shem. Nevertheless, *Antiquities* offers unmitigated approval for Joshua and the annihilation of the Canaanites (e.g., 5.118, 120, 132–133), with God promising that there will be total conquest without Israelite casualties as long as the people obey the directives given to them (5.37).

are orchestrated by Israel's appointed leaders, and when they are not (as in the cases of *A.J.* 1.337–341 and 20.118–136). The consistent assertion throughout the laws and narrative accounts is that the populace submit to the guidance of their appointed leaders, whether for peace *or* for violence.

Thus, the ethical content of *A.J.* 1.337–341 and the effects of the representations of *A.J.* 1.337–341 stand somewhat in tension with each other. As argued above, the account's diversified representations of the Shechemites delegitimize the violence done to all of the city's inhabitants when only one man's actions were criminal. In light of the ethos promoted by *Antiquities* as a whole, however, if Jacob had approved the massacre (as he does in Jubilees), the violence would have been not only permissible but required.[241] Authoritative assertions of aristocratic or oligarchic rule as divinely upheld open a Pandora's box of dangers, including political license for oppression, subjugation, and violence, often against the weakest or most marginalized members of society. On one hand, it would be somewhat unfair to hold Josephus's political ideals, strongly informed by his interpretation of the Judean Torah and personal experiences, against the critical lens of post-twentieth-century ideas about healthy political ideologies.[242] On the other hand, comparatively engaging the *Judean Antiquities*' central thesis about the preeminence of the Judean constitution and its laws *is* precisely what the narrator hopes his readers will do. Echoing Polybius, who sets forth Rome's constitution in *Universal History*, Josephus invites his readers to assess (δοκιμάζειν) the laws of Moses as set forth by himself (*A.J.* 1.15; cf. Polybius, *Hist.* 6.1.4–5).[243] As noted above, however, this investigation's chief aim is to observe and reflect on the representational models of self and other present in this ancient

---

241. To make matters more complex, Josephus venerates other individuals, such as the prophets Elijah (9.18–28) and Jeremiah (10.103–104), who took a stand *against* God-appointed leaders deemed wicked, indicating that there are some exceptions to the rule of blind obedience. In reference to Josephus's many contradictions, within his own writings or his contradictions to his source texts, Feldman fittingly quotes Walt Whitman's "Song of Myself": "Do I contradict myself? Very well, then, I contradict myself: I am large; I contain multitudes" ("Reshaping of Biblical Narrative," 74).

242. Furthermore, if we take the narrator's reflections as Josephus's own, then after the utter devastation of homeland and holy city, the historian Josephus was convinced that one of the reasons such horrors befell them was due to the breaches of their own divinely given political constitution, which included the requirement that the populace submit to its leaders.

243. Mason, "Introduction to the *Judean Antiquities*," xxiv.

history, not to call its political or ideological standpoints into conversations with modern political ethics. For now, let it suffice to acknowledge that the ethical content of the *Judean Antiquities*—specifically, the ethical message of blind obedience to aristocratic rule explicitly promoted by its presentation of the Judean πολιτεία—somewhat undermines the effects of the history's diversified representation of the corporate self and other in *A.J.* 1.337–341.

6.2. Curses and Caveats: Samari(t)ans in *Antiquities*, a Cautionary Tale

Just as the ethical imperative behind *A.J.* 1.337–341 is not readily apparent until viewed in light of Josephus's whole composition, the ethical effects of the representation of cultural others in the account are called into question when contextualized within the whole of *Antiquities*. Above, I argued that within 1.337–341, Josephus's diverse representation of those deemed Shechemite and the *Antiquities'* central message of God's πρόνοια work together as a corrective to the strong boundary between Israel and other that Jubilees draws with its history, especially in chapter 30. This isolated corrective works to delegitimize violence against whole people groups for the offenses of a few in their midst, while also upholding the importance of an individual's choices over their origins—prioritizing ethos over ethnos. In the broader history narrated by *Antiquities*, there are virtuous and villainous people found among the prediluvian population, the ancient Israelites, the Judean kings, and imperial rulers over Jehud/Judea, including the Romans.[244] Everyone is allotted a great degree of choice. That is, everyone *except* the postexodus Canaanites and the Samari(t)ans. While a full analysis of *Antiquities'* representation of Canaanites in the postexodus/conquest period unfortunately lies beyond the scope of this study,

---

244. E.g., prediluvian population (Abel versus Cain, *A.J.* 1.52–66), ancient Israelites (Phinehas versus Zimri, 4.131–155), Israelite and Judean kings (as in the biblical accounts, assessments of virtue and vice vary from Saul to Zedekiah), the Macedonian conqueror Alexander is acclaimed as Godfearing (11.325–347), and the Herodians are a mixed bag (books 14–20). Although Josephus's primary audience was likely among the Roman elite (see *A.J.* 1.6–13) even the Romans received a balanced treatment. "All over his account of Judaea under Roman rule we find the same, specific attitude towards the Romans: the fair and reasonable governors are portrayed with sympathy, as Caesar, Augustus, Claudius, Vitellius and Petronius, whereas the governors hostile to the Jews are censured, as Crassus, Gaius Caligula, Sabinus, Pilatus, Cumanus, Felix, Albinus, and Florus" (Bilde, "Causes of the Jewish War," 188–89).

the parallels between the clash at Shechem in 1.337–341 and the first-century conflicts in Samaria in 20.118–136 necessitate a consideration of the representation of Samari(t)ans as well as that of the Shechemites. In this section, I first briefly address the curse of Canaan as depicted in *A.J.* 1.139–142, arguing that it undermines the central ethical message of *Antiquities*, though it does not erase the corrective impact of the Shechemites' diversity in 1.337–341. Then I look at *Antiquities*' representation of the Samari(t)ans and argue that the irredeemably negative depiction of Josephus's present-day other wholly undermines the corrective offered by his diverse representations of other national groups.

6.2.1. Curses: The Canaanites and God's πρόνοια

The central ethical message of God's πρόνοια over creation, to reward those who choose the good and punish those who depart from it, is undermined by *Antiquities*' pronouncement that all Canaanites, regardless of behavior or choice, lie under Noah's curse. While this does not erase the diversity and humanity represented among the Shechemites in *A.J.* 1.337–341, it certainly problematizes their representation. Following his source material in Genesis, Josephus notes that the Shechemites were Canaanites, and that as descendants of Canaan, they were cursed by Noah, a curse that God honors (1.142). Mention of the curse by Josephus, however, serves to justify the later divine mandate for the postexodus generation to take the land rather than legitimize a timeless mandate to annihilate any other people groups as defiled or condemned. As in Genesis, the Canaanites' first introduction comes in tandem with the curse placed on Canaan and his descendants by Noah, who was offended at the deeds of Ham, Canaan's father (Gen 9:20–27; *A.J.* 1.141–142). Although faithful to his sources by recounting this curse on the people, Josephus does not extend the curse to other nations or render it as a spiritual or eternal phenomenon, like the "eternal destruction" awaiting all Canaanites in Jubilees.

Though narrower in scope, damage is still done. As in Gen 9, it is Canaan's father, Ham, not Canaan himself, who committed the offense against Noah (see Gen 9:20–27, *A.J.* 1.139–142). Josephus offers the explanation that Noah did not curse his own son Ham "because of his kinship to him," so he cursed Ham's descendants instead (1.142)! Such an explanation upholds the innocence of poor Canaan and his many children. Nevertheless, according to Josephus, God honored the righteous Noah's words and "pursued the children of Canaan" (1.142). As in Genesis, God speaks a prophetic revelation to Abraham that his descendants will possess Canaan (1.185), which is repeated to his male heirs, as in Genesis, to Isaac (1.191, 235) and to Jacob (1.280–282). The Canaanites are thus *not* depicted as an inherently wicked people, yet they are the natives of the land promised to the Hebrews, and from the point of their introduction in the historical narrative, they are marked for destruction. The Canaanites are the exceptions to the rule of God's πρόνοια, then—a people not permitted the freedom of ethical choice but cursed from the start.

6.2.2. Caveats: The Samari(t)ans, According to Josephus

According to the *Judean Antiquities*, there is no such thing as a good Samari(t)an.[245] Although a degree of difference is employed in the representation of almost any other people group, Samari(t)ans are, according to their representation in *Antiquities*, wholly reprobate.[246] In Josephus's first introduction of the people, he identifies them as Cuthians from Cuthah in Persia, deported and settled in Samaria under Assyrian rule in the late eighth century BCE.[247] Josephus describes them as inherently deceptive and opportunistic, and emphasizes their difference, that they are *not* Judean:

> They are kinsmen to change, for when they observe the Judeans doing well, they claim to be descendants of Joseph and to have a relationship with them from the beginning, but when they see them falling, they say they are in no way related to them, and that the Judeans have no right of kindness or family with them, but they declare themselves sojourners from another country. (*A.J.* 9.291)

In Josephus's presentation of the postexilic efforts to rebuild Jerusalem and Judea, the Samari(t)ans are perennial enemies of the Judean efforts: "The Samarians, being hatefully and maliciously disposed toward [the Judeans], perpetrated many evil deeds against the Judeans" (11.114). Paul Spils-

---

245. Josephus frequently alternates between *Samaritan* and *Samarian* to refer to the people who inhabited the region of Samaria during the postexilic period.
246. For a careful study of all the boundary crafting Josephus's representation of the Samari(t)ans accomplishes, see Sung Uk Lim, "Josephus Constructs the Samari(t)ans: A Strategic Construction of Judaean/Jewish Identity through the Rhetoric of Inclusion and Exclusion," *JTS* 64 (2013): 404–31.
247. Josephus, of course, does not use such a dating scheme.

bury and Chris Seeman assert that "the hatred of the Samarians" forms a "theme" within *Antiquities*, especially saturated in book 11.[248] All consideration of diversity dissolves when it comes to the Samari(t)ans, who are continuously depicted as wholly villainous and false.

The high concentration of reference to Samari(t)ans in book 11 forms a unique midway pinpoint on which Josephus hangs the parallel of *A.J.* 1.337–341 and 20.118–136: it is also in book 11 that the "mother city" of the Samari(t)ans[249] is identified as none other than Shechem (*A.J.* 11.340), and Josephus therefore also refers to them as "Shechemites" (11.342, 344). These Samari(t)an "Shechemites" of the late fourth century BCE are disparaged by Josephus, who describes them as a mix between the descendants of deceptive Cuthians and "defectors from the Judean nation," who, according to Josephus, chose the bribes of Sanballat, governor of Samaria, over the upholding of Judean priestly regulations.[250] The henceforth ethnically mixed group collectively claims Judean heritage when they see them honored by Alexander the Great after his visit to Jerusalem, and the narrator asserts,

> For these are the sort [of people] the Samarians are by nature [τὴν φύσιν].... When the Judeans are in adversity, they deny kinship—confessing then in truth—but when they see a glimmer of fortune about them, they immediately claim their fellowship, saying they belong to them and that they descend from Joseph and are born of Ephraim and Manasseh. (11.341)

This negative portrait remains unmitigated until the Samari(t)ans' reappearance in book 20, in which they again emerge as the ever-adversaries of the Judeans in both Galilee and Judea. While no voice speaks from heaven

---

248. Paul Spilsbury and Chris Seeman, *Judean Antiquities 11*, FJTC 6a (Leiden: Brill, 2017), 37.

249. Specifically, during the conquest of Alexander the Great.

250. Proper observance of priestly laws and regulations was highly valued by Josephus and considered essential to the well-being of the nation. Breaches of proper observance by extension posed a threat to the nation. In book 20, when he describes how many Levites obtained permission from the Sanhedrin to wear linen garments, Josephus comments that it too was a cause of the Roman destruction that followed: "All these things were in opposition to the laws of our country, which, whenever they have been transgressed, it was not *ever* possible to avoid punishments" (*A.J.* 20.218, italics signifying the multiple negatives that are used for emphasis in this passage).

to condemn the population of Samaria to smithereens, the authoritative narrator of Josephus's history has monochromatically limited this entire people group to the role of deceptive villain through their multigenerational representation in the *Antiquities*. Any magnanimity or equality that the central thesis of *Antiquities* promotes is paradoxically dissolved when it comes to Samari(t)ans. They are not free to choose or to change but are the (despicable) way they are "by nature [τὴν φύσιν]." Thus *Antiquities*' irredeemably negative representation of the Samari(t)ans, Josephus's present-day other, wholly undermines the corrective offered by his diverse representations of the ancient Shechemites and other national groups. The efforts of *Antiquities* to re-present the past become a cautionary tale to present-day national history tellers, who, while knowingly working to rectify the dangerous and damaging representations inherited from their own culture's dominant national histories, may unwittingly depict *other* othered identities with unchecked bias.

7. Conclusions

This investigation offers reflections from Judean antiquity on the ethical impact of representation in authoritative history-telling, either academic or otherwise. Academic histories, by nature of their authorship by degree-holding and highly trained historians, carry somewhat of an authoritative weight. Nonacademic, public-facing histories also maintain various claims to reliability, yet what exists on the page (or screen) of such narratives is often highly selective and highly interpreted. Although the fruits of stringent academic historical inquiry have their limited spheres of influence, the public at large receives their sense of the past through more public-facing history that, like Jubilees and *Judean Antiquities*, is highly interpretive and often hides its source material beneath the floorboards of its authoritatively presented narrative.

Although the author of Jubilees and the historian Josephus likely did not reflect on this matter, I posit that the role of national history tellers involves the ethical responsibility to represent their national subjects (who are, in essence, groups of diverse individuals and intersecting subidentities) and the "others" to those national subjects (who are also groups of diverse individuals and intersecting subidentities) conscientiously. While it stands to reason that any given national history need not be taken up by a population but may be resisted or retold as a new narrative, the self-presentation of national histories *as reliable accounts* bring an ethical weight to their representations. The potential for national histories to be taken up and thus have a shaping effect on great numbers of people adds to their ethical force. This is why critical consideration of representation in national histories is so important. The representational models found in Jub. 30 provide reflections on the dangers of monolithic depictions of national groups. Jubilees' corporate representations of Israelites and Shechemites present a stark binary of good and evil nations that works to dissolve diversity and diplomacy, instead promoting violence. The irrefutable rightness of Israel and the irredeemable wickedness of their other(s) are presented as being true depictions for all time, thus perpetuating deprecating views of othered identities to future generations who would take up these representations as authoritative.

The differing representational models of the *Judean Antiquities* prove to be *less* dangerous in places and ethically problematic in others. Josephus's representation of Israelite self and Shechemite other in *A.J.* 1.337–341 incorporates diversity and complexity among both identities. This representational model, within the context of *A.J.* 1, is coupled with a worldview that promotes all humans (somewhat) equitably as ethical agents and serves to correct the damaging representations of his predecessor. The *Antiquities* as a whole, however, ultimately preserves and promotes harmful bias against Josephus's contemporary ethnic other, the Samari(t)ans. In doing this, the resulting history upholds the idea that some people groups can be inherently bad,[251] even if they may be the exception to the general rule. Thus, I find that unchecked bias can produce distortedly homogenous and denigrating representations that have the potential to be damaging, even in work that may correct dangerous representations inherited from previous generations.

---

251. Or, in the case of the Canaanites noted above, cursed or destined for destruction.

4
THE AGENT(S) OF AN ETHICAL SHIFT: THE RE-PRESENTATION OF GENESIS 34 IN MANUSCRIPTS A AND F OF *ASENETH*

> And these are the names of the descendants of Israel, who came into Egypt, Jacob and his sons ... with his daughter Dinah.
> —Genesis 46:8, 15

1. Introduction

In the action-filled narrative of *Aseneth* 22–29,[1] the events of Gen 34 are briefly referred to twice (Jos. Asen. 23.2, 14); the characters of Gen 34, however, especially Simeon, Levi, and their brothers, permeate the narrative as central figures in a "new" story, which also takes up the themes of offense (ὕβρις) and revenge (ἐκδίκησις). As Angela Standhartinger notes,

---

1. As noted in chapter 1, the manuscript tradition attests to several names for this ancient work. Early modern scholarship adopted the name Joseph and Aseneth, but Ross Kraemer argues that *Aseneth* is more fitting, as the narrative centers on the female protagonist throughout (*When Aseneth Met Joseph*, 3). Ahearne-Kroll has followed suit (*Aseneth of Egypt*, 1 n. 1). I agree that *Aseneth* is a more fitting title for the work, and it reflects the earliest attestation of its title found in the Syriac, which was simply labeled "Of Aseneth."
  Unlike chapters 1–21, chapters 22–29 take place after the marriage of Joseph and Aseneth during the years of plenty and are set in the years of famine, after Joseph's family has come to Egypt. Therefore, chapters 22–29 are often referred to as *Aseneth*'s part 2. As Gordon Zerbe notes, the sword (ῥομφαία), which is not mentioned in part 1, features prominently in part 2 alongside repeated instances of the axiom "do not repay evil for evil": "As soon as the theme of 'the sword' is introduced into the story [in ch. 23], counterbalancing teaching on non-retaliation and the refusal to use the sword is presented" (*Non-retaliation*, 75).

"The ethical problem that Genesis 34 set for Judeo-Hellenistic interpreters—namely how the annihilation of an entire city by Simeon and Levi can be justified—is solved here in an original way."[2] In Standhartinger's reading, the axiom spoken by Aseneth in chapter 28 ("by no means, brother, will you repay evil for evil") indicates that the text renounces all forms of violent retaliation and teaches universal forgiveness.[3] Yet as this chapter demonstrates, the ways in which *Aseneth* engages with the evaluative gap of Gen 34 is not that simple, and each manuscript responds to the ethical problem of violent retaliation uniquely.

Many scholars have written about the axiom of nonretaliation ("do not repay evil for evil") repeatedly found in *Aseneth* in comparison with other works of ancient Jewish and Christian literature,[4] but few have grappled with the complex picture of nonretaliation presented through the story's heroine and heroes. In both reconstructed critical editions of *Aseneth*, the "short text" of Marc Philonenko (Phil) and the "long text" of Christoph Burchard (*KritHer*),[5] a tension exists between the spoken axiom of nonre-

---

2. "Das ethische Problem, das Gen 34 den jüdisch-hellenistischen Auslegungen stellt, nämlich wie die Vernichtung einer ganzen Stadt durch Simeon und Levi gerechtfertigt werden kann, wird hier auf eine originelle Weise gelöst." See Angela Standhartinger, "'Um zu Sehen die Töchter des Landes' die Perspektive Dinas in der Jüdischehellenistichen Diskussion um Gen 34," in *Religious Propaganda and Missionary Completion in the New Testament World: Essays Honoring Dieter George*, ed. Lukas Bormann, Kelly Del Tredici, and Angela Standhartinger (Leiden: Brill, 1994), 112.

3. Standhartinger, "'Um zu Sehen,'" 112, 114.

4. Chesnutt, Klassen, and Piper have mainly engaged with the nonretaliatory axiom itself, especially as spoken by Levi in 23.9, not noting the tension between his words and actions in that chapter and the rest of the narrative. See Randall Chesnutt, *From Death to Life: Conversion in Joseph and Aseneth* (Sheffield: Sheffield Academic, 1995), 107; William Klassen, *Love of Enemies: The Way to Peace* (Minneapolis: Fortress, 1984); John Piper, *Love Your Enemies: Jesus' Love Command in the Synoptic Gospels and the Early Christian Paraenesis* (Wheaton, IL: Crossway, 2012), 37–39. Even Nir asserts that by having both Levi and Aseneth speak the axiom to not repay evil for evil, "the story's stance is decisive" on an unmitigated picture of nonretaliation. See Rivka Nir, "'It Is Not Right for a Man Who Worships God to Repay His Neighbor Evil for Evil': Christian Ethics in *Joseph and Aseneth* (Chapters 22–29)," *JHS* 13 (2013): 5. Writing before Zerbe's 1993 investigation, Burchard considered "the ethics of *JosAs*" to be "a neglected field" of scholarship. See Christoph Burchard, "The Present State of Research on Joseph and Aseneth," in *Gesammelte Studien Zu Joseph and Aseneth* (Leiden: Brill, 1996), 310.

5. Philonenko claims to prioritize Greek MSS B and D and the Slavic witnesses, which are shorter than the text of family Mc and *a* and Burchard's previous family *b*

taliation and the use of violence for both vengeance and defense of the pious by Levi, Simeon, Benjamin, and the other sons of Leah. The axiom "do not repay evil for evil" is spoken and enforced among the brothers of Joseph by Levi (Phil/*KritHer* 23.9, 12; 29.3) and Aseneth (Phil/*KritHer* 28.10, 14), yet Levi threatens Pharaoh's son at swordpoint while boasting about how "the Lord avenged the insult" (ἐξεδίκησε κύριος [ὁ θεὸς] τὴν ὕβριν) of the Shechemites through his and Simeon's swords (Phil/*KritHer* 23.14). In addition, the first cycle of Aseneth's deliverance from the armed men pursuing her is accomplished through Benjamin's deadly stone-throwing capabilities (Phil/*KritHer* 26.8–27.7) and a prophetically informed attack by the well-armed sons of Leah (Phil/*KritHer* 26.5–6, 27.6–7).

Very few scholars note this tension, and those who do have come to differing conclusions. Jill Hicks-Keeton reads Levi and his brothers as falling short of the story's ideal ethic of offering and preserving life "unremittingly."[6] She argues that the ethic of "not repaying evil for evil" is perfectly displayed only by Aseneth in the story, whereas the various sons of Israel (apart from Joseph) "either (1) try to kill each other, (2) desire to kill each other and/or Egyptians or (3) actually kill Egyptians."[7] Even Levi, who enforces nonretaliation to Simeon (23.9) and stays Benjamin's hand from dealing Pharaoh's son the deathblow (29.4), demonstrates this ideal ethic imperfectly in Hicks-Keeton's reading when he boasts of his prior vengeance against the Shechemites.[8] Gordon Zerbe's investigation of the ethic of nonretaliation in *Aseneth* examines "the exhortations or themes of non-retaliation" as they are displayed by both Aseneth *and* Levi, who are the dual heroes of part 2 (Jos. Asen. 22–29).[9] Relying on Burchard's reconstructed text, he attends to the nuanced presentation of nonretaliation by the exemplary figures of Aseneth and Levi in conversation with messages of nonretaliation in other Hellenistic Jewish writings (i.e., Letter of Aristeas,

---

(Syr., Arm., L2, FW, G, Ngr, L1, E). Philonenko claims the shorter manuscripts (B, D, and Slav.) preserve the oldest version of *Aseneth* (*Joseph et Aséneth*, 3–26). See also Christoph Burchard, "The Text of *Joseph and Aseneth* Reconsidered," *JSP* 14 (2005): 83–96. Burchard prioritizes the earliest witnesses, the Syriac, Armenian versions, and L2, and the Greek MSS FW, G, Ngr over family *a* (see below) and family *d* (Greek MSS B, D, and the Slavic witnesses; see *Joseph und Aseneth*).

6. Jill Hicks-Keeton, *Arguing with Aseneth: Gentile Access to Israel's Living God in Jewish Antiquity* (Oxford: Oxford University Press, 2018), 61.

7. Hicks-Keeton, *Arguing with Aseneth*, 61.

8. Hicks-Keeton, *Arguing with Aseneth*, 61.

9. Zerbe, *Non-retaliation*, 26.

Philo, Pseudo-Phocylides, 3 Maccabees, Wisdom of Solomon). I engage with many of his arguments below. Each of these scholars, however, was dealing with the editorially constructed texts, neither of which undistortedly reflects any extant *Aseneth* manuscript.[10]

Building on the foundations of Jonathon Stuart Wright's investigation into the extant Greek manuscripts of *Aseneth*, the analysis below takes a new philological approach to *Aseneth* and compares MSS A and F.[11] To date, these manuscripts have received little scholarly attention as literary creations in their own right due to a preference for critical editions that aim to reconstruct the original Ur-text. Both MS A and MS F of *Aseneth*

---

10. Even among manuscript families, no extant text of *Aseneth* completely agrees with the other, and in places there are wide divergences in characterization, dialogue, word choice, and even plot elements. Based on this diversity, Ahearne-Kroll argues, "To depend on either reconstruction alone disregards the individual adaptations and differences between manuscripts and manuscript families.... The witnesses provide multiple tellings of a fairly fixed storyline, not multiple copies of a fairly fixed text" (*Aseneth of Egypt*, 75, 124).

11. Wright, "After Antiquity." In this chapter, and in the appendix, I rely on Wright's editions for the Greek text of MSS A and F. The first critical edition of *Aseneth* was published by Batiffol in 1889, relying heavily on MS A, with an apparatus indicating variants in Greek MSS B, C, and D. Wright's edition of family *a* amends some faults in Battifol's text of A (see "After Antiquity," 140). Though digital scans of the manuscript were consulted, I base my analysis primarily on the text of A as provided by Wright's edition. Likely due to the conflict in Eastern Europe affecting not only the Ukraine but all its neighboring nations, including Romania, attempts to gain access to MS F were unsuccessful. I am indebted to Wright for making available the text of F through his edition of FW in "After Antiquity." In F, *Aseneth* is located in the middle of a miscellany of theological works, which are mostly sermons, and follows the *Life of Joseph*. This is also the case for its sister text, W. The new philological approach takes each manuscript as an artifact that can shed light on how the story of *Aseneth* was retold and interacted with in its unique cultural setting. Such an approach is a strong departure from previous *Aseneth* research, which has either evaluated manuscripts on the basis of their usefulness in reconstructing the "original" Second Temple period text from Hellenistic Judaism or primarily engaged with reconstructions that belie the fluidity that exists in the various witnesses. See Bernard Cerquiglini, *Éloge de la variante: Histoire critique de la philologie* (Paris: Seuil, 1989); Matthew James Driscoll, "The Words on the Page: Thoughts on Philology, Old and New," in *Creating the Medieval Saga: Versions, Variability, and Editorial Interpretations of Old Norse Saga Literature*, ed. Judy Quinn and Emily Lethbridge (Odense: University Press of Southern Denmark, 2010), 87–104; Liv Ingeborg Lied and Hugo Lundhaug, *Snapshots of Evolving Traditions: Jewish and Christian Manuscript Culture, Textual Fluidity, and New Philology* (Berlin: De Gruyter, 2017).

uniquely re-present the events and characters of Gen 34 to shape the ethical content of the story and to promote a nuanced ethos of nonretaliation for their audiences. Comparing MSS A and F removes us from the world of ancient Judaism, since they represent Aseneth's story as it was encountered by the middle Byzantine church and sixteenth-/seventeenth-century Romanian monastics, respectively. MS A, found in a *menologion*, frames *Aseneth* as a hagiography to be read aloud annually to a Byzantine congregation on her saint day (December 13), and MS F of the Radu-Vodă monastery was read either corporately or individually by seventeenth-century Romanian monastics.[12] As noted in chapter 1, MSS A and F represent popular iterations of *Aseneth* as encountered in middle to late Byzantium and in seventeenth- to nineteenth-century Romania, respectively.[13]

In both manuscripts, the characters of Gen 34 are cast into a new story with thematic and plot-related parallels to Gen 34, and their actions and words serve to craft a picture of an ideal nonretaliatory ethos. In this chapter, I argue that the heroine is assigned the role of Dinah in Jos. Asen. 22–29, but whereas Dinah of Genesis remains permanently hidden though narratorial reticence, Aseneth's voice and actions are foregrounded and contribute to the promotion of the unique ethos of nonretaliation promoted by each manuscript. Each text features Aseneth as an inspirational model, with Simeon and Levi as supporting characters who stimulate the audience's ethical reflection in different ways: Simeon acts as a foil to the ethical ideal and must be restrained and instructed by Levi (in MS A) or Aseneth (in both). In MS A, Aseneth receives instruction from Levi, who first promotes an ethos of nonretaliation nuanced by contingencies for the legitimate use of violence in certain circumstances by certain people. In MS F, however, Levi's role is significantly diminished, supporting the message that even defensive and protective violence is illegitimate for the one who worships God (θεοσεβής).[14] Instead of Levi, it is Aseneth who intro-

---

12. Wright, "After Antiquity," 141; Burchard, "Joseph and Aseneth in Rumania," 542–45.

13. Burchard, *Joseph und Aseneth*, 22; Burchard, "Joseph and Aseneth in Rumania," 540. To my knowledge, there are no published English translations of these manuscripts, and although they were once a lively part of the ritual life of their communities, they are now carefully preserved in archives and accessible by a limited few. For this reason, I provide a translation of chapters 1 and 22–29 of manuscripts A and F in an appendix.

14. Though sometimes translated as "Godfearer," I agree with Burchard and Chesnutt that this translation encourages a false association with φοβούμενοι τὸν

duces and enforces an ethos of nonretaliation that precludes the use of violence for retribution or self-defense in MS F.

Throughout this chapter, I offer reflections on how these texts craft the relational spaces[15] in which they encountered their original audiences. MSS A and F each invite their audiences, through different means, into a narrative in-between[16] to encounter the unfolding of their unique answers to the ethical quandary of retaliatory violence. MSS A and F also seize on both the ethical potential of stories to enrich an audience's ethical imagination and the power of communal identity to shape ethical inclinations. Attention is paid to the unique force that each manuscript of *Aseneth* exerts on its audience in the space of encounter, and how that force works to expand and influence their audiences' sense of ethical possibilities available to them.[17] Both manuscripts aim to expand their audience's sense of not only what is possible but what is *preferable* for the God-worshiper when it comes to retaliation and violence. The communal nature of the relational spaces crafted by the texts in which to face their audiences exerts a unique force on them. By so crafting a communal interaction, Aseneth's story became for the audiences not just *a* story but *their* story. By extension, the nonretaliatory ethos demonstrated by its centralized characters was put forth as not just *an* ethos but *their* ethos.

2. Aseneth as a New Dinah in A and F

As argued in chapter 2, the absence of Dinah's voice in Gen 34 parallels the absence of narratorial evaluation on the male characters and their actions, including Simeon and Levi's retributive violence against the Shechemites. In a creative extension of this parallel, the voice of Aseneth, whose role

---

θεόν, "Godfearers" (Chesnutt, *From Death to Life*, 100–101). In contrast to the more common term, εὐσεβής, meaning "pious" or "devout," the initial θεός emphasizes the divine object of one's devotion. For this reason, I translate the term "God-worshiper." Burchard argues, "The word *theosebēs* is something like a technical term in JosAsen; it is used to designate the Jews who revere the one and only God and observe appropriate ethical standards." See Christoph Burchard, "Joseph and Aseneth," *OTP* 2:206. It is reasonable to assume that in the Christian contexts in which *Aseneth* A and F were read, the term may have taken on Christian connotations through its contextual relocation.

15. See ch. 1, §1.
16. See ch. 1, §1.
17. Meretoja, *Ethics of Storytelling*, 90–97. See introduction and below.

is paralleled to Dinah's,[18] becomes a conduit in both MSS A and F for the enforcement of the two uniquely nuanced ethics of nonretaliation that each of these texts promotes. The following sections elucidate how Aseneth functions in each manuscript to articulate a unique nonretaliatory ethos, while this section describes the parallels made between her character and that of Dinah.

Dinah, daughter of Leah, is not present as a character in either version of *Aseneth*, yet in a sense Aseneth becomes a "new Dinah."[19] Her position in the family and the dangers that befall her are paralleled in part 2 of *Aseneth* to those of Dinah in Gen 34. Yet unlike Dinah, Aseneth is foregrounded with agency, action, and speech.[20] The audience is privy to her perspective and hears her voice, which is a powerful change agent in both stories.

---

18. See also Hicks-Keeton, *Arguing with Aseneth*, 61–65. As Hicks-Keeton notes, "Whereas in Genesis Dinah is the female victim and the brothers' swordsmanship is featured (though approached with ambivalence), in *Joseph and Aseneth* the title heroine stands in for Dinah as the woman pursued (this time unsuccessfully)" (126). The role of Dinah as victim is more apparent, however, in Jub. 30 than in Gen 34 (see ch. 2). I hold that *Aseneth* assumes a reading of Gen 34 that is in line with the interpretation found in Jub. 30, in which all the Shechemites were guilty, Dinah was a victim of assault and "defiled" by Shechem, and Simeon and Levi were agents of God's vengeance. This reading is evinced by the majority of manuscripts' renderings of Jos. Asen. 23.14, including MS A. MSS F's and W's alterations to the role of Levi, however, call his perspective in 23.14 into question and omit any mention of Dinah's "defilement." See below for further discussion.

19. In MS A, Dinah is mentioned in the speech of Simeon and Levi as they recall "our sister Dinah, who Shechem son of Hamor defiled" (23.14 A). In MS F, however, Dinah is never mentioned. Simeon and Levi declare that "the Lord avenged the insult of the Shechemites" with their swords, but what that insult was goes unnamed (23.14 F). I am not the first to note that Aseneth becomes a new Dinah. See Standhartinger, "Um zu Sehen," 107–12; Hicks-Keeton, *Arguing with Aseneth*, 126.

20. Standhartinger also reads Aseneth as fulfilling the role of Dinah and providing Dinah's perspective that was missing in Gen 34. Standhartinger, working with the reconstructed text of Philonenko, claims that Aseneth introduces "a new ethic to the expression (eine neue Ethik zum Ausdruck)" ("do not repay evil for evil") that "teaches universal forgiveness (allgemeine Vergebung lehrt)" (Standhartinger, "Um zu Sehen," 112). As argued below, the texts in MSS A and F offer a more nuanced ethos of nonretaliation than what Standhartinger proposes. While the language of "sparing" (φείσασθαι) a wrongdoer is used in reference to withholding violent punishment (e.g., 28.10), "forgiving" (ἀφεῖναι) is not. Furthermore, Standhartinger's analysis of Aseneth in Philonenko's text as the teacher of a new ethic accords more with her presentation in MS F than in MS A, as demonstrated below.

In effect, Aseneth becomes a new, illuminated Dinah, brought out of the shadows and into the spotlight of her own story.

In both MSS A and F, Aseneth takes Dinah's place among the children of Israel. In part 1 (chs. 1–21), she is grafted into the family of Israel through repentance toward "the God Most High" and through marriage to Joseph (Jos. Asen. 21.1–9; 22.3, 8; cf. Gen 41:45). In both manuscripts, Jacob blesses Aseneth (Jos. Asen. 22.8–9) and Aseneth falls on his neck as Joseph does in Gen 46:29.[21] Whereas Dinah is not included in Jacob's blessings of his children in Gen 49, Aseneth receives his blessing and greets him as if she were a long-lost member of the family.[22] MS A further strengthens the paternal connection when Aseneth declares to Joseph, "Your father Israel is like my father [ὁ πατήρ σου 'Ισραὴλ ὡς πατήρ μού ἐστιν]" (22.3 A). Like Dinah, Aseneth is uniquely tied to Simeon and Levi. Although they are not maternally linked in *Aseneth*, the same men who took up the role of avengers of wrong in Dinah's story are the leaders and spokesmen among their brothers who rush to Aseneth's aid when she is in danger (Jos. Asen. 26–28).

---

21. See also Gen 33:4, 45:14–15. In each instance of the family members embracing, with reference to the neck, it represents a moment of reconciliation after years of separation. In Gen 33:4, it is Esau who greets Jacob this way; in Gen 45, it is Joseph and Benjamin who embrace; and in Gen 46:29, Joseph is reunited with his father, who thought him long dead. In this way, Jacob, though meeting Aseneth for the first time, receives her as a long-lost daughter.

22. Some early medieval Jewish traditions (e.g., Pirqe R. El. 38, Midr. Gen. 1.97) make the connection between Aseneth and Dinah genealogically, with Aseneth being the daughter of Dinah and Shechem. See Victor Aptowitzer, "Asenath, the Wife of Joseph: A Haggadic Literary-Historical Study," *HUCA* 1 (1924): 243–47. The text of *Aseneth*, however, does not assume this tradition. Aseneth is referred to only as Pentephres's daughter. Though her mother remains unnamed, there is no indication that the reader is to infer a biological connection to the Israelites, but her identity as an Egyptian woman is emphasized in part 1 (3.6, 4.10). In her lamentations of chapter 11, Aseneth claims that her father and her mother have disowned her because she rejected the Egyptian gods (11.5). This allows her to claim orphanhood and appeal to the God who is "father to the fatherless" (11.13; see Ps 68:5). Early in part 1, the reader is told that Aseneth was born on the same night as the other seven female παρθένοι who attend her (2.6 A and F). The elaborate picture that chapter 2 paints of their shared tower intimates seclusion from the rest of the world from the time of their birth. The description of Aseneth in 1.5, however, likens Aseneth's physical traits to the Hebrew matriarchs Sarah, Rebekah, and Rachel, leaving open the possibility of creative connections.

4. The Agent(s) of an Ethical Shift

Like Dinah of Genesis, Aseneth is seen and desired by the son of the ruler of the land. Pharaoh's son is first introduced in relation to the female object of his desire, Aseneth. After hearing reports of her beauty, Pharaoh's son begs his father, the ruler of Egypt, to arrange their marriage (1.7), in a scene that is reminiscent of Shechem's plea to his father Hamor:

> And the firstborn son of Pharaoh heard about [Aseneth] and earnestly entreated his father to give her to him as a wife. (1.7a A, 1.7 F)

> And he clung to the soul[23] of Dinah, the daughter of Jacob.... Shechem said to Hamor, his father, "Get this girl as a wife for me." (Gen 34:3–4 LXX)

Unlike Dinah in Genesis, however, Aseneth's perspective on the matter is made explicit. Before meeting Joseph and before her transformation, she desires to marry the firstborn son of Pharaoh (Jos. Asen. 4.11). Although she had never seen Pharaoh's son or interacted with him (2.6), in her pride (4.12) she spurns the idea of marrying Joseph, whom she considers below her station as "the son of a shepherd from the land of Canaan" (4.10), and demands that she marry "the firstborn son of the king" (4.11) instead. After her encounter with Joseph, she comes to recognize him as highly stationed indeed, referring to him as "the son of God" (6.5 F, 6.2 A).[24] During her dramatic confession and repentance, she declares to God that she loves Joseph more than her own life (ψυχή, 13.15) and "rejoices with great joy" when the heavenly messenger announces that she will marry him (15.9–11). Thus, the audience knows that Aseneth has exchanged her desire to be wed to the son of Pharaoh for the desire to be with Joseph when Pharaoh's son sees her from afar at the start of chapter 23 (cf. Gen 34:2)[25] and begins to plot a scheme to "take" her by force. Unlike his counterpart Shechem, however, Pharaoh's son does not succeed in "taking" the woman he desires.

---

23. Gk. τῇ ψυχῇ.

24. In MSS A and F, Aseneth alternatively refers to Joseph in chapter 6 as "a son of God" or "the son of God." She uses the indefinite expression in 6.6 A and 6.3 F, and the definite in 6.2 A and 6.5 F. In 23.10 A, Levi says that Joseph is "like a son of God," and in 23.10 F, Levi says "Joseph our brother is like the firstborn son of God."

25. At which point Aseneth is, unlike Dinah, a married woman and a mother (Jos. Asen. 21.8–9) and is anxious at the idea of being apart from her husband Joseph (26.1).

Dinah's voice is never heard in Gen 34, yet Aseneth's voice pervades the narrative in *Aseneth*. In part 2, her voice displays power and authority, and acts as a catalyst. Aseneth cries to heaven twice (Jos. Asen. 26.8, 27.10), and twice she is delivered from attack. When Pharaoh comes to "take" her, she trembles with fear and calls on God for help (26.8). In both MSS A and F, Aseneth is delivered from his grasp through the actions of Benjamin and the sons of Leah. Immediately afterward, when the sons of Bilhah and Zilpah come near with swords drawn, intending to kill Aseneth, she cries to God again (27.10), and God intervenes directly by dissolving their weapons and causing the attackers to cower in fear (27.11–12). In response to their pleas for mercy, she restrains and instructs the vengeful sons of Leah, preserving her assailants from further harm (28.10–11, 14). Furthermore, it is Aseneth's voice that restrains Simeon and the sons of Leah from violently retaliating against the brothers who had plotted against Aseneth and aided Pharaoh's son in assaulting her. Stretching out her right hand, she says to Simeon, "By no means, brother,[26] shall you repay evil for evil" (Jos. Asen. 28.14). As argued in chapter 2, Dinah's perspective is centralized by its absence in Gen 34, yet the reader remains uninformed of what her perspective may have been with regard to her brothers' actions. Aseneth, who is paralleled to Dinah in multiple ways, clearly speaks against violent retaliation on her own enemies. Her voice carries weight among the family, and her will is heeded, despite some initial resistance on Simeon's part (28.12–13). In each version of *Aseneth*, Aseneth's voice and actions support a uniquely nuanced ethos of nonretaliation. The following sections examine the pictures of nonretaliation put forth in MSS A and F, and how Aseneth serves to elucidate the nonretaliatory ethos of each manuscript.

3. Manuscript A

MS A, through its hagiographical form and liturgical context, welcomes its audience into an annual, communal experience of reflection on the complex narrative whole of *Aseneth* and its exemplary characters. As mentioned above, MS A's *Aseneth* is crafted into a liturgical hagiography, one of many hagiographical works within a *menologion*, intended to be read aloud to a Byzantine congregation on Aseneth's saint day.

---

26. MS F has the plural address, "brothers."

4. The Agent(s) of an Ethical Shift 193

Through this contextual situating, MS A shapes the relational space of encounter to be a communal and public one. Annually, through this collective auditory experience, a common world was created in which the members of the congregation encountered the various possibilities of violence and nonretaliation that the focal characters of *Aseneth* display. Thus, the in-between for MS A's original audience was not only relational but physical, liturgical, and ritual. Its tangibility and immanency allowed for the community of individuals to engage the story together, while the generic expectations of hagiography "taxed"[27] the readers with a demand to consider the saint and other venerated characters as ethical models.

3.1. A Nuanced Ethos of Nonretaliation with Concessions for Legitimate Uses of Violence

Through the exemplary models of Levi and Aseneth, and in contrast to Levi's near-foil Simeon, part 1 of *Aseneth* MS A promotes an ethos of nonretaliation rooted in the theological concept of God as the God who avenges wrongs.[28] In MS A, Levi is the first character to articulate and promote the nonretaliatory ethos (ch. 23), and Aseneth follows suit (ch. 28). There is tension, as noted above, between the spoken ethical axiom of Levi ("it is not fitting for a θεοσεβής ἀνήρ to repay evil for evil," 23.9

---

27. "Texts tax readers with ethical duties which increase in proportion to the measure with which they are taken up" (Newton, *Narrative Ethics*, 292). The generic function of Byzantine hagiography as narratives from which to draw edification is well accepted by modern scholars, as well as explicitly attested in many of the hagiographical works themselves. See Stephanos Efthymiadis and Nikos Kalogeras, "Audience, Language, and Patronage in Byzantine Hagiography," in *Genres and Contexts*, vol. 2 of *The Ashgate Research Companion to Byzantine Hagiography*, ed. Stephanos Efthymiadis (Farnham, UK: Ashgate, 2011), 258.

28. Zerbe, *Non-retaliation*, 75. Zerbe reads divine warfare texts, such as Exod 14:13–14; Deut 3:22; 20:1, 3b–4; 2 Chr 20:15–17, as undergirding this theological designation of God as warring on behalf of his people (*Non-retaliation*, 78). To this, one may add the many references in the HB to God as the "God of vengeance" (אל נקמות/ὁ θεὸς ἐκδικήσεων, as an "avenging God," or as the one who brings vengeance (e.g., Ps 94:1 [LXX 93:1]; Nah 1:2; Deut 32:35, 41, 43; Isa 35:4). These theological concepts from the Hebrew Scriptures serve to undergird the ethical messages of both MS A and MS F. This is also reflected in Burchard's reconstruction, which Zerbe analyzes: "While the edifying theme of divine deliverance is significant in its own right, it also functions to ground the second major message of the story, the ethical lesson" (*Non-retaliation*, 75).

A) and his threats of violence against Pharaoh's son (23.13), boasting of past acts of vengeance (23.14), as well as his actions in mustering his brothers against Aseneth's attackers (26.6). This apparent incongruity between speech and action, however, serves to elucidate the full extent of MS A's ethos of nonretaliation.[29] This ethos does not preclude the use of violence in extreme cases but includes (1) the role of the θεοσεβής as an agent of God's vengeance on the wicked (23.14) and (2) the use of force to protect the pious when under attack (26.6, 27.1–6). MS A's ethos of nonretaliation also (3) discourages doing harm to a fallen or defeated enemy. Through the model of Aseneth in chapter 28, the granting of clemency is promoted, and, especially through the example of Levi in chapter 29, so is doing kindness to one's fallen or defeated enemy.

By framing *Aseneth* as a hagiography, MS A exalted *Aseneth* to its middle Byzantine audience as a saint from ancient, biblical times from whom to draw inspiration. MS A is among the earliest extant Greek witnesses of *Aseneth*, and the earliest full manuscript of family *a*, dating to the eleventh or twelfth century.[30] Its elevated style and framing of *Aseneth* as hagiography is shared by the four other extant manuscripts in its family.[31] MS A is thus representative of how Aseneth's story was encountered by many Byzantine churches and monastic communities from at least the tenth to the fifteenth centuries.[32] MS A, and the other manuscripts in

---

29. Zerbe, *Non-retaliation*, 76.

30. Family *a* consists of six manuscripts, O, A, P, Q, C, and R (Wright, "After Antiquity," 141–45). Only MSS A, P, and Q offer the full text. MSS C and R preserve partial texts, ending abruptly at 10.5 and 5.1, respectively. MS O preserves the title and incipit shared with other manuscripts in the family, and is, like MS A, a *menologion* (Burchard, *Joseph und Aseneth*, 22). Burchard dismissed family *a*'s text as being valuable for reconstructing the original *Aseneth* due to its "Greecianization (Gräzisierung)," or elevated style (24). The stylistic amplification of family *a*'s *Aseneth* was likely the result of the ninth- and tenth-century revival and renewal of hagiographical compositions in the middle Byzantine period (23). See also Efthymiadis and Kalogeras, "Audience, Language, and Patronage," 261–65. Other eleventh-century manuscripts include the M palimpsest of Burchard's family Mc and B of MSS family *d* (Wright, "After Antiquity," 8). The only older Greek manuscript is O, dating to the tenth century, of which unfortunately only the title and incipit in the table of contents has survived (141–42).

31. See Wright, "After Antiquity," 147–13.

32. "[In his 1889 edition,] Battifol largely reproduce[d] the internal divisions in A and these provide[d] the majority of his chapter divisions. Reissler's versification of *Jos. Asen.*, taken over by Burchard, often follows the punctuation of A. Thus A still exerts some influence over how the story is read today" (Wright, "After Antiquity," 142).

4. The Agent(s) of an Ethical Shift

family *a*, title the story, "The Life [βίος] and Confession [ἐξομολόγησις] of Aseneth, Daughter of Pentephre, Priest and Satrap of Heliopolis and Narrative [διήγησις] [of] How the All-Beautiful Joseph Took Her as a Wife." The hagiography ends with a quotation from Gen 50:22b–26, describing Joseph's death and burial, with an additional statement about Aseneth's death and burial, followed by a liturgical trinitarian invocation.[33] Wright proposes that the labeling of *Aseneth* as βίος and family *a*'s formulaic ending serve the purpose of shaping *Aseneth* to be "more in line with the hagiographic literature it was read in amongst."[34]

In part 2 of MS A's *Aseneth*, the figure of Levi is upheld as a heroic model and ethical exemplar in addition to Aseneth. Though Aseneth is the protagonist "saint" of MS A, both Joseph and Levi feature prominently in part 1 and part 2, respectively. In addition, Joseph and Levi are each labeled as a θεοσεβής, or God-worshiper,[35] and they each instruct Aseneth in the ways of God. For example, Joseph instructs her on the proper behavior regarding kissing for the θεοσεβής ἀνήρ in 8.5–8.6 and the θεοσεβής γυνή in 8.7 A, and Levi reads and reveals the "writings written in heaven [γράμματα γεγραμμένα ἐν τῷ οὐρανῷ]" to Aseneth in 22.13 A. Joseph is offstage distributing grain for much of part 2, but Levi is depicted as sharing a special relationship with Aseneth from the moment of his introduction in chapter 22:

καὶ ἦν Λευὶς ἐκ δεξιῶν τῆς Ἀσενὲθ καὶ Συμεὼν ἐξ εὐωνύμων. ἐκράτησε δὲ Ἀσενὲθ τὴν χεῖρα Λευὶ διότι ἠγάπα αὐτὸν σφόδρα ὑπὲρ πάντας τοὺς ἀδελφοὺς Ἰωσὴφ καὶ ὡς ἄνδρα προφήτην καὶ θεοσεβῆ καὶ φοβούμενον τὸν κύριον· ἦν γὰρ ἀνὴρ συνιὼν καὶ προφήτης ὑψίστου καὶ αὐτὸς ἑώρα γράμματα γεγραμμένα ἐν τῷ οὐρανῷ καὶ ἀνεγίνωσκεν αὐτὰ καὶ ἀπεκάλυπτεν αὐτὰ τῇ Ἀσενὲθ κρυφῇ διότι καὶ αὐτὸς Λευὶς ἠγάπα τὴν Ἀσενὲθ πάνυ καὶ ἑώρα τὸν τόπον τῆς καταπαύσεως αὐτῆς ἐν τοῖς ὑψίστοις. (22.13)

---

33. Ἐτελεύτησεν δὲ καὶ Ἀσενὲθ μετὰ τὴν κοίμησιν Ἰωσὴφ προβεβήκιαν καὶ πλήρης [ἡμερῶν] ὑπάρχουσα καὶ ἐτάφη πλησίον Ἰωσὴφ τοῦ ταύτης μνηστῆρος. ὑπὲρ δὲ τούτων ἁπάντων δοξάσομεν τὸν πατέρα καὶ τὸν υἱὸν καὶ τὸ ἅγιον πνεῦμα νῦν καὶ ἀεὶ καὶ εἰς τοὺς αἰῶνας τῶν αἰώνων ἀμήν. See translation in appendix.

34. Wright, "After Antiquity," 151. See also Martin Hinterberger, "Byzantine Hagiography and Its Literary Genres: Some Critical Observations," in Efthymiadis, *Ashgate Research Companion*, 29–32.

35. Joseph in 4.7 A (by Pentephres) and Levi in 22.13 A. This term is also used in MS F (see note 14 and below).

> And Levi was on the right of Aseneth and Simeon on [her] left. Aseneth grasped Levi's hand because she loved him exceedingly above all Joseph's brothers and because[36] [he was] a prophetic man and a God-worshiper and feared the Lord. For he was a man of understanding and a prophet of the Most High, and he saw writings that were written in heaven and read them and revealed them to Aseneth in secret, because Levi himself also loved Aseneth very much and saw the place of her rest in the highest [heavens]. (22.13)

Aseneth had first received instruction from Joseph, called "the son of God" in 6.2 A, and then received revelations of the "unspoken mysteries of God [τὰ ἀπόρρητα τοῦ θεοῦ]" from the godly messenger (ὁ θεῖος ἄγγελος)[37] in 16.13–14. In part 2, it is Levi, "a man of understanding and a prophet of the Most High," who instructs Aseneth and reveals divine mysteries to her.[38] MS A's Aseneth thus models a willingness to receive instruction from divinely appointed authorities, one of whom is Levi. Levi's actions and instructions to his brothers in chapters 23, 26, and 29, therefore, serve to articulate and demonstrate what is fitting behavior for the θεοσεβής.

In chapter 23, Levi first exemplifies nonretaliation as "not repaying evil for evil," which he demonstrates and enforces in his interaction with Pharaoh's son. Pharaoh's son summons Simeon and Levi, hoping for them to aid him in his plan "to make war against Joseph and to kill him with [the] sword and to take Aseneth as a wife" (23.4). Pharaoh's son chooses Simeon and Levi based on their renown as warriors in their destruction of Shechem (cf. Gen 34):

> τότε ἀπέστειλεν ἀγγέλους ὁ υἱὸς Φαραὼ καὶ ἐκάλεσε πρὸς ἑαυτὸν Συμεὼν καὶ Λευί· οἱ δὲ ἐλθόντες καὶ σταθέντες ἐνώπιον αὐτοῦ λέγει αὐτοῖς ὁ υἱὸς

---

36. In this dependent clause, the relative ὡς functions as a causal conjunction. See Herbert Smyth, *Greek Grammar* (Cambridge: Harvard University Press, 1956), 671 (§3000).

37. MS A uses this term for the ἄνθρωπος in 14.4; 15.2; 16.3, 5, 15; 17.2, 4. In MS A, he is described as "a man in every way like Joseph, with the robe and the crown and the royal staff" (14.9 A), but in MS F, no such connection is made.

38. As Zerbe has also noted, the role of Levi as seer and teacher is also prevalent in the Testaments of the Twelve Patriarchs, especially T. Reu. 6.8–12; T. Levi 2–5, 14–18; T. Naph. 6.8 (*Non-retaliation*, 76). The oldest roots of this tradition may be found in Deut 33:8–11 in Moses's blessing of Levi's descendants, addressed to God, "They will teach Jacob your rules and Israel your *torah*" (Deut 33:10a).

4. The Agent(s) of an Ethical Shift 197

Φαραὼ ὁ πρωτότοκος Γινώσκω ἐγὼ ὅτι σήμερον ὑμεῖς ἐστὲ ἄνδρες δυνατοὶ ὑπὲρ πάντας ἀνθρώπους ἐπὶ τῆς γῆς καὶ ἐν ταῖς δεξιαῖς ὑμῶν ταύταις κατέστραπται ἡ πόλις τῶν Σικημιτῶν καὶ ἐν ταῖς δυσὶ ῥομφαίαις ὑμῶν κατεκόπησαν τριάκοντα χιλιάδες ἀνδρῶν πολεμιστῶν. (23.2)

Then Pharaoh's son sent messengers and summoned Simeon and Levi to himself. After they came and stood before him, the firstborn son of Pharaoh said to them, "I myself know that you today are men mightier than all peoples on the earth, and with these right hands of yours the city of the Shechemites was overthrown, and with your two swords thirty thousand warriors were cut down." (23.2)

After trying to entice Simeon and Levi to assist him in his plan with the promise of riches and slaves (23.3), Pharaoh's son threatens them with death if they do not comply (23.5–6). In response to his harsh words, Simeon is offended and ready to respond violently, but Levi interferes:

ὁ δὲ Συμεὼν ἦν ἀνὴρ θρασὺς καὶ τολμηρὸς καὶ ἐνεθυμήθη βαλεῖν τὴν χεῖρα αὐτοῦ τὴν δεξιὰν ἐπὶ τὴν κοπὴν τῆς ῥομφαίας αὐτοῦ τοῦ ἑλκῦσαι αὐτὴν ἐκ τοῦ κολεοῦ αὐτῆς καὶ πατάξαι τὸν υἱὸν Φαραὼ διότι σκ[λ]ηρὰ λελάληκεν αὐτοῖς.

εἶδεν οὖν Λευὶ τὴν ἐνθύμησιν τῆς καρδίας αὐτοῦ ὅτι ἦν ἀνὴρ προφήτης καὶ ἐπάτησεν τῷ ποδὶ αὐτοῦ τὸν δεξιὸν πόδα Συμεὼν καὶ ἔθλιψεν σημαίνων αὐτῷ τοῦ παύσασθαι αὐτὸν ἀπὸ τῆς ὀργῆς αὐτοῦ.

ὁ δὲ Λευὶ τῷ Συμεὼν ἡσύχως ἔλεγεν· Ἵνατι σὺ θυμοῦσαι πρὸς τὸν ἄνδρα τοῦτον; ἡμεῖς ἄνδρες ἐσμὲν θεοσεβεῖς καὶ οὐ προσήκει ἡμῖν ἀποδοῦναι κακὸν ἀντὶ κακοῦ. (23.7–9)

Now, Simeon was a rash and daring man, and he wanted to put his right hand on the hilt of his sword to draw it from its sheath and strike Pharaoh's son because he had spoken to them harshly.

Therefore, Levi saw the intention of his heart because he was a prophetic man and stepped on the right foot of Simeon with his [own] foot and pressed, signaling to him to cease from his anger.

Levi spoke quietly to Simeon, "Why are you furious toward this man? We are God-worshiping men, and it is not fitting for us to repay evil for evil." (23.7–9)

In contrast to his brother Simeon, Levi responds "with frankness and gentleness of heart" (μετὰ παρρησίας ἐν πραότητι καρδίας) when he declares to Pharaoh's son why they cannot help:

ἱνατί λάλει ὁ κύριος ἡμῶν τὰ ῥήματα ταῦτα; ἡμεῖς τοίνυν ἐσμὲν ἄνδρες θεοσεβεῖς καὶ ὁ πατὴρ ἡμῶν ἔστιν φίλος θεοῦ τοῦ ὑψίστου καὶ ὁ ἀδελφὸς ἡμῶν ἔστιν ὡς υἱὸς τοῦ θεοῦ.

καὶ πῶς ποιήσομεν ἡμεῖς τὸ πονηρὸν τοῦτο ῥῆμα τοῦ ἁμαρτῆσαι ἐνώπιον τοῦ θεοῦ ἡμῶν καὶ τοῦ πατρὸς ἡμῶν Ἰσραὴλ καὶ ἐνώπιον τοῦ ἀδελφοῦ ἡμῶν Ἰωσήφ; (23.10–11)

Why is our lord saying these things? Furthermore, we are God-worshiping men, and our father is a friend of God the Most High, and our brother [Joseph] is like a son of God.

And how can we do this wicked thing, to sin before our God and our father Israel and before our brother, Joseph? (23.10–11)

To Simeon, Levi teaches that to be θεοσεβής is to not "repay evil for evil" by responding to the harsh threats of an overlord with anger-induced violence. To Pharaoh's son, he asserts that their identity as ἄνδρες θεοσεβεῖς involves respecting those who are honored as God's friends and children. Therefore, they cannot aid in any plots against them, for to do so would be sin.

Furthermore, in chapter 23, Levi's continued speech teaches that although the ways of the θεοσεβής are usually peaceable, there are extreme circumstances in which God himself works through the θεοσεβής to exact revenge. This is seen in his seemingly paradoxical assertions of verses 12–14:

καὶ νῦν ἄκουσον τῶν ῥημάτων μου· οὐ προσήκει ἀνδρὶ θεοσεβεῖ ἀδικεῖν ἄνθρωπόν τινα κατ' οὐδένα τρόπον· ἐὰν δέ τις ἀδικεῖν βούλεται ἄνδρα θεοσεβῆ οὐκ ἀμύνεται αὐτῷ ὁ ἀνὴρ ἐκεῖνος ὁ θεοσεβής διότι ῥομφαῖα οὐκ ἔστιν ἐν ταῖς χερσὶν αὐτοῦ.

καὶ σὺ μὲν φύλαξαι ἔτι λαλῆσαι περὶ τοῦ ἀδελφοῦ ἡμῶν Ἰωσὴφ τὰ ῥήματα ταῦτα· εἰ δὲ ἐπιμένεις τῇ βουλ[ῇ]³⁹ σου τῇ πονηρᾷ ἰδοὺ αἱ ῥομφαῖαι ἡμῶν ἐσπασμέναι κατενώπιόν σου.

τότε εἵλκυσαν τὰς ῥομφαίας αὐτῶν Συμεὼν καὶ Λευὶ ἐκ τῶν κολεῶν αὐτῶν καὶ εἶπον· Ὁρᾷς τοίνυν τὰς ῥομφαίας ταύτας; ἐν ταύταις ταῖς δυσὶ ῥομφαίαις ἐξεδίκησεν κύριος τὴν ὕβριν Σικιμιτῶν ἣν ὕβρισαν τοὺς υἱοὺς Ἰσραὴλ διὰ τὴν ἀδελφὴν ἡμῶν Δῖναν ἣν καὶ ἐμίανεν Συχὲμ ὁ υἱὸς Ἐμμώρ. (23.12–14)

And now, hear *my* words! It is not fitting for a God-worshiping man to wrong any person in any way. But if someone desires to wrong a God-

---

39. MS A βουλήσει.

worshiping man, that God-worshiping man will not defend himself[40] against him, for a sword is not in his hands.

And as for you, be wary of speaking these things any longer about our brother Joseph. If you continue in your wicked plan, behold! Our swords are drawn against you.

Then Simeon and Levi drew their swords from their sheaths and said, "Now, do you see these swords? With these two swords, the Lord avenged the insult of the Shechemites with which they insulted the sons of Israel on account of our sister Dinah, whom Shechem son of Hamor also defiled." (23.12–14)

---

40. There is some debate about the translation of the negated verb ἀμύνω, here in the middle form. In the active voice, it can mean "to keep off," "to defend," or "to aid," while in the middle it indicates "to defend oneself" or "to avenge oneself" (*LSJ*, 87). For a majority of translators, including Riessler, Burchard, Brooks, and Klassen, this phrase (οὐκ ἀμύνεται αὐτῷ) is rendered according to its middle verb form with either "does not avenge himself upon him (the injurer)" or "will not defend himself before him (the injurer)" (Zerbe, *Non-retaliation*, 82 n. 88). In these examples, the dative is used with this verb to indicate the person for or from whom danger is averted (see LSJ, 87). Zerbe argues for translating the middle verb with the active meaning "to assist" here, with αὐτῷ acting as a dative of advantage, indicating the person being assisted (*Non-retaliation*, 82 n. 88). He renders the phrase, "If anyone wants to injure a(nother) God-worshipper, that (former) God-worshipper will not assist him (the injurer), because a sword is not in his hands" (82 n. 88). Ahearne-Kroll's translation also renders the verb this way. See Patricia Ahearne-Kroll, "Joseph and Aseneth," in Feldman, Kugel, and Schiffman, *Outside the Bible*, 2573. Zerbe's reading, however, would necessitate the first "God-worshipping man" that "someone desires to wrong" as being different from "that God-worshipping man" that is the subject of the verb ἀμύνεται, as indicated by his parenthetical insertions, but even he admits that "there is no certainty that the sequence is supposed to refer to two separate God-worshippers—ἐκεῖνος may simply be emphatic" (*Non-retaliation*, 82 n. 88). While Zerbe's rendering certainly offers "the least conflict between 23.13–15 and the rest of the story; cf. 26.6; 27.6," I find that the phrase "a sword is not in his hands" poses a conflict that remains between these words of Levi and later actions and words. I argue that the use of the middle form of ἀμύνω in the following chapter undergirds the rendering of this verb as "defend himself." In 24.7, Pharaoh's son declares to Dan, Gad, Naphtali, and Asher that they "should not die like women but be men and avenge yourselves on your enemies [ἀμύνεσθε τοὺς ἐχθροὺς ὑμῶν]!" The verb is used in the middle sense with the accusative, and contextually, Pharaoh's son is attempting to gain the brothers' assistance to attack Joseph, who he deceitfully claims is actively plotting with the Pharaoh to kill the brothers (24.8–12). Pharaoh's son frames Joseph and Pharaoh as the "enemies" of the sons of Bilhah and Zilpah, and incites them to avenge themselves by responding to the (false) threat with an attack of their own.

Within the span of a breath, Levi declares that the God-worshiping man does not defend himself against those who would seek to wrong him, "because a sword is not in his hands," and then he, the self-proclaimed θεοσεβής ἀνήρ, brandishes his own sword with a threat. In line with Jub. 30's version of the events at Shechem,[41] Levi and Simeon declare that "with these two swords, the Lord avenged the insult of the Shechemites." By this, Levi the prophetic revealer and instructor of heavenly writings displays the nuances of the ethos of the θεοσεβής. As Zerbe notes, "While stressing non-retaliation and the rejection of the sword, the author admits that in some extreme cases the sword can be used as a legitimate instrument of divine vengeance."[42]

Verse 13 is a pivot point in the chapter, a resounding, unspoken "however" in which Levi makes clear to the tyrannical Pharaoh's son that a θεοσεβής will *not* sit idly by when God's friends and children are harmed by an enemy. In MS A, Levi and Simeon remind Pharaoh's son of one such time, when their sister Dinah was defiled[43] by Shechem, and "God avenged the insult" through their swords. Pharaoh's son began the conversation with reference to this event (23.2),[44] stating it as evidence of the military prowess of the brothers. Simeon and Levi interpret that event afresh for Pharaoh's son—it was not their fight but the Lord's vengeance against a wrong done to them on account of their sister. Zerbe concludes that "Levi here proclaims that the swords of the pious may become the legitimate instruments of divine vengeance."[45] This God-given role of the θεοσεβής is emphasized when the swords themselves "were flashing like a flame of fire [ἤστραπτον ὥσπερ φλόγα πυρός]," the same words used to describe the appearance of the chariot from heaven in Jos. Asen. 17.8 (ἦν

---

41. The account of Gen 34 presented by *Aseneth*'s Levi and Simeon in 23.14 A agrees with Jub. 30 in three ways: (1) all of the Shechemites are to blame for the "insult," (2) the Lord works through Simeon and Levi to punish the Shechemites for their offense (Jub. 30.6), and (3) that offense is the defiling of Dinah.

42. Zerbe, *Non-retaliation*, 76. Zerbe used Burchard's reconstruction as a base text. The reconstructed texts of both Burchard and Philonenko have this tension between Levi's spoken words in 23.12 and the brothers' actions and threats in 23.13–14.

43. See notes 18 and 19 above.

44. It is never clear whether the number of Shechemite "warriors" (30,000) that Pharaoh's son recounts as slain by Simeon and Levi is exaggerated for the point of flattery, reflects an exaggerated report of their exploits that has reached him, or is meant to be taken as accurate. Simeon and Levi do not comment on the number itself.

45. Zerbe, *Non-retaliation*, 82.

4. The Agent(s) of an Ethical Shift 201

... ὥσπερ φλόγα πυρός).⁴⁶ Pharaoh's son gets the message; "exceedingly afraid," trembling, and nearly blinded, "he fell upon his face to the ground beneath their feet" (23.15).

Later in MS A, Levi and his freeborn brothers⁴⁷ demonstrate a second nuance of the ethos of the θεοσεβής: violence is legitimate for the θεοσεβής when used to defend the pious from attack. In Aseneth and Joseph's parting scene (26.1–4), Joseph assures her that "the Lord is with you and will himself guard you like the apple of his eye from every evil."⁴⁸ As the action pans out, it becomes clear that the Lord's guard over Aseneth is in part accomplished through the ἀδελφοί θεοσεβεῖς. The first cycle of Aseneth's deliverance comes through a series of miraculous strikes by Benjamin and the sons of Leah. In chapters 24–25, Pharaoh's son enlists the aid of the sons of Bilhah and Zilpah to prepare a 2,050-man ambush against Aseneth (24.18–19). She was to be traveling with an armed force of six hundred men and fifty forerunners (24.15, 26.5), and their plan was to cut down the guards, take Aseneth for Pharaoh's son, and kill Joseph and his young

---

46. The tradition that Simeon and/or Levi received special swords from heaven with which to slaughter the Shechemites is also preserved in Jdt 9:2 and T. Levi 5.3 (Kugel, *Traditions of the Bible*, 428–29). This may indicate a connection with God's own blazing sword of vengeance in Deut 32:41; in YHWH's oath of vengeance on his enemies (Deut 32:40–42), he declares, "I will sharpen my sword like lightning, and my hand will grasp judgment, and I shall repay justice to [my] enemies and those who hate me I shall repay!" (παροξυνῶ ὡς ἀστραπὴν τὴν μάχαιράν μου, καὶ ἀνθέξεται κρίματος ἡ χείρ μου, καὶ ἀνταποδώσω δίκην τοῖς ἐχθροῖς, καὶ τοῖς μισοῦσίν με ἀνταποδώσω).

47. *Aseneth* draws a distinction between the sons of Leah and Rachel and the sons of Bilhah and Zilpah, who are labeled as their slaves by the narrator (Ζελφὰς καὶ Βάλας τῶν παιδίσκων Λείας καὶ Ῥαχιήλ, 22.11). At the first introduction of the slave-born sons, they are further distinguished by their disdain for the narrative's revered couple, Joseph and Aseneth: "Simeon and Levi (the sons of Leah only) escorted them, but the sons of Bilhah and Zilpah, the slaves of Leah and Rachel, did not also escort them because they resented and hated them [Joseph and Aseneth]" (22.11 A). It is this animosity that Pharaoh's son is able to capitalize on when he spins a deceitful tale in chapter 24 to frighten Dan, Gad, Naphtali, and Asher into working together to destroy Joseph and take Aseneth. Their willingness to comply with the plan further distinguishes them as foils (and enemies) to their θεοσεβεῖς brothers.

48. "And Joseph said to her, 'Have courage and do not fear, but rather go away rejoicing because the Lord is with you and will himself guard you like the apple of [his] eye from every evil'" (καὶ εἶπεν αὐτῇ ὁ Ἰωσήφ· θάρσει καὶ μὴ φοβοῦ ἀλλὰ μᾶλλον ἄπελθε χαίρων καθόλου μηδένα πτοουμένη διότι κύριος μετὰ σοῦ ἐστὶν καὶ αὐτός σε διαφυλάξει ὡς κόρην ὀφθαλμοῦ ἀπὸ παντὸς κακοῦ, 26.2 A).

children (24.19). When the first part of their plan—the killing of the 650 guards—is underway, however, word miraculously comes to Levi, the prophet, who immediately prepares his brothers for action:

ὡς δὲ ἔφθασεν Ἀσενὲθ ἐπὶ τὸν τόπον τοῦ χειμάρρου μετὰ τῶν ἑξακοσίων ἀνδρῶν ἐξαίφνης ἐξῆλθον οἱ περὶ τὸν υἱὸν Φαραὼ ἐκ τῆς ἐνέδρας αὐτῶν καὶ συνέμιξαν πόλεμον μετὰ τῶν ἀνδρωντῶν ὄντων μετὰ Ἀσενὲθ καὶ κατέκοψαν αὐτοὺς πάντας ἐν ταῖς ῥομφαίαις αὐτῶν καὶ τοὺς προδρόμους αὐτῆς πάντας ἀπέκτειναν· ἡ δὲ Ἀσενὲθ ἔφυγεν μετὰ τοῦ ὀχήματος αὐτῆς.

τότε ἔγνω Λευὶ ὁ υἱὸς Λίας ταῦτα πάντα τῷ πνεύματι ὡς προφήτης καὶ εἶπεν τοῖς ἀδελφοῖς αὐτοῦ τὸν κίνδυνον Ἀσενὲθ καὶ εὐθέως ἔλαβεν ἕκαστος αὐτῶν τὴν ῥομφαίαν ἐπὶ τὸν μηρὸν αὐτοῦ καὶ τὰς ἀσπίδας αὐτῶν ἐπὶ τοὺς βραχίονας αὐτῶν καὶ τὰ δόρατα ἐν ταῖς δεξιαῖς αὐτῶν χερσὶν καὶ κατεδίωξαν ὀπίσω τῆς Ἀσενὲθ δρόμῳ πολλῷ. (26.5-6)

When Aseneth arrived at the place of the wadi with six hundred men, instantaneously those around the son of Pharaoh came out from their hiding place and mixed in battle with the men who were with Aseneth. And they cut them all down with their swords and they killed all her forerunners. But Aseneth fled with her chariot.

Then Levi the son of Leah knew all these things by the spirit as a prophet and told his brothers [about] Aseneth's danger, and immediately each of them took [a] sword on his thigh and their shields on their arms and spears in their right hands and they pursued after Aseneth with much speed. (26.5-6)

Zerbe notes that "the story ... assumes that it is advisable and legitimate for Aseneth to have armed escorts (22.11; 24.15) for her protection,"[49] but what he does not note is that they are useless when the attack comes. Every armed guard of Aseneth falls, but the God-worshiping sons of Leah, notified of the attack through divine revelatory means, succeed:

τότε οἱ υἱοὶ Λίας· Ρουβὴν καὶ Συμεὼν· Λευὶ καὶ Ἰούδας· Ἰσάχαρ καὶ Ζαβουλών· κατεδίωξαν ὀπίσω τῶν ἀνδρῶν τῶν ἐνεδρασάντων τῇ Ἀσενὲθ καὶ ἐπέπεσον αὐτοῖς ἄφνω καὶ κατέκοψαν αὐτοὺς πάντας· καὶ ἀπέκτειναν οἱ ἓξ ἄνδρες δισχιλίοις. (27.6)

Then the sons of Leah—Reuben and Simeon, Levi and Judah, Issachar and Zebulun—pursued after the men who lied in wait for Aseneth and

---

49. Zerbe, *Non-retaliation*, 86–87.

fell on them suddenly and cut them all down. And the six men killed two thousand.⁵⁰ (27.6)

What the six hundred armed guards could not do, the six θεοσεβεῖς accomplished. This miraculous deliverance, prompted by a divine revelation, serves to affirm the message that the θεοσεβής has a legitimate role as defender of the pious under attack.⁵¹

MS A further upholds the idea that defensive violence enacted by a θεοσεβής is legitimate and God-ordained. It does so through narration of another miraculous defense that happens by human means, which is told in a way that echoes a biblical tale of divine deliverance through a human hero. Before Leah's sons arrive in 27.6, Aseneth, fleeing ahead on her chariot from the slaughter of her armed guards, is met by Pharaoh's son and his fifty cavalry men (26.7): "And upon seeing him, Aseneth was very afraid and trembling and called on the name of the Lord her God" (26.8). In response to this prayer, a miraculous intervention⁵² ensues, in which the previously unmentioned Benjamin leaps out from Aseneth's chariot and strikes Pharaoh's son with a round stone taken from the nearby wadi (λίθον ἐκ τοῦ χειμάρρου στρογγύλον, 27.2): "He hurled it down toward the son of Pharaoh and struck his left temple [τὸν κρόταφον αὐτοῦ τὸν εὐώνυμον]. And it wounded him with a deep wound" (27.2b). Many interpreters note that this episode alludes to 1 Sam 17, in which the young David, after taking smooth stones from the nearby wadi (λίθους λείους ἐκ τοῦ χειμάρρου, LXX 1 Sam 17:40), hurls one against Goliath the Philis-

---

50. MS A (and its relative, MS P) has καὶ ἀπέκτειναν οἱ ἓξ ἄνδρες δισχιλίοις ἑβδομήκοντα ἕξ, "and the six men killed 2,076," a curiously specific number that does not reflect the data given previously in the narrative (24.18 and 24.20 attest to a total of 2,000 men).

51. Zerbe has made the connection that this accords with Philo's view of the legitimate use of the sword. Though in many of his writings, and *On Joseph* in particular, Philo writes against violent retaliation for wrongs, in *Spec.* 4.7–10, Philo affirms, "The sword can legitimately be used as an instrument of self-defense and justice" (Zerbe, *Non-retaliation*, 104). Zerbe categorizes *Aseneth* along with Philo's writings as texts from the "the Egyptian Diaspora." Both texts share a special emphasis on the ethos of nonretaliation applying to relations between fellow Judeans (e.g., Philo, *Ios.* 239–240; Jos. Asen. 28.10, 14; Zerbe, *Non-retaliation*, 104).

52. As Standhartinger puts it, Aseneth is "saved out of the hands of Pharaoh by a miracle of Benjamin" ("Sie selbst wird jedoch aus den Händen des Pharaos durch ein Wunder Benjamins gerettet") ("Um zu Sehen," 111).

tine and knocks him out with one hit to the head (1 Sam 17:49).⁵³ The miraculous nature of Benjamin's stone throwing is further emphasized by his ability to do it again, fifty more times: "Benjamin, having run up upon a rock, said to Aseneth's driver, 'Give me stones from the wadi!' And once he had given him fifty stones, Benjamin hurled the stones and killed the fifty men who were with Pharaoh's son. The stones all sunk through their temples" (27.4–5). In 1 Sam 17, David continually boasts in God's ability to "deliver [him] out of the hand of this uncircumcised Philistine," for "the battle belongs to the Lord" (1 Sam 17:37, 47; see also 17:45–46).⁵⁴ While Benjamin says nothing more than "Give me stones from the valley!" the echoes of the evoked text carry with it the associations of David's God-empowered victory over Goliath.⁵⁵ When it comes to non-Israelite enemy attacks, "the battle belongs to the Lord," yet the victory is accomplished through human weaponry. Aseneth's prayers are answered with the actions of Leah's sons and Benjamin.

---

53. E.g., Standhartinger, "Um zu Sehen," 111; Ahearne-Kroll, *Aseneth of Egypt*, 174–75; Zerbe, *Non-retaliation*, 78–80; Hicks-Keeton, *Arguing with Aseneth*, 80–87. Further strengthening the parallel to David, Benjamin is also described in regard to his youth and beauty, as well as his unique strength and fear of God: "He was a young boy, and he was ruddy with a beautiful appearance" (αὐτὸς ἦν παιδάριον, καὶ αὐτὸς πυρράκης μετὰ κάλλους ὀφθαλμῶν, 1 Sam 17:42b LXX). "Now, Benjamin was a young boy, strong as an eighteen-year-old, and there was an unspeakable beauty on him and power like a lion's cub. And he exceedingly feared God" (ἦν δὲ Βενιαμὶν παιδαρίον ἰσχυρὸν ὡς δεκακαίοκτω καὶ ἦν επ' αὐτῷ κάλλος ἄρρητον καὶ δύναμις ὡς σκύμνον λέοντος· ἦν δὲ καὶ φοβούμενος τὸν θεὸν σφόδρα, 27.1 A). The tribe of Judah is connected to lion imagery in Jacob's blessing of Judah in Gen 49:8–12, notably 49:9, which reads, "Judah is a lion's cub" (LXX σκύμνος λέοντος Ιουδα). Here in *Aseneth* A, Benjamin is further connected to David through this imagery associated with his ancestral tribe.

54. Most LXX witnesses, with the exception of the Alexandrine text, omit 1 Sam 17:12–31, in which David asks the cowering Israelite men, "What is to be done for the man who smites that Philistine and takes away the reproach of Israel?" and Eliab's accusations of David's pride. Thus, David in most LXX versions is less tainted by the possibility of vainglorious motivations.

55. See Ziva Ben-Porat, "The Poetics of Literary Allusion," *PTL* 1 (1976): 105–28. In Ben-Porat's theory, "Allusion consists not only in the echoing of an earlier text but in the utilization of the marked material for some rhetorical or strategic end." See Benjamin Sommers, *A Prophet Reads Scripture: Allusion in Isaiah 40–66* (Stanford, CA: Stanford University Press, 1998), 15. I use the term *echo* here to indicate the marker that allows a reader to indicate the source of the allusion, contrary to Sommers's technical use of the term.

4. The Agent(s) of an Ethical Shift 205

These divine deliverances, enacted through human agents, are further legitimized through their parallel to the direct intervention of God that follows. In the second cycle of deliverance, God acts directly on Aseneth's attackers, who are fellow Israelites. After witnessing the sons of Leah destroy their force of two thousand and Benjamin take out Pharaoh's son and his men, the sons of Bilhah and Zilpah, fleeing from before their brothers, conspire a getaway plan: "Come! Let's kill Aseneth and Benjamin and flee into the thicket of these reeds" (27.8). The threat of their violence, Aseneth's prayer for deliverance, and God's divine intervention follow in quick succession:

καὶ ἦλθον ἐπὶ Ἀσενὲθ ἐσπασμένας ἔχοντες τὰς ῥομφαίας αὐτῶν αἵματος πλήρεις.

ἰδοῦσα δὲ αὐτοὺς Ἀσενὲθ ἐφοβήθη πάνυ καὶ εἶπεν· Κύριος ὁ θεὸς ὁ ζωοποιήσας με καὶ ῥυσάμενός με ἐκ τῶν εἰδώλων καὶ τῆς φθορᾶς τοῦ θανάτου καθὼς μοι εἶπας ὅτι εἰς τὸν αἰῶνα ζήσεται ἡ ψυχή μου ῥῦσαί με καὶ νῦν ἀπὸ τῶν ἀνδρῶν τούτων τῶν πονηρῶν.

καὶ ἤκουσεν κύριος ὁ θεὸς τῆς φωνῆς Ἀσενὲθ καὶ εὐθέως αἱ ῥομφαίαι τῶν ἐναντίων ἐξέπεσον ἐκ τῶν χειρῶν αὐτῶν ἐπὶ τὴν γῆν καὶ ἐτεφρώθησαν. (27.9–11)

And they came on Aseneth, holding their drawn swords, covered with blood.
Upon seeing them, Aseneth was very afraid and said, "Lord God—who made me alive and rescued me from the idols and the destruction of death—just as you said to me that 'your soul will live into eternity'—rescue me even now from these wicked men!"
And the Lord God heard Aseneth's voice and immediately the swords of [her] opponents fell from their hands on the ground and were burned to ash. (27.9–11)

This second deliverance comes through the direct intervention of God, who burns up the swords of Aseneth's attackers. Whereas Simeon and Levi's swords were able to burn with divine flame and not be consumed (23.15), the swords of their "wicked" brothers are destroyed by it. It is at this point of direct intervention that the sons of Bilhah and Zilpah affirm God's role in Aseneth's protection: "Having seen this marvelous wonder, they were afraid and said, 'The Lord is waging war against us on behalf of Aseneth!'" (28.1). These two parallel cycles of deliverance, first through the hands of the ἄνδρες θεοσεβεῖς and then through the direct intervention of God, both operate to fulfill Joseph's promise to Aseneth in 26.2, that the Lord would guard her "from every evil."[56]

The ethos of nonretaliation in MS A, through the model characters of Aseneth and Levi, also discourages doing harm to a fallen enemy, promoting instead the granting of clemency. In chapter 23, this is briefly shown by Levi, after Pharaoh's son has fallen at his feet in fear: "Then Levi stretched out his right hand and grasped him, saying, "Arise and do not fear. Only be wary of continuing to speak any wicked thing about our brother Joseph" (23.16 A). In chapter 28, Aseneth models this ethos of mercy by protecting the defeated and repentant sons of Bilhah and Zilpah from further harm. After realizing that God is fighting on Aseneth's behalf, they "fell on their faces," "paid obeisance to Aseneth," and beg her, "Have mercy on us, your servants!" (28.3). Anathea Portier-Young notes the parallels between the brothers' pleas and Aseneth's prayers to God in chapters 12–13.[57] As Aseneth fell before God in her chamber in part 1, the brothers here fall to the ground, declaring themselves to be "humble and afflicted" (τοὺς ταπεινοὺς καὶ ἀθλίους, 28.4), echoing Aseneth's previous cries to God as "the humble one" (ἡ ταπεινὴ, 11.14) and "the afflicted Aseneth" (ἡ ἀθλία Ἀσενὲθ, 12.5). As she confessed her sins to God (12.3–5, 13.10–13) and asked God to "have mercy" (ἐλέησον, 12.14) and to "save" her (ῥῦσαί, 12.7a), so too the brothers confess their wrongs (28.3) and beg, "Have mercy on us ... and save us" (ἐλέησον ἡμᾶς ... καὶ ῥῦσαι ἡμᾶς, (28.4). God's answer to Aseneth's plea was met by the appearance of a divine messenger, who spoke words of comfort to her: "Have courage, Aseneth, and do not fear" (θάρσει Ἀσενὲθ καὶ μὴ φοβοῦ, 14.11). Aseneth responds to the brothers in the same way, θαρσεῖτε καὶ μὴ φοβεῖσθε ὑμεῖς (28.7).[58] In short, she extends to them the mercy that she herself had previously received from God. Dan, Gad, Naphtali, and

---

56. These two parallel cycles of deliverance also affirm Naphtali and Asher's fears, spoken before the conflict to their older brothers, Gad and Dan, to attempt to dissuade them from taking part in the son of Pharaoh's scheme (25.5–6): "If you intend to act wickedly against [Joseph], he will cry to the Most High and He will send fire from heaven and consume you. And the angels of God will war against you" (25.6). But it is Aseneth, Joseph's "wife from eternity" (21.3), who cries to God and is rescued with God's fire from heaven, which mercifully consumes their swords rather than their bodies.

57. Anathea Portier-Young, "Sweet Mercy Metropolis: Interpreting Aseneth's Honeycomb," *JSP* 14 (2005): 156.

58. Portier-Young, "Sweet Mercy Metropolis," 156.

4. The Agent(s) of an Ethical Shift

Asher fear their brothers, the sons of Leah, who were still after them in hot pursuit, but make a case to Aseneth to protect them. They claim that the Lord's recompense—their humiliation and the dissolving of their swords—has been sufficient:

ὁ δὲ κύριος ἀνταπέδωκεν ἡμῖν κατὰ τὰ ἔργα ἡμῶν.

διὰ τοῦτο δεόμεθά σου ἡμεῖς οἱ δοῦλοί σου ἐλέησον ἡμᾶς τοὺς ταπεινοὺς καὶ ἀθλίους καὶ ῥῦσαι ἡμᾶς ἐκ τῶν χειρῶν τῶν ἀδελφῶν ἡμῶν διότι αὐτοὶ γενήσονται ἔκδικοι τῆς σῆς ὕβρεως καὶ αἱ ῥομφαῖαι αὐτῶν κατέναντι ἡμῶν εἰσίν·

καὶ οἴδαμεν ὅτιοί ἀδελφοὶ ἡμῶν ἄνδρες εἰσὶν θεοσεβεῖς καὶ μὴ ἀποδιδόντες κακὸν ἀντὶ κακοῦ τινὶ ἀνθρώπῳ.

λοιπὸν γενοῦ ἴλεως τοῖς δούλοις σου δέσποινα ἐνώπιον αὐτῶν. (28.3b–6)

The Lord has repaid us according to our deeds.

Because of this, we your slaves are begging you, have mercy on us, the humble and afflicted ones, and save us from the hands of our brothers because they have become avengers of your insult and their swords are against us!

And we know that our brothers are God-worshiping men and do not repay evil for evil to any person.

Therefore, be gracious to us, your slaves, mistress, before them. (28.3b–6)

The tension between the ethos of the θεοσεβεῖς to "not repay evil for evil" and the role of the θεοσεβεῖς as avengers of insult (ἔκδικοι τῆς ὕβρεως) is seen here.[59] Although the sons of Leah consider themselves defeated and acknowledge that the ethos of their θεοσεβεῖς brothers is to "not repay evil for evil to any person," it does not disqualify them from the role of divinely appointed agents of God's vengeance. This is affirmed by the fear and urgency behind their plea; they believe themselves to truly be in danger. Aseneth responds with a pledge of protection:

καὶ εἶπεν αὐτοῖς Ἀσενέθ· θαρσεῖτε καὶ μὴ φοβεῖσθε ὑμεῖς ἀπὸ τῶν ἀδελφῶν ὑμῶν· διότι αὐτοὶ θεοσεβεῖς ἄνδρες ὑπάρχουσι καὶ φοβούμενοι τὸν κύριον·

---

59. Jos. Asen. 28.5 is extant in only four manuscripts (A, P, and Q of family *a*, and B). MSS P and Q are both very similar texts to MS A and frame *Aseneth* as a hagiography. The other manuscripts in family *a*, MSS C and R, were not copied fully, and both end abruptly at 10.5 and 5.1, respectively. B is considered, in Burchard's schema, part of family *d* (Wright, "After Antiquity," 8).

πορεύθητε δὴ εἰς τὴν ὕλην τοῦ καλάμου τούτου ἕως οὗ ἐξιλεώσομαι αὐτοὺς ὑπὲρ ὑμῶν καὶ καταπαύσωτὴν ὀργὴν αὐτῶν ἀνθ' ὧν ὑμεῖς μεγάλα τετολμήκατε κατ' αὐτῶν· πλὴν ἴδοι κύριος καὶ κρινεῖ ἀναμέσον ἐμοῦ τὲ καὶ ὑμῶν. (28.7)

And Aseneth said to them, "Have courage and do not be afraid of your brothers, because they are God-worshiping men and ones who fear the Lord. Now, go into the thicket of these reeds until I appease them on your behalf and put an end to the anger of those whom you dared [to commit] great things against. However, the Lord himself will also judge between me and you." (28.7)

In the same way Levi spoke to Pharaoh's son a parting warning to "be wary of continuing to speak any wicked thing about our brother, Joseph" (23.16), Aseneth bids her enemies to "have courage and do not fear" but leaves them with a parting reminder meant to keep them from attempting anything "daring" again: "The Lord will judge between me and you."[60] Aseneth, like the divine messenger and her tutor Levi before her, when confronted with her enemies cowering before her feet, extends mercy to them with the words, "Have courage and do not be afraid." She offers them a place to safely hide and a promise to dissuade their brothers from avenging this wrong.

---

60. Gerhard Delling first noted the parallels between the phrase "the Lord will judge between me and you" (κρινεῖ ἀναμέσον ἐμοῦ τὲ καὶ ὑμῶν) and its use in LXX 1 Sam 24:16 ("Einwirkungen der Sprache der Septuaginta," 43). The phrase also occurs in Gen 16:5 LXX, Exod 5:21, 2 Chr 24:22, and Jdt 7:24, but as Zerbe has argued, here in *Aseneth*, "it seems especially to be an allusion to the story of the encounter between Saul and David in 1 Sam 24" (*Non-retaliation*, 91). In it, David finds Saul defenseless while relieving himself in the cave in which David and his men are hiding. When presented with this opportunity, David spares the enemy who sought his life and declares, "The Lord will judge between me and you, and he will avenge me from you, and my hand will not be against you" (δικάσαι κύριος ἀναμέσον ἐμοῦ καὶ σοῦ· καὶ ἐκδικήσαι μοι* ἐκ σοῦ· καὶ ἡ χείρ μου οὐκ ἔσται ἐπὶ σέ (1 Sam 24:16 LXX [*Zerbe's emendation, LXX σοι]). Saul responds with a declaration of what David has done, essentially describing his action as *not* "repaying evil for evil": "You are more righteous than I, because you have repaid me good, but I have repaid you evil" (Δίκαιος σὺ ὑπὲρ ἐμέ, ὅτι σὺ ἀνταπέδωκάς μοι ἀγαθά, ἐγὼ δὲ ἀνταπέδωκά σοι κακά, 1 Sam 24:18 LXX). Zerbe notes these parallels with *Aseneth* and concludes, "This story ... provided our author not only with a precedent for non-retaliation, restraint, and mercy toward a defenseless enemy, but also with a precedent for deferring justice to God" (*Non-retaliation*, 91).

4. The Agent(s) of an Ethical Shift 209

In 28.9–14, Aseneth undergirds the ethos of "do not repay evil for evil" with three foundational reasons for refraining from vengeance: (1) the Lord is already fighting against their enemies, and God's actions are sufficient (28.10); (2) the Lord avenges hubris done by a "neighbor"; and (3) the "enemies" are their brothers and "neighbors" in that they are fellow offspring of Israel. When the sons of Leah arrive, they are unaware of the miraculous deliverance that transpired and are "seeking their brothers, the sons of the slave-women, to do away with them" (28.9). Aseneth pleads on behalf of the sons of Bilhah and Zilpah:

καὶ εἶπεν πρὸς αὐτοὺς Ἀσενέθ· δέομαι ὑμῶν φείσασθαι τῶν ἀδελφῶν ὑμῶν καὶ μὴ ἀποδώσητε αὐτοῖς κακὸν ἀντὶ κακοῦ· ὁ γὰρ κύριος διέσωσέν με ἀπ' αὐτῶν· καὶ ἔθραυσε τὰς μαχαίρας αὐτῶν καὶ τὰς ῥομφαίας ἐκ τῶν χειρῶν αὐτῶν· καὶ ἰδοὺ τετήκασι καὶ ἐτεφρώθησαν ἐπὶ τὴν γῆν ὥσπερ κηρίον ἀπὸ προσώπου πυρός· καὶ ἔστιν τοῦτο ἡμῖν ἱκανὸν ὅτι κύριος πολεμεῖ αὐτοῖς ὑπὲρ ἡμῶν.

λοιπὸν φείσασθαι ὑμεῖς τῶν ἀδελφῶν ὑμῶν διότι ἀδελφοὶ ὑμῶν εἰσιν καὶ αἷμα τοῦ πατρὸς ὑμῶν Ἰσραήλ. (28.10–11)

And Aseneth said to them, "I beg you to spare your brothers and do not repay them evil for evil. For the Lord preserved me from them and shattered their blades and the swords from their hands. And look! They have melted and were burned to ash on the ground like honeycomb before the face of a fire. And this is enough for them that the Lord is warring against them on our behalf.

So then, you are to spare your brothers because they are your brothers and the blood of your father Israel." (28.10–11)

Aseneth assures the θεοσεβεῖς that their avenging roles are not necessary in this case because the Lord has already intervened. What is left is to show mercy and "spare" them. Most of the brothers seem to be convinced, for they show no opposition to Aseneth. Levi is in full agreement and even comes close to kiss her hand "because he knew what she wanted to save the men from the wrath of their brothers" (28.15). Yet he keeps secret the whereabouts of the sons of Bilhah and Zilpah, "for he was afraid lest in their wrath [ὀργῇ] they may cut down their brothers" (28.17). Here, as in chapter 23, anger (ὀργή) is a passion that seems to war against the ideal ethos of the θεοσεβής. Simeon, who is characterized as rash and angry in 23.7–9, questions Aseneth's intercessory plea for mercy, prompting an opportunity for her to, like Levi, become a teacher and enforcer of the ethos:

καὶ εἶπεν αὐτῇ Συμεών· Ἵνα τί ἡ δέσποινα ἡμῶν λαλεῖ ἀγαθὰ ῥήματα ὑπὲρ τῶν ἐχθρῶν αὐτῆς;

οὐχὶ ἀλλὰ μᾶλλον κατακόψωμεν αὐτοὺς μεληδὸνὲν ταῖς ῥομφαίαις ἡμῶν διότι ἐβουλεύσαντο κακὰ περὶ τοῦ ἀδελφοῦ ἡμῶν Ἰωσὴφ καὶ τοῦ πατρὸς αὐτῶν Ἰσραὴλ καὶ κατὰ σοῦ δέσποινα ἡμῶν σήμερον.

τότε ἐξέτεινεν Ἀσενὲθ τὴν χεῖρα αὐτῆς τὴν δεξιὰν καὶ ἥψατο τῆς γενιάδος τοῦ Συμεὼν καὶ καταφιλήσας αὐτὸν εἶπεν· Μηδαμῶς ἀδελφὲ ἀποδώσῃς κακὸν συινώμην αὐτοῖς ἀντὶ κακοῦ τὸν πλησίον σου διότι κύριος ἐκδικήσει τὴν ὕβριν ταύτην· αὐτοὶ τοίνυν ἀδελφοὶ ὑμῶν εἰσὶν καὶ γένος τοῦ πατρὸς ὑμῶν Ἰσραὴλ καὶ ἔφυγον μήκοθεν ἀπὸ προσώπου ὑμῶν. λοιπὸν συγγνώμην αὐτοῖς ἀπονείματε. (28.12–14)

And Simeon said to her, "Why is our lady[61] saying good things about her enemies?

"No, but rather let's cut them down in order with our swords because today they plotted evil concerning our brother Joseph and our father Israel and against you, our lady!"

Then Aseneth stretched out her right hand and touched Simeon's beard. And having kissed him, she said, "By no means, brother, will you repay *your neighbor* evil for evil because the Lord will avenge this insult. Moreover, they are your brothers and offspring of your father Israel, and they fled far from your presence. Therefore, impart pardon to them." (28.12–14)

Accomplished with a kiss rather than a foot-stomping, Aseneth's rebuke draws attention to the familial relationship between the offenders and the would-be avengers. This repeated focus on their blood relationship (here and above in 28.11) and the mention of "your neighbor" echo the Levitical injunction against seeking vengeance:[62]

Οὐκ ἐκδικᾶταί σου ἡ χείρ καὶ οὐ μηνιεῖς τοῖς υἱοῖς τοῦ λαοῦ σου καὶ ἀγαπήσεις τὸν πλησίον σου ὡς σεαυτόν. Ἐγώ εἰμι Κύριος.

---

61. Or "mistress." Also in 28.13.

62. This connection has also been noted by Zerbe (*Non-retaliation*, 89). In MS A, unlike in Philonenko's reconstructed text, this is the only place where the axiom of nonretaliation is modified by the phrase "to your neighbor." Philonenko, following MS B, includes "to your neighbor" in 23.9, as well, and the narrator refers to Pharaoh's son as Levi's "neighbor" in 23.10. In MS A, the only characters referred to as "neighbor" are the other sons of Israel. In MS F, the phrase "to your neighbor" does not occur at all.

4. The Agent(s) of an Ethical Shift

Your hand shall not avenge yourself and you shall not be wroth against the sons of your People. And you shall love *your neighbor* as yourself. I am the Lord. (Lev 19:18 LXX)

Aseneth, having first received Levi's teachings (22.13), becomes the teacher and enforcer of this ethos of nonretaliation among the brothers.

Immediately after Aseneth's words and Levi's affirmation of her choice to spare his brothers (28.15–17; see above), Levi demonstrates and expounds on the ethos of nonretaliation as it pertains to defeated enemies who are *not* "neighbors" or "brothers." Pharaoh's son, who had fallen on the ground "seemingly half-dead" (ἡμιθανὴς τυγχάνων) after being hit by Benjamin (27.3), revives: "And Pharaoh's son arose from the ground, sat up, and spat blood from his mouth" (29.1). Benjamin rushes forward to finish him off:

καὶ δραμὼν ἐπ' αὐτὸν Βενιαμὶν ἔλαβεν τὴν ῥομφαίαν αὐτοῦ καὶ ἑλκύσας αὐτὴν ἐκ τοῦ κολεοῦ τοῦ υἱοῦ Φαραώ· ὁ γὰρ Βενιαμὶν ῥομφαίαν οὐκ ἦν φορῶν ἐπὶ τῶν μηρῶν αὐτοῦ ἠβουλήθη πατάξαι ἐπὶ τοῦ στήθους τὸν υἱὸν Φαραώ. (29.2)

And after running up to him, Benjamin took his sword. And having drawn it from the son of Pharaoh's sheath (for Benjamin did not have a sword on his thighs), he wanted to strike the son of Pharaoh's chest. (29.2)

Benjamin, who had been paralleled with 1 Sam 17's David earlier in chapter 27, here runs forward to finish off his Goliath in like manner, taking the sword of his enemy to deliver the deathblow.[63] What Levi does next is a deliberate reversal of the 1 Sam 17 story it alludes to:[64]

τότε ἔδραμεν ἐπ' αὐτὸν Λευὶ καὶ κρατήσας τῆς χειρὸς αὐτοῦ εἶπεν· Μηδαμῶς ἀδελφὲ ποιήσῃς τὸ ἔργον τοῦτο διότι [ἡμεῖς][65] ἄνδρες ἐσμὲν θεοσεβεῖς καὶ οὐ

---

63. Immediately after Goliath falls to the ground after being hit by the smooth wadi stone that David hurled at him: "David ran and came upon him and he [David] took his [Goliath's] sword and killed him" (ἔδραμε Δαυὶδ καὶ ἐπέστη ἐπ'αὐτὸν καὶ ἔλαβε τὴν ῥομφαίαν αὐτοῦ [Goliath's] καὶ ἐθανάτωσεν αὐτόν, 1 Sam 17:51a LXX).

64. This has been noted by other interpreters. For example, Zerbe writes, "Here we have a significant rewriting of scriptural tradition and its implicit morality" (*Nonretaliation*, 79).

65. MS A ὑμεῖς.

προσῆκόν ἐστιν ἀνδρὶ θεοσεβεῖ ἀποδοῦναι κακὸν ἀντὶ κακοῦ· οὐδὲ πεπτωκότα καταπατῆσαι οὐδὲ ἐκθλίψαι τὸν ἐχθρὸν αὐτοῦ ἕως θανάτου.

καὶ νῦν ἀπόστρεψον τὴν ῥομφαίαν εἰς τὸν τόπον αὐτῆς καὶ δεῦρο βοήθησόν μοι καὶ θεραπεύσωμεν αὐτὸν ἀπὸ τοῦ τραύματος τούτου καὶ ἐὰν ζήσῃ ἔσται ἡμῶν φίλος καὶ ὁ πατὴρ αὐτοῦ Φαραὼ ἔσται ὡς πατὴρ ἡμῶν. (29.3–4)

Then Levi ran up to him [Benjamin], and having grasped his hand, he said, "By no means, brother, should you do this thing! Because we are God-worshiping men and it is not fitting for a God-worshiping man to repay evil for evil, nor to trample one who has fallen, nor to press his enemy unto death.

"And now, return your sword to its place and come help me, and we may heal him from this wound. And if he lives, he will be our friend, and his father Pharaoh will be like our father." (29.3–4)

Unlike the previous group of enemies, Pharaoh's son does not display repentance or plead for mercy, but his humbled status is indicated by the state of his wounded body. He is "seemingly half-dead" (27.3 A), and when he revives, "blood ran down on his mouth" (29.1 A). Levi repeats the now-familiar axiom, "It is not fitting for a God-worshiping man to repay evil for evil," but uses the opportunity to expound on what that entails in the case of a fallen enemy. Here, mercy is to be granted, in that the defeated opponent is spared his life. In addition, kindness is to be extended ("we may heal him from his wound"), with a hope for reconciliation and even familial-like relations ("if he lives, he will be our friend, and his father Pharaoh will be like our father"). Strikingly, the enemy has done nothing to display a change in his animosity or desire for reconciliation, but Levi proceeds to demonstrate the ethos he has just spoken. He helps Pharaoh's son up off of the ground and washes the blood from his face (29.5). He then "bound bandages on his wound" and brings him to his father, Pharaoh. When Pharaoh hears from Levi "all the things that followed and what happened," he honors Levi by bowing to him on the ground and blessing him (29.6).

3.2. Some Conclusions on Manuscript A

As demonstrated above, MS A not only offers a possibility of nonretaliation to its audience but also promotes it. MS A does so subtly and situationally through the lauded and exemplary characters of Levi and Aseneth. New ethical possibilities are put forth by the words and actions of the leading characters as they navigate various situations, and are meant to be enticing and inspiring. For example, in chapter 23 A, Levi demonstrates the possibility of responding to an overlord's threats with calm composure instead of rash action. In chapters 28–29 of MS A, Aseneth and Levi present the possibility of extending mercy and kindness to humbled foes in lieu of exacting further recompense. The exemplary character of Levi also demonstrates that it *is* possible for the θεοσεβής to use the sword and wield violence in certain situations, including defending the pious (chs. 26–27), and acting as God's agent of vengeance (chs. 23, 28).[66] MS A's ethos of nonretaliation, which holds pious restraint and legitimated uses of violence in tension, spoke to a middle Byzantine audience whose imperial religion was Christianity. At this time, the empire was engaged in frequent wars with neighboring Arab states, and the hagiographies of military saints were being rewritten to emphasize their heroism, and their images were spread widely through various artistic media.[67] MS A presents the hagiography of an Old Testament matriarch, not that of a military saint. Nevertheless, the ethos articulated and demonstrated by Levi and Aseneth in MS A honored and legitimized the Byzantine arms bearer as an agent of God's vengeance while promoting the use of restraint or the display of mercy in certain situations. The public reading of this narrative instigated a corporate reflection on this societal role and its responsibilities.

In part 2 of A's *Aseneth*, it is both Levi and Aseneth who demonstrate the nuances of the ethos of nonretaliation that A promotes. For

---

66. In the previous chapter, I explored the dangers of Jubilees' narrative representation of Simeon and Levi as historical figures who operated as agents of God's wrath. It is not a stretch to assert that similar dangers loom here in the representations of MS A's *Aseneth* and the legitimization it potentially provides to the violent. Taken from another perspective, however, one may argue that MS F's idealization of Aseneth's nonresistance to the attackers aiding her would-be rapist provides an equally dangerous ethos, especially for women. The project of this chapter, however, is not to evaluate the ethical ideals of MSS A and F and the narrative means through which they are communicated, but rather to analyze and compare them with sensitivity to how these manuscripts functioned within their cultural contexts. Nevertheless, I would be remiss not to acknowledge this troubling aspect of MS A's *Aseneth*.

67. Monica White, "Military Saints," in *The Concise Encyclopedia of Orthodox Christianity*, ed. John Anthony McGuckin (Oxford: Wiley Blackwell, 2014), 312–13; Christopher Walter, *Warrior Saints in Byzantine Art and Tradition* (Aldershot, UK: Ashgate, 2003).

the θεοσεβής ἀνήρ, "not repaying evil for evil" does not preclude the use of violence, because, somewhat paradoxically, the special role of the θεοσεβής as God's instruments of vengeance is upheld; MS A affirms that the θεοσεβής ἀνήρ does not "repay evil for evil," which is God's role, but God sometimes accomplishes his role through the θεοσεβής (23.14, 28.4), as well as by direct intervention (27.11). In addition, MS A's ethos of non-retaliation upholds the legitimacy of the use of violence by the θεοσεβής to protect the pious from harm, as witnessed in the defense of Aseneth via the miraculous stone-slinging of Benjamin (27.1–5) and the powerful charge of Leah's sons, led by a Spirit-informed prophet (26.6, 27.6). Furthermore, the ethos of "not repaying evil for evil" involves granting life and clemency to defeated enemies (28.7, 10, 14), and showing them kindness (28.7, 15–17, 29.3–5), especially if they are kinspeople. It is also likely that in its Byzantine ecclesiastical context, "kinspeople" could, by extension, include fellow citizens or fellow Christians.[68] Both Levi, the heralded prophet, teacher, and revealer of heaven's written mysteries, and Aseneth, to whom the "unspoken mysteries of God" were revealed (16.14), teach and display the nuances of this ethos among the sons of Israel.

Within the functional context of MS A,[69] there may have been a felt implicit emphasis on Aseneth's manifestation of the ethos as a θεοσεβής γυνή. Aseneth lives and promotes the ethos of "not repaying evil for evil"

---

68. Literary and artistic evidence from the early Byzantine Empire suggests that "Byzantium was a predominantly Christian state whose inhabitants shared a profoundly religious view of the world. Most people saw their culture as fitting into an uninterrupted historical development stretching from the Old Testament kingdoms to the prophesized return of the Christ at the end of worldly time." See Marcus Rautman, *Daily Life in the Byzantine Empire* (Westport, CT: Greenwood, 2006), 1. At this time, universal chronicles became a common genre, connecting the Byzantine society to the biblical timeline in an ongoing sequence (2). Christianity provided a unifying identity for the diverse population of the empire throughout its many generations. There is evidence to suggest that by the turn of the tenth century—within a century of the composition of MS A—there was imperial promotion of Byzantine identity as God's "chosen people." See Meredith Riedel, *Leo VI and the Transformation of Christian Byzantine Identity: Writings of an Unexpected Emperor* (New York: Cambridge University Press, 2018), 154–73. This chosenness involved an appropriation of chosenness through the association of "Constantinople as the New Jerusalem and the people of Byzantium as the New Israel" (164).

69. That is, as a hagiography of Aseneth read annually on her saint's day.

without doing violence at all, in either self-defense or revenge. If she is the exemplary saint for the audience to meditate on, she demonstrates herself to be a willing recipient of God's teachings, delivered through his specially appointed leader (Joseph), direct revelation (through the godly messenger), and his prophet (Levi). She also teaches and enforces the ethos, first introduced by Levi (23.9), among the Israelites, who likely represented the church or empire for the Byzantine audience.[70] Though there are many biblical traditions in which the female protagonist (e.g., Deborah, Jael, Judith) takes up her sword (or tent peg) against her enemies, it is notable that Aseneth does not do so here. She relies on God through prayer alone, and God brings deliverance either through the armed, God-worshiping men or through direct, miraculous intervention. It could also be that the two central figures of MS A's part 2 offer a gendered ethos of nonretaliation, with Aseneth as a model for the θεοσεβής γυνή and Levi for the θεοσεβής ἀνήρ. There is nothing explicit in the text that would support this, but nothing to refute it either. The Byzantine audience of MS A's *Aseneth* may have been of mixed genders, gathered in corporate church services, or in a monastic community of only men or only women.[71] Whatever the gender makeup of the audience, men and women were free to draw edification from either Aseneth or Levi's demonstration of the ethos, for both are exalted as exemplary characters through their positive assessments by the narrator.

4. Manuscript F

MS F may have also been read aloud in a corporate gathering, yet we cannot be certain whether this was how it was used in the Radu-Vodă monastery. The manuscript was copied at the monastery in Bucharest, which

---

70. See note 68 above.
71. Efthymiadis and Kalogeras, "Audience, Language, and Patronage," 247–84; Alice-Mary Talbot, "A Comparison of the Monastic Experiences of Byzantine Men and Women," *GOTR* 30 (1985): 10–20. In accordance with extant evidence, although literary production was not as prevalent among female monastics as their male counterparts, literacy was certainly well documented and encouraged (Talbot, "Comparison of the Monastic Experiences," 12–13). Monastic libraries differed in size and variety from monastery to monastery, as did the valuation of certain texts. See Nigel Wilson, "The Libraries of the Byzantine World," *GRBS* 8 (2003): 62–65. The reformation of *Aseneth* as a hagiography may have led to an increase in its popularity and circulation, due to its annual liturgical function.

was destroyed in the late sixteenth century during a Turkish invasion and restored in 1614.[72] As the monks returned from their neighboring places of refuge, they worked to repopulate their library with valued works, in which *Aseneth* was included. Aseneth's story is located in the middle of a miscellany of theological works, mostly sermons, and follows Ephraem's *Life of Joseph*.[73]

Whether read corporately or used for private reading and reflection, MS F's *Aseneth* rhetorically constructs a communal narrative in-between for its audience through a series of direct addresses by the narrator. The several second-person plural addresses (after 7.6, framing 21, and after 29) construct a sense of communal inclusion to the reader. In this relational space, the readers or hearers may enter it together, regardless of temporality and spatial dimensions. MS F assumes its monastic Christian audience and claims them as included in its fellowship; all who read MS F are directly addressed by the narrator as "brothers" and included in the community of story experiencers that is crafted by this rhetoric. As kinsmen in Christ, brothers to one another and to the text, they are explicitly exhorted to adhere to the nonretaliatory ethos demonstrated by Aseneth in the narrative. The force of this exhortation is bolstered by the assertion of communal identity bestowed on the audience by the narrator, in essence claiming that as God-worshipers who "live from him" (epilogue F), this is how the collective should conduct themselves.

4.1. Exalting Aseneth as the Agent of an Ethical Shift

MS F's *Aseneth* is shaped to diminish the tension between the axiom of nonretaliation ("do not repay evil for evil") and the use of violence for defense and revenge in some circumstances. Through a series of systematic omissions, MS F exalts Aseneth as the teacher and exemplar of nonretaliation, over and above Levi, to the effect that Levi's threats and actions in chapters 23, 26, and 27 are presented as *un*acceptable conduct, falling short of the ideal that is fully displayed in Aseneth. Due to these

---

72. Wright, "After Antiquity," 105; "The History of the Monastery," Radu Voda Monastery Official Website, https://tinyurl.com/SBL6710c.

73. Its sister text, W, also follows the *Life of Joseph*. Most of these are sermons by Ephraem in Greek or John Chrysostom. See "România, Bucuresti, Biblioteca Academiei Române (BAR), Ms Grec 0966," Pinakes: Textes et manuscrits grecs, https://tinyurl.com/SBL6710d.

omissions, Aseneth inhabits the role of teacher to Levi as well as his brothers. Through the final exhortations of the narrator, the audience is left with a clear expectation for what is required— an expectation that is modeled by Aseneth alone. As Aseneth's modeling of nonretaliation is emphasized, the ethos of legitimate uses of violence in extreme cases, including the role of the θεοσεβής as agent of God's vengeance, is diminished. Tension remains, however, as MS F somewhat paradoxically affirms that God *does* deliver through acts of human violence but makes clear that defensive or retributive violence is not fitting for the audience.

I am not arguing that the copyist of MS F made the changes to the narrative and characterization discussed below, or that the audience would have been aware of any alterations. Although MS F dates to six centuries later than MS A, there is no evidence to suggest literary dependence of MS F on MS A.[74] Furthermore, most but not all of the formal features discussed below are also found in MS F's sister text, MS W. It is therefore likely that the changes happened at the level of an earlier *Vorlage*. I use the terms *omission* and *extension* because in this chapter, I place MS F in dialogue with the earlier text, MS A. MS A's depiction of Levi in 22.13 and his speech in 23.9 are also found in the earliest witnesses to *Aseneth* in Syriac and Armenian, making it the oldest extant and most popular character depiction of Levi in the literary record. Although employing terminology of "omission" and "extension" for comparative reasons, I am making the case that the unique form of MS F's *Aseneth* highlights Aseneth as an ethical exemplar over and above Levi, which drastically affects the ideal ethos promoted by the narrative.

MS F systematically exalts Aseneth over Levi as an exemplary character and ethical authority through a series of omissions. Focus on Aseneth is maintained from the start of the narrative. The story begins at modern versification's 1.3, omitting the story's setting in the "first year of plenty" and the description of Joseph's whereabouts. Instead, MS F begins with an

---

74. See Burchard, *Joseph und Aseneth*, 17–25; and Barbara Uta Fink's proposed stemma in *Joseph und Aseneth: Revision des griechischen Textes und Edition der zweiten lateinischen Übersetzung*, FSBP 5 (Berlin: de Gruyter, 2008). Although I follow Ahearne-Kroll's criticisms of linear reconstructions of the manuscript transmission of *Aseneth*, Burchard's textual comparisons and Fink's stemma both attest to the strong literary and stylistic differences between MSS A and F that suggest F's *Vorlage* was transmitted independently from the stylistic changes that family *a* employed.

introduction of Pentephres and his daughter Aseneth.⁷⁵ More importantly, Levi is still introduced as a man of understanding and a prophet of the Most High in MS F, but his role as revealer of God's mysteries is erased. Aseneth alone has the mysteries of God revealed to her by fiery impartation⁷⁶ from the ἄνθρωπος of heaven:

> καὶ ἐκάλεσεν αὐτὴν πρὸς αὐτὸν καὶ ἐξέτεινε τὴν χεῖραν αὐτοῦ τὴν δεξιάν καὶ ἔθηκεν ἐπὶ τὴν κεφαλὴν αὐτῆς. καὶ ἐφοβήθη Ἀσυνὲθ τὴν χεῖρα τοῦ ἀνθρώπου διότι σπινθῆρες ἐπήδουν ἀπὸ τῆς χειρὸς αὐτοῦ ὡς ἀπὸ σιδήρου καχλάζαντος. καὶ ἐπέβλεψεν Ἀσυνὲθ ἀτενίζουσα τοῖς ὀφθαλμοῖς αὐτῆς εἰς τὴν χεῖρα τοῦ ἀνθρώπου.
>
> καὶ ἐγέλασεν ὁ ἄνθρωπος καὶ εἶπεν τῷ Ἀσυνὲθ· Μακαρία σὺ εἶ διότι ἀπεκαλύφθη σοι τὰ μυστροῦ τοῦ ὑψίστου καὶ μακάριοι πάντες οἱ προσκείμενοι κυρίῳ τῷ θεῷ σου ἐν μετανοίᾳ. (16.13–14)

> And he called her to himself and stretched out his right hand and placed it on her head. And Aseneth was afraid of the man's hand because sparks were leaping from his hand as from crackling iron. And Aseneth, looking intensely, looked with her eyes at the man's hand.
>
> And the man laughed and said to Aseneth, "Blessed are you because the mysteries of the Most High have been revealed to you, and blessed are all who are devoted to the Lord your God in repentance." (16.13–14)

As in MS A, Levi is introduced in chapter 22 as sitting at Aseneth's right hand (22.12) when she and Joseph are escorted home from visiting Jacob.⁷⁷

---

75. Joseph is not even mentioned until chapter 3. In MS F, *Aseneth* follows the *Life of Joseph*. This popular pairing is well attested in every Greek manuscript family and the Armenian manuscripts, leading Burchard to suggest that the two were paired at a very early stage (*Joseph und Aseneth*, 33). Unfortunately, since there has been little text-critical work done on the *Life of Joseph*, it is difficult to determine the relationship between MS F's version of *Aseneth* and MS F's version of the *Life of Joseph* in comparison to other manuscript versions and pairings.

76. A very similar scene is found in 16.13–14 A. In 16.15 F, however, Aseneth does not eat of the honeycomb that the messenger hands her, whereas in MS A, she eats of it. In both texts, the declaration that Aseneth has received the mysteries of God comes after the messenger places his hands on Aseneth's head and precedes the eating or holding of the honeycomb.

77. In MS A, Simeon sits at her left hand. In MS F, Joseph has that position.

4. The Agent(s) of an Ethical Shift

κρατοῦσα τὴν δεξιὰν χεῖρα τοῦ Λευὶ καὶ ἠγαπησεν Ἀσυνὲθ τὸν Λευὶ σφόδρα ὅτι ἦν Λευὶς προσκείμενος πρὸς κύριον τὸν θεὸν καὶ ἦν ἀνὴρ συνιῶν καὶ ὑψίστου προφήτης καὶ ὀξέως βλέπων τοῖς ὀφθαλμοῖς αὐτοῦ. (22.13)

Aseneth grasped the right hand of Levi and loved Levi very much because Levi was devoted to the Lord God, and he was a man of understanding and the Most High's prophet and saw openly with his eyes. (22.13)

Levi is celebrated for his devotion to God, his understanding, and his prophetic abilities, but here in MS F he is not Aseneth's teacher. This is a departure not only from Levi's role as it exists in MS A and family *a* but also from the earliest and most text-critically valued witnesses, the Syriac, Armenian, and Latin 436 manuscripts.[78] Though Levi is lauded with positive characteristics,[79] from the point of his introduction his role as instructor of Aseneth is omitted.

In chapter 23, Levi's role as instructor is further diminished. In 23.8, Levi still operates as a "prophetic man," able to see the intentions of Simeon's heart; however, his hushed rebuke about what is fitting for the θεοσεβής ἀνήρ is omitted:

καὶ εἶδε Λευὶς τὴν ἐνθύμησιν αὐτοῦ τῆς καρδίας αὐτοῦ διότι ἦν Λευὶς ἀνὴρ προφήτης καὶ ἐπάτησε Λευὶς τῷ ποδὶ αὐτοῦ τὸ πόδα τὸν δεξιὸν τοῦ Συμεὼν καὶ ἐξέθλιψε καὶ ἐσήμανεν αὐτῷ τοῦ παύσασθαι ἀπὸ τῆς ὀργῆς αὐτοῦ.

καὶ εἶπε Λευὶς· Ἵνα τί λαλεῖ ὁ κύριος ἡμῶν κατὰ τὰ ῥήματα ταῦτα; καὶ ἡμεῖς ἐσμὲν ἄνδρες θεοσεβεῖς καὶ ὁ πατὴρ ἡμῶν φίλος θεοῦ τοῦ ὑψίστου καὶ Ἰωσὴφ ὁ ἀδελφὸς ἡμῶν ὡς υἱὸς τοῦ θεοῦ πρωτότοκος. (23.8, 10)

And Levi saw the intention of his heart because Levi was a prophetic man. And Levi stepped with his foot on the right foot of Simeon and pressed it and signaled to him to cease from his anger.

And Levi said [to Pharaoh's son], "Why is our lord saying these things? And we are God-worshiping men, and our father is a friend of God the Most High, and Joseph our brother is like the firstborn son of God." (23.8, 10)

---

78. Burchard, *Joseph und Aseneth*, 276–77.
79. Devotion to the Lord is a high value of MS F's narrative, as evinced in the words of the ἄνθρωπος in 16.14.

While Levi still moves to keep Simeon from acting on his anger, he does not instruct him that "we are God-worshiping men, and it is not fitting for us to repay evil for evil" (23.9 A). The first character to instruct the sons of Israel and enforce the ethos of nonretaliation ("do not repay evil for evil") among them is Aseneth in chapter 28 (see below).

Levi's speech to Pharaoh's son is shortened in MS F, to the effect that the threatening nature of his words is enhanced based on the expectation that the θεοσεβής will harm the person who desires to wrong him. In 23.10 A, Levi speaks "with frankness and gentleness of heart," increasing the contrast between him and his hot-headed brother. In 23.10 F, there is no reference to Levi's emotive state. Levi still rejects the plan of Pharaoh's son, calling it "a wicked thing" and "utterly sinning" before God (23.11), but verse 12 is crafted into a threat. The text of MS A is included below for comparison.

> καὶ νῦν ἄκουσον τῶν ῥημάτων μου· οὐ προσήκει ἀνδρὶ θεοσεβεῖ ἀδικεῖν ἄνθρωπόν τινα κατ᾽ οὐδένα τρόπον. ἐὰν δέ τις ἀδικῆσαι βούλεται ἄνδρα θεοσεβῆ οὐκ ἀμύνεται αὐτῷ ὁ ἀνὴρ ἐκεῖνος ὁ θεοσεβὴς διότι ῥομφαία οὐκ ἔστιν ἐν ταῖς χερσὶν αὐτοῦ.
>
> καὶ σὺ μὲν φύλαξαι ἔτι λαλῆσαι περὶ τοῦ ἀδελφοῦ ἡμῶν Ἰωσὴφ τὰ ῥήματα ταῦτα· εἰ δὲ τί πράξεις τῇ βουλῇ σου τῇ πονηρᾷ ἰδοὺ αἱ ῥομφαῖαι ἡμῶν ἐσπασμέναι κατενώπιόν σου. (23.12–13 A)

And now, hear my words! It is not fitting for a God-worshiping man to harm any person in any way. But if someone desires to harm a God-worshiping man, that God-worshiping man does not avenge himself because a sword is not in his hands.

And you! Be wary of speaking these things any longer about our brother Joseph. If you do anything with your wicked plan, behold! Our swords are drawn against you! (23.12–13 A)

> καὶ νῦν ἄκουε τῶν ῥημάτων μου. οὐ προσήκει ἀνδρὶ θεοσεβεῖ ἀδικεῖν πάντα ἄνθρωπον κατουδένα τρόπον. ἐὰν δέ τις ἀδικῆσαι βούλεται ἄνδρα θεοσεβῆ χερσὶν αὐτοῦ—
>
> καὶ σὺ μὲν φύλαξον λαλῆσαι περὶ τοῦ ἀδελφοῦ ἡμῶν Ἰωσὴφ κατὰ τὰ ῥήματα. εἰ δὲ σὺ[80] ἐπιμένεις τῇ πονηρᾷ βουλῇ ταύτῃ[81] ἰδοῦ αἱ ῥομφαῖαι ἡμῶν ἐνώπιόν σου. (23.12–13 F)

---

80. The text of MS F has a lacuna here. MS W reads ἰ δὲ σὺ (Wright, "After Antiquity," 2:191).

81. The text of MS F has a lacuna here. MS W reads βουλῇ ταύτῃ (Wright, "After Antiquity," 2:191).

4. The Agent(s) of an Ethical Shift 221

And now, hear my words! It is not fitting for a God-worshiping man to harm any person in any way. But if someone desires to harm a God-worshiping man with his hands—[82]

And you! Be wary of speaking about our brother Joseph in accordance with these things. But if you remain in this wicked plan, behold! Our swords are against you! (23.12–13 F)

As noted above, MS A's conditional statement in 23.12 enforces the ethos of nonretaliation that Levi introduced in 23.9 A, that a θεοσεβής ἀνήρ does not repay evil for evil.[83] In MS F, however, no such ethos has been introduced. Instead, Levi communicates that while the usual conduct for θεοσεβεῖς such as themselves is to harm no one, responding with violence on one who acts as an enemy is common practice. In other words, the θεοσεβής does not start a fight, but if provoked, he will retaliate. Levi's unfinished sentence adds force to the threat that follows it; "If someone desires to wrong a God-worshiping man with his hands—" finds its apodosis in the unsheathing of swords that follows in 23.14:[84]

---

82. MS W concludes with a septuagintism, "let him surely die" (θανάτῳ ἀποθανείτω).

83. MS Latin 436 agrees with MS A ("The faithful one does not defend himself because there is no sword in his hand," *non defendit se fidelis quia gladius in manu eius non est*), but the Syriac and Armenian witnesses indicate that there *is* a sword in the hand of God-worshiper, and he is ready to use it for vengeance (see Burchard, *Joseph und Aseneth*, 286–87).

84. For the grammatically typical construction of a threat, one would expect εἰ paired with a subjunctive verb, rather than ἐάν with the present indicative βούλεται here (Smyth, *Greek Grammar*, 525–26). Indeed, one would expect any conditional construction beginning with ἐάν to be followed by a subjunctive verb. MS F, however, frequently interchanges ε and η, due to iticism. It is clear from MS F's comparison with other manuscripts that the omission of an apodosis leaves a grammatically awkward construction. I am suggesting that it may *function* here as an unfinished threat that complements the following general conditional phrase ("if you remain in this wicked plan, behold! Our swords are against you!"). As in Exod 7:27 LXX; 9:2, in which God threatens Pharaoh with plagues using general conditional constructions, the condition of Jos. Asen. 23.13 F functions as a threat: "If you are not willing to send [them] out, behold! I will strike all your country with frogs" (εἰ δὲ μὴ βούλει σὺ ἐξαποστεῖλαι ἰδοὺ ἐγὼ τύπτω πάντα τὰ ὅριά σου τοῖς βατράχοις, Exod 7:27 LXX); "If you are not willing to send my people out … behold! the hand of the Lord come upon your livestock in the fields" (εἰ μὲν οὖν μὴ βούλει ἐξαποστεῖλαι τὸν λαόν μου … ἰδοὺ χεὶρ κυρίου ἐπέσται ἐν τοῖς κτήνεσίν σου τοῖς ἐν τοῖς πεδίοις, Exod 9:2–3). In Jos. Asen. 23.13, the apodosis also begins with ἰδού, perhaps intentionally evoking these threats

> καὶ εἵλκυσαν τὰς ῥομφαίας αὐτῶν Συμεὼν καὶ Λευὶς ἐκ τῶν θησαυρῶν αὐτῶν καὶ εἶπον· Ἰδοὺ ἑώρακας τὰς ῥομφαίας ταύτας; ἐν ταύταις ταῖς δυσὶ ῥομφαίαις ἐξεδίκισε κύριος τὴν ὕβριν τῶν Σικήμων. (23.14)

> And Simeon and Levi drew their swords from their stores and said, "Behold! Do you see these swords? With these two swords the Lord avenged the insult of the Shechemites." (23.14)

Chapter 23 F thus crafts the words and actions of Levi to indicate that he *upholds* an ethos of violent retaliation before Aseneth introduces another way in chapter 28 (see below). There is no tension between the nonretaliatory axiom that Levi whispers to Simeon, because Levi does not speak it. Here, taking vengeance with the sword is something that both brothers boast of doing in the past, and it is something they are prepared to do in the present. In MS A, the recourse to violence is presented as fitting for an extreme case that went *against* the usual ethos of nonretaliation and going unarmed. MS F's Levi is armed and ready to avenge a wrong. Pharaoh's son speaks a threat and flashes a sword (23.5–6), and Levi responds with an unmitigated threat and a flash of a sword (23.12–14).

MS F also somewhat diminishes the legitimacy of Levi and his freeborn brothers' rally to Aseneth's defense. In MS A, Levi's awareness of Aseneth's plight is clearly given through the divine medium of prophecy:

> τότε ἔγνω Λευὶ ὁ υἱὸς Λίας ταῦτα πάντα τῷ πνεύματι ὡς προφήτης καὶ εἶπεν τοῖς ἀδελφοῖς αὐτοῦ τὸν κίνδυνον Ἀσενέθ καὶ εὐθέως ἔλαβεν ἕκαστος αὐτῶν τὴν ῥομφαίαν ἐπὶ τὸν μηρὸν αὐτοῦ...(26.6 A)

> Then Levi, the son of Leah, knew all these things by the spirit[85] as a prophet, and he told Aseneth's danger to his brothers. And immediately each of them took his sword on his thigh... (26.6 A)

---

against the hard-hearted Pharaoh of Exodus. The threat of Exod 10:4 LXX is made with a future more vivid conditional construction: "If you are not willing to send my people out, behold! Tomorrow I will bring upon this land a great locust swarm upon all your country" (ἐὰν δὲ μὴ θέλῃς σὺ ἐξαποστεῖλαι τὸν λαόν μου, ἰδοὺ ἐγὼ ἐπάγω ταύτην τὴν ὥραν αὔριον ἀκρίδα πολλὴν ἐπὶ πάντα τὰ ὅριά σου). One could expect Jos. Asen. 23.12 F's unfinished conditional construction to reflect the beginning of a present general condition or a future more vivid condition, either of which may *function* as a threat due to context.

85. Or "in [his] spirit."

4. The Agent(s) of an Ethical Shift

The revelation is imparted before even Aseneth becomes aware of the danger (26.7) or calls on the Lord for help (26.8). As is fitting with MS A's full picture of the θεοσεβής, Levi works in tandem with God to protect the pious, taking up arms when necessary. By contrast, MS F does not relate whence Levi's knowledge of the plot against Aseneth comes:

καὶ Λευὶς ἀνήγγειλε τοῖς ἀδελφοῖς αὐτοῦ τοῖς υἱοῖς Ἰσραηλ λέγων τὸν κίνδυνον τῆς Ἀσυνὲθ καὶ ἔλαβεν ἕκατος τὴν ῥομφαίαν αὐτοῦ...(26.6 F)

And Levi announced to his brothers, the sons of Israel, telling Aseneth's danger. And each took his sword... (26.6 F)

Though in 22.13 F, Levi is characterized as "a prophet of the Most High," it is not clear that his gifting is at work in this scenario. The informational gap created by MS F casts doubt on the legitimacy of the brothers' response to take up arms and begin the chase.

The characterization of Levi and his freeborn brothers as avengers of wrong is furthered in chapter 28 F through the words of their brothers, the sons of Bilhah and Zilpah. In their plea to Aseneth for mercy and salvation, the sons of Bilhah and Zilpah do not acknowledge their brothers as θεοσεβεῖς or mention that, as such, they typically "do not repay evil for evil" (cf. 23.5 A). Instead, they cry, "Have mercy and save us from the hands of our brothers because they are by you as avengers of the insult [ἔκδικοι τῆς ὕβρεως], and their swords are against us!" (28.4 F). Aseneth's response, as in MS A, is meant to comfort them. She assures them that the brothers are θεοσεβεῖς and fearers of God (φοβούμενοι τόν θεὸν), yet sends them into the reeds until she is able to "appease them" on the defeated brothers' behalf and until the sons of Leah "put an end to their anger" (23.7). At this point in MS F's narrative, the axiom "do not repay evil for evil" has not been introduced. There is no hope or expectation that the sons of Leah will not avenge the wrongs of their brothers. Instead, they are acting fully in accordance with the ethos of retaliation as put forth by MS F's Levi in chapter 23.

Thus, when Aseneth greets the sons of Leah, she is the first character to introduce the ethos of nonretaliation among the Israelites:

καὶ κατέβη Ἀσυνὲθ ἐκ τοῦ ὀχήματος τῆς σκεπαστῆς αὐτῆς καὶ ἐδεξιώσατο αὐτοὺς μετὰ δακρύων. καὶ αὐτοὶ πεσόντες ἐπὶ πρόσωπον προσεκύνησαν αὐτὴν ἐπὶ τὴν γῆν καὶ ἔκλαυσαν μετὰ φωνῆς μεγάλης καὶ ἐζήτουν τοὺς ἀδελφοὺς αὐτῶν.

> καὶ εἶπεν αὐτοῖς Ἀσυνὲθ· Φείσασθε τῶν ἀδελφῶν ὑμῶν καὶ μὴ ποιήσειτε κακὸν ἀντὶ κακοῦ. κύριος γὰρ συνετήρησέ με ἐξ᾽αὐτῶν καὶ ἔθραυσε τὰς ῥομφαίας αὐτῶν. ἰδοὺ τετήκασιν ἐπὶ τὴν γῆν· ὥσπερ κηρὸς ἀπὸ προσώπου πυρὸς . καὶ ἔσται τοῦτο ἱκανὸν αὐτοῖς τοῦ πολεμῆσαι κύριον πρὸς αὐτούς.
>
> καὶ ὑμεῖς φείσασθε αὐτοῖς ὅτι ἀδελφοὶ ὑμῶν εἰσὶ καὶ αἷμα τοῦ πατρὸς ὑμῶν Ἰσραηλ. (28.9–11)

> And Aseneth came down from the chariot, her shelter, and greeted them with tears. And they, falling on [their] faces, bowed to her on the ground and cried with a loud voice and were seeking their brothers.
>
> And Aseneth said to them, "Spare your brothers, and do not repay evil for evil. For the Lord kept me from them and shattered their swords. Look, they have melted on the ground like wax from the face of a fire. And this will be enough for them, for the Lord to war against them.
>
> "And you, spare them because they are your brothers and the blood of your father Israel." (28.9–11)

As in MS A, MS F's Aseneth argues that God's action on her behalf has been sufficient and that there is no need to "repay evil for evil" to their brothers. Rather, they are to spare them and show them mercy. In MS F, however, Aseneth's position as the initial teacher of this ethos is unique. She has uniquely been privy to the mysteries of God (16.14) and has experienced the mercy of God, who, in response to her pleas (12.4, 12.12) spared and saved *her* rather than repay her wrongs (she confesses speaking "wicked words" and "blasphemies" about Joseph in 6.7 and 13.13 and admits to idolatry in 12.5). All of the brothers, Levi included, are introduced to this ethos of nonretaliation and mercy through Aseneth. When Simeon objects in 28.12–13, she expounds on what nonretaliation entails with a phrase that is unique to MS F.[86] After she responds gently—with a kiss—to Simeon with the negative injunction, "By no means, brothers, shall you do evil for evil" (μηδαμῶς ἀδελφοὶ ποιήσετε κακὸν ἀντὶ κακοῦ), she enforces a positive ethic: "Give to the Lord the avenging of their insult" (τῷ κυρίῳ δόσεις ἐκδίκησιν τὴν ὕβριν αὐτῶν, 28.14). Not only are the brothers to accept that God's "warring against them" has been sufficient, but they are instructed to yield the right of vengeance to God.

---

86. It is also found in MS F's sister text, MS W, with which MS F shared a *Vorlage*, and their "cousin" G.

4. The Agent(s) of an Ethical Shift

MS F's *Aseneth* is thus shaped to accord with a New Testament ethos of nonretaliation as articulated by Paul (Rom 12:17, 1 Thess 5:15) and 1 Pet 3:9,[87] but particular resonance is found with Rom 12:17–21:

μηδενὶ κακὸν ἀντὶ κακοῦ ἀποδιδόντες, προνοούμενοι καλὰ ἐνώπιον πάντων ἀνθρώπων· εἰ δυνατὸν τὸ ἐξ ὑμῶν, μετὰ πάντων ἀνθρώπων εἰρηνεύοντες· μὴ ἑαυτοὺς ἐκδικοῦντες, ἀγαπητοί, ἀλλὰ δότε τόπον τῇ ὀργῇ, γέγραπται γάρ· ἐμοὶ ἐκδίκησις, ἐγὼ ἀνταποδώσω, λέγει κύριος. ἀλλ' ἐὰν πεινᾷ ὁ ἐχθρός σου, ψώμιζε αὐτόν· ἐὰν διψᾷ, πότιζε αὐτόν· τοῦτο γὰρ ποιῶν ἄνθρακας πυρὸς σωρεύσεις ἐπὶ τὴν κεφαλὴν αὐτοῦ. μὴ νικῶ ὑπὸ τοῦ κακοῦ ἀλλὰ νίκα ἐν τῷ ἀγαθῷ τὸ κακόν.

Repay no one evil for evil, consider what is honorable before all people. If it is in your power, be at peace with all people. Do not avenge yourselves, beloved, but give place for wrath, for it is written, "'Vengeance is mine, I will repay,'[88] says the Lord," but "if your enemy is hungry, feed him. If he thirsts, give him drink. For by doing this, you will heap coals of fire upon his head."[89] Do not be overcome by evil, but overcome evil with good.

Both MS F and Rom 12 hold that the role of avenger of wrongs belongs to God, and the role of the faithful is to leave room for God to fulfill that role. The emphasis on doing good instead of evil to one's enemies, or "overcoming evil with good," is also displayed in the final scenes of *Aseneth* (see below).

---

87. "See that no one repays evil for evil to anyone, but always pursue the good for one another and for everyone" (ὁρᾶτε μή τις κακὸν ἀντὶ κακοῦ τινι ἀποδῷ, ἀλλὰ πάντοτε τὸ ἀγαθὸν διώκετε [καὶ] εἰς ἀλλήλους καὶ εἰς πάντας, 1 Thess 5:15); cf. Matt 5:39. In the Sermon on the Mount, Jesus articulates an ethos of nonresistance and nonretaliation without the use of the "evil for evil" phrase: "But I say to you, do not oppose the wicked, but whoever strikes you on your right cheek, offer the other to him also" (ἐγὼ δὲ λέγω ὑμῖν μὴ ἀντιστῆναι τῷ πονηρῷ· ἀλλ' ὅστις σε ῥαπίζει εἰς τὴν δεξιὰν σιαγόνα [σου], στρέψον αὐτῷ καὶ τὴν ἄλλην, Matt 5:39). First Peter 3:9's injunction against repaying evil for evil is found within the context of a reflection on Jesus's exemplary life rather than his teachings: "When he was reviled, he did not revile in response, when he suffered, he did not threaten, but continued entrusting himself to the One who judges justly" (ὃς λοιδορούμενος οὐκ ἀντελοιδόρει, πάσχων οὐκ ἠπείλει, παρεδίδου δὲ τῷ κρίνοντι δικαίως, 1 Pet 2:23).

88. Deut 32:35 LXX.

89. Prov 25:21–22.

In MS F, Aseneth and Levi's roles are reversed from those found in MS A. She is the tutor of the divine mysteries of nonretaliation and mercy, and he is the willing pupil, who receives her instruction and enforces it among his brothers. Levi is the first—and perhaps the only—brother to take up Aseneth's teaching. The resistance of Simeon, as in MS A, acts as a contrast to the acceptance of the ethos by the "man of understanding" (22.13 F). Levi "comes from afar" and kisses Aseneth's right hand, because "he knew that she wanted to save the men" (28.15 F). The distance of space that he crosses in F reflects the shift in his ethos from one far from nonretaliation to one embracing it. As in MS A, he keeps secret the whereabouts of the sons of Bilhah and Zilpah to protect them (28.16–17). In the following scene, Levi enforces to Benjamin the ethos of nonretaliation that Aseneth introduced. When Benjamin runs up to take the sword of Pharaoh's son and strike, Levi's words and actions echo Aseneth's:

καὶ ἔδραμεν ἐπ' αὐτὸν Λευὶ καὶ ἐκράτησε τῆς χειρὸς αὐτοῦ καὶ εἶπε· Μηδαμῶς ἀδελφὲ μὴ ποιήσεις τὸ πρᾶγμα τοῦτο διότι ἡμεῖς θεοσεβεῖς ἐσμὲν καὶ οὐ προσῆκεν κακὸν ἀντὶ κακοῦ ἀποδοῦναι οὐδὲ πεπτωκότα πατῆσαι οὐδὲ ἐκθλίψαι τὸν ἐχθρὸν ἕως θανάτου. (29.3)

And Levi ran up to him and seized his hand and said, "By no means, brother! You should not do this thing, because we are God-worshiping, and it is not fitting to repay evil for evil or to tread on the one who has fallen or to press the enemy unto death." (29.3)

His first exhortation parallels Aseneth's rebuke to Simeon in 28.14 (see above). The following elaborations that indicate it is not fitting "to tread on the one who has fallen or to press the enemy unto death," in the context of MS F, describe what Aseneth has just demonstrated with her actions. Instead of allowing the sons of Leah to finish off their brothers, who had plotted murder against Joseph and her children and aided her would-be rapist, she had shown and enforced mercy after their defeat. Levi articulates this kind of ethos with his words to Benjamin. Just as Aseneth had helped the sons of Bilhah and Zilpah by hiding them, Levi suggests to Benjamin that they help Pharaoh's son by caring for his wound (29.4). As Aseneth had affirmed the familial ties between the defeated enemies and their would-be avengers, Levi speaks hopefully about Pharaoh's injured son to the would-be avenger, Benjamin: "He will be our friend after these things, and his father Pharaoh will be like our father" (29.4). Since MS F's Aseneth is the one who first

4. The Agent(s) of an Ethical Shift

introduces the ethos of nonretaliation and mercy to one's defeated enemy, Levi becomes characterized as *her* student, who both receives her instruction and the model of her example and passes it on to his brother.

In addition to the focalization of Aseneth throughout the episodes of the narrative at the expense of Levi, exhortative inserts of MS F draw the audience's attention to both Aseneth and Joseph as exemplary figures, not Levi.[90] In MS F, an opening focus on Aseneth and several narratorial insertions (between 7.6 and 7.7, before and after ch. 21, and an epilogue after ch. 29) centralize her as an exemplary figure. All who read the story are directly addressed as "brothers," are exhorted to observe the main characters, Joseph and Aseneth, and are urged to follow the example they set. The direct addresses distill the theological and ethical messages for the audience, for example, by drawing attention to Joseph's self-control (σωφροσύνη) in chapters 7 and 21, and Aseneth's repentance, ascetic practices, and acknowledgment of the living God (ἐπέγνω θεὸν ζῶντα) in chapter 21. In chapter 7, the first direct address to the audience follows the narrator's description of Joseph's adamant refusal of the seductive intentions of "all the daughters and wives of the officials and satraps of all of Egypt" (7.3–5). The narrator instructs the audience to observe and follow in Joseph's example through the love and fear of God:

ἴδετε ἐγκράτειαν καὶ ἀποχὴν τῆς ἁμαρτίας. ... ὁ τοῦ θεοῦ ἔρως ἐνίκα τῶν γυναικῶν πάντων τὸν πόθον καὶ τὴν φιλίαν. ὀξύτερος γὰρ ἦν ὁ τοῦ θεοῦ ἔρως ... καὶ ἡμεῖς μιμησώμεθα τὸν πρὸ τῆς χάριτος τὸν πρότους εὐαγγελίου.

Observe self-control and abstinence from sins.... The love of God conquered the longing and fondness for all women. For the love of God was more potent ... and we should imitate the one before grace, the one before the gospel.

---

90. Wright also notes Levi's diminished role in MS F's *Aseneth* ("After Antiquity," 219). He also notes the diminishing of Levi's role in MS E and L1, and suggests that "the explanation for the reduction in Levi's character and importance could be a loss of interest in a figure that held little importance for the redactor or his audience. It could also be to avoid having Levi take attention away from Aseneth as the central character." I posit that Levi's diminished role in MS F is accomplished through systematic omissions that alter the ethical ideal put forth by the narrative, an ideal that is exemplified primarily by Aseneth.

Each of the narrator's insertions situate the characters of the narrative—here, Joseph—as being "before grace" and "before the gospel." Their lives, however, are read as models for the Christian, male monastic audience—those "after grace" and "after the gospel"[91]—to imitate. In the insertions of chapter 21, Joseph and Aseneth are models of self-control and humble repentance, respectively. The final exhortations that make up the epilogue of MS F's *Aseneth* draw attention heavenward, to the "life-loving, all-compassionate Lord" (ὁ φιλόψυχος πανοικτίρμων κύριος) as he acted in the lives of Joseph and Aseneth in the story. God "had compassion [ᾤκτειρε]" on Joseph, "protected [him] like an apple of the eye [ὡς κόρην ὀφθαλμοῦ διετήρησε],"[92] and "made [him] king and lord of all Egypt" (βασιλέα καὶ κύριον πάσης γῆς Αἰγύπτου πεποίηκε) because Joseph "protected self-control [τὴν σωφροσύνην φυλάξας] and did not bow down to the gods of the Egyptians [θεοὺς τῶν Αἰγυπτίων μὴ προσκυνήσας]." The audience is called to reflect on "how God saved Aseneth from the darkness of idols and led her to the knowledge of God" (πῶς τὴν Ἀσυνὲθ ἐκ σκότους εἰδώλων ἐρρύσατο καὶ εἰς θεοῦ ἐπίγνωσιν ἤγαγε) and how "he saved her from the snares and hands of the son of Pharaoh" (αὐτὴν ... ἐκ τῶν παγίδων καὶ χειρῶν τοῦ υἱοῦ Φαραὼ ἐρρύσατο). Levi is never mentioned in the exhortations as a role model. The narrational addresses focus on Joseph and Aseneth as MS F's exemplary figures, and the theo-

---

91. The first insertion of chapter 21 (after 21.10) puts it this way: "These things are necessary also for us to remember. The things before grace. The things before the gospel. So that we may also richly receive the things asked for like they did, or even more richly, as we have also enjoyed greater grace and gifts."

92. This phrase κόρην ὀφθαλμοῦ, idiomatically referring to a protected person or nation as a pupil of God's eye, finds biblical precedent in Deut 32:10 and Ps 17:8 (see also Zech 2:8). In these verses, God protects Israel "as the apple of his eye" (ὡς κόραν ὀφθαλμοῦ/ כְּאִישׁוֹן עֵינוֹ, Deut 32:10), or the psalmist calls on God to protect him "like the apple of your eye" (ὡς κόραν ὀφθαλμοῦ, Ps 16:8 LXX /כְּאִישׁוֹן בַּת עַיִן, Ps 17:8). The English translation of אִישׁ (lit. "little man," perhaps referring to the reflection of someone in another's pupil) or κόρη as "apple" follows the KJV, which introduced the idiom into English expression to the extent that translating the phrase "apple of the eye" is more colloquially accepted than "pupil of the eye" in English. In *Aseneth* (MSS A and F), Nephtali and Asher describe God's protection of Joseph in these terms, stating that God "protects him like an apple of [his] eye" in 25.5. Also, Joseph promises Aseneth that "the Lord is with you and he will guard you like an apple of [his] eye" in 26.2 A and F. Thus, when MS F's narrator makes mention in the epilogue of this phrase, he is harking back to its usage in the narrative and likely alluding to its biblical usage as well.

logical message of the epilogue is that the Lord is great, as is his power to save those who trust him.

The foundation of MS F's unmitigated ethos of nonretaliation is the theological idea of God as the all-powerful one who works vengeance on behalf of those who trust him. The final insertion of chapter 21, which comes directly before the beginning of part 2, introduces a thematic assertion that part 2 takes up and demonstrates: "Out of many griefs and dangers and circumstances the Lord of All delivers and guards" (ἐκ πολλῶν ἀνιαρῶν καὶ κινδύνων καὶ περιστάσεων ῥύεται καὶ φθλάσσει ὁ πάντων κύριος). This precept undergirds Aseneth's model of nonretaliation that MS F promotes. In addition, the message of God's greatness and role as avenger of wrongs immediately precedes and undergirds the final exhortation of the narrator:

μέγας κύριος· καὶ μεγάλη ἰσχὺς αὐτοῦ ὅτι ἐρρύσατο γυνὴ ἐκ χειρός στερεωτερῶν αὐτῆς καὶ ἀπὸ ἐνέδρας ἐναντιων· καὶ πονηρῶν ἀνδρῶν καὶ βασκάνων· καὶ ἐκεινοι μὲν ἔπεσον· αὕτη δὲ ἀνέστη καὶ ἀνορθώθη· καὶ κατεπάτησε τοὺς ἐχθροὺς αὐτῆς·

καὶ ἡμεῖς τοίνυν ἀδελφοὶ ἐὰν μὴ αὐτοὺς ἐκδικῶμεν ἀπὸ τῶν ἐναντίων ἐχθρῶν ἡμῶν ἀλλ' εἰς θεὸν τὴν ἐκδίκησιν ἀνατίθωμεν καὶ ἐπιφέρωμεν λαμπρὰ τὰ νικητρια ἐξ'αὐτοῦ ἔζωμεν καὶ οὐ μόνον ἤρεμον καὶ ἡσύχιον βίον ζήσωμεν ἀλλὰ καὶ τῶν ἐνθέν δε ἀπαναστάντες εἰς σκηνὰς αἰωνίους καὶ ἀτελευτή τους καταξεῖ ἡμᾶς ὁ τῶν ὅλων δημιουργός καὶ βασιλεύς.

Great is the Lord! And great is his power that he saved a woman from the hand of those stronger than her and from the opposing ambush and from wicked and malicious men. And while they fell, she arose and was restored. And he trampled her enemies.

And we, furthermore, brothers, if we do not avenge ourselves from our opposing enemies but offer up the vengeance to God, and if we also bear shining prizes of victory, then we are living from him. And let us not only live a quiet and restful life, but also departing from there, the artisan and king of the whole creation will appoint us into eternal and endless tents.

Aseneth's salvation from the power of her opposing enemies in the story serves as evidence to the faithfulness of God to act as avenger in the lives of the audience. Also, Aseneth's decidedly nonviolent way of dealing with her enemies is the prime example of the ethos promoted to the audience. The nonretaliatory ethos of MS F, however, also comes with a promise, "endless tents" given by God in eternity. These are the final words of the narrator, followed only by a trinitarian doxology. By concluding with this message, the narrator emphasizes the ethical takeaway for the audience: to not avenge themselves but, like Aseneth, through prayers for deliverance and through displays of mercy to enemies, to "offer up vengeance to God."

4.2. Manuscript F: Conclusions and Remaining Tension

In MS F, three elements work together to forefront an ethos of nonretaliation that precludes the use of violence in any situation and invites the audience to a radical dependence on God that makes room for the miraculous: (1) the diminishment of Levi's role, (2) the primacy of Aseneth as the model of nonretaliation, and (3) the direct narrational addresses, which exhort the audience to follow her example. Through systematic omissions, Levi in MS F is not a receiver or revealer of God's mysteries, as Aseneth is. He does not teach, nor is he associated with[93] an ethos of nonretaliation. In MS F, Aseneth and Levi do not promote a complementary ethos for the θεοσεβής. Instead, Aseneth's complete dependence on God and the mercy she shows to her would-be attackers is contrasted with Levi and Simeon's boasting of the slaughter at Shechem and their purported role as "avengers of insult." The narratorial addresses exhort the audience to act in accordance with Aseneth's example, based on the theological claims that are drawn from the narrative: "The Lord is great" and "The Lord of All delivers and guards" those who believe in (or trust in) him "out of many griefs and dangers and circumstances."[94] For the monks of Bucharest in the late sixteenth and early seventeenth centuries, "griefs and dangers" were prevalent as their city faced waves of invasions by Turkish armies, Christian *voivodes*, and the Tartars.[95] Through this narrative shaping and these narratorial claims, MS F works to expand the possibility for the miraculous in the lives of its audience. It does this by promoting a nonretaliatory—and essentially nonviolent—ethos of "living a quiet and restful life" by "not avenging ourselves from our opposing enemies but offering up the vengeance to God" (epilogue F). Rather than retaliation, the pious are called to instead do acts of kindness to their enemies, thereby demonstrating a

---

93. The sons of Bilhah and Zilpah's words in 28.5 A are not present in MS F, so "not repaying evil for evil" is not attributed to Levi or the sons of Leah in MS F until it is introduced and enforced by Aseneth in 28.10, 14 F.

94. MS F epilogue; F chapter 21 insertion.

95. "History of the Monastery."

4. The Agent(s) of an Ethical Shift

deep faith in a God who intervenes in human affairs. By affirming this nonretaliatory and nonviolent ethos through the exemplary figure of Aseneth, MS F asserts that Aseneth's reality of miraculous deliverance can become the audience's reality, "living from [God]" in this life and receiving eternal blessings in the heavenly afterlife (epilogue F).

Tension remains, however, between MS F's ideal ethos of nonretaliation as demonstrated by Aseneth and the epilogue's attribution of God's agency in human violence. The final exhortatory epilogue, partially quoted above, praises God for delivering Aseneth from the opposing ambush and trampling all her enemies. The moment referred to is not only the miraculous melting of the swords in 27.11 F, but the epilogue also mentions Pharaoh's son and "the great multitude" of attackers from which Aseneth was delivered:

> καὶ πάλιν πῶς καὶ αὐτὴν ὁ φιλόψυχος πανοικτίρμων κύριος ἐκ τῶν παγίδων καὶ χειρῶν τοῦ υἱοῦ Φαραὼ ἐρρύσατο καὶ ἐκ πολλοῦ πλήθους διέσωσε καὶ ἐκ τῶν ἀδελφῶν τοῦ Ἰωσὴφ

> And again [you have heard] how the life-loving, all-compassionate Lord saved her from the snares and hands of Pharaoh's son and preserved [her] from the great multitude and from the brothers of Joseph.

Both cycles of deliverance, then, are declared to be the work of God. Benjamin's wounding of Pharaoh's son and slaying of his guardsmen are here interpreted as *the Lord* saving Aseneth "from the snares and hands of Pharaoh's son." The sons of Leah's slaying of two thousand men is presented as *the Lord* preserving Aseneth "from the great multitude."[96] Thus, MS F does not deny that God works deliverance through human weaponry and warfare but rather affirms it. The ideal ethos for MS F's audience to follow, however, is still emphatically presented through the model of Aseneth, who alone was armed with nothing but prayer.

---

96. This is the case, even though MS F, in contrast to MS A and the manuscripts of text family *b*, did *not* indicate that Levi and the brothers' response to Aseneth's plight was initiated by revelation or direction from God (see 26.6 F and above). Where MS A has 2,076, F has 2,000, which concurs with the number in chapter 24.

5. Conclusions

In both MSS A and F, part 2 of *Aseneth* assumes the events of Gen 34 as background (Jos. Asen. 23.4, 14), and re-presents its characters in a new plot that echoes and revises elements of Gen 34. These unique re-presentations found in MSS A and F functioned to promote a nuanced ethos of nonretaliation to their audiences, the middle Byzantine populace and seventeenth-century Romanian monastics, respectively. As they recast some of Gen 34's central figures into a new drama, MSS A and F also re-presented to their audiences a question that Gen 34 left unanswered, namely, How is one to evaluate the retributive violence of Simeon and Levi against the Shechemites? As mentioned above, Standhartinger, working with the reconstructed text of Philonenko, asserts that *Aseneth* solves what she calls this "ethical problem" of Gen 34 in an original way.[97] What this investigation has shown, however, is that each manuscript of *Aseneth* surveyed here answers this question prompted by the silences of Gen 34 uniquely, by promoting its own nuanced ethos of nonretaliation. In addition, they each do so in part through the voice and agency of the character of Aseneth, who functions as a new Dinah.

In MS A, Levi most fully displays the nuanced ethos of nonretaliation the text promotes. He functions as teacher of that ethos to Simeon (23.9 A), Aseneth (22.13 A), and Benjamin (29.4 A). He displays self-control in the face of an enemy's threat (23.8–13 A) and models that the ethos of the θεοσεβής is to "not repay evil for evil," yet nuances this ethos with his actions. Levi in MS A thus displays that defending the pious (26.6, 27.6) and operating as God's agent of vengeance (23.14) are both legitimate roles of the θεοσεβής. Aseneth's words complement Levi's in MS A, as they both serve to demonstrate the full extent of MS A's ideal ethos. As the new Dinah in MS A, Aseneth upholds Levi's authority as revealer of God's mysteries, implicitly affirming his assessment of the slaughter at Shechem as God working vengeance through the θεοσεβεῖς.

There is a decisive break in MS F between what was acceptable conduct among the God-worshiping Israelites before and after Aseneth's revelatory teaching. In MS F, Levi self-identifies as θεοσεβής (23.10), but the narrator does not affirm this (22.13 F). The characterization of Levi as "devoted to the Lord God" (προσκείμενος πρὸς κύριον τὸν θεόν, 22.13) in MS F casts him

---

97. Standhartinger, "Um zu Sehen," 112.

in a positive light,[98] but his threats and boasts of past vengeance in chapter 23 occur before Aseneth's introduction of the ethical ideal for the θεοσεβής to "not repay evil for evil" in 28.10 and 28.14. Aseneth, not Levi, is the recipient of God's mysteries in MS F (16.14; cf. 22.13), and the ethos she promotes comes as a reformation to the vengeance that Levi and Simeon boast of in 23.14. Thus, MS F's Aseneth, as a new Dinah, indirectly offers judgment against the retaliatory violence of Levi and Simeon at Shechem.

Simeon serves as a foil to the models of each manuscript's ethical ideal. In MS A, his anger and rashness to "repay evil for evil" is contrasted to Levi's composure and teachings in chapter 23, and Simeon's resistance to spare his brothers in chapter 28 is contrasted with Aseneth's display of nonretaliation and mercy. In MS F, Simeon is most contrasted with Levi in chapters 28–29. Where Levi displays acceptance (28.15–17 F) and appropriation (29.3–5 F) of Aseneth's teaching to "not repay evil for evil," Simeon displays resistance (28.12–13 F).

MSS A and F uniquely created narrative in-betweens for each of their audiences to collectively inhabit and engage with the dramatic unfolding of Aseneth's story, including the ethical situations and ideal ethos it was shaped to present. Relational space for such engagement was orchestrated through the corporate experience of a liturgical reading (MS A) or through direct and inclusive narrational addresses (MS F). MSS A and F bound their respective audiences to one another and to the text by the communal identity asserted on them either contextually or rhetorically. In these negotiated communal encounters, each text exerted its own unique force on its audience. In liturgical and physical space orchestrated by generic categorization and overt evaluations, MS A offers an invitation to imagine new possibilities of relational and ethical behavior. The audience of MS A is somewhat gently invited to consider the ethical possibilities that the exemplary characters, Levi and Aseneth, demonstrate in a variety of circumstances. There is both freedom and constraint, however, for while MS A refrains from direct exhortations for adoption of its ideal ethos, it exerts its authority by nature of the collective, ecclesiastical encounter it demands. MS F, on the other hand, binds its audience candidly and vigorously with several measures. The narrator of MS F appealed to the audience as one who shared in their common identity as "brother," enforcing a relational

---

98. In 16.14, in every Greek manuscript, a blessing is pronounced on "all who are devoted to the Lord" in repentance: μακάριοι πάντες οἱ προσκείμενοι κυρίῳ τῷ θεῷ (σου, F) ἐν μετανοίᾳ (διὰ μετανοίας, Q).

space of kinship between reader(s) and text, claiming an identity tied up in their obligation to their common Lord and to one another. This narrator not only sought his audience's consideration but directly exhorted them to live in nonretaliation and nonviolence like Aseneth, thereby making room in their own lives for the possibility of the miraculous. Thus, through a comparative analysis of these two influential manuscripts of *Aseneth*, we witness the agency of stories to shape their audiences with varying degrees of force, playing an "ontological role"[99] in constructing social identities and illustrating ethical associations—ways of being in the world—that are bound up with those identities.

---

99. Meretoja, *Ethics of Storytelling*, 119.

5
Conclusion

> People do not always live well with stories. If narrative analysis does not improve the quality of companionship between humans and stories, then it has failed.
> —Arthur Frank, *Letting Stories Breathe*

> Take [this story]. It's yours. Do with it what you will. Tell it to your children. Turn it into a play. Forget it. But don't say in the years to come that you would have lived your life differently if you had heard this story. You've heard it now.
> —Thomas King, *The Truth about Stories*

1. Genesis 34, Told and Told Again

Considering Gen 34 as a story encountered through the lens of narrative ethics has shed light on why the ambiguity-rich features of the narrative have for over two millennia compelled readers to grapple with the multiple perspectives and unanswered ethical quandaries it presents. As chapter 2 argued, Gen 34 is a tapestry woven of covert narration, semantic ambiguity, multiperspectivity, and reticence. Together, these features form a complex pattern with several loose ends, resisting finalization while inviting audience engagement. Characters are sparsely outlined, their threads unfinished, allowing for the audience to imagine multiple ways in which they may be filled in. Two gaping holes—central informational gaps—appear in the composition: the perspective of Dinah and the evaluation of the retributive violence of Simeon and Levi. Whether audiences have been conscious of it or not, these holes have demanded their active participation. For some, they have acted as mirrors; audiences have seen their own perspectives and evaluations reflected back to them in the silent spaces of the narrative. For others, the holes have felt like missing puzzle pieces, and they have searched for those missing pieces in other biblical narratives, the Mosaic law, or socioanthropological studies. Others, claiming and acknowledging their agency as readers, have carved out their own puzzle pieces, fitted them into the tapestry, and tied its loose strings with precision, in essence making Gen 34 their own.

In their compositions, Josephus and the author(s) of Jubilees take the threads hanging from Gen 34 and weave two very different tapestries. It is impossible to say *how* they perceived the central informational gaps of Gen 34[1] or what types of readers they may have been. Both of their *new* compositions, however, reflect deep and active engagement with the uncertainties of Gen 34 in light of the issues facing their present generation. Jubilees composes a rigidly framed story, tightly tying the loose threads taken from Gen 34. This new story, Jub. 30, functions as a warning against exogamous relations by centering a motif taken from the "original" story. Any mention of circumcision, however, is left behind. Pulling strands from Deuteronomy's assessment of the Canaanite nations, Jubilees stitches the Shechemites as eternally base villains, cursed and condemned by God. The Israelites, on the other hand, are woven with the purest threads of holiness; every action they take, including the unreserved slaughter of the Shechemites, is lauded by the hosts of heaven.

Josephus also incorporates intermarriage as a central element of the work he crafted for his first-century audience. Yet he sketches each of his characters uniquely, more closely reflecting their diverse presentations in Gen 34 and clothing them, as it were, in contemporary garb to reflect the social and political divisions of his generation. The Shechemites are a diverse mix of foreigners ruling over the Israelites in the land, not unlike the Romans to whom the *Antiquities* was addressed. The ruler, King Hamor, is ultimately benevolent but ignorant to the ways of the Israelite people, while his son the prince is the one who grievously offends the plebeian Israelites by raping Dinah. Thus, the common people of Shechem are innocent victims when retribution is meted out for their prince's crime. Similarly, the Israelite division between a wise, wary father and his unruly sons in *A.J.* 1.337–341 reflected the first-century divisions between the

---

1. While neither author supplied the perspective of Dinah, it is likely that both assumed without question that she was raped, due to the way they both represent the encounter with Shechem as rape (see ch. 3). It is possible that the lack of Dinah's perspective, on the matter of whether she was raped, or on the matter of what she hoped for or desired, was not a *perceived* gap for the author(s) of Jubilees and Josephus.

5. Conclusion

cautious, elite Judean leadership and a reckless, raging populace depicted by Josephus in *A.J.* 20. Josephus, like Jubilees, also leaves out the motif and mention of circumcision but maintains and emphasizes the generational and social divisions of the Genesis narrative.

Chapters 22–29 of *Aseneth* reflect an audience's choice to take up the loom scaffolding of Gen 34 and weave into it something new. *Aseneth*'s characters overlie where those of Gen 34 once stood. Aseneth is a new Dinah, threatened by the violent, erotically motivated attack of Pharaoh's son, a new Shechem. Simeon and Levi are stitched wearing the garb of Hellenistic heroes,[2] but they continue in their role as avengers of offense against the daughter of Israel. Episode by episode, the evaluative gap of Gen 34—the evaluation of Simeon and Levi's violent retaliation—is addressed as *Aseneth*'s characters demonstrate how the godly should respond in various situations of offense. While the original text of *Aseneth* remains elusive, later retellings of this ancient romance bear witness to creative ways in which audiences encountered the story and made their mark on it as they passed it on, re-presenting it to their own communities. The middle Byzantine MS A presents Aseneth's story as a hagiography, upholding her as an exemplary saint, along with the pious, divinely gifted Levi. MS F, copied for the edification of seventeenth-century Romanian monastics, is heavily framed with direct addresses to its audience that steadily confirm the ethical importance of what is pictured in the narrative.

Each of these later works thus reflects direct, active engagement with the nuanced composition of Gen 34 in unique and creative ways. The ambiguities and silences of the biblical narrative itself demanded such activity. In one way, the storytellers behind Jubilees, *Judean Antiquities*, and *Aseneth* MSS A and F are first and foremost readers who have encountered Gen 34 and responded to its demands. Yet these readers became storytellers, stepping forth to create something new with what they took from the encounter. Although the ways in which they color their characters and retell the plot differ to better address their contemporary audiences, each later work fills in a central narrative gap that Gen 34 left: the evaluation of the retributive violence of Simeon and Levi.

---

2. See Gillian Glass, "A Daughter of Hebrews and Hellenes: Epiphany in *Aseneth* and Contemporary Ancient Greek Literature" (PhD diss., University of British Columbia, 2022).

2. Deciding *Dinah*:
Evaluating the Retributive Violence of Simeon and Levi

Jubilees, *Judean Antiquities*, and *Aseneth* MSS A and F all explicitly and uniquely weigh in on the retributive violence of Simeon and Levi in ways that promoted an ethos to their contemporary readers, an ethos that is bound up in the identity each text claims for its audience. Each narrative takes up a central gap of Gen 34—the lack of an explicit evaluation of Simeon and Levi's retributive violence on the Shechemites—and creatively fills that gap in ways that assert an ideal ethos for its contemporary audience. Furthermore, the aforementioned manuscripts of *Aseneth* engage with the evaluative gap and unanswered questions in Gen 34 regarding retributive violence by centralizing the voice of Aseneth as a new Dinah, reflecting the parallel between Dinah's silence and the narrator's reticence in the biblical narrative.

While Jubilees' re-presentation of Gen 34 serves as an occasion to elucidate the laws against exogamous relations with non-Israelites, by celebrating Simeon and Levi's actions, it implicitly promotes violence against any peoples understood to be God's enemies. The purpose of the entire message of Jub. 30 is that the audience—future generations of Israelites—will not sin or transgress the laws this episode contains, namely, laws against exogamous relations (Jub. 30.15, 21–22). Simeon and Levi's actions, on the one hand, demonstrate the destruction of which all transgressors of God's laws are deserving (30.22). On the other hand, the celebration of these men upholds them as ethical exemplars. Simeon and Levi's retributive violence, which in Jub. 30 involves the annihilation of *all* the Shechemites, is celebrated by the authoritative voice of heaven as "right—justice and revenge against the sinners" (30.23). In Jub. 30.6, their actions are divinely backed, for "the Lord handed [the Shechemites] over to Jacob's sons." While the text does not explicitly authorize future generations of Israel to annihilate non-Israelites, it champions the Israelite forefathers who did. Their actions are recorded as "a just act" (30.17) and "a blessing" (30.23), and Levi's eagerness to carry out revenge "on all who rise against Israel" earns him and his descendants the priesthood forever (30.18). By exalting Simeon and Levi as exemplary and blessed in the sight of heaven, rewarded for their violence against non-Israelite offenders, the text promotes such an ethos of violent vengeance for its Israelite-identifying audience.

Although the narrator of *Antiquities* regularly moralizes his episodic history, drawing attention to the virtues and vices of his diverse cast of historical characters, with Simeon and Levi he refrains from direct evaluation. As chapter 3 argued, it is when the brothers' actions in *A.J.* 1.337–341 are read in light of *Antiquities*' presentation of the Judean law and in connection with the paralleled account in 20.118–136 that it becomes clear that their choices are to be disparaged. It is not their violence or even their thirst for vengeance, however, that is problematic in *Antiquities* but their impertinence. Various leaders of Judean history are lauded for their vindictive violence, when they act with the authority that their status affords them (e.g., Abraham, 1.178; Moses, 3.42–60; Phineas, 4.152–155; and Samson, 5.295–317). Simeon and Levi, however, are under the authority of their father, the patriarch of Israel. When they act without the knowledge or permission (1.340) of their leader, they do so as those who transgress the law and "despise God" (4.181, 215). In Josephus's efforts to convince his elite, Greek-speaking audience that the Judean πολιτεία is the most excellent of political systems,[3] Simeon and Levi represent a perennial problem facing ruling authorities: the dangers of a reckless and rebellious populace, who resist the authority of their superiors. The "problem" of the populace is one that is repeated throughout the *Antiquities*' Judean history up to Josephus's own generation and likely reflected the concerns of his audience, whom he paints as social and political elites concerned for the best ways of ordering life and nation. For such an audience, *Antiquities*' πολιτεία, framed with exhortations to obey political elites as *divinely appointed* authorities (*A.J.* 4.177–195, 4.309–319), becomes an attractive option indeed.

The connection between the reticence regarding the ethical evaluation of the brothers in Gen 34 and the perspective of Dinah is bolstered by both MS A and MS F of *Aseneth*. As chapter 2 argued, the silence of Dinah, whose name may be faithfully rendered "judicial decision" or "she decides," artfully parallels the narratorial silence with regard to evaluating Simeon and Levi's retributive violence toward the Shechemites. Aseneth, as the new Dinah in MSS A and F, helps to demonstrate with her words and actions the ethical ideal of each story with regard to violence and vengeance. In both of these narratives, it is Aseneth who is presented as the focal figure from whom to draw ethical inspiration. In MS A, this focalizing is accomplished through the framing of the story as her hagiography, and in MS F, through the introductory focus on her and the ethical exhortations that draw at-

---

3. See ch. 3.

tention to her words and actions. Thus, it is through the centralized voice of Aseneth—the new Dinah—that these narratives evaluate Simeon and Levi's retributive violence at Shechem. Furthermore, they promote their own unique ethos regarding retributive violence through rhetorical moves that work to shape their audiences and the space of encounter.

The nuanced ethos of nonretaliation that MS A promotes is supported by not only the voice of Aseneth but also its explicit evaluation of Simeon and Levi's retribution on the Shechemites. Levi declares that when he and his brother destroyed Shechem, it was "the vengeance of the Lord on the hubris of the Shechemites" enacted through their swords (Jos. Asen. 23.14 A). Levi's words are upheld as reliable, for he is introduced in MS A with a stream of laudatory descriptors; he is a prophetic man, God-worshiping and fearing the Lord, a man of understanding and a prophet of the Most High, privy to divine writings, which he reveals to Aseneth (22.13 A). That Aseneth receives and later enforces his teachings is suggestive to the audience that it would be wise to do the same. This positive evaluation of Simeon and Levi's violent retribution on the Shechemites undergirds an aspect of the ethos promoted by MS A, that the θεοσεβής may rightly serve as an agent of God's vengeance on "his enemies," preventing or avenging wrongs done by foreigners against God's people. In the latter chapters of *Aseneth* MS A, Simeon and Levi demonstrate again, together with their brothers, the sons of Leah, that attacking foreigners who attempt hubris on the pious is part and parcel of the identity of the God-worshiper. On the other hand, Aseneth restrains the brothers from avenging an insult done by or attempted by "a neighbor" in an allusion to the Levitical law proscribing vengeance on a fellow Israelite (Lev 19:18). Instead, she promotes showing mercy, affirming that "the Lord will avenge this insult" (Jos. Asen. 28.14). MS A allows its audience to contemplate the distinction between neighbor and foreigner, even as it decisively evaluates Simeon and Levi's retribution on the Shechemites as divinely ordained.

MS F's proscription of all retributive violence begins with its somewhat ambiguous recollection of Simeon and Levi's vengeance on the Shechemites. As in MS A, Levi claims they acted as instruments of God, saying, "With these two swords the Lord avenged the hubris of the Shechemites" (23.14 F). Levi, however, is diminished as an ethical exemplar in MS F. Although devoted to God (22.13 F), he is not a teacher of divine revelations, and the authority of his speech in chapter 23 is therefore more tenuous. Aseneth alone has received divine revelations (16.13–16 F), and it is she who introduces the ethos of not repaying evil for evil (28.14 F).

Aseneth's teaching is unqualified with the phrase "to a neighbor"; rather, she promotes and teaches a universal ethos of nonretaliation to the sons of Israel. Retrospectively, then, the audience may infer that Simeon and Levi's actions at Shechem would be negatively evaluated by the heroine of this story. Her teaching and the example of her behavior in the second round of deliverance—in which God himself intervenes on Aseneth's behalf—is explicitly upheld by the narrator as the only proper response for the audience. By not defending herself but "offering up" or "giving over" vengeance to God, she was protected by the God who saves and "wages war" on behalf of the faithful (28.1, epilogue F). Even so, the narrator describes the first round of deliverance, in which the sons of Leah cut down the hordes of attackers with swords and stones, as "the all-compassionate Lord" saving Aseneth "from the snares and hands of the son of Pharaoh" (epilogue F), leaving open the possibility that God does indeed work through human violence, and therefore possibly confirming Levi's assessment of the sacking of Shechem. Therefore, MS F supports a negative assessment of Simeon and Levi's retributive violence against Shechem as proscribed behavior for the brethren, but it also supports a positive assessment through affirming the idea that God can and does work through human instruments to do violence on behalf of the pious. While the tension between these interpretations remains, what is made certain is that the Romanian monastic audience, as brethren in Christ, are to collectively walk in the ways of Aseneth—to not oppose enemies but to "offer up the vengeance to God" (epilogue F).

3. Narrative Capacity and Force

These four re-presentations of Gen 34 display the capacity of stories to shape their audience's sense of identity and ethical responsibility. In each unique tale, crafted for a specific audience, claims are made regarding the identity of that audience through generic choices, character representations, and/or rhetorical moves. Jubilees, by presenting itself as Moses's record of a divine dictation[4] for later generations of Israelites, claims its second-century BCE Judean readers as such and as responsible for its divinely revealed contents (Jub. 1.4–5). Through narrative

---

4. The monological narrator, the angel of the presence, is backed by the authority of his heavenly status and the heavenly writings, which he received from the hand of God himself (Jub. 1.27–29).

representation, Jubilees gathers the disparate, dispersed, and disenfranchised Judeans of the second century BCE as a unified people. As Israel's descendants, they are called to be holy, a tentative status that can be lost by improper conduct, resulting in their destruction (21.21–24).[5] Thus, the demand Jubilees places on its second-century BCE Judean audience is high: ultimate acceptance and observance of the ordinances and behaviors stipulated therein.

By contrast, in *Judean Antiquities*, Josephus gently shapes the identity of his audience as Greek speakers who are eager to know about the history and πολιτεία of the Ἰουδαῖοι, likening them to Ptolemy II as elite governors and lovers of learning (A.J. 1.10–12, 19).[6] Honoring his readers as philosophers and statesmen, Josephus invites them to enact an examination (ποιεῖσθαι τὴν ἐξέτασιν) of his work, particularly how it reveals the pure virtue of God and the ways in which people ought to imitate that virtue through obedience to the legislations revealed to Moses (1.23–24). *Antiquities* is explicitly crafted to persuade its audience that the Judean history is useful and beneficial for all (1.3–4), and that the πολιτεία it reveals and reflects on is most excellent, holding the key to individual and national εὐδαιμονία (1.20).[7]

More subtly, MS A of *Aseneth*, by labeling its exemplary characters as God-worshiping (θεοσεβής) and virtuous, offers that identity to the gathered members of the Byzantine church it encounters. By framing *Aseneth* as a hagiography, assigned for annual public reading, MS A gathers the audience through its situational performance to contemplate the βίος of this "Old Testament" saint. MS A therefore inspires rather than indoctrinates, yet, for those desirous of taking up the identity of θεοσεβής, the message regarding their ethical comportment is clear. With a far more assertive rhetoric, MS F of *Aseneth* directly and repeatedly claims its

---

5. Non-Israelites are cast as innate sinners and divinely doomed (Jub. 21.21–24). Following the ways of the nations (Jub. 21.21–24) or having intercourse with them (Jub. 30.15) will lead to the defilement and the destruction of the Israelite people; they will be no better off than the rest of sinful humanity.

6. Furthermore, by mention of the qualities of Epaphroditus, the likely patron of the work and the source from whom Josephus claims to have received "the courage" to undertake it, the audience is cast as philosophically minded, with a desire for what is virtuous, beautiful, and useful (A.J. 1.8–9).

7. A.J. 1.24 also asserts that it is revealed by God and therefore harmonious with the nature of the universe.

readers as "brothers," or kinsmen in Christ.[8] The familial, communal identifying force on the audience is strong and continuous, and it is on the basis of this assigned identity that the narrator of MS F makes explicit demands on his audience's thoughts and behavior.[9]

This comparative literary-ethical analysis of Gen 34 and the later texts as both companions and craftspersons of story has drawn focus to narrative choices made concerning narration, genre, characterization, representation, and rhetoric, and what ethical force those choices may exert on an audience. With each choice of these storytellers, there is a unique force placed on the audience, a force bearing ethical potential for contemplation, indoctrination, persuasion, inspiration, or exhortation. While attending to the shaping power of stories is essential in understanding how they identify, inform, and act on human consciousness, audiences, of course, are free to encounter each story with powers of their own.

4. Living Well With Stories

As mentioned in the introduction, a central aim of applying the theories of narrative ethics and socionarratology to the study of Gen 34 and its literary descendants has been to improve the quality of companionship between present-day humans and the biblical narrative, both as readers and as storytellers. With regard to the biblical narrative, this engagement has resisted the prevailing tendency to solidify or solve what the text leaves fluid or puzzling. Rather, this approach highlights the artistry of Gen 34 in inviting its readers to engage deeply with its "sparsely sketched foreground"[10] while allowing the gaping background to spark imagination and ethical engagement. Yet as the long history of biblical interpretation

---

8. Although MS F was adapted from a *Vorlage* that included such direct addresses, its contextual use in a seventeenth-century monastery in Bucharest also supported the communal constitution of its audience.

9. In the sections of direct narratorial address, the narrator exhorts his brothers to "observe" the exemplary behaviors of Joseph or Aseneth, or to "observe" certain theological implications of the story. Furthermore, in the final epilogue, the narrator makes clear, with the force of communal inclusion, what the brethren ("we") should do when faced with "opposing enemies" (Jos. Asen. epilogue F), a frequent plight of the inhabitants of Romania's capital city in the late sixteenth and early seventeenth centuries ("History of the Monastery").

10. Alter, *Art of Biblical Narrative*, 143. While the quoted phrase is Alter's, he is referencing Erich Auerbach's "Odysseus's Scar," in which Auerbach argues that the

attests, "People do not always live well with stories."[11] As Frank argues, "Stories are rarely if ever bad in themselves. What go badly are story-person-situation companionships."[12] While the dialogical explorations above have reflected on how stories act on their audiences, shaping the ways in which encounter with story occurs, they also highlight the ethical capacity and responsibility of humans as companions of story, and biblical story in particular.

The biblical narrative overflows with ethical potential through its silences and nuanced multiperspectivity, yet those same features coupled with its unique authority make it prone to being weaponized[13] through interpretive practice. On the one hand, of the five narratives analyzed in this book, Gen 34 may be considered the least dangerous. By fostering dialogical engagement, it resists finalization and activates its readers' ethical agency. The demand placed on the readers for engagement affirms their identity as ethical agents, while granting them freedom to exert that agency in whatever ways they choose. On the other hand, the openness with which Gen 34 meets its readers may make the biblical narrative the most dangerous of them all. Endowed with authority in multiple religious traditions by its canonicity as Scripture, Gen 34 leaves gaps and unfinished strands for anyone to take up and "do with them what they will."[14] In drawing on the authority of the biblical text, *consciously or unconsciously*, readers and biblical storytellers may precipitate "violent personal and social practices," committing what Cottrill terms "interpretive violence."[15]

---

biblical narrative's lack of foregrounded narrative details leaves it open to many interpretive possibilities. See ch. 2, §5.

11. Frank, *Letting Stories Breathe*, 19. See introduction, §1. See also Suzanne Scholtz, *Rape Plots: A Feminist Cultural Study of Genesis 34* (New York: Lang, 2002), 45–61; Stephen Haynes, *Noah's Curse: The Biblical Justification of American Slavery* (Oxford: Oxford University Press, 2002).

12. Frank, *Letting Stories Breathe*, 147.

13. This is a slight emendation from Cottrill's assertion that "the process of interpretation itself is like a potential weapon, with the capacity to enforce violence by virtue of the Bible's cultural and religious authority" (*Uncovering Violence*, 20). Here I suggest that the text itself can become the weapon, through the process of biblical storytelling.

14. See Thomas King epigraph above. Whatever Gen 34 may have been at the time of its composition, for millions of readers in Jewish and Christian traditions today, it holds a "unique kind of authority" as a sacred text (Cottrill, *Uncovering Violence*, 20).

15. Cottrill, *Uncovering Violence*, 20.

The biblical narrative meets its audience with depictions of violence narrated with ambiguity and artful silences, thus offering itself to its readers with dangerous risk.

Biblical narrative, as with any narrative, leaves its readers inherently responsible. As the epigraphic quotation from Thomas King above asserts, readers, though free to "do with a story what they will," nevertheless are ethically bound as a result of narrative encounter. Reading, like storytelling, is a "consequential ethical activity,"[16] with personal and corporate ramifications. Readers come to the relational space of narrative encounter with a manifold force of their own. Exerted consciously or unconsciously, a reader's power resides in the willingness to be vulnerable before the text, to yield to the force with which the story exerts on their encounter and be "caught up in"[17] a story. Yet readers may also interpret, resist, recontextualize, or even reshape the story by retelling it for their own ends and purposes. The re-presentations of Gen 34 attest to readers who exerted their own unique force on the biblical story, essentially remaking it for their own generations. Although narratives themselves wield power through narrational features and representational choices, and by shaping the relational space in which story meets audience, readers ultimately determine where the story will go from there. The impetus of readers to retell biblical narratives is just as strong today as it was two thousand years ago.[18] I hope that by reflecting on the power that both stories and readers hold and by making narrative encounter and narrative re-presentation a more conscious exercise, this generation of readers and storytellers may become better companions of biblical narratives. By engaging with biblical narratives in ways that mitigate interpretive violence and maximize ethical potential, perhaps we may emplot ourselves into a better future.

---

16. Cottrill, *Uncovering Violence*, 149.
17. Frank, *Letting Stories Breathe*, 157.
18. See ch. 1, §1.

Appendix

Translation of Chapters 1, 22–29 of *Aseneth* Manuscripts A and F

1. The Texts

Although excerpts from the texts of MSS A and F are engaged in the analysis of chapter 4, here I provide translations of chapters 1 and 22–29 of the texts in parallel. Of the two, MS A is more well known. In 1889, Pierre Battifol based his critical edition on the text of MS A, noting variations from other known Greek manuscripts of *Aseneth* in the apparatus. MS A is also available via a somewhat hazy digital scan through the Digital Vatican Library, though for this translation I primarily consulted Jonathon Stuart Wright's presentation of the text, which amends some minor faults in Battifol's text of A.[1] The full Greek text of MS F has only recently been made available by Wright, who has produced a critical edition of MS F and its sister text, MS W, presenting the texts of the manuscripts in all of their orthographic originality. The manuscript of F is currently housed in the Biblioteca Academiei Române in Bucharest, Romania, and efforts to access it have been unsuccessful due to the recent turmoil in the region. In this translation, I follow Burchard's versification despite the awkwardness it sometimes creates in MS F (e.g., 1.3, 23.8–10) and offer the relevant Greek quotations in the analysis found in the later sections. I provide my translations of chapter 1 and chapters 22–29 here in parallel columns followed by translation notes.

2. Translations

A	F
The Life [βίος] and Confession [ἐξομολόγησις] of Aseneth, Daughter of Pentephre, Priest and Satrap of Heliopolis and Narrative [διήγησις] [of] How the All-Beautiful Joseph Took Her as a Wife.	A Select Account [λόγος] from the Ancient Book concerning Aseneth
1.1 Now, in the first year of plenty, in the second month, on the fifth of the month, Pharaoh sent Joseph out to go about all the land of Egypt.	
1.2 And in the fourth month of the first year, on the eighteenth of the month, Joseph came to the district of Heliopolis, and he was gathering the grain of that country like the sand of the sea.	
1.3 There was a certain man in that city by the name of Pentephres, who was a priest of Heliopolis and a satrap of Pharaoh and ruler of all the satraps and the nobles of Pharaoh. This man was exceedingly rich and very prudent and gracious, and he was even Pharaoh's adviser because he was intelligent beyond all the nobles of Pharaoh.	1.3 There was a certain man in Egypt, a satrap of Pharaoh. And this [man] was a ruler of all the satraps and nobles of Pharaoh. And the man was exceedingly rich and prudent and gracious, and he was Pharaoh's adviser, [being] intelligent. And the name of this man was Pentephres, priest of Heliopolis.
1.4 He had a daughter, a παρθένος[2] by the name of Aseneth, [who was] eighteen years old. [She was] tall and voluptuous and exceedingly beautiful in appearance, beyond every παρθένος on the earth.	1.4 And ...[3] the name Aseneth, who was about ... [W: eight and] ten years, ... beyond all παρθένοι...
1.5 Now, this Aseneth had no one like her among the virgins of the daughters of the Egyptians, but she was in every way like the daughters of the Hebrews.	1.5 And she had no one ... but she was in everything like the daughters of the Hebrews, Sarah and Rachel and Rebekah.

Appendix: Translation of *Aseneth* Chapters 1, 22–29

She was tall like Sarah and voluptuous like Rebekah and beautiful like Rachel.	
1.6 And the report of her beauty ran throughout all that land, even until the limits of the earth, so that from this, all the sons of the nobles and the satraps were wanting to court [μνηστευθῆναι] her. Not only them, but even sons of the kings, all young men and powerful. And there was much strife among them because of her, and they were attempting to battle for her.	**1.6** And the report of her beauty went away on all the land, and all sons of the people and sons of all the satraps and sons of all the kings were singing of her. And there was much strife among them concerning Aseneth, and they were attempting battle against one another for her.
1.7 And even the firstborn son of Pharaoh heard about her and earnestly entreated his father to give her to him as a wife. And he said to him, "Give to me, father, Aseneth, the daughter of Pentephres, the foremost man of Heliopolis, as a wife."	**1.7** And the firstborn son of [Pharaoh] heard about her, and he earnestly entreated his father to give [her] to him as a wife.
1.8 And his father Pharaoh said to him, "Why do you seek a wife inferior [ἐλάχιστον] to you, though you are a king of all this land?	**1.8** And Pharaoh said, "Why are you seeking a wife less [ἧττον] than you? And you are to be king of all the land!
1.9 No! But look, the daughter of Iakim, the king of Moab, is betrothed to you, and she is a queen and exceedingly beautiful in appearance. Therefore, take for yourself this one as a wife."	**1.9** No! Look, the daughter of the king of Moab, and she is exceedingly beautiful."
2.1 Aseneth was disdaining and despising all men, being boastful and arrogant…	**2.1** And Aseneth was despising and disdaining all the men, and she was boastful and arrogant toward every person…
22.1 And when the seven years of plenty passed, the seven years of famine began to come.	**22.1** And the seven years of plenty passed, and the times of the famine came.
22.2 And when Jacob heard about Joseph his son, he came to Egypt with	**22.2** And Jacob heard about Joseph his son, and he went down into Egypt,

all his kindred in the second year of the famine, in the second month, on the twenty-first day of the month, and settled [κατῴκησεν] in the land of Goshen.⁴	he and all his kindred, and settled [ὄρκησεν] in the land of Goshen.⁵
22.3 And Aseneth said to Joseph, "I will go and see your father, because your father Israel is like my father and God."	**22.3** And Aseneth said, "I am going and I will see your father because the father Israel is like God to me."⁶
22.4 And Joseph said to her, "Go with me and see my father."	**22.4** But Joseph said, "Go with me and see my father."
22.5 And Joseph and Aseneth came to Jacob in the land of Goshen, and the brothers of Joseph met them and prostrated to them with their face(s) on the ground.	**22.5** And Joseph and Aseneth came in the land of Goshen to Jacob … [W: and the brothers of Joseph met them and prostrated themselves] toward them with their face(s) on the ground.
22.6 Then they both came before Jacob. And Jacob was sitting on his bed, and he was old, advanced in age.	**22.6** And Israel was sitting on his bed.
22.7 And upon seeing him, Aseneth was amazed [ἐθαμβήθη] by his beauty, because Jacob was exceedingly beautiful to see and his old age was like the youthful season of a man. And his head was all white like snow, and the hairs of his head were completely thick and exceedingly full, and his beard was white, down to his chest. His eyes were joyous and flashing, his sinews and his shoulders and his arms were like an angel's, his thighs and his calves and his feet were like a giant's.	**22.7** And Aseneth saw him and was amazed [ἐξεθαμβήθη] because he was exceedingly beautiful, and his old age was like the youthful season of a man.
22.8 Then, upon seeing him thus, Aseneth was amazed and falling, she prostrated to him with her face on the ground. And Jacob said to Joseph, "Is this my daughter-in-law, your wife? She will be blessed by God the Most High."	**22.8** And she prostrated herself … on the ground. And Jacob said to Joseph, "Is this my daughter-in-law? She is blessed by God the Most High."

22.9 Then Jacob summoned her to himself and he blessed her and kissed her. And Aseneth stretched out her hands and grasped Jacob's neck-sinews and hung on his neck and kissed him.	**22.9** And he summoned her and blessed her, and Aseneth straightened the neck of Jacob and hung from its sinews.
22.10 And after these things, they ate and drank, and then in this way, both Joseph and Aseneth went to their house:	**22.10** And after these things, Joseph and Aseneth went to their house.
22.11 Simeon and Levi (the sons of Leah only) escorted them, but the sons of Bilhah and Zilpah, the slaves of Leah and Rachel, did not also escort them because they resented and hated them.	**22.11** And the brothers of Joseph (the sons of Leah only) escorted them. But the sons of Zilpah and Bilhah, the slaves of Leah and Rachel, did not also escort them because they resented and hated him.
22.12 And Levi was at the right hand of Aseneth, and Simeon was on the left.	**22.12** And Levi was at the right hand of Aseneth, and Joseph at the left.
22.13 And Aseneth grasped Levi's hand, because she loved him exceedingly above all the brothers of Joseph, and he was like a prophetic man and God-worshiping and fearing the Lord. For he was a man of understanding and a prophet of the Most High, and he would see writings written in heaven and read them, and he secretly revealed them to Aseneth because Levi himself also loved Aseneth very much, and he would see the place of her rest in the highest places.	**22.13** Grasping the right hand of Levi, Aseneth loved Levi very much because Levi was devoted to the Lord God, and he was a man of understanding and prophet of the Most High and saw openly with his eyes.
23.1 And it happened when Joseph and Aseneth were passing by, having departed from Jacob, the firstborn son of Pharaoh saw them from the wall, and upon seeing Aseneth he became fervid over her because of her surpassing beauty.	**23.1** And it happened when Joseph and Aseneth were passing by, the firstborn son of Pharaoh saw her. And was stricken [by] Aseneth and became deeply distraught and sick because of her beauty and he said, "It will not be this way!"
23.2 Then the son of Pharaoh sent messengers and summoned Simeon	**23.2** And the son of Pharaoh sent messengers and summoned Simeon

and Levi. And after they came and stood before him, the firstborn son of Pharaoh said to them, "I myself know that today you are men mightier than all peoples on the earth, and with these right hands of yours the city of the Shechemites was overthrown, and with your two swords thirty thousand warriors were struck down.	and Levi. And the men came to him and stood before him. And the son of Pharaoh said, "I myself know that you are men mightier than all peoples, and you overthrew the cities of Shechem, and with these two swords thirty myriads of warriors were struck down.
23.3 And today I will take you as companions for myself, and I will give you much gold and silver, both male slaves and female slaves, and houses and great properties. Support me in battle and do mercy with me because I have been very insulted [ὑβρίσθην πάνυ] by your brother Joseph, since he took Aseneth to wife and she was betrothed to me from the beginning.	**23.3** Behold! I will take you as companions, and I will give you gold and silver, male slaves and female slaves, and donkeys [ὄνους] and great estates if you do this thing and have mercy on me because I am suddenly insulted [ὑβρίζομαι ταχέως] by your brother Joseph because he took my wife Aseneth, who was pinned down by me from the beginning.
23.4 And now come with me and I will war against Joseph to kill him with my sword, and I will take Aseneth to wife, and you will be to me brothers and faithful friends.	**23.4** And now come! Together oppose your brother, and I will kill him with my sword, and I shall have Aseneth as a wife, and you will be to me brothers and faithful friends.
23.5 But if you do not listen to my words, I will kill you with my sword!"	**23.5** But if you shrink back from my plan, behold! My sword is ready for you!"
23.6 And after he said these things, he unsheathed his sword and showed it to them.	**23.6** And right when he was saying these things, he unsheathed [his] sword and he showed it to them. But as Simeon and Levi heard these things, they were exceedingly wounded, because the son of Pharaoh spoke to them in the manner of a tyrant.
23.7 Now Simeon was a rash and daring man, and he wanted to put his right hand on the handle of his sword to draw it from its sheath and strike the son of Pharaoh because he had spoken harshly to them.	**23.7** And Simeon was rash and daring, and he wanted to strike him because he spoke to them harshly.

23.8 Levi indeed saw the intention of his heart because he was a prophetic man, and he stepped with his foot on the right foot of Simeon and pressed, signaling to him, to stop him from his anger.	**23.8** And Levi saw the intention of his heart because Levi was a prophetic man. And Levi stepped with his foot on the right foot of Simeon and pressed it and signaled to him to cease from his anger.[7]
23.9 And Levi spoke quietly to Simeon, "Why are you furious toward this man? We are God-worshiping men, and it is not fitting for us to repay evil for evil."	
23.10 Then Levi spoke to the son of Pharaoh with frankness and in gentleness of heart, "Why is our lord saying these things? Moreover, we are God-worshiping men, and our father is a friend of the Most High God, and our brother is like a son of God.	**23.10** And Levi said, "Why is our lord saying these things? And we are God-worshiping men, and our father is a friend of the Most High God, and Joseph our brother is like the firstborn son of God.
23.11 And how could we do this wicked thing, to sin before our God and our father Israel and before our brother Joseph?	**23.11** And how could we utterly sin [by doing] this wicked thing before God and before our father and before our brother Joseph?
23.12 And now, hear *my* words! It is not fitting for a God-worshiping man to wrong any person in any way. But if someone desires to wrong a God-worshiping man, that God-worshiping man will not defend himself, because a sword is not in his hands.	**23.12** And now, hear *my* words! It is not fitting for a God-worshiping man to wrong any person in any way. But if someone desires to harm a God-worshiping man with his hands—[8]
23.13 And you, be wary of speaking these things any longer about our brother Joseph. If you continue in your wicked plan, Behold! Our swords are drawn against you!"	**23.13** And you, be wary of speaking about our brother Joseph in accordance with these things.... Behold! Our swords are before you!"
23.14 Then Simeon and Levi drew their swords from their sheaths and said, "Now, do you see these swords? With these two swords, the Lord avenged the insult of the Shechemites	**23.14** And Simeon and Levi drew their swords from their stores and said, "Behold! Have you seen these swords? With these two swords the Lord avenged the insult of the Shechemites."

with which they insulted the sons of Israel, because of our sister Dinah, whom Shechem son of Hamor also defiled."

23.15 And the son of Pharaoh, upon seeing the drawn swords, was exceedingly afraid and trembled with his whole body because they were flashing like a flame of fire, and his eyes became dim, and he fell on his face to the ground beneath their feet.	23.15 And the son of Pharaoh saw their swords, and he was exceedingly afraid and trembled because their swords were flashing like a flame of fire. And the eyes of the son of Pharaoh grew dim, and he fell on his face to the ground beneath their feet.
23.16 Then, Levi stretched out his right hand and grasped him, saying, "Arise, and do not fear. Only be wary of continuing to speak any wicked thing about our brother Joseph."	23.16 And Levi stretched out his hand and raised him, saying, "Arise, and do not be afraid. But[9] be wary to not speak wickedly about our brother Joseph."
23.17 And thus Simeon and Levi went out from his presence.	23.17 And Simeon and Levi went out from the presence of the son of Pharaoh.
24.1 Therefore, the son of Pharaoh remained, being full of fear and pain because he feared the brothers of Joseph. And he was once more exceedingly maddened on account of Aseneth's beauty and was pained even more.	24.1 And the son of Pharaoh was full of fear and pain. Because he feared Joseph and his brothers Simeon and Levi. And he was depressed with extreme pain, from Aseneth's superabundantly great beauty.
24.2 Then his servants spoke to him in [his] ear, "Look, the sons of Bilhah and the sons of Zilpah, the slaves of Leah and Rachel, Jacob's wives, are at great enmity with Joseph and Aseneth and hate them. These will be for you in everything, in accordance with your will."	24.2 Then his servants spoke, saying, "Look, the sons of Bilhah and Zilpah, the slaves of Leah and Rachel, Jacob's wives, are at enmity with Joseph and envy him, and they will be in accordance with your will."
24.3 Therefore, the son of Pharaoh immediately having sent messengers, he summoned them, and they came to him in the first hour of the night and stood before him. And he said	24.3 And the son of Pharaoh sent and summoned them. And the son of Pharaoh said to them, "I've got a word for you, because you are powerful men."

to them, "I have learned from many [people] that you are powerful men."	
24.4 And Dan and Gad the older brothers said to him, "Then let our lord speak to his slaves what he desires so that your slaves may hear and act according to your will."	**24.4** And Gad and Dan[10] the older brothers said to him, "Then let our lord speak, and we will act according to your word."
24.5 Then, the son of Pharaoh rejoiced with an exceedingly great joy and said to his slaves, "Now, withdraw from me a little while because I have a secret word for these men."	**24.5** And the son of Pharaoh rejoiced with great joy. And he said to his slaves, "Now, withdraw from me a little while because I have a secret word for these men."
24.6 And they all withdrew.	**24.6** And they all withdrew.
24.7 Then the son of Pharaoh was deceptive and said to them, "Look now, blessing and death are before your face. Therefore, you take the blessing rather than the death because you are powerful men and should not die like women but be men! and repay [ἀμύνεσθε][11] your enemies.	**24.7** And the son of Pharaoh said to them, "Look, blessing and death are before your face. Take the blessing rather and not the death because you are powerful men and should not die like women but should be men and repay [ἀμύνασθαι] your enemies.
24.8 For I myself have heard Joseph your brother saying to Pharaoh, my father, that 'Dan and Gad and Nephtali and Asher are not my brothers but children of my father's slaves. Indeed, I am waiting for my father's death and I will remove them and all their offspring from the earth. They will never inherit with us, because they are children of slaves.	**24.8** I heard your brother Joseph saying to my father Pharaoh—because Joseph said about you that 'they are children of my father's slaves and they are not my brothers. And I am waiting for my father's death and I will wipe out them and all of their offspring. And they will never inherit together with us because they are children of a slave.
24.9 For these sold me to the Ishmaelites, and I will strip them in accordance with their insult that they wickedly did against me. Only let my father die [first].'	**24.9** And they sold me to the Ishmaelites,[12] and I will destroy them in accordance with the insult that they wickedly did to me. Only let them die before me [πρὸ ἐμοῦ].'
24.10 And my father Pharaoh commended him for these things and said	**24.10** And my father the Pharaoh praised him and said to him, 'You have

to him, 'You have spoken well, child. As for the rest, take from me powerful men and go out stealthily to meet them, in the way that they did for you, and I will be a helper for you.'"	spoken well. And take men, powerful in battle and good [καλούς], and I will be a helper for you.'"
24.11 And when Dan and Gad heard these things from the son of Pharaoh, they were very disturbed and exceedingly pained and said to him, "We beg you, lord, help us! For, from now on, we are your household slaves and servants, and we are ready to die with you!"	**24.11** And when the men heard these words, they were disturbed and pained and said to the son of Pharaoh, "We beg you, lord, help us!
24.12 And the son of Pharaoh said, "I myself will be helper to you if you listen to my words."	
24.13 And they said to him, "Command us what you want and we will act according to your will."	**24.13** We are your slaves. Command us and we will act according to your will."
24.14 And the son of Pharaoh said to them, "I will kill my father Pharaoh on this night because Pharaoh is like a father to Joseph and he said [he would] help him against you. But you will kill Joseph, and I will take Aseneth to wife for myself, and you will be my brothers and co-heirs of everything mine. Only [μόνον] do this thing [first]."	**24.14** And the son of Pharaoh said to them, "I will kill my father on this night because Pharaoh is like Joseph's father, and I will take Aseneth to wife for myself, and [you] will be brothers and co-heirs to me. Only [πλήν] do this thing [first]."
24.15 And Dan and Gad said to him, "We are your slaves today and we will do everything that you have commanded us. And we have heard Joseph saying to Aseneth, 'Go tomorrow to your field of our inheritance because it is the time [καιρός] of the vine harvest.' And he sent men powerful in battle with her, six hundred [of them], and fifty forerunners with her.	**24.15** And Gad and Dan[13] said, "We are your slaves today and we shall do what you have commanded us. And we have heard Joseph saying to Aseneth, 'Go tomorrow into your field of our inheritance, because it is the time [ὥρα]...' And he sent with her six hundred men powerful in battle [and] fifty forerunners.

24.16 Now, therefore, listen to us, and we will speak to our lord."	**24.16** Now, listen to us, and we shall speak with our lord."
24.17 And they had spoken to him all of their words [λόγους] in secret.	**24.17** And they spoke all of the message [λόγου] in secret.
24.18 Then the son of Pharaoh had given to the four brothers five hundred men each, and he appointed them as their rulers and commanders.	**24.18** And the son of Pharaoh gave to those four five hundred men each, and he stationed them as their rulers and commanders.
24.19 And Dan and Gad said to him, "We are your slaves today, and we will do everything that you have commanded us. We will go during the night and lie in wait in the valley and hide in the thicket of the reeds. And you, take with you fifty archers on horses and go in front of her at a distance. And Aseneth will come and fall into our hands, and we will cut down the men who are with her, but she will flee in front with her chariot and will fall into your hands, and you will do with her just as [καθώς] your soul desires. And after these things we will also kill Joseph while he is grieving for Aseneth, and likewise we will kill his children before his eyes." The firstborn son of Pharaoh having therefore heard these things, he rejoiced exceedingly and he sent them out, [with] two thousand men of war with them.	**24.19** And Gad and Dan said, "We are your slaves today and we will do what you have commanded us. We will go during the night and lie in wait [in] the valley and hide in the thicket of the reeds. And take with you fifty cavalry archers and go in front at a far distance. And Aseneth will come and fall into our ambush, and we will cut down those with her. And Aseneth will flee in front by chariot into your hands, and you will do with her just as [καθά] your soul desires. And after these things, we will kill Joseph while he is grieving for Aseneth, and we will kill his children before his eyes." And ... [W: the son of Pharaoh] rejoiced ... [W: when he heard these words and sent] them ... [W: out] and two ... [W: thousand men of war with them].[14]
24.20 And when they came to the valley, hiding in the thicket of reeds, they had [divided] in four companies. And they sat on the far side of the valley—so that with regard to the division in front on one side, and on either side of the road five hundred men were distributed. And likewise, on this side of the valley the rest stayed and sat. And they were in the thicket of the	**24.20** And they went ... [W: into the valley and] hid in the thicket of the reeds. And they sat across the valley, and in front were five hundred on the other side, between them the road was flat.[15]

reeds. On either side of the road five hundred men were distributed. And the road between them was flat and wide.

25.1 Then the son of Pharaoh arose on this night and went to his father's bedchamber to kill him with a sword. Therefore, his father's guards were preventing him from entering to his father and said to him, "Why do you come forth, lord?"	**25.1** And the son of Pharaoh arose on that night and went for his father's death, to kill his father with a sword.
25.2 And the son of Pharaoh said to them, "I desire [that] I shall see my father because I am going to harvest my newly planted vineyard."	
25.3 And the guards said to him, "Your father is suffering with pain and laid awake the whole night, and now he is resting. And he said to us, 'Do not let anyone enter this [room], not even if it is my firstborn son.'"	**25.3** And his father's guards said, "Your father has a headache and laid awake the whole night, and now he is resting a little while. And your father said, 'Let no one come near me, not even my firstborn son.'"
25.4 But he, having heard these things, went away in fury and immediately took men, cavalry archers, fifty in number. And he went away in front of them, just as Dan and Gad had told him.	**25.4** And hastening, the son of Pharaoh went away and took the fifty cavalry archers and went away in front of them.
25.5 But the younger brothers Nephtali and Asher were speaking to their older brothers, to Dan and Gad, saying, "Why are you acting wickedly again against our father Israel and against our brother Joseph? And God protects him like an apple of [his] eye. Look, haven't you sold Joseph once? And today, he is king of all the land of Egypt and savior and grain provider!	**25.5** Accordingly, the younger brothers Nephtali and Asher spoke to their older brothers, to Dan and Gad, saying, "Why are you acting wickedly again against your father and our brother Joseph? And the Lord protects him like an apple of [his] eye. Look, haven't you sold him once? And behold! Today he is king of the land and savior and grain provider!
25.6 Now, therefore, if you intend to act wickedly against him, he will cry	**25.6** And now, if you again try … he will send fire from heaven and it will

Appendix: Translation of *Aseneth* Chapters 1, 22–29

to the Most High, and he will send fire from heaven and consume you. And the angels of God will war against you."	consume you. And the angels of God will war and will destroy you."
25.7 Then their older brothers were angered against them and said, "And shall we die like women? No way!"	25.7 And their older brothers were angered, saying, "Otherwise, we shall die as women!"
25.8 And they went out to meet Joseph and Aseneth.	
26.1 And Aseneth arose at dawn and said to Joseph, "I will go to the field, just as you said, of our inheritance. But my soul is exceedingly anxious because you are separating from me."	26.1 And Aseneth arose at dawn and said to Joseph, "We will go, just as you said, to the field of inheritance. And my soul is anxious because you are separating from me."
26.2 And Joseph said to her, "Have courage and do not fear, but rather go away rejoicing completely, distraught by nothing, because the Lord is with you, and he will guard you like an apple of [his] eye from all evil.	26.2 And Joseph said to her, "Have courage and do not fear, but go because the Lord is with you, and he will guard you like an apple of [his] eye from every wicked deed.
26.3 And I will go on my grain-distribution [route], and I will give grain to all the people in the city. And no person will be destroyed by famine in the land of Egypt."	26.3 Therefore, I myself will go on my grain-distribution [route], and I will give bread to all the people, and all the land will not be ruined from the face of the Lord."
26.4 Then Aseneth went on her way and Joseph on his grain distribution.	26.4 And Aseneth went on her way and Joseph on the grain distribution.
26.5 And when Aseneth arrived at the place of the valley with six hundred men, instantaneously those around the son of Pharaoh came out from their hiding place and mixed in battle with the men who were with Aseneth. And they cut them all down with their swords and they killed all her forerunners. But Aseneth fled with her chariot.	26.5 And Aseneth came on the place of the valley, and six hundred men [were] with her. And the ambushers rushed forth from the hiding places and mixed with the men of Aseneth and cut them down by [the] edge of a knife and they killed all her forerunners. And Aseneth fled ahead with her chariot.
26.6 Then Levi the son of Leah knew all these things by the spirit as[16] a	26.6 And Levi announced to his brothers, the sons of Israel, telling Aseneth's

prophet. And he told Aseneth's danger to his brothers, and immediately each of them took [a] sword on his thigh and their shields on their arms and spears in [their] left hands, and they pursued after Aseneth with much speed.	danger. And each took his sword and their shields and spears in their hands and pursued after Aseneth with quick speed.
26.7 And as Aseneth fled ahead, behold! The son of Pharaoh encountered her, and fifty cavalry men with him.	**26.7** And Aseneth fled ahead and behold! The son of Pharaoh met her, and fifty cavalry men with him.
26.8 And upon seeing him, Aseneth was very afraid and was trembling and called on the name of the Lord her God.	**26.8** And Aseneth saw him and was afraid and exceedingly troubled, and she called on the name of the Lord her God.
27.1 And Benjamin was sitting with her on the chariot on [her] left [δεχίων]. And Benjamin was a little boy as strong as an eighteen-year-old. And there was an unspeakable beauty on him and power like a lion cub's. And he exceedingly feared God.	**27.1** And Benjamin sat on the left [εὐονύμων = εὐωνύμον] of Aseneth in her chariot. And Benjamin was a little boy, an eighteen-year-old boy, large and strong, and there was an unspeakable beauty in him and strength like a lion's cub. And he exceedingly feared the Lord.
27.2 Then Benjamin leapt down from the chariot and took a round stone from the valley, and having filled his hand, he hurled it down toward the son of Pharaoh and struck his left temple. And it wounded him with a deep wound.	**27.2** And he leapt down from the chariot and took a round stone from the valley, and it filled his hand. And he hurled it over against the son of Pharaoh, and it struck his left temple. And it wounded him with a deep wound.
27.3 And he fell on the ground, seemingly half-dead.	**27.3** And the son of Pharaoh fell.
27.4 And whether it was so, Benjamin, having run up upon a rock, said to Aseneth's driver, "Give me stones from the valley!"	**27.4** And Benjamin leapt and went up on the rock. And he said to Aseneth's driver, "Give me stones from the valley!"
27.5 And he had given him fifty stones. And by hurling the stones,	**27.5** And he gave him forty-eight stones. And he hurled the forty-eight

Benjamin killed the fifty men who were with the son of Pharaoh. The stones all sunk through their temples.	stones, and with them he struck forty-eight men of the son of Pharaoh's men. And all the stones sunk into their temples.
27.6 Then the sons of Leah—Reuben and Simeon, Levi and Judah, Issachar and Zebulun—pursued after the men who were lying in wait for Aseneth and fell on them suddenly and cut them all down. And the six men killed 2,076.	**27.6** And [the] sons of Leah—Reuben, Simeon, Levi, Judah, Issachar, Zebulun—pursued after the men who were lying in wait. And they fell on them suddenly and cut down all the men. And the six men killed two thousand.
27.7 And the sons of Bilhah and Zilpah fled from their presence and said, "We've been destroyed by our brothers, and the son of Pharaoh has died by the hand of Benjamin the little boy, and all those with him will be destroyed by the hand of the boy Benjamin!"	**27.7** And his brothers, the sons of Bilhah and Zilpah, fled from their presence and said, "We've been destroyed by our brothers, and the son of Pharaoh has died by the hand of Benjamin, and all those with him have been destroyed by the one hand of the little boy Benjamin!
27.8 Therefore, the rest left behind said, "Come! Let's kill Aseneth and Benjamin and let's flee into[17] the thicket of these reeds."[18]	**27.8** And now, Come! Let's kill Aseneth and Benjamin and let's flee into the thicket of these reeds."[19]
27.9 And they came on Aseneth, holding their drawn swords, covered with blood.	**27.9** And they came, having drawn their swords, covered with blood.
27.10 And upon seeing them, Aseneth was very afraid and said, "The Lord God who made me alive and rescued me from the idols and the destruction of death, just as you said to me that 'in the [eternal] age, your soul will live,' rescue me even now from these wicked men!"	**27.10** And Aseneth saw them and was afraid and said, "Lord, who brought me back to life from death, saying to me, 'In the [eternal] age, your soul will live,' rescue me from the hands of these men!"
27.11 And the Lord God heard the voice of Aseneth, and immediately the swords of the opponents fell from their hands on the ground and burned to ashes.	**27.11** … [W: And the Lord heard the voice of Aseneth …] from their hands on the ground and burned to ashes.

28.1 And the sons of Bilhah and Zilpah, having seen this marvelous wonder, were afraid and said, "The Lord is waging war against us on behalf of Aseneth!"	**28.1** And the sons of Bilhah and Zilpah saw these great things, and they were afraid and said, "The Lord is waging war on us for Aseneth!"
28.2 Then falling on [their] face[s] toward the ground, they paid obeisance to Aseneth and said, "Have mercy on us your servants because you are our lady and queen!	**28.2** And they fell on [their] face[s] on the ground and paid obeisance to her and said, "Have mercy on us your servants because you are our lady and queen!
28.3 And although we acted wickedly, doing evil to you and against our brother Joseph, the Lord has repaid us according to our deeds.	**28.3** And we acted wickedly to you and the Lord has repaid us according to our deeds.
28.4 Because of this, we your servants are begging you—have mercy on us, the humble and afflicted ones, and save us from the hands of our brothers because they have become avengers of your insult and their swords are against us!	**28.4** And now, we your servants are begging—have mercy on us and save us from the hands of our brothers because they are by you as avengers of the insult [ἔκδικοι τῆς ὕβρεως] and their swords are against us!"
28.5 And we know that our brothers are God-worshiping men and do not repay evil for evil to any person.	
28.6 Therefore, be gracious to your slaves, Lady, before them."	
28.7 And Aseneth said to them, "Have courage and do not be afraid of your brothers, because they are God-worshiping men and ones who fear the Lord. Go now into the thicket of this reed until I appease them regarding you and I put an end to the anger of those against whom you have dared [to commit] great things against them. However, the Lord himself will also judge between me and you."	**28.7** And Aseneth said to them, "Have courage and do not be afraid of your brothers because they are God-worshiping men and ones who fear God. But go into the thicket of this reed until I appease these [men] about you and they put an end to their anger, because you have dared [to commit] a great thing against them. Therefore have courage and do not fear … [W: However, God judges between me and you."]

28.8 Then Dan and Gad fled into the thicket of reed, but their brothers, the sons of Leah, came running like stags with much haste against them.	**28.8** And they fled … Dan and his brothers. And behold! The sons of Leah came running like three-year-old stags.
28.9 And Aseneth came down from the protection of her chariot and greeted them with tears. And they, falling, paid her obeisance on the ground and cried with a loud voice. And they were seeking their brothers the sons of the slave-women to do away with them.	**28.9** And Aseneth came down from the shelter of her chariot and greeted them with tears. And they, falling on [their] face[s], paid her obeisance on the ground and they cried with a loud voice. And they were seeking their brothers.
28.10 And Aseneth said to them, "I beg you to spare your brothers and do not repay them evil for evil. For the Lord preserved me from them and shattered their blades and the swords from their hands. And look! They have melted and were burned to ash on the ground like honeycomb before the face of a fire. And this is enough for them that the Lord is warring against them on our behalf.	**28.10** And Aseneth said to them, "Spare your brothers and do not do evil for evil. For the Lord kept me from them and shattered their swords. Look! They have melted on the ground, like wax from the face of a fire. And this is enough for them, for the Lord to have warred against them.
28.11 So then, you are to spare your brothers because they are your brothers and the blood of your father Israel."	**28.11** And you, spare them because they are your brothers and the blood of your father Israel."
28.12 And Simeon said to her, "Why does our lady speak good things on behalf of her enemies?	**28.12** And Simeon said to her, "Why does our lady speak to us good [things] on behalf of her enemies?
28.13 No, but rather let's cut them down in order with our swords because today they plotted evil concerning our brother Joseph and our father Israel and against you, our lady."	**28.13** No, but let's cut them down with our swords because today first, they plotted against us and against our father and against our brother—now this twice—and against you, our lady and queen."
28.14 Then Aseneth stretched out her right hand and touched Simeon's beard and having kissed him, said, "By no means, brother, will you repay evil	**28.14** And Aseneth spoke to him and stretched out her right hand and kissed him and said, "By no means, brothers, shall you do evil for evil. Give to the

for evil [to] your neighbor because the Lord will avenge this insult [ὕβριν]. Moreover, they are your brothers and offspring of your father Israel and they fled far from your presence. Therefore, impart pardon to them."	Lord the avenging of their insult. And they are your brothers and are of the offspring of your father."
28.15 Then having come toward her, Levi kissed her right hand because he knew that she wanted to save the men from the wrath of their brothers so that [they would] not kill them.	**28.15** And Levi came from afar and kissed her right hand and knew that she wanted to save the men.
28.16 And [he knew that] they were nearby in the thicket of the reed.	**28.16** And [he knew that] they were nearby in the thicket of the reed.
28.17 And his brother Levi, though knowing this, did not report it to his brothers. For he was afraid lest in their wrath they may cut down their brothers.	**28.17** And their brother Levi, though he knew this, did not report it to his brothers. For he was afraid lest in their wrath they would cut them down.
29.1 And the son of Pharaoh rose from the ground and sat and spat blood from his mouth. The blood ran down on his mouth.	**29.1** And the son of Pharaoh rose from the ground and sat up, and blood was falling from his mouth.
29.2 And Benjamin, after running toward him, took his sword, having drawn it from the son of Pharaoh's sheath. For Benjamin was not carrying a sword on his thigh, he desired to strike on the son of Pharaoh's chest.	**29.2** And Benjamin ran up to him and took his sword and drew it up from its place because Benjamin himself did not have a sword on his thigh. And he drew his sword and wanted to strike the son of Pharaoh's chest.
29.3 Then Levi ran up to him and, having seized his hand, said, "By no means, brother, should you do this act because we[20] are God-worshiping men, and it is not fitting for a God-worshiping man to repay evil for evil, nor to trample one who has fallen, nor to press his enemy to death.	**29.3** And Levi ran up to him and seized his hand and said, "By no means, brother! You should not do this thing, because we are God-worshiping, and it is not fitting to repay evil for evil, nor to tread [on] the one who has fallen, nor to press the enemy to death.
29.4 And now, return your sword to its place and come help me, and we	**29.4** And now, return your sword to its place and come help me, and we may

may heal him from this wound. And if he lives, he will be our friend, and his father Pharaoh will be like our father."	heal him from his wound. And if he lives, he will be our friend after these things, and his father Pharaoh will be like our father."
29.5 Then, Levi raised up the son of Pharaoh from the ground and washed the blood from his face. And he bound bandages on his wound and put him on his horse and conveyed him to his father Pharaoh, narrating to him all the things that followed and what had happened.	29.5 And Levi raised up the son of Pharaoh and washed the blood from his face. And he put bandages [on] his wound and put him on his horse and conveyed him to his father Pharaoh. And he narrated to him all the things that his son had done.
29.6 And Pharaoh, after getting up from his throne, paid obeisance to Levi on the ground and blessed[21] him.	29.6 And Pharaoh got up from [his] throne.
29.7 Now, after the third day passed, the son of Pharaoh died from the stone from Benjamin by which he was wounded.	29.7 And on the third day, the son of Pharaoh died from the wound of [caused by] the stone of Benjamin.
29.8 And Pharaoh mourned his firstborn son exceedingly, whence Pharaoh became ill from the pain. And he died 109 years [of age]. And he left his diadem to the all-beautiful Joseph.	29.8 And Pharaoh mourned his firstborn son and became ill from the mourning. And he died, ninety-nine years [of age]. And he left the diadem of the kingdom to Joseph
29.9 And Joseph reigned in Egypt alone for forty-eight years. And after these things, Joseph handed over the diadem to the eager younger [son of] Pharaoh, who was at breast when Pharaoh the elder died. And Joseph was from then on like a father to the younger son of Pharaoh in the land of Egypt until his end, glorifying and praising God.	29.9 for forty-eight years in Egypt. After these things, Pharaoh handed over the diadem to a younger [son] from the offspring of Pharaoh in Egypt.
Epilogue A And Joseph lived for 110 years, and Joseph saw the children of Ephraim until the third generation, and the sons of Machir, Manasseh's son, were born on the lap of Joseph.	**Epilogue F** You have heard everything, brothers: How the Lord did not neglect to distinguish all those who believed in him. And how the one who was sold by his brothers and taken captive was

And Joseph said to his brothers, "I am dying. But God will surely visit you and lead us up out of this land into the land that God swore to our fathers, to Abraham and Isaac and Jacob."

And Joseph adjured the sons of Israel, saying, "At the time of the visitation, when God will visit you, gather my bones together from here with their grave-soil and take them out with you."

And Joseph died, being 110 years old, and they buried him in the tomb of the kings in Egypt.

And Aseneth also died after the death-sleep of Joseph, being advanced and full of days, and she was buried near Joseph, her suitor [μνηστῆρος].

On behalf of these things, we will glorify the Father and the Son and the Holy Spirit, now and forever and into the ages of the ages, Amen.

carried off into Egypt and thrown into prison, and falsely accused by his mistress, and having guarded self-control [σωφροσύνη], he also did not bow to the gods of the Egyptians.

How the one who desires mercy had compassion on this one, and as an apple of the eye, he guarded [him], and made [him] king and lord over all the land of Egypt. And he prepared his brothers to bow.

And how he saved Aseneth from the darkness of idols, and led her to the knowledge of God.

And again [you have heard] how the life-loving, all-compassionate Lord saved her from the snares and hands of the son of Pharaoh, and preserved [her] from the great multitude and from the brothers of Joseph.

Verily, to cry out that beautiful prophetic word, who will speak of the mighty deeds of the Lord? Who will make known all of his praises?[22]

And again, great is the Lord! And great is his power that he saved a woman from the hand of those stronger than her and from the opposing ambush and from wicked and malicious men. And while they fell, she arose and was restored. And he trampled her enemies.

And we, furthermore, brothers, if we do not avenge ourselves from our opposing enemies but offer up the vengeance to God, and if we also bear shining prizes of victory, then we are living from him.[23] And let us not only live a quiet and restful life but also, having departed from there, the artisan and king of the whole creation will appoint us into eternal and endless tents, to whom it is fitting, all glory and honor and devotion together to the Father, and the Son, and the Holy Spirit, now and forever into the ages of ages, Amen.

Notes

1. Wright, "After Antiquity," 1:140.
2. Often translated "virgin," παρθένος carried multiple connotations in classical Greek and Hellenistic literature, referring to a young unmarried woman, a young married woman, goddesses, or even, on occasion, chaste males (e.g., Jos. Asen. 4.7, where it refers to Joseph, emphasizing his sexual abstention and self-control, and Rev 14:4). "When referring to women, *Aseneth* uses the … connotation of the young female, but the genre of this narrative produces more expectations regarding the nature of female *parthenoi*. In ancient Greek novels, chastity is an outward sign of noble youth, and *parthenos* especially describes the female protagonist, so a female *parthenos* in *Aseneth* is a heterosexually innocent woman who is unmarried, capable of producing offspring, and from a wealthy household" (Ahearne-Kroll, "Joseph and Aseneth," 2530). For this reason, I have followed Ahearne-Kroll's convention and left the term transliterated rather than translated.
3. The text of MS F has several lacunae, which are indicated in this translation with ellipses. When the sister text of MS W offers a plausible suggestion of what MS F may have, the text of MS W is provided in brackets.
4. Gk. ἐν γῇ Γεσέμ. Also in 22.5 A.
5. Gk. ἐν γῇ Γεσέμ. Also in 22.5 F.
6. Or "is like a god to me."
7. There is no versification in the original manuscripts, and no breaks between what is labeled here in MS F as verse 8 and verse 10.
8. See discussion in ch. 4.
9. Gk. καί.
10. MS F "Dad."
11. See discussion in ch. 4.
12. MS F "Israelites." This is likely an error, and I have provided instead the text of MS W.
13. MS F "Dad."
14. This portion of the manuscript has been damaged.
15. Here the text is corrupt and difficult to determine.
16. Or "like."
17. Lit. "upon."
18. Lit. "this reed."
19. Lit. "this reed."
20. Wright's emendation. Gk. ὑμεῖς.

21. Or "praised." Gk. εὐλόγησεν.
22. Lit. "who will make heard."
23. See 1 John 2:6.

Bibliography

Abbot, Abiel. *Traits of Resemblance in the People of the United States of America and Ancient Israel*. Repr. as pages 3–25 in *The American Republic and Ancient Israel*. Edited by Moshe David. New York: Arno, 1977.

Ahearne-Kroll, Patricia D. *Aseneth of Egypt: The Composition of a Jewish Narrative*. EJL 53. Atlanta: SBL Press, 2020.

———. "Joseph and Aseneth." Pages 2525–89 in *Outside the Bible: Ancient Jewish Writings Related to Scripture*. Edited by Louis H. Feldman, James L. Kugel, and Lawrence H. Schiffman. Lincoln: University of Nebraska Press, 2013.

———. "*Joseph and Aseneth* and Jewish Identity in Greco-Roman Egypt." PhD diss., University of Chicago Divinity School, 2005.

Alter, Robert. *The Art of Bible Translation*. Princeton: Princeton University Press, 2019.

———. *The Art of Biblical Narrative*. Rev. and updated ed. New York: Basic Books, 2011.

———. *Pen of Iron: American Prose and the King James Bible*. Princeton: Princeton University Press, 2010.

Aptowitzer, Victor. "Asenath, the Wife of Joseph: A Haggadic Literary-Historical Study." *HUCA* 1 (1924): 239–306.

Attridge, Harold. *The Interpretation of Biblical History in the "Antiquitates Judaicae" of Flavius Josephus*. Missoula, MT: Scholars Press, 1990.

Auerbach, Erich. "Odysseus' Scar." Pages 3–23 in *Mimesis: The Representation of Reality in Western Literature*. Translated by Willard R. Trask. Princeton: Princeton University Press, 1968.

Bader, Mary Anna. *Sexual Violation in the Hebrew Bible: A Multi-methodological Study of Genesis 34 and 2 Samuel 13*. StBibLit 87. Berlin: Lang, 2006.

Bar-Efrat, Shimon. *Narrative Art in the Bible*. Sheffield: Sheffield Academic, 1989.

Bechtel, Lyn M. "What if Dinah Is Not Raped? (Genesis 34)." *JSOT* 62 (1994): 19–36.

Begg, Christopher. "Genesis in Josephus." Pages 303–29 in *The Book of Genesis: Composition, Reception, and Interpretation*. Edited by Craig Evans, Joel N. Lohr, and David L. Petersen. VTSup 152. Leiden: Brill, 2012.

———. *Judean Antiquities, Books 5–7*. FJTC 4. Leiden: Brill, 2005.

Ben-Porat, Ziva. "The Poetics of Literary Allusion." *PTL* 1 (1976): 105–28.

Berger, Klaus. *Das Buch der Jubiläen*. JSHRZ 2.3. Gütersloh: Mohn, 1981.

Berlin, Adele. "Literary Approaches to Biblical Literature: General Observations and a Case Study of Genesis 34." Pages 45–75 in *The Hebrew Bible: New Insights and Scholarship*. Edited by Frederick E. Greenspahn. New York: New York University Press, 2008.

———. *Poetics and Interpretation of Biblical Narrative*. Winona Lake, IN: Eisenbrauns, 1994.

Bilde, Per. "The Causes of the Jewish War according to Josephus." *JSJ* 10 (1979): 179–202.

———. *Flavius Josephus between Jerusalem and Rome: His Life, His Works, and Their Importance*. Sheffield: JSOT Press, 1988.

Birch, Dom. "Why We Need an Ethics of History Writing." Doing History in Public, December 6, 2016. https://tinyurl.com/SBL6710a.

Bochner, Arthur P. *Coming to Narrative: A Personal History of Paradigm Change in the Human Sciences*. Walnut Creek, CA: Left Coast, 2014.

Bolen, Derek M., and Tony E. Adams. "Narrative Ethics." Pages 618–29 in *The Routledge International Handbook on Narrative and Life History*. Edited by Ivor Goodson, Ari Antikainen, Pat Sikes, and Molly Andrews. New York: Routledge, 2017.

Booth, Wayne C. *The Company We Keep: An Ethics of Fiction*. Berkeley: University of California Press, 1988.

Bouque, Linda B. *Defining Rape*. Durham, NC: Duke University Press, 1989.

Breisach, Ernst. *Historiography: Ancient, Medieval, and Modern*. Chicago: University of Chicago Press, 1993.

Brody, Howard, and Mark Clark. "Narrative Ethics: A Narrative." *HCRSR* 44 (2014): S7–S11.

Bruner, Edward M. "Ethnography as Narrative." Pages 139–55 in *The Anthropology of Experience*. Edited by Victor W. Turner and Edward M. Bruner. Chicago: University of Illinois Press, 1986.

———. "Introduction." Pages 3–32 in *The Anthropology of Experience.* Edited by Victor W. Turner and Edward M. Bruner. Chicago: University of Illinois Press, 1986.
Burchard, Christoph. "Joseph and Aseneth." *OTP* 2:177–248.
———. "Joseph and Aseneth in Rumania." *JSJ* 39 (2008): 540–49.
———. "The Present State of Research on Joseph and Aseneth." Pages 297–320 in *Gesammelte Studien zu Joseph and Aseneth.* Leiden: Brill, 1996.
———. "The Text of *Joseph and Aseneth* Reconsidered." *JSP* 14 (2005): 83–96.
Burchard, Christoph, assisted by Carsten Burfeind and Uta Barbara Fink. *Joseph und Aseneth.* PVTG 5. Leiden: Brill, 2003.
Cerquiglini, Bernard. *Éloge de la variante: Histoire critique de la philologie.* Paris: Seuil, 1989.
Chapman, Cynthia R. *The House of the Mother: The Social Roles of Maternal Kin in Biblical Hebrew Narrative and Poetry.* New Haven: Yale University Press, 2016.
Charles, R. H. *The Book of Jubilees or Little Genesis: Translated from the Editor's Ethiopic Text and Edited, with Introduction, Notes, and Indices.* London: Black, 1902.
———. *The Ethiopic Version of the Hebrew Book of Jubilees.* Oxford: Clarendon, 1895.
Charlesworth, James. *The Pseudepigrapha and Modern Research.* SCS 7. Atlanta: Scholars Press, 1981.
Chesnutt, Randall D. *From Death to Life: Conversion in Joseph and Aseneth.* Sheffield: Sheffield Academic, 1995.
Cohen, Shaye J. D. *The Beginnings of Jewishness: Boundaries, Varieties, Uncertainties.* Berkeley: University of California Press, 1999.
Coleman, Monica A. *The Dinah Project: A Handbook for Congregational Response to Sexual Violence.* Eugene, OR: Wipf & Stock, 2010.
Collins, John J. "The Genre Apocalypse Reconsidered." *ZAC* 20 (2016): 21–40.
———. "Introduction: Towards the Morphology of a Genre." *Semeia* 14 (1979): 1–20.
Cottrill, Amy. *Uncovering Violence: Reading Biblical Narratives as an Ethical Project.* Louisville: Westminster John Knox, 2021.
Crawford, Sidnie White. *Rewriting Scripture in Second Temple Times.* Grand Rapids: Eerdmans, 2008.
Cruikshank, Julie. *The Social Life of Stories: Narrative and Knowledge in the Yukon Territory.* Lincoln: University of Nebraska Press, 1998.

Delling, Gerhard. "Einwirkungen der Sprache der Septuaginta in 'Joseph und Aseneth.'" *JSJ* 9 (1978): 29–56.

Diamant, Anita. *The Red Tent*. New York: St. Martin's, 1997.

Driscoll, Matthew James. "The Words on the Page: Thoughts on Philology, Old and New." Pages 87–104 in *Creating the Medieval Saga: Versions, Variability and Editorial Interpretations of Old Norse Saga Literature*. Edited by Judy Quinn and Emily Lethbridge. Odense: University Press of Southern Denmark, 2010.

Efthymiadis, Stephanos, and Nikos Kalogeras. "Audience, Language, and Patronage in Byzantine Hagiography." Pages 247–84 in *Genres and Contexts*. Volume 2 of *The Ashgate Research Companion to Byzantine Hagiography*. Edited by Stephanos Efthymiadis. Farnham, UK: Ashgate, 2011.

Endres, John C. *Biblical Interpretation in the Book of Jubilees*. CBQMS 18. Washington, DC: Catholic Biblical Association of America, 1987.

Epstein, Louis. *Marriage Laws in the Bible and Talmud*. Cambridge: Harvard University Press, 1942.

Feldman, Louis H. "Josephus as a Biblical Interpreter: The 'Aqedah.'" *JQR* 75 (1984–1985): 212–52.

———. "Josephus' Portrait of Moses." *JQR* 82 (1992): 285–328.

———. "The Reshaping of Biblical Narrative in the Hellenistic Period: A Review Essay." *IJCT* 8 (2001): 60–79.

Fewell, Danna Nolan, and David M. Gunn. "Tipping the Balance: Sternberg's Reader and the Rape of Dinah." *JBL* 110 (1991): 193–211.

Fink, Barbara Uta. *Joseph und Aseneth: Revision des griechischen Textes und Edition der zweiten lateinischen Übersetzung*. FSBP 5. Berlin: de Gruyter, 2008.

Fishbane, Michael. *Biblical Interpretation in Ancient Israel*. Oxford: Clarendon, 1988.

Fitzpatrick, John C., ed. *The Writings of George Washington from the Original Manuscript Sources, 1745–1799*. Washington, DC: U.S. Government Printing Office, 1931.

Fowler, Alastair. *Kinds of Literature: An Introduction to the Theory of Genres and Modes*. Cambridge: Harvard University Press, 1982.

Frank, Arthur W. *Letting Stories Breathe: A Socio-narratology*. Chicago: University of Chicago Press, 2010.

———. "Notes on Socio-narratology and Narrative Therapy." *JNFT* 2 (2017): 3–19.

———. "Philoctetes and the Good Companion Story." *Enthymema* 16 (2016): 119–27.
Gager, John. "Pseudo-Hecataeus Again." *ZNW* 60 (1969): 130–39.
Gallant, Robert. "Josephus's Expositions of Biblical Law: An Internal Analysis." PhD diss., Yale University, 1988.
Ganz, Marshall. "Public Narrative, Collective Action, and Power." Pages 273–87 in *Accountability through Public Opinion: From Inertia to Public Action*. Edited by Sina Odugbemi and Taeku Lee. Washington, DC: World Bank, 2011.
Geller, Steven. *Sacred Enigmas: Literary Religion in the Hebrew Bible*. New York: Routledge, 1996.
Giere, Samuel D. *A New Glimpse of Day One: Intertextuality, History of Interpretation, and Genesis 1.1–5*. Berlin: De Gruyter, 2009.
Ginzberg, Louis. *Legends of the Jews*. 7 vols. Philadelphia: Jewish Publication Society, 1969.
Glass, Gillian. "A Daughter of Hebrews and Hellenes: Epiphany in *Aseneth* and Contemporary Ancient Greek Literature." PhD diss., University of British Columbia, 2022.
Goldstein, Jonathan. "The Date of the Book of Jubilees." *PAAJR* 50 (1983): 63–86.
Graybill, Rhiannon. *Texts after Terror: Rape, Sexual Violence, and the Hebrew Bible*. Oxford: Oxford University Press, 2021.
Halpern-Amaru, Betsy. "Flavius Josephus and the Book of Jubilees: A Question of Source." *HUCA* 72 (2001): 15–44.
Hansen, Julie. "The Ethics of Storytelling: Narrative Hermeneutics, History, and the Possible." *MS* 13 (2020): 350–54.
Harrington, Anne. *The Cure within: A History of Mind-Body Medicine*. New York: Norton, 2008.
Hartner, Marcus. "Multiperspectivity." Pages 353–63 in *Handbook of Narratology*. Edited by Peter Hühn, Jan Christoph Meister, and Wolf Schmid. Berlin: De Gruyter, 2014.
Hata, Gohei. "The Abuse and Misuse of Josephus in Eusebius' *Ecclesiastical History*, Books 2 and 3." Pages 91–102 in *Studies in Josephus and the Varieties of Ancient Judaism: Louis H. Feldman Jubilee Album*. Edited by Shaye J. D. Cohen and Joshua J. Schwartz. AJEC 67. Leiden: Brill, 2007.
Hayes, Catherine. *Gentile Impurities and Jewish Identities: Intermarriage and Conversion from the Bible to the Talmud*. Oxford: Oxford University Press, 2002.

———. "Impurity, Intermarriage, and Conversion in Second Temple Sources." Pages 68–91 in *Gentile Impurities and Jewish Identities: Intermarriage and Conversion from the Bible to the Talmud*. Oxford: Oxford University Press, 2002.

———. "Intermarriage and Impurity in Ancient Jewish Sources." *HTR* 92 (1999): 3–36.

Haynes, Stephen. *Noah's Curse: The Biblical Justification of American Slavery*. Oxford: Oxford University Press, 2002.

Hicks-Keeton, Jill. *Arguing with Aseneth: Gentile Access to Israel's Living God in Jewish Antiquity*. Oxford: Oxford University Press, 2018.

Hinterberger, Martin. "Byzantine Hagiography and Its Literary Genres: Some Critical Observations." Pages 25–60 in *Genres and Contexts*. Volume 2 of *The Ashgate Research Companion to Byzantine Hagiography*. Edited by Stephanos Efthymiadis. Farnham, UK: Ashgate, 2011.

"The History of the Monastery." Radu Voda Monastery Official Website. https://tinyurl.com/SBL6710c.

Johnson, Sylvester. "New Israel, New Canaan: The Bible, the People of God, and the American Holocaust." *USQR* 59 (2005): 25–39.

Joseph, Alison L. "'Is Dinah Raped?' Isn't the Right Question: Genesis 34 and Feminist Historiography." *JHS* 19 (2019): 27–37.

———. "Understanding Genesis 34:2: 'Innâ.'" *VT* 66 (2016): 663–68.

Josephus, Flavius, Étienne Nodet, Gilles Berceville, André Paul, and Elizabeth Warschawski. *Les Antiquités Juives: Introduction et text, Livres I à III*. Paris: Cerf, 1990.

Kato, Teppei. "Ancient Chronography on Abraham's Departure from Haran: Qumran, Josephus, Rabbinic Literature, and Jerome." *JSJ* (2019): 178–96.

Kelley, Donald R. *Faces of History: Historical Inquiry from Herodotus to Herder*. New Haven: Yale University Press, 1998.

Kennedy, George A., trans. *Progymnasmata: Greek Textbooks of Prose Composition and Rhetoric*. WGRW 10. Atlanta: Society of Biblical Literature, 2003.

Klassen, William. *Love of Enemies: The Way to Peace*. Minneapolis: Fortress, 1984.

Klopper, Frances. "Rape and the Case of Dinah: Ethical Responsibilities for Reading Genesis 34." *OTE* 23 (2010): 652–65.

Kraemer, Ross Shepard. *When Aseneth Met Joseph: A Late Antique Tale of the Biblical Patriarch and His Egyptian Wife, Reconsidered*. Oxford: Oxford University Press, 1998.

Kugel, James L. "Jubilees." Pages 272–465 in *Outside the Bible: Ancient Jewish Writings Related to Scripture*. Edited by Louis H. Feldman, James L. Kugel and Lawrence H. Schiffman. Lincoln: University of Nebraska Press, 2013.

———. "On the Interpolations in the *Book of Jubilees*." *RevQ* 94 (2009): 215–72.

———. *Traditions of the Bible: A Guide to the Bible as It Was at the Start of the Common Era*. Cambridge: Harvard University Press, 1998.

Laqueur, Richard. *Der jüdische Historiker Flavius Josephus*. Darmstadt: Wissenschaftliche Buchgesellschaft, 1920.

Legaspi, Michael C. "Job's Wives in the *Testament of Job*: A Note on the Synthesis of Two Traditions." *JBL* 127 (2008): 71–79.

Leslau, Wolf. *Comparative Dictionary of Ge'ez*. Wiesbaden: Harrassowitz, 2006.

Lewy, Hans. "Hekataios von Abdera περὶ Ἰουδαίων." *ZNW* 31 (1932): 117–32.

Lied, Liv Ingeborg, and Hugo Lundhaug. *Snapshots of Evolving Traditions: Jewish and Christian Manuscript Culture, Textual Fluidity, and New Philology*. Berlin: De Gruyter, 2017.

Lim, Sung Uk. "Josephus Constructs the Samari(t)ans: A Strategic Construction of Judaean/Jewish Identity Through the Rhetoric of Inclusion and Exclusion." *JTS* 64 (2013): 404–31.

Mason, Steve. "Introduction to the *Judean Antiquities*." Pages xiii–xxxvi in *Judean Antiquities, Books 1–4*. FJTC 3. Leiden, Brill: 2004.

———. "Introduction to the *Life* of Josephus." Pages xiii–liv in *Life of Josephus*. FJTC 9. Leiden: Brill, 2001.

———. "'Should Any Wish to Inquire Further' (*Ant.* 1.25): The Aim and Audience of Josephus' *Judean Antiquities/Life*." Pages 64–103 in *Understanding Josephus: Seven Perspectives*. Edited by Steve Mason. Sheffield: Sheffield Academic, 1998.

Meretoja, Hanna. *The Ethics of Storytelling: Narrative Hermeneutics, History, and the Possible*. Oxford: Oxford University Press, 2018.

Miller, Carolyn. "Genre as Social Action." *QJS* 70 (1984): 151–67.

Mroczek, Eva. *The Literary Imagination in Jewish Antiquity*. Oxford: Oxford University Press, 2016.

"Muslims in America after 9/11, Part II." 9/11 Memorial and Museum. https://tinyurl.com/SBL6710b.

Myres, John L. *Herodotus: Father of History*. Oxford: Clarendon, 1953.

Najman, Hindy. "Interpretation as Primordial Writing: Jubilees and Its Authority Conferring Strategies." Pages 39–72 in *Past Renewals: Interpretive Authority, Renewed Revelation, and the Quest for Perfection in Jewish Antiquity*. Leiden: Brill, 2010.

Newton, Adam Zachary. *Narrative Ethics*. Cambridge: Harvard University Press, 1995.

Nickelsburg, George. *Jewish Literature between the Bible and the Mishnah: A Historical and Literary Introduction*. 2nd ed. Minneapolis: Fortress, 2005.

Nida, Eugene. "Fewer Words and Simpler Grammars Mean More Headaches." *BT* 33 (1982): 134–37.

———. "Principles of Translation as Exemplified by Bible Translating." *BT* 10 (1959): 148–64.

Niederhoff, Burkhard. "Perspective—Point of View." Pages 692–705 in *Handbook of Narratology*. Edited by Peter Hühn, Jan Christoph Meister, and Wolf Schmid. Berlin: De Gruyter, 2014.

Nir, Rivka. "'It Is Not Right for a Man Who Worships God to Repay His Neighbor Evil for Evil': Christian Ethics in *Joseph and Aseneth* (Chapters 22–29)." *JHS* 13 (2013): 1–29.

———. *Joseph and Aseneth: A Christian Book*. Sheffield: Sheffield Phoenix, 2012.

Parry, Robin. *Old Testament Story and Christian Ethics: The Rape of Dinah as a Case Study*. Milton Keynes, UK: Paternoster, 2004.

Phelan, James. "Narrative Ethics." Pages 531–46 in *Handbook of Narratology*. 2nd ed. Edited by Peter Hühn, Jan Christoph Meister, and Wolf Schmid. Berlin: De Gruyter, 2014.

Philonenko, Marc. *Joseph et Aséneth: Introduction, texte critique, traduction et notes*. StPB 13. Leiden: Brill, 1968.

Piper, John. *Love Your Enemies: Jesus' Love Command in the Synoptic Gospels and the Early Christian Paraenesis*. Wheaton, IL: Crossway, 2012.

Polletta, Francesca. "Contending Stories: Narrative in Social Movements." *QS* 21 (1998): 419–41.

Popkin, Jeremy D. *From Herodotus to H-Net: The Story of Historiography*. 2nd ed. Oxford: Oxford University Press, 2021.

Portier-Young, Anathea. "Sweet Mercy Metropolis: Interpreting Aseneth's Honeycomb." *JSP* 14 (2005): 133–57.

Potok, Chaim. *The JPS Torah Commentary: Genesis*. Philadelphia: Jewish Publication Society, 1989.

Powell, Mark Allan. *What Is Narrative Criticism?* Minneapolis: Fortress, 1990.
Rad, Gerhard von. *Genesis: A Commentary.* Translated by John H. Marks. Philadelphia: Westminster, 1972.
Rassmussen, Carl G. *Zondervan Atlas of the Bible.* Rev. ed. Grand Rapids: Zondervan, 2010.
Rautman, Marcus. *Daily Life in the Byzantine Empire.* Westport, CT: Greenwood, 2006.
Ravid, Liora. "Issues in the Book of Jubilees." PhD diss., Bar Ilan University, 2001.
Reed, Justin. "The Injustice of Noah's Curse and the Presumption of Canaanite Guilt." Paper presented at the Annual Meeting of the Society of Biblical Literature, November 2020.
———. "The Injustice of Noah's Curse and the Presumption of Canaanite Guilt: A New Reading of Genesis 9:18–29." PhD diss., Princeton University, 2020.
Richie, Ian D. "The Nose Knows: Bodily Knowing in Isaiah 11:3." *JSOT* 87 (2000): 59–73.
Richter, David H. "Review of *Narrative Ethics*." *MFS* 42 (1996): 247–50.
Ricoeur, Paul. "The Human Experience of Time and Narrative." *RP* 9 (1979): 17–34.
———. *Time and Narrative.* Vol. 3. Translated by Kathleen McLaughlin and David Pellauer. Chicago: University of Chicago Press, 1988.
Riedel, Meredith. *Leo VI and the Transformation of Christian Byzantine Identity: Writings of an Unexpected Emperor.* New York: Cambridge University Press, 2018.
Ritschl, Dietrich. *Zur Logik der Theologie: Kurze Darstellung der Zusammenhänge Theologischer Grundgedanken.* Munich: Kaiser, 1984.
"România, Bucuresti, Biblioteca Academiei Române (BAR), Ms Grec 0966." Pinakes: Textes et manuscrits grecs. https://tinyurl.com/SBL6710d.
Rönsch, Hermann. *Das Buch der Jubiläen oder die Kleine Genesis.* Repr., Amsterdam: Editions Rodopi, 1910.
Ryan, Marie-Laure. "Toward a Definition of Narrative." Pages 22–35 in *The Cambridge Companion to Narrative.* Edited by David Herman. Cambridge: Cambridge University Press, 2007.
Scholz, Susanne. *Rape Plots: A Feminist Cultural Study of Genesis 34.* New York: Lang, 2002.
———. "What Really Happened to Dinah: A Feminist Interpretation of Genesis 34." *LD* (2001): 1–15.

Schubert, Friedemann. *Tradition und Erneuerung: Studien zum Jubiläenbuch und seinem Trägerkreis*. EHGIH 771. Frankfurt: Lang, 1998.
Shemesh, Yael. "Rape Is Rape Is Rape: The Story of Dinah and Shechem (Genesis 34)." *ZAW* 119 (2007): 2–21.
Singer, Wilhelm. *Das Buch der Jubiläen oder die Leptogenesis*. Repr., Amsterdam: Editions Rodopi, 1910.
Smith, Philip. *Why War? The Cultural Logic of Iraq, the Gulf War, and Suez*. Chicago: University of Chicago Press, 2005.
Smyth, Albert H., ed. *Writings of Benjamin Franklin*. New York: Macmillan, 1905–1907.
Smyth, Herbert. *Greek Grammar*. Cambridge: Harvard University Press, 1956.
Somers, Margaret. "The Narrative Constitution of Identity: A Relational and Network Approach." *ThSoc* 23 (1994): 605–49.
Sommers, Benjamin. *A Prophet Reads Scripture: Allusion in Isaiah 40–66*. Stanford, CA: Stanford University Press, 1998.
Speiser, E. A. *Genesis*. 2nd ed. AB 1. Garden City, NY: Doubleday, 1964.
Spilsbury, Paul, and Chris Seeman. *Judean Antiquities 11*. FJTC 6a. Leiden: Brill, 2000.
Standhartinger, Angela. "'Um zu Sehen die Töchter des Landes' Die Perspektive Dinas in der Jüdischehellenistichen Diskussion um Gen 34." Pages 89–116 in *Religious Propaganda and Missionary Completion in the New Testament World: Essays Honoring Dieter George*. Edited by Lukas Bormann, Kelly Del Tredici, and Angela Standhartinger. Leiden: Brill, 1994.
Sternberg, Meir. "Biblical Poetics and Sexual Politics: From Reading to Counterreading." *JBL* 111 (1992): 463–88.
———. *The Poetics of Biblical Narrative: Ideological Literature and the Drama of Reading*. Bloomington: Indiana University Press, 1985.
Tal, Abraham. "Introduction and Commentaries on Genesis." Pages 1–226 in *BHQ Gen*.
Talbot, Alice-Mary. "A Comparison of the Monastic Experiences of Byzantine Men and Women." *GOTR* 30 (1985): 10–20.
Teeter, Andrew. "On 'Exegetical Function' in Rewritten Scripture: Innerbiblical Exegesis and the Abram/Ravens Narrative in Jubilees." *HTR* 106 (2013): 373–402.
Thackeray, Henry St. John. *Josephus: The Man and the Historian*. New York: Ktav, 1929.

Toker, Leona. *Eloquent Reticence: Withholding Information in Fictional Narrative*. Lexington: University Press of Kentucky, 1993.
Toombs, Lawrence E. "Clean and Unclean." *IDB* 1:641–48.
VanderKam, James C. *The Book of Jubilees*. 2 vols. CSCO 510-11. Leuven: Peeters, 1989.
———. *Jubilees: A Commentary on the Book of Jubilees*. Minneapolis: Fortress, 2018.
———. "The Origins and Purposes of the *Book of Jubilees*." Pages 3–24 in *Studies in the Book of Jubilees*. Edited by Mattias Albani, Jörg Frey, and Armin Lange. Tübingen: Mohr Siebeck, 1997.
———. "Recent Scholarship in the Book of Jubilees." *CurBR* 6 (2008): 405–31.
VanderKam, James, and Jozef T. Milik. "Jubilees." Pages 1–185 in *Qumran Cave 4 VIII Parabiblical Texts, Part 1*. Edited by James VanderKam. Oxford: Clarendon, 1994.
Vermes, Geza. *The Complete Dead Sea Scrolls in English*. Rev. ed. London: Penguin Books, 2011.
Walter, Christopher. *Warrior Saints in Byzantine Art and Tradition*. Aldershot, UK: Ashgate, 2003.
Weems, Renita. *Battered Love: Marriage, Sex, and Violence in the Hebrew Prophets*. Minneapolis: Fortress, 1995.
Westermann, Claus. *Genesis 12–36: A Commentary*. London: SPCK, 1986.
White, Michael, and David Epston. *Narrative Means to Therapeutic Ends*. New York: Norton, 1990.
White, Monica. "Military Saints." Pages 312–13 in *The Concise Encyclopedia of Orthodox Christianity*. Edited by John Anthony McGuckin. Oxford: Wiley-Blackwell, 2014.
Wilson, Nigel. "The Libraries of the Byzantine World." *GRBS* 8 (2003): 53–80.
Wolde, Ellen van. "Does 'innâ Denote Rape? A Semantic Analysis of a Controversial Word." *VT* 52 (2002): 528–44.
Wood, Henry. *The Histories of Herodotus: An Analysis of the Formal Structure*. The Hague: Mouton, 1972.
Wright, Jonathon Stuart. "After Antiquity: Joseph and Aseneth in the Manuscript Transmission: A Case Study for Engaging with What Came after the Original Version of Jewish Pseudepigrapha." 2 vols. PhD diss., University of Oxford, 2018.
Zahn, Molly. "Genre and Rewritten Scripture: A Reassessment." *JBL* 131 (2012): 271–88.

———. *Genres of Rewriting in Second Temple Judaism.* Cambridge: Cambridge University Press, 2020.

Zeitlin, Solomon. "The Origin of the Pharisees Reaffirmed." *JQR* 59 (1969): 255–67.

Zerbe, Gordon. *Non-retaliation in Early Jewish and New Testament Texts: Ethical Themes in Social Contexts.* Sheffield: Sheffield Academic, 1993.

Ancient Sources Index

Hebrew Bible/Old Testament		16:6	31
		16:14	77
Genesis		16:13	23
1	90, 117, 122	17	64
1:1–5	21	17:4–8	64
2–4	118	17:10	64
4	102	17:12–13	64
4:8	102	17:14	64
4:19	29	18	77–78
6:6	66–67	18:12	78
9	117, 140, 178	19:32	30
9:18–29	140	19:33	30
9:20–21	118	19:35	30
9:20–27	178	20	23, 70
10:15	159	20:32	158, 160
10:15–18	140	21	70, 77
10:15–19	23	21:21	29
10:16	159	21:22–34	23
10:17	140	21:32	126
10:19	158	22	51, 107
11:29	29	22:14	23
11:31	126	23	73, 159
12	70, 77	24	47, 65, 75, 78
12:1	132	24:57–58	77
12:5	29	24:58	34
13:11–12	159	24:61	24
14:12	29	25	60, 70
14:16	23	25:23	78
14:18	159	25:28	70, 78
15	8, 111	26	23
15:13	31	26:4–5	126
16	31, 70, 77	26:6–9	70
16:3	29	26:10	30
16:4	31	26:18–20	126
16:5	208	26:18–21	160

Genesis (continued)

26:18	126
26:33	37
27	148
27:5–13	78
27:15	148
27:33–34	70
27:35	70
27:41	70
27:41–45	22, 61
27:46	65
28:1	65
28:11	126
28:19	23
29	60, 70
29–30	78
30	54, 68
30:15	30
31:21–33	70
31:22–24	61
31:50	32
32–33	22
32:6–8	61
32:22–32	63
32:30	23
33	19, 109
33:4	190
33:12–14	63
33:18	23
33:18–20	53
33:19	47, 160
33:18–20	76
33:18–34:31	19–22, 46
34	1–9, 14–81, 94–95, 97, 104, 106–7, 109–11, 116, 122–25, 130–31, 135, 137–40, 144–45, 147–50, 153–57, 183–84, 187–89, 192, 196, 200, 232, 235–39, 241, 243–45
34:1	46–47, 53–54, 75, 111
34:2	20, 22, 28–32, 38–39, 42, 47–48, 50, 54–55, 58, 67, 76, 105, 110, 138, 191
34:3	43, 47, 54–56, 59, 139
34:3–4	26, 191
34:4	46–47, 59, 73
34:4–24	73
34:5	41, 43, 45, 47–48, 52–53, 59–61, 63, 78, 135, 156
34:5–6	48
34:6	47
34:6–7	66
34:7	30, 42–43, 47, 62, 66, 136, 156
34:8	46, 55, 63
34:8–10	55, 58, 139
34:9	22, 29, 58
34:10	26, 58
34:11	46, 63
34:11–12	54–55, 58
34:11–13	60
34:12	22
34:12–13	139
34:13	25, 37, 41, 43, 45, 47–48, 53, 61–63, 66, 136, 150
34:13–17	63
34:14	25, 46–47, 62
34:14–17	63, 65–66
34:16	22
34:17	22, 26, 46–47
34:18	47, 53, 59
34:19	43–44, 47, 54–56, 58–60
34:20	47
34:20–23	58–59, 139
34:20–24	139
34:21	22
34:23	22, 60
34:24	47
34:25	22, 26, 28–32, 47–48, 62, 150
34:25–26	67
34:25–29	66
34:26	41, 47, 76
34:27	37, 41, 43, 45, 47–48, 53, 66, 139, 150
34:27–29	156
34:29	22, 29
34:30	22, 61, 69, 71, 136, 150, 156
34:30–31	150
34:31	46, 66, 69
35:1	62
35:1–5	78
35:5	62, 106, 137

Ancient Sources Index 283

35:9	62	14:19	95		
35:9–13	62	17:15	23		
35:11–12	62	19:5–6	132		
35:15	23	20:12	39		
35:18	23	21:12–14	171		
35:22	30, 134	22:15	161		
36:6	27	22:15–16	56–57		
36:20	23	22:16	57		
36:29	23	22:16–17	39, 56, 58, 108		
37	49, 71, 107	22:17	57		
38	34, 65, 71	23:32	123		
38:15	73	24	90, 117, 122		
39:12	30	29:44	121		
39:14	30	34	23		
41:45	190	34:11–16	66, 112, 123		
42–43	71	34:15–16	135		
42:45	65				
45	190	Leviticus			
45:14–15	190	8	121		
46:8	183	11	41		
46:10	65, 79	12:1–5	117		
46:15	79, 183	12:1–8	40		
46:29	190	15:18	30		
47:11–12	71	15:24	30		
48:9	29	15:25	40		
49	68, 145, 190	16:29	31, 39		
49:4	134	16:31	31		
49:5–7	68, 136	18:24	135		
49:6	145	18:24–29	135		
49:8–12	204	19:3	39		
50:15	71	19:18	69, 211, 240		
50:15–16	71	21:6–15	132		
50:21	54	21:16	133		
50:22b–26	195	21:11	134		
		22:4	40		
Exodus					
2	149	Numbers			
2:5	24	3:5–51	121		
2:11–15	98	5:13	30, 41		
5:21	208	5:19	30		
7:27	221	6:9	40		
9:2–3	221	20	149		
10:4	222	20:8–11	98		
14	95	22:15	44		
14:13–14	193	23:11	30		

Genesis (cont.)

23:27–28	29
25	173
30:14	39

Deuteronomy

2:12	23
2:22	23
3:22	193
4:2	97
7	3, 23, 65–66, 68, 142
7:1	65
7:1–4	67
7:1–7	112
7:2	67
7:2–3	66
7:6	132
7:16	135
19:11–13	171
20:1	193
20:3–4	193
20:10–14	175
20:13–18	158
20:18	135
20:19	57
21:14	32
22:19	24
22:20–21	34
22:21	42
22:22–27	39
22:23–24	34–35
22:24	35
22:25	32, 35
22:25–27	34–35
22:26–27	35
22:28–29	39, 56–58, 108, 161
22:29	32, 57
25:5–10	34, 133
25:19	69
27:20	134
28	113
30	113
32:10	228
32:35	69, 193, 225
32:40–42	201
32:41	193, 201
32:43	193
32:51–52	98
33:8–10	196
33:10	122, 196

Joshua

7:15	42
8:23	57

Judges

6:24	23
11:5	30
17:6	37
18:10	26
19:3	56
19:23–24	42
20:6	42
20:10	42

Ruth

2:6	24
2:13	55

1 Samuel

2:22	30
9:6	26
9:11	24
15:15	42
16:11	30
17	203–4, 211
17:12–31	204
17:37	204
17:40	203
17:42	204
17:45–46	204
17:47	204
17:49	204
17:51	211
22:14	26
24	208
24:16	208
24:18	208

Ancient Sources Index

2 Samuel
- 5:1–12   159
- 13   2–3, 32, 34
- 13:11   30
- 13:12   42
- 13:14   30, 32, 57
- 13:16   39, 57
- 13:20   32, 57
- 19:7   55–56
- 23:19   44
- 23:23   44

1 Kings
- 13:4   57
- 21:25   38

2 Kings
- 2:22   37
- 17:24–31   145
- 17:24–41   142
- 24:12   142

1 Chronicles
- 11:21   44
- 11:25   44

2 Chronicles
- 20:15–17   193
- 24:22   208
- 32:6–8   55

Ezra
- 9:1   135
- 9:1–2   142
- 9:2   132
- 10:18–44   142

Esther
- 2   29
- 2:4   24
- 2:7   29
- 2:8   29

Job
- 42:8   42

Psalms
- 17:8   228
- 35:13   31
- 68:5   190
- 76:2   159
- 94:1   193

Proverbs
- 1:8   39
- 20:22   69
- 24:29   69
- 25:21–22   225

Isaiah
- 6:13   132
- 9:16   42
- 11:3   28
- 22:18   26
- 23:8   26
- 32:6   42
- 35:4   193
- 40:1–2   55
- 40:2   56
- 45:1   98
- 58:3   31

Jeremiah
- 2:23   41
- 29:23   42

Ezekiel
- 16   11
- 16:44   53
- 18:16   41
- 20:30   41
- 23   11
- 23:8   30
- 33:26   41

Daniel
- 6–12   113
- 7:25   118

Hosea
- 2:16   56

Hosea (*cont.*)
5:3   41

Nahum
1:2   193

Zechariah
2:8   228
13:2   41

Deuterocanonical Books

Tobit
4:12   145
10:10   27

Judith
7:24   208
9   145
9:1–14   6
9:2   25, 145, 201
9:2–4   145

Sirach
50:25–26   145

1 Maccabees
1:11   120
1:11–15   120
1:43–45   118

4 Maccabees
2:19–20   145

Pseudepigrapha

Aseneth
1   187, 247
1–21   183, 190
1.1   248
1.2   248
1.3   217, 247–48
1.4   248
1.5   190, 248–9
1.6   249
1.7   191, 249
1.8   249
1.9   249
2   190
2.1   249
2.6   190–91
3   218
3–26   185
3.6   190
4.7   195, 268
4.10   190–91
4.11   191
4.12   191
5.1   207
6.2   191, 196
6.3   191
6.5   191
6.7   224
7   227
7.3–5   227
7.6   145, 216, 227
7.7   227
8.5–8.6   195
8.7   195
10.5   207
11   190
11.3   190
11.5   190
11.14   206
12–13   206
12.3–5   206
12.4   224
12.5   206, 224
12.7   206
12.12   224
12.14   206
13.10–13   206
13.13   224
13.15   191
14.4   196
14.9   196
14.11   206
15.2   196
15.9–11   191
16.3   196

Ancient Sources Index

16.5	196	23.10	191, 210, 219, 220, 232, 253
16.13–14	196, 218	23.10–11	198
16.13–16	240	23.11	220, 253
16.14	214, 224, 233	23.12	185, 200, 220–22, 253
16.15	196, 218	23.12–13	220–21
17.2	196	23.12–14	198, 222
17.4	196	23.13	194, 200, 221, 253
17.8	200	23.13–14	200
21	216, 227–30	23.13–15	199
21.1–9	190–91	23.14	145, 183, 185, 189, 194, 200, 214, 221–22, 232–33, 240, 253–54
21.3	206		
21.10	228	23.15	201, 205, 254
22	195, 218	23.16	206, 208, 254
22–29	4, 17, 183, 185, 187, 237, 247	23.17	254
22.1	249	24	201
22.2	249–50	24–25	201
22.3	190, 250	24.1	254
22.4	250	24.2	254
22.5	250, 268	24.3	254–55
22.6	250	24.4	255
22.7	250	24.5	255
22.8	250	24.6	255
22.8–9	190	24.7	199, 255
22.9	251	24.8	255
22.10	251	24.8–12	199
22.11	201–2, 251	24.9	255
22.12	218, 251	24.10	255–56
22.13	195–96, 211, 216, 219, 223, 226, 232–33, 240, 251	24.11	256
		24.12	256
23	183, 191, 193, 196, 198, 206, 209, 213, 216, 219, 222–23, 233, 240	24.13	256
		24.14	256
23.1	251	24.15	201–2, 256
23.2	183, 197, 200, 251–52	24.16	257
23.3	197, 252	24.17	257
23.4	196, 232, 252	24.18	203, 257
23.5	223, 252	24.18–19	201
23.5–6	197, 222	24.19	202, 257
23.6	252	24.20	203, 257–8
23.7	223, 252	25.1	258
23.7–9	196, 209	25.2	258
23.8	219, 253	25.3	258
23.8–10	247	25.4	258
23.8–13	232	25.5	228, 258
23.9	184–85, 193, 210, 215, 217, 220–21, 232, 253	25.5–6	206
		25.6	206, 258–59

Aseneth (cont.)

25.7	259
25.8	259
26	196, 216
26–27	213
26.1	259
26.1–4	201
26.2	201, 206, 228, 259
26.3	259
26.4	259
26.5	201, 259
26.5–6	185, 202
26.6	194, 199, 214, 222–23, 231–32, 259–60
26.7	203, 223, 260
26.8	192, 203, 223, 260
26.8–27.7	185
27	211, 216
27.1	204, 260
27.1–5	214
27.1–6	194
27.2	203, 260
27.3	211–12, 260
27.4	260
27.4–5	204
27.5	260–61
27.6	199, 202–3, 214, 232, 261
27.6–7	185
27.7	261
27.8	261
27.9	261
27.9–11	205
27.10	192, 261
27.11	214, 231, 261
27.11–12	192
28	184, 193–94, 206, 220, 222–23, 233
28–29	213, 233
28.1	205, 241, 262
28.2	262
28.3	206, 262
28.3–6	207
28.4	206, 214, 223, 262
28.5	207, 230, 262
28.6	262
28.7	206, 208, 214, 262
28.8	263
28.9	209, 263
28.9–11	223–24
28.9–14	209
28.10	185, 189, 203, 209, 214, 230, 233, 263
28.10–11	192, 209
28.11	210, 263
28.12	263
28.12–13	192, 224, 233
28.12–14	210
28.13	210, 263
28.14	185, 192, 203, 214, 224, 226, 230, 233, 240, 263–64
28.15	209, 226, 265
28.15–17	211, 214, 233
28.16	264
28.16–17	226
28.17	209, 264
29	194, 196, 216, 227
29.1	211–12, 264
29.2	211, 264
29.3	185, 226, 264
29.3–4	212
29.3–5	214, 233
29.4	185, 226, 232, 264–65
29.5	212, 265
29.6	212, 265
29.7	265
29.8	265
29.9	265

Jubilees

1.4–5	241
1.5–1.17	115
1.13	115
1.16	114
1.27	95
1.27–29	241
1.29	95–96
2	121, 133–34
2.8–9	116
2.19–20	119, 132
2.19–22	133

Ancient Sources Index

2.25–28	133	22.20	143
2.26	116	22.20–21	140
2.28	133	22.21–22	140
3	134	23	114
3.1	118	23.21	134
3.8	117	23.22	114
3.9–14	117	23.26	114
3.28	146	23.30	114
4	134	25.2–18	133
4.22	134	28.24	105
6.13–14	116	30	4, 16, 41, 61, 65–68, 72, 81–82, 104, 110–12, 122, 124, 131, 133–39, 143–46, 158, 182, 189, 200, 236, 238
6.23–28	117		
6.32	116, 119		
6.32–38	119		
6.34	119	30.1	23
6.35	119	30.1–4	104–5
7.1–3	118	30.2	105, 110, 139
7.7	118	30.3	25, 136
7.20–39	116	30.4	139
7.38–39	121	30.5	25, 139
8–9	140	30.5–6	123, 137
9.14–15	141	30.5–22	116
10.29	141	30.6	140, 200, 238
10.29–34	140	30.7–10	112, 124, 143
10.30–32	141	30.8–9	144
10.33	141	30.10	95
10.35–36	141	30.11	116
11	8	30.11–12	123
12.25–26	121	30.11–16	66
15	111, 121	30.14–15	124, 144
15.28	121	30.15	134, 238, 242
15.33–34	121	30.17	139, 238
16.1	95	30.17–20	67, 140
16.5	134	30.18	238
16.16–18	133	30.18–20	121
16.24–29	133	30.20	140
16.26	133	30.21–22	124, 238
20.1–10	116	30.22	238
21	135	30.23	139–40, 151, 238
21.1–25	116	30.23–26	104–5
21.1–26	121	30.25	136–37, 150
21.21–24	242	30.26	137
21.21–25	119	32.1	121
22.10–18	133	32.3–9	121
22.10–24	116	32.19	133

Jubilees (cont.)		4Q320–330	119
33	135		
33.4	134	4Q337	119
33.7–9	134		
33.9	134	Temple Scroll	
33.10	134	LVII, 15–19	145
33.14	134		
33.15	134	Ancient Jewish Writers	
33.18	95		
35.18–27	116	Josephus, *Antiquitates judaicae*	
36.1–11	116	1	147, 152, 156, 158, 163–64, 182
45.13–16	136	1.1–26	152
45.14	146	1.3	102, 166
45.15	116	1.3–4	242
45.16	121–22	1.4	100, 166
47.5	146	1.5	92, 97, 127
47.10	95	1.6–13	177
48.13	95	1.8–9	242
		1.8–13	148
Testament of Levi		1.9	92, 102, 127, 163, 166
2–5	196	1.10–12	242
2.1	6	1.12	127
5.1–7.4	6	1.14	98, 128–29, 149, 162–63, 166–67, 170
5.3	145, 201		
6	145	1.15	130, 163, 176
6.3–6	145	1.15–29	96
6.4–5	145	1.16–23	99
7	145	1.17	97, 148
14–18	196	1.19	242
		1.20	129, 242
Testament of Job		1.21	130
45.3	145	1.23	130
		1.23–24	242
Testament of Naphtali		1.24	242
6.8	196	1.25	101, 130
		1.27–2.200	148
Testament of Reuben		1.38–40	98
6.8–12	196	1.41	146
		1.50	146
Dead Sea Scrolls		1.52–55	163
		1.52–66	177
4Q216	113	1.53	103
		1.60	103
4Q252	119	1.60–66	166
		1.61	103

Ancient Sources Index

1.70	110	1.267–275	148, 167
1.83	98	1.277	126, 159
1.93	98, 100	1.277–278	152
1.94	99	1.278	160, 167
1.94–95	99	1.280–282	179
1.107	99	1.280–284	167
1.108	99	1.283	167
1.110–112	166	1.299	152
1.115–117	166	1.327	167
1.118–119	99	1.337	54, 110–11, 124, 154, 158, 160, 162
1.128–129	92		
1.136	160	1.337–338	145
1.139–142	178	1.337–339	152
1.141–142	178	1.337–341	4, 16, 68–69, 81–82, 97, 107–10, 124–25, 130–31, 147–48, 150–51, 153–55, 157–58, 160, 164–67, 169–70, 176–78, 180, 182, 236, 239
1.142	175, 178		
1.154–157	152		
1.156–157	103		
1.158	99		
1.159	99	1.338	65, 124, 161
1.159–160	99	1.338–339	161
1.162	149	1.339	25, 124
1.171–179	153	1.339–40	25
1.176	158	1.340	150, 153–54, 172, 239
1.177	172	1.341	150, 156, 167, 169
1.178	173, 239	2–4	157
1.179	173	2.2–10	152
1.180	159	2.12	166
1.183	167	2.18	149
1.185	179	2.18–20	166
1.191	167, 179	2.21–31	107
1.192	111, 152	2.33	149
1.194	167	2.34	110
1.194–196	166	2.35	149
1.207	110, 126, 160	2.40–260	149
1.207–212	153	2.91	152
1.222	167	2.173	149
1.223–236	107	2.194	146
1.226	162	2.208	110
1.235	179	2.224	146
1.237	159	2.248	110, 174
1.239	150	2.252	174
1.256	167	2.307	110
1.259–262	153	2.327–329	157, 164
1.260–261	126, 160	3–4	152
1.266	159	3.11–13	157

Josephus, *Antiquitates judaicae* (cont.)		4.252	108, 161
3.17	110	4.277	170
3.40–61	173	4.278	170
3.42–60	239	4.292	175
3.43	173	4.293	175
3.44–46	173	4.293–301	174–75
3.44–47	173	4.296	175
3.47	173	4.297	175
3.49	173	4.300	158
3.60	173	4.309–319	172, 239
3.213	97	4.324–331	149, 157
3.295–299	149, 164	5	158
3.317	92, 149	5.12	110
3.328–329	98	5.37	175
4	170	5.60–61	175
4.1–12	175	5.65–67	175
4.2	175	5.107	158
4.6	175	5.117–118	175
4.7	175	5.118	175
4.11–56	164	5.120	175
4.56	110	5.132–133	175
4.87	173	5.157	110
4.87–88	173	5.198	149
4.87–94	173	5.295	174
4.131–155	177	5.295–297	174
4.141	173	5.295–317	239
4.141–164	173	5.296	110
4.145–150	173	5.317	174
4.152–153	173	6	151
4.152–155	239	6.36	171
4.154	174	6.84–85	171
4.154–155	174	6.230	97
4.155	110	7.61	159
4.177–195	172, 239	7.101–103	99
4.181	172, 239	7.172	110
4.182	173	7.290–291	151
4.186–187	172	7.294	110
4.196–292	175	7.326	110
4.196–301	170–71	9	151
4.197	92, 97, 171	9.18–28	176
4.198	92	9.70	110
4.214	171	9.242	97
4.215	172, 239	9.289	110
4.223	171	9.291	179
4.251–252	110	10	151

10.20	99	20.51	110
10.103–104	176	20.116	125
10.218	97	20.118–136	148, 151, 153–57, 165–
10.219–226	99		67, 170, 176, 180, 239
10.269–281	98	20.119	154
10.281	96	20.120–121	155
11	151, 180	20.121	125, 155, 172
11.1	98	20.122	155–56
11.5	98	20.123	156
11.111	171	20.127	110, 154
11.114	179	20.129	167
11.325–347	177	20.135	168
11.340	180	20.135–136	168
11.341	180	20.139	111, 152
11.342	180	20.145–146	111, 152
11.344	180	20.160	168
12	151	20.161	155
13.5	110	20.165–166	169
13.171–173	129	20.167	168
13.299–300	152	20.172	168
13.391	110	20.173–178	153
14–17	151	20.176	152
14–20	177	20.178	153
14.1–3	92, 100	20.193–194	125
14.186–187	92	20.201	125
15.122	110	20.202–203	125
15.302	110	20.214	168
15.310	110	20.218	169, 180
16.175	92	20.234	171
17.254	92	20.252	168
17.276	110	20.252–258	153
18.9	168	20.259–262	89
18.12–18	129	20.259–268	96, 152
18.100	110	20.260	101
19.221–278	152	20.261	101
19.249	110	20.262	92
20	125, 147, 152–53, 169, 180, 237	20.263	101
20.2	153	20.264	101
20.2–4	153	20.266	102
20.17–96	128, 152, 163	20.267	101
20.22–23	152		
20.29	110	Josephus, *Bellum judaicum*	
20.34–48	111, 152–53	1.2	92
20.39	152	1.3	92
20.48	152	1.6	92

Josephus, *Bellum judaicum* (cont.)
2.232	154
2.232–246	154–55
2.233	154
2.235	155
3.132–336	174
4.128–134	169
5.412–415	169

Josephus, *Contra Apionem*
2.287	128

Josephus, *Vita*
1	92
3–7	102
8–12	102
12	92
80	102
208–211	102
425	102
430	102

Philo, *De Iosepho*
239–240	203

Philo, *De migratione Abrahami*
39.223–235	6

Philo, *De mutatione nominum*
36.193–200	6

Philo, *De sacrificiis Abel et Caini*
3.10	102
4.14	102

Philo, *De specialibus legibus*
4.7–9	203

Theodotus
frag. 4	145
frag. 7	145
frag. 8	145

New Testament

Matthew
5:39	225
23:35	102

Acts
23:7–8	91

Romans
12	225
12:17	225
12:17–21	225

Ephesians
1:1–3	132

1 Thessalonians
5:15	225

Hebrews
11:4	102

1 Peter
2:23	225
3:9	225

1 John
2:6	268
3:12	102

Revelation
14:4	268

Rabbinic Works

Genesis Rabbah
1:97	190
22:5	102
57:4	145
80	6, 53
80:5	24
80:8	145

Pirqe Rabbi Eliezar
38   190

Targum Neofiti   30
  Gen 34   145
  Gen 34:31   145

Targum Onqelos
  Gen 34:1   145

Targum Pseudo-Jonathan   30, 102

Yerushalmi Bava Batra
  15:2   145

Early Christian Works

Ambrose, *De officiis ministrorum*
  1.25   6

Eusebius, *Praeparatio evangelica*
  9.22.4   108

Jerome, *Epistula* 22
  25   6

Syncellus, *Chronological Excerpts*
  55   99

Greco-Roman Literature

Dionysius of Halicarnassus, *De Thucydide*
  5   97
  8   97

Lucian, *Quomodo historia conscribenda sit*
  47   97

Polybius, *Historiae*
  6.1.4–5   163, 176

Modern Authors Index

Abbot, Abiel 13
Adams, Tony E. 11
Ahearne-Kroll, Patricia D. 7–8, 21, 183, 186, 199, 204, 217, 268
Alter, Robert 21–22, 51–53, 59, 243
Aptowitzer, Victor 190
Attridge, Harold 102–3, 129, 162–63, 167
Auerbach, Erich 49, 51, 243–44
Bader, Mary Anna 2–4, 19, 30, 33, 40, 42, 57–58, 65
Bar-Efrat, Shimon 30, 36–38, 45, 50
Bechtel, Lyn M. 2–3, 15, 28–31, 43, 45, 55–56, 58–59, 62, 65–67, 70
Begg, Christopher 21, 148, 174
Ben-Porat, Ziva 204
Berger, Klaus 120
Berlin, Adele 2, 49, 52, 72
Bilde, Per 151, 168, 177
Birch, Dom 82
Bochner, Arthur P. 10
Bolen, Derek M. 11
Booth, Wayne C. 3, 7
Bouque, Linda B. 28
Breisach, Ernst 89
Brody, Howard 137
Bruner, Edward M. 9, 82, 86–88, 164
Burchard, Christoph 7, 17, 184–85, 187–88, 193–94, 199–200, 207, 217–19, 221, 247
Burfiend, Carsten 17
Clark, Mark 137
Cerquiglini, Bernard 186
Chapman, Cynthia R. 46–48
Charles, R. H. 105, 112–13, 122
Charlesworth, James 108
Chesnutt, Randall D. 184, 187–88
Cohen, Shaye J. D. 7, 93
Coleman, Monica A. 33
Collins, John J. 90–91
Cottrill, Amy 5, 244–45
Crawford, Sidnie White 85
Cruikshank, Julie 10
Delling, Gerhard 21, 208
Diamant, Anita 72
Driscoll, Matthew James 186
Efthymiadis, Stephanos 193–95, 215
Endres, John C. 120
Epstein, Louis 135
Epston, David 10
Feldman, Louis H. 24, 92–93, 97–99, 102–3, 108, 126, 129, 148–49, 159–60, 167, 171, 173, 175–76, 199
Fewell, Danna Nolan 2–4, 55–58, 61, 66–67, 70, 72, 74
Fink, Barbara 17, 217
Fishbane, Michael 142
Fitzpatrick, John C. 89
Fowler, Alastair 84
Frank, Arthur W. 1, 9–12, 19, 86, 137–38, 161–62, 235, 244–45
Gager, John 100
Gallant, Robert 171
Ganz, Marshall 9
Geller, Steven 68
Giere, Samuel D. 21
Ginzberg, Louis 146
Glass, Gillian 237
Goldstein, Jonathan 113
Graybill, Rhiannon 4, 28, 33–34, 36

Gunn, David M. 2–4, 55–58, 61, 66–67, 70, 72, 74
Halpern-Amaru, Betsy 146–47
Hansen, Julie 9
Harrington, Anne 1
Hartner, Marcus 71–72
Hata, Gohei 93
Hayes, Catherine 65, 132–33, 135
Haynes, Stephen 244
Hicks-Keeton, Jill 185, 189, 204
Hinterberger, Martin 195
Johnson, Sylvester 12
Joseph, Alison L. 3, 29, 32, 34, 41, 76
Kalogeras, Nikos 193–94, 215
Kato, Teppei 85
Kelley, Donald R. 89
Kennedy, George A. 7
Klassen, William 184, 199
Klopper, Frances 33
Kraemer, Ross Shepard 7–8, 183
Kugel, James L. 1, 4, 24–25, 91, 95, 111–12, 144–47, 199, 201
Laqueur, Richard 126
Legaspi, Michael C. 79
Leslau, Wolf 105–106
Lewy, Hans 100
Lied, Liv Igenborg 186
Lim, Sung Uk 179
Lundhaug, Hugo 186
Mason, Steve 89, 92, 101–2, 126–30, 151–52, 163, 176
Meretoja, Hanna 10, 13, 138, 188, 234
Milik, Jozef T. 113
Miller, Carolyn 86
Mroczek, Eva 8
Myres, John L. 151
Najman, Hindy 96
Newton, Adam Zachary 4–6, 12, 19, 93–94, 193
Nickelsburg, George 113
Nida, Eugene 22
Niederhoff, Burkard 40
Nir, Rivka 7, 184
Nodet, Étienne 107, 169
Parry, Robin 3–4, 15
Phelan, James 10
Philonenko, Marc 21, 184–85, 189, 200, 210, 232
Piper, John 184
Polletta, Francesca 10–11, 86
Popkin, Jeremy D. 82, 85, 89–90, 109
Portier-Young, Anathea 206
Potok, Chaim 57
Powell, Mark Allan 19
Rad, Gerhard von 31
Rassmussen, Carl G. 159
Rautman, Marcus 214
Ravid, Liora 113
Reed, Justin 140
Richie, Ian D. 28
Richter, David H. 12, 131
Ricoeur, Paul 11
Riedel, Meredith 214
Ritschl, Dietrich 36
Rönsch, Hermann 113
Ryan, Marie-Laure 1
Scholz, Susanne 33, 55–56, 77
Schubert, Friedemann 122
Seeman, Chris 180
Shemesh, Yael 33
Singer, Wilhelm 113
Smith, Phillip 11, 83–84, 143
Smyth, Albert H. 89
Smyth, Herbert 196, 221
Somers, Margaret 9, 82, 86
Sommers, Benjamin 204
Speiser, E. A. 30, 60, 73
Spilsbury, Paul 180
Standhartinger, Angela 183–84, 189, 203–4, 232
Sternberg, Meir 2–3, 15, 24, 30, 36, 41–43, 45, 54–56, 61–62, 65–69, 76
Tal, Abraham 30
Talbot, Alice-Marie 215
Teeter, Andrew 8
Thackeray, Henry St. John 126
Toker, Leona 15, 74–75
Toombs, Lawrence E. 40
VanderKam, James C. 95, 104, 106, 112–13, 115, 117–20, 122, 144

Vermes, Geza	119
Walter, Christopher	213
Weems, Renita	11
Westermann, Claus	3, 27, 31, 62
White, Michael	10
White, Monica	213
Wilson, Nigel	215
Wolde, Ellen van	29–31
Wood, Henry	151
Wright, Jonathon Stuart	17, 186–87, 194–95, 207, 216, 220, 227, 247, 268
Zahn, Molly	84–86, 90
Zeitlin, Solomon	122
Zerbe, Gordon	7, 21, 183, 185, 193–94, 196, 199–200, 202–3, 208, 210–11